Social security policies in industrial countries

Social security policies in industrial countries

A comparative analysis

Margaret S. Gordon
University of California, Berkeley

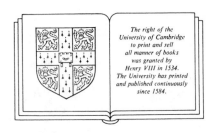

*The right of the
University of Cambridge
to print and sell
all manner of books
was granted by
Henry VIII in 1534.
The University has printed
and published continuously
since 1584.*

CAMBRIDGE UNIVERSITY PRESS

Cambridge
New York   New Rochelle   Melbourne   Sydney

Published by the Press Syndicate of the University of Cambridge
The Pitt Building, Trumpington Street, Cambridge CB2 1RP
32 East 57th Street, New York, NY 10022, USA
10 Stamford Road, Oakleigh, Melbourne 3166, Australia

First published 1988

Printed in the United States of America

Library of Congress Cataloging-in-Publication Data
Gordon, Margaret S.
Social security policies in industrial countries : a comparative
analysis / Margaret S. Gordon.
p.   cm.
Bibliography: p.
ISBN 0-521-33311-3
1. Social security.   I. Title.
HD7101.G67   1988
368.4–dc19   88-6516

British Library Cataloguing in Publication Data
Gordon, Margaret S.
Social security policies in industrial
countries : a comparative analysis
1. Industrialised countries. Social security
I. Title
368.4′009172′2

ISBN 0 521 33311 3

Contents

Contents

Preface

When I first conceived the plans for this book in the mid-1960s, social security programs were experiencing expansion and liberalization throughout the industrial world. Now, two decades later, in an environment of retarded economic growth and severe unemployment, the need for social security expenditures to mitigate the impacts of unemployment and economic deprivation has increased enormously, but the capacity of governments to meet this need is being severely limited because of the necessity of budgetary restraint. The result is a constant conflict, and, in conservative and right-wing circles, a growing tendency to place the blame for persistent unemployment on the generosity of the ''welfare state.''

My aim in this volume is to provide a comparative analysis of social security policies in industrial countries, not simply in their general outlines, but in their major features, including the scope and adequacy of benefits and the structure of financing provisions in each of the main types of social security programs – pension programs, health benefit programs, unemployment and manpower programs, children's allowances and family policies, and public assistance.

Included are 28 industrial countries. I have omitted a few of the smaller industrial countries, such as Iceland, Luxemburg, and Portugal, as well as industrial countries in Latin America. It goes without saying, of course, that I cannot possibly cover all the details of the programs of 28 countries. And yet, for certain statistical purposes, such as social security expenditures as a percentage of gross domestic product (GDP), it is extremely useful to analyze the data for as many as 28 countries. It is equally useful for the purpose of identifying prevailing patterns and trends in the basic structure of programs – for example, the trend toward two-tiered or three-tiered systems in national pension programs.

At the same time, I have selected for emphasis the countries that have been innovators in developing various types of policies. Thus, in discussing the evolution of old-age pension programs, for example, I have treated in some detail the earliest old-age insurance program, in Bismarck's Germany, and contrasted it with the old-age assistance approach first adopted in Denmark. The major focus of the book, however, is not on the early history of social

security policies, but on developments and trends in the period since World
War II.

There have been a number of exceedingly useful comparative studies of
social security policies in relatively recent years, on which I have drawn extensively, but from which my study differs significantly. Wilensky (1975) and
others have illuminated the reasons for differences in social security spending
in relation to GDP, in some cases covering both industrial and less developed
countries, but, for the most part, such studies have not been concerned with
the details of social security policies. Also very useful have been a number of
studies, such as those of Rimlinger (1971) and Heclo (1974), that have provided a penetrating historical analysis of differences in the evolution of policies in several countries – Britain and Sweden in the case of Heclo, and
Britain, Germany, Russia, and the United States in the case of Rimlinger.

Another invaluable group of studies are concerned with particular types of
policies, such as Abel-Smith's studies of health benefit policies (e.g., Abel-
Smith, 1984), the series of volumes by Kamerman and Kahn (e.g., 1978) on
family policies, and a number of others. From studies such as these, I have
benefited immensely.

In an attempt to keep my study within manageable proportions, I have
concentrated not only on major types of social security policies but also on
those relating to employed workers or to the population in general. For example, I have not discussed, except in passing, the numerous programs for
special groups of workers in France or the special programs for farm workers
in some countries. Nor have I included programs for public employees or
veterans, which, of course, are important in their own right but are not what
we have in mind when we consider controversies over major social security
policies.

Also largely omitted, though important in some countries, are subsidized
housing policies, simply because any attempt to consider such policies would
immensely add to the scope of the volume and the complexity of my task.
And, for the same reasons, I have not attempted comprehensive coverage of
social services, although I have emphasized, for example, the importance of
child care services in relation to family policies.

Another omission is any detailed treatment of administration of social security policies, although I refer occasionally to the differences between countries in which administration is highly centralized and those in which it is
regionalized, delegated partly or wholly to states or provinces, or supervised
by committees representing labor, management, and the public. Not that these
differences are unimportant, but detailed treatment of them would add to the
complexity of the study and interfere with the main focus on policies.

Some readers may wonder why I have included a rather lengthy chapter on
labor market policies in a book on social security, but it is abundantly clear

that countries with vigorous and consistent labor market policies have succeeded in reducing unemployment, rehabilitating the disabled, and in other ways reducing the number of people dependent on income maintenance. Several recent studies, in fact, have come to the conclusion that minimum income guarantees need to be closely associated with vigorous labor market policies.

Finally, unlike many writers in this field, I rarely use the term "welfare state." One reason is that, in the American context, it can be confusing because when we speak of "welfare" we often have in mind our major public assistance program, Aid to Families with Dependent Children. A more important reason is increasing awareness of the persistence of poverty, even in relatively affluent countries, and of the disturbing spread of such problems as homelessness in recent years.

And lastly, the social security policies covered in this study are only one important aspect of the so-called welfare state; other important aspects – educational policies, for example – are beyond the scope of this volume, except insofar as they involve vocational training as a part of labor market policy.

Perhaps the most important point is that very few countries have actually achieved a welfare state. The reasons for this are complex, and one of my purposes is to illuminate them.

Acknowledgments

My work on this project has stretched over several decades, beginning in the early 1960s with my study of *Retraining and Labor Market Adjustment in Western Europe* (1965b), which was part of a large-scale study of unemployment and the American economy from 1962 to 1966, financed by a grant from the Ford Foundation to the Institute of Industrial Relations, University of California, Berkeley. Later the Ford Foundation provided a modest grant to the institute to support my research on comparative social security policies, but work on that project was interrupted for ten years while I served as associate director of the Carnegie Commission on Higher Education and its successor, the Carnegie Council on Policy Studies in Higher Education. That experience, however, was not without relevance to this project, especially my work on Carnegie Council... (1979) and on *Youth Education...* (Gordon, with Trow, 1979).

In more recent years, I have become indebted to numerous individuals who have assisted my research in various ways. I am especially indebted to those who arranged my schedule of interviews in Bonn, Geneva, London, Ottawa, and Stockholm, at various times from 1983 to 1986. They have included Professor Wilhelm Krelle, University of Bonn; Mr. G. Tamburi, chief of the Social Security Department of the ILO, Geneva; Mr. David Richardson, director of the branch office of the ILO in London; Ms. Carol MacKinnon, assistant director of the ILO branch office in Ottawa; and Ms. MariAnne Walz, of the Swedish Institute in Stockholm. I also received special assistance in getting access to various documents from Ms. Kathleen F. Lee of the Commission of European Communities in Brussels and from Ms. Ilene Zeitzer of the Office of International Policy, U.S. Social Security Administration in Washington.

Valuable as were my interviews with experts in London and the other cities that I visited, at least equally useful were the numerous documents and books that I picked up on the way or arranged to have sent to me. The stack of publications that I received from officials in Canada Health and Welfare after my visit to Ottawa was nearly a foot high and could scarcely be read in its entirety, but at least it brought me up to date on many aspects of Canadian policy.

xiii

I feel strongly indebted to the late Barbara N. Armstrong, Professor of Law, University of California, Berkeley (reputed to have been the first female professor of law in the United States) whose pioneering work on comparative social security policies in industrial countries (Armstrong, 1932) played an important role in my decision to undertake such a study many years later. Barbara also arranged for me to conduct a study group of the San Francisco League of Women Voters on health insurance in 1939, at a time when a health insurance bill had been introduced in the California legislature – introducing me not only to my first study of a proposed social insurance program but also to the intense controversy surrounding the proposal.

I owe a very special debt to Dr. Paul Fisher, former director of the international policies staff of the U.S. Social Security Administration, for his careful reading of the first draft of this volume, at a time when it had not yet benefited from the extensive cutting that it later received. He made many valuable suggestions, not all of which I could follow because of the need to hold down the overall length of the volume. Chapter 5 (which was originally written as an article though never published as such) also benefited from useful comments by the late Wilbur J. Cohen, former U.S. Secretary of Health, Education, and Welfare; and from Dr. Ida C. Merriam, former director, and Ms. Lenore E. Bixby, former deputy director, of the Office of Research and Statistics, U.S. Social Security Administration.

My two economist sons deserve thanks, also: Robert J. Gordon, for sending me relevant papers from the numerous conferences he attends and for useful comments on the first six chapters, which he read the last time he was in Berkeley; and David M. Gordon, for carrying out on his computer the multiple regressions that are discussed in Chapter 2.

One of the complications involved in writing about comparative social security policies is that they are constantly subject to change, especially in this era when high unemployment and budgetary deficits in numerous countries have forced belt tightening and retrenchment. For this reason, I have had to establish a cutoff date, beyond which I would not attempt to cover new developments. The reader will find that many of my generalizations about the prevalence of various policies relate to the year 1985, since they are largely based on the most recent issue of *Social Security Programs Throughout the World, 1985* (USSSA, 1986), although I have used numerous other sources. I have also tried, however, to take account of significant developments, such as the important amendments adopted in Britain in 1986, at least to the end of 1986.

Finally, it seems appropriate to add that a study of this kind would have been all but impossible to carry out without access to *Social Security Programs Throughout The World*, published biennially, even though I have also used numerous other sources. Also of basic importance is *The Cost of Social Security*, published every few years by the International Labor Office (ILO), as well as numerous other publications of both the ILO and the Organization for Economic Cooperation and Development (OECD).

Berkeley, California   Margaret S. Gordon
October 1987

Abbreviations

Cited in the text and appearing in the reference list are many references to journals and publications of organizations that are especially concerned with social security issues. In order to reduce the length of the list of references, *unsigned* articles in such journals will be cited in abbreviated form in the text only, and such organizations will be listed by their initials in caps. The following journals and organizations are involved:

European Community or Communities (EC)
European Economic Community (EEC)
International Labor Office (ILO)
International Labor Review (ILR)
International Social Security Association (ISSA)
International Social Security Review (ISSR)
Organization for Economic Cooperation and Development (OECD)
Social Security Bulletin (SSB)
Social and Labor Bulletin (S&LB)
U.S. Social Security Administration (USSSA)

CHAPTER 1

Postwar developments

The trend toward more integrated systems

World War II proved to be an important turning point in the history of social security. To be sure, social security programs had experienced substantial development in industrial countries in the 50 years since the adoption of social insurance in Bismarck's Germany in the 1880s, but the programs were often limited in coverage, provided meager benefits, and were fragmented in the sense that coverage and eligibility varied from one program to another (Laroque, 1948). Morever, under the strain of the Great Depression of the 1930s, unemployment insurance systems (where they existed) broke down and had to be supplemented or replaced by assistance and relief programs.

Allied leaders sensed that the will to fight and win the war among their peoples depended not only on the determination to overcome the Axis Powers but also on the conviction that life would be more rewarding after the war than in the difficult years of the 1930s.

Even before the United States entered the war, President Franklin D. Roosevelt, attempting to persuade Congress to step up aid to the Allied Powers, was one of the first to give voice to a set of wartime objectives, when he proclaimed the "Four Freedoms" on January 6, 1941. They included freedom of speech, religious freedom, freedom from want, and freedom from fear (Filler, 1964, 241–2).

Much the same aims were expressed in a joint declaration, known as the Atlantic Charter, by the President and Prime Minister Winston Churchill of Great Britain when they met secretly off the Newfoundland coast in August 1941. The fifth goal of the Atlantic Charter called for "the fullest collaboration between all nations in the economic field with the object of securing, for all, improved labor standards, economic advancement, and social security" (Filler, 1964, 245).

Another development that was influential in stimulating postwar expansion and improvement of social security programs was the resolution adopted by the International Labor Organization (ILO) in 1944, which pledged the organization "to promote programs for extending social security measures to pro-

1

vide a basic income to all in need of such protection and comprehensive medical care'' (*ILR*, 1944, *50* [July]: 6).

According to Laroque (1948), the term ''social security,'' which came into general use after World War II, was first used in the U.S. Social Security Act of 1935. However, Perrin (1984a) pointed out that although the words may have been used first in the American legislation, the concept of a social security system was first embodied in the comprehensive New Zealand legislation of 1938.

Social security, as now generally understood, includes all types of income maintenance programs, as well as health benefits, whether in the form of health insurance or the provision of free health care, as in the British National Health Service. I have also included labor market policies because they are an integral part of policies aimed at preventing dependency.

Closely related to the goal of more comprehensive social security was the goal of full employment. In fact, full employment, sustained economic growth, and the expansion of social security went hand in hand – especially in Western Europe – in the 1950s and 1960s, but the course became much more difficult in the 1970s and 1980s, as countries grappled with much higher inflation rates, slower growth, and rising unemployment in what came to be known as ''stagflation.''

One of the striking aspects of the 1950s and 1960s was the fact that economic growth rates were considerably higher in the continental countries of Western Europe than in the United States, Canada, and the United Kingdom. As Maddison pointed out in his comprehensive study of economic growth:

In continental Europe the decade of the 1950s was brilliant, with growth of output and consumption, productivity, investment and employment surpassing any recorded historical experience, and the rhythm of development virtually uninterrupted by recession. . . . In North America and the United Kingdom, the 1950s were no worse or better than many periods in the past, but in view of the continental experience, it seemed like stagnation.

(Maddison, 1964, 25)

Maddison went on to point out that the action of governments in sustaining high and steady levels of demand and investment was a major reason for the postwar acceleration of growth.

Another influence that should be kept in mind was the U.S. program of Marshall Plan aid to the war-damaged countries of Western Europe from 1948 to 1951.

The oil crisis of the mid-1970s was a major factor in bringing about a retardation of growth, even more in some of the continental countries than in the United States because the former were more dependent on imported oil. Responsible as it was for an acceleration of inflation rates, it tended to lead to more conservative economic policies in an effort to combat inflation, to growing skepticism about Keynesian expansionist policies, and in some cases to the embracing of monetarism. Even so, it seems probable that the high growth rates of the 1950s and 1960s could not have been sustained into the indefinite future even without the oil crisis, as competition from Japan and later from other Asian countries became more formidable.

In his more recent study of comparative growth, covering six industrial countries (chiefly the larger countries) in the 1973–82 period, Maddison (1983) found that there were three main causes of decelerated growth:

1. A longer-term decline in productivity growth potential as the follower countries (Europe and Japan) converged on the performance levels of the leader (the United States)
2. Inevitable "cyclical" losses in output and employment as countries adjusted to important "system shocks" (the collapse of the Bretton Woods fixed exchange system and the 12-fold increase in oil prices)
3. Losses due to a change in the "establishment view" of macropolicy tasks and instruments (i.e., a shift, at least in some countries, away from Keynesian policies and toward more restrictive policies)

Numerous critics attack rigidities in European economies as a major factor in explaining persistent unemployment, and the phrase "Eurosclerosis" has been coined to characterize the problem. Others dispute this interpretation, as we shall see in Chapter 11, whereas still others refer, instead, to the "crisis" in Western Europe, a crisis that is more severe than anything experienced since the Great Depression. For example, Jacques Delors, currently the president of the Commission of the European Communities, has identified three main elements in the crisis, with particular reference to EEC countries: (1) a crisis of adaptation, resulting from the failure to meet the challenge of a lag of five to ten years behind the United States and Japan in adopting advanced technologies; (2) a crisis of regulation, in which "mixed" economies have not been functioning well since the end of the 1960s; and (3) a crisis of identity, characterized by a tendency of the EEC to react defensively to problems, rather than to develop imaginative long-range plans and goals (Delors, 1984).

During World War II, country after country appointed commissions or committees to develop plans for an improved social security system after the war. By far the most influential of these was the Committee on Social Insurance and Allied Services, appointed by the British Government in June 1941 and chaired by Sir William Beveridge. In a well-established British tradition, found also in such British Commonwealth countries as Australia and Canada, the committee's report, which came to be known as the Beveridge Report, was signed by the chairman alone (*Social Insurance and Allied Services*, 1942). This procedure protected the civil servants who staffed the committee from identification with recommendations that might prove controversial.

Beveridge paid tribute to the comprehensiveness of Britain's existing income maintenance programs but at the same time noted certain weaknesses:

Provision for most of the many varieties of need through interruption of earnings and other causes that may arise in modern industrial communities has already been made in Britain on a scale not surpassed and hardly rivalled in any other country of the world. In one respect only of first importance, namely limitation of medical services, both in the range of treatment which is provided and in respect of the classes of persons for whom it is provided, does Britain's achievement fall seriously short of what has been accomplished elsewhere: it falls short also in its provision for maternity and funerals and through the defects of its system for workmen's compensation.

(*Social Insurance and Allied Services*, 1942, 5–6)

The Beveridge Report envisaged an integrated and comprehensive social security system – sometimes characterized as guaranteeing security "from the cradle to the grave" – that was not confined to workers but in some respects embraced the entire population. All employees would be eligible for unemployment and disability benefits, pensions on retirement, medical treatment, and funeral expenses. The self-employed would be eligible for all of these except unemployment and disability benefits during the first weeks of disability. Other persons of working age not gainfully occupied would receive all except unemployment and disability benefits. Housewives would be eligible for maternity grants, benefits for widowhood and separation, and old-age pensions by virtue of their husband's contributions. Finally, persons below working age would receive children's allowances, to be financed from general revenues.

Unemployment, disability, and retirement benefits would be at the same flat rate, and that rate would provide the income necessary for subsistence. There would be a single, combined, weekly contribution by employers, employees, the self-employed, and persons of working age who were not gainfully occupied, to cover the benefits for which the various groups were eligible. Curiously, however, in a provision that reflected the pervasiveness of the concept of dependency of a wife, married women workers were allowed to opt out of making contributions, which most of them chose to do, and this meant that they were eligible only for the benefits that could be received by housewives (cf. Abel-Smith, 1983a). The contributions, like the benefits, were on a flat-rate basis.

Medical treatment would be provided for all citizens by a national health service, and postmedical rehabilitation treatment would be provided for all persons capable of benefiting from it. For the limited number of cases of need not covered by social insurance, national assistance would be available.

Unlike the comprehensive recommendations developed in some other countries, which were adopted only in part and sometimes after lengthy delays, the Beveridge plan was adopted practically in its entirety, with only minor modifications, very soon after the end of the war. Embraced by the Labor Party, which came into power in 1945, its adoption went smoothly. In 1946, the National Insurance Act, the Family Allowances Act, and the National Health Service all received parliamentary approval. They were followed by the National Assistance Act of 1948, which spelled out a unified and humane program of assistance to the needy.

One important deviation from the Beveridge recommendations was the decision of the government to provide weekly benefits that were below the standard deemed necessary for subsistence, along with an announced intention to raise the benefits gradually to a subsistence level over time.

The entire concept of flat-rate benefits and flat-rate contributions embodied in the Beveridge plan eventually came under attack, and provisions for earnings-related supplements were adopted. However, the Thatcher government removed the earnings-related supplements to unemployment and sickness benefits in 1981, and proposed phasing out the earnings-related supplements to retirement benefits in 1985 – a proposal that proved controversial and was greatly modified under 1986 amendments.

The concept of flat-rate benefits included in the Beveridge Report was deemed egalitarian and consistent with British social security traditions, but it was proposed at a time when wages had been comparatively stable or falling for several decades and when the steadily rising wages of the postwar period were not anticipated. As they became accustomed to rising wage levels, workers became reluctant to look forward to a sharp drop in income during periods of unemployment or disability, or at the time of retirement. Particularly unworkable were the flat-rate contributions, which had to be held down to a level that would not be an undue burden for low earners, and could not easily be raised to meet benefit needs in a period of rising wages and prices. They were also extremely regressive, extracting a larger percentage of wages from low than from high earners. Under legislation adopted in 1975, earnings-related contributions from employers and employees, plus a government supplement, provide for all social insurance programs combined, even though some of the benefits are on a flat-rate basis.[1]

In Western Europe, plans were developed, in a number of occupied countries during the war, for more comprehensive social security legislation, often in discussions between employers and union members, who are usually referred to as the "social partners" in Europe (a term that is unfamiliar in the United States). In Belgium, even before the end of the war, a legislative order of December 1944 provided for substantial revision and expansion of its social security programs (Miry, 1945). Under a series of ordinances and laws

---

[1] Supplementary earnings-related contributions for sickness and unemployment insurance had been adopted earlier.

adopted in 1945 and 1946, France abolished the former social insurance and family allowance funds for workers in commercial and industrial enterprises, replacing them by a system of local and regional social security funds, which were to administer compulsory government health and sickness insurance, invalidity insurance, old-age insurance, and employment injuries insurance under the general supervision of the National Social Security Fund (Laroque, 1948; Durand, 1953).

Czechoslovakia, which had had a relatively comprehensive social insurance system before the war, adopted a much more unified system in 1948 – destined, after the Communists took over the government in 1949, to be changed gradually to conform somewhat more closely to the Soviet pattern.[2] Other countries that adopted significant social security changes soon after the end of the war were Ireland, Italy, Norway, Sweden, and Yugoslavia.

Both Australia and Canada had appointed parliamentary commissions during the war, which developed plans for broader social security systems, but major changes were destined to occur slowly, especially in the controversial area of hospital and medical care (*ILR*, 1943, *47* [April]: 591–612; Marsh, 1943; Kewley, 1973). Canada did, however, adopt a children's allowance system in 1944, whereas in Australia, which had adopted children's allowances in 1941, a constitutional amendment was presented to the voters and approved in 1946, confirming the power of the federal government to enact legislation with respect to a broad range of social security programs.

In the United States, which had adopted its Social Security Act in 1935, the Wagner–Murray–Dingle bill, introduced in Congress in 1943, would have greatly expanded the social security program to provide for federal health insurance, as well as temporary disability and maternity insurance, and would have federalized the federal–state unemployment insurance system (*ILR*, 1945, *52* [July]: 88–90). However, strong opposition from the U.S. Chamber of Commerce, the American Medical Association, private insurance companies, and business interests generally, not only succeeded in defeating the proposed legislation, but continued throughout the postwar period to block federal legislation in these fields, except for the compromise leading to the adoption of Medicare and Medicaid in 1965, providing health insurance for the elderly and means-tested medical assistance for the poor. Nevertheless, the Social Security Act was amended frequently until it provided for broad coverage and a moderately liberal system of insurance for the aged, survivors, and disabled.

Family allowances

One of the most dramatic developments of the 1940s and 1950s was the adoption of family allowances systems, providing benefits according to the number

---

[2] Some of the information on Czechoslovakia that I shall be using is based on interviews in Prague in 1966.

of children in a family and frequently referred to as "children's allowances," in country after country. Such programs had existed in seven of the countries included in this study before the war, chiefly in Europe, dating from the 1930s, and in most cases related to employment in the sense that they covered employees with children and were financed by employers. By the late 1950s, nearly all of the countries included in this study had adopted family allowance schemes.

There is little question that the recommendation for family allowances in the Beveridge Report played an important role in stimulating the adoption of family allowances systems, and also in ensuring that many of the new programs were universal – applying to all children regardless of the employment status or income of the parent(s), or at least applying to all residents with several children. Beveridge clearly favored such an approach, as his arguments for children's allowances indicated (*Social Insurance* . . . , 1942, 154–5):

First, it is unreasonable to seek to guarantee an income sufficient for subsistence, while earnings are interrupted by unemployment or disability, without ensuring sufficient income during earning. Social insurance should be part of a policy of a national minimum. But a national minimum for families of every size cannot in practice be secured by a wage system, which must be based on the product of a man's labor and not on the size of his family. . . . Second, it is dangerous to allow benefit during unemployment or disability to equal or exceed earnings during work. But, without allowances for children, during earning and not-earning alike, this danger cannot be avoided. . . . the gap between income during earning and during interruption of earning should be as large as possible for every man. It cannot be kept large for men with large families, except either by making their benefit in unemployment and disability inadequate, or by giving allowances for children in time of earning and not-earning alike.

In addition . . . there are arguments arising from consideration of numbers of population and care of children. With its present rate of reproduction, the British race cannot continue; means of reversing the recent course of the birth rate must be found. It is not likely that allowances for children . . . will, by themselves, provide that means and lead parents who do not desire children to rear children for gain. But children's allowances can help to restore the birth rate, both by making it possible for parents who desire more children to bring them into the world without damaging the chances of those already born, and as a signal of the national interest in children. . . .

As to the source of children's allowances, the view taken here is that they should be non-contributory, provided wholly out of taxation, and not to any extent by insurance contributions.

The rationale for children's allowances will be considered more fully in Chapter 13, along with differences in the systems adopted in various countries and the changing course of policies relating to them. Suffice it to say at this point that although the real benefit provided per child was allowed to erode in a good many countries in the 1950s and 1960s, there was a reversal of this trend in some countries in the 1970s, along with a movement to target child benefits at least to some extent toward low-income families.

Other early postwar developments

Apart from the growth of children's allowance systems, the major developments of the late 1940s and 1950s included (1) the expansion and liberalization of pension programs, which emerged from the war either greatly weakened or seriously inadequate in relation to postwar wage and price levels, (2) the rounding out of social security systems by adoption of programs, especially health and unemployment benefits, where none had existed before, (3) the replacement of voluntary by compulsory programs, especially in health, work injury, and unemployment benefit systems, and (4) provisions for indexing of benefits – that is, adjustment to changing wage and/or price levels – either on an automatic basis or on the basis of a requirement for systematic review.

By 1961, nearly all of the countries included in this study had comprehensive social security programs. Provision for medical care was limited in some countries and a significant group of countries had no provision for unemployment benefits. Except for Israel, however, the countries that lacked unemployment benefits were all in the Soviet bloc, where socialist policies aimed at eliminating unemployment or at least maintaining that it did not exist.

During the 1960s, the movement toward two-tiered pension systems, which began with Sweden in the late 1950s, continued, with Canada, Britain, Denmark, Finland, and Norway adopting either earnings-related or employment-related supplements to their flat-rate pension systems. Contributing in a somewhat different way to the movement toward two-tiered or even three-tiered systems were guaranteed minima for the elderly and liberalization of public assistance systems.

In the health benefits field, notable developments in the 1960s were the federal legislation on medical insurance in Canada in 1966, and adoption of the Medicare and Medicaid systems in the United States in 1965.

In Eastern Europe, two developments in Czechoslovakia were forerunners of changes that were to spread in the Soviet bloc in the 1970s. The first was a rounded program to encourage population growth through an increase in the duration of maternity benefits, a provision that a mother who stayed at home to rear a child up to the third birthday would be credited with periods of work (for social insurance purposes), and a lowered age of retirement for women who had reared children. The second was a group of measures aimed at encouraging older workers to continue working beyond pensionable age as a means of helping to meet manpower shortages (Pisca, 1965).

Clearly one of the most significant developments of the 1960s was the adoption of the ''war on poverty'' in the United States, not so much for its immediate effects, which were quite limited, but for the heightened interest in the persistence of poverty in industrial countries that it stimulated. It seems likely that the intensified interest in combatting poverty in this country played a role in stimulating a similar development in several other countries, especially in the British Commonwealth, although increased awareness in other countries would probably have developed sooner or later regardless of what was happening in the United States.

The legislation directly associated with the war on poverty was the Economic Opportunity Act, signed by President Lyndon B. Johnson in August 1964. Transmitting the proposed legislation to Congress five months earlier, he urged Americans as "citizens of the richest . . . nation in the history of the world" to declare war on poverty.[3]

During the 1950s, in the United States and most other industrial countries, concern about poverty had not been very widespread. The general assumption was that gradual improvement of income maintenance programs and maintenance of full employment would eliminate poverty. To be sure, certain writers – notably Galbraith (1958) in the United States and Titmuss (1958) in Great Britain – called attention to the inadequacy of measures to reduce poverty. There also was keen awareness of poverty in old age among social gerontologists.

In retrospect, however, it seems clear that the civil rights movement played a decisive role in dramatizing the problem of poverty, especially among minority groups, in the early 1960s. In addition, the publication of Michael Harrington's *The Other America* (1962) – a vivid portrayal of the incidence of poverty among underprivileged groups in the United States – was notable, perhaps because it influenced President Kennedy, who had been disturbed by the poverty he saw when campaigning in West Virginia, to urge the Council of Economic Advisers to investigate the problem more thoroughly (Levy, 1980, 19).

Partly because of cost considerations, and partly because there was little support for income maintenance programs among some of those who were influential in developing plans for the war on poverty, the Economic Opportunity Act did not include provisions for improving income maintenance programs, which at the time were quite limited, but placed its emphasis on aiding the disadvantaged to improve their labor market skills.

A significant aspect of the war on poverty was the development of intensive research into the causes of poverty on the part of social scientists in the United States and a number of other countries. Younger economists in this country disputed orthodox concepts, such as the marginal productivity theory of wages, and developed a "dual labor market theory," distinguishing between the primary labor market, in which workers have full-time stable jobs and generous

---

[3] Quoted in Levitan (1969, 3), a volume that provides an illuminating discussion of the antecedents and development of the war on poverty. See also M. S. Gordon, ed. (1965a).

fringe benefits, and the secondary labor market, in which jobs are nonunion-
ized, temporary or part-time or both, with low wages and little or no fringe
benefits, except for those that are legally mandatory (see, e.g., D.M. Gordon,
1972; Doeringer and Piore, 1977; and D. M. Gordon, Edwards, and Reich,
1982). Minority and other disadvantaged workers tend to be in the secondary
labor market.

Another offshoot of the war on poverty was to arouse interest, especially
among economists, in the negative income tax, a version of a guaranteed
minimum income that originated with Edgeworth, the British economist, in
the late nineteenth century, and was revived by economist Milton Friedman
in the United States in his *Capitalism and Freedom* (1962). This proposal and
related versions of a guaranteed minimum income will be discussed in Chapters 13 and 14, where we shall find that concepts embodied in the negative
income tax and in related tax credit proposals have influenced modifications in
policies affecting low-income groups, even though no country has adopted a
comprehensive negative income tax or tax credit system involving the entire
population.

The 1970s and 1980s

The economic developments of the 1970s and 1980s gradually undermined
the financial strength of at least some social security programs and created an
environment that was much less favorable to their expansion than in the preceding two decades. Economic growth was less stable, inflation rates were
far higher, and there was a decided trend toward higher unemployment rates
in nearly all market-oriented industrial countries, especially after 1973.

Inflation created a problem for social security programs, many of which
were indexed, especially in years when prices rose more sharply than wages.
Since the chief sources of revenue for most social insurance programs were
the earnings-related contributions paid by employers and employees, revenue
tended to become insufficient to meet the increase in benefits, which in most
countries were linked to price changes. The problem was especially serious
for health benefit programs because many countries experienced sharply increasing medical costs, at rates that exceeded the rise in the overall consumer
price index.

Rising unemployment exacerbated the financial problems not only by increasing the burden of unemployment insurance and assistance but also by
reducing the social insurance revenue derived from contributory employer and
employee taxes.

In spite of all this, the changes enacted in social security programs during
the 1970s were primarily of an expansionary character. Rising costs were met
initially for the most part by raising taxes (Zeitzer, 1983). It was not until

toward the end of the decade that serious "belt tightening" began to appear, in the form of modifications and delays in indexing and in measures to control hospital and medical costs and to impose more charges on patients. In the early 1980s, as unemployment rates rose to heights that in many countries were unprecedented in the postwar period, changes designed to bring costs under greater control continued.

Major improvements in pension programs were adopted in at least 11 of our countries during the 1970s, while there was also a pronounced trend toward liberalization of early retirement provisions, especially in Western Europe. The move to encourage early retirement was by and large a response to rising unemployment, and especially to a serious problem of youth unemployment that developed in Western Europe in the late 1970s and continued into the 1980s. Unemployment rates varied from country to country, however, and the youth unemployment rate tended to be high where overall unemployment was high. It had been high throughout the 1970s in this country.

Along with liberalized early retirement policies, programs aimed directly at improving job opportunities for youth were expanded and liberalized in many cases. Sometimes the liberalized early retirement provisions and the measures aimed at youth unemployment were directly linked, as in Belgium, where special prepension benefits were provided for older workers who voluntarily withdrew from employment, on condition that the employer hired a worker under age 30 as a replacement, not necessarily in the same job (Tracy, 1978). Somewhat similar approaches, though differing in detail, were adopted in Finland, West Germany, Spain, and the United Kingdom.

Also noteworthy among developments in the 1970s was increased emphasis on measures to overcome poverty in several countries. One indication of this trend was the adoption of minimum income guarantees for public assistance recipients in Austria and Belgium and for low-income families in France. Other manifestations were the issuance of a White Paper on Income Security in Canada in 1970, a British Green Paper in 1972 that proposed a broadly based system of tax credits, and the 1975 report of the Australian Government Commission on Inquiry into Poverty, which recommended a guaranteed minimum income plan for Australia. Among these reports, the Canadian White Paper had the most significant impact on legislation, although changes occurred only gradually over the course of the 1970s.

Also related to the goal of stamping out poverty were a number of changes in family allowance systems and tax policies in relation to children, designed to target more benefits toward low-income families. Related to these shifts in family allowance systems were a number of changes designed to make it financially more feasible for mothers to stay at home to care for young children. Both Hungary and Poland adopted changes in the 1970s that were similar to those we discussed with respect to Czechoslovakia in the 1960s, changes that appeared to be at least partly motivated by a desire to maintain population growth. Similar changes also occurred in Western Europe and among British Commonwealth countries, where they were more likely to be influenced by both the women's liberation movement and the drive to overcome poverty. Attracting widespread attention in other countries was an amendment to Sweden's health insurance scheme in 1973, which converted maternity insurance to parents' insurance, making it possible for a father to be eligible for a cash benefit if he stayed at home to care for a newborn child. The policy has been gradually liberalized since its original adoption and several other countries have adopted similar programs. It is probably no accident that this movement started in the country in which the Myrdals developed comprehensive recommendations for a family policy in the 1930s. We shall have much more to say about various aspects of increased interest in family policies in Chapter 13.

One of the most striking developments of the 1970s was an increase throughout the industrialized world in the proportion of single-parent families, usually headed by the mother, although the trend had been underway earlier. More frequent separations and divorces, as well as a marked decline in the traditional social stigma associated with cohabitation, and a rise in the frequency of illegitimate births were responsible. Liberalized policies to benefit single-parent families were adopted in response to this development in a number of countries.

Another important development of the 1970s and early 1980s was a move to impose compulsory standards on private pension plans, especially in relation to financing and vesting provisions, and in a few European countries the adoption of legislation to make pension plans mandatory. The whole question of the relationship between national pension programs and private employer pension plans has become a matter of controversy and will be discussed at length in Chapter 8.

The growth of expenditures

Throughout the postwar period there has been a persistent trend toward rising social security expenditures as a percentage of gross domestic product (GDP) – a trend that has been implied by liberalization of programs that we have been discussing. The tendency toward rising expenditures accelerated in the 1970s under the impact of stagflation, although, as we have seen, toward the end of the decade and in the early 1980s efforts were made in a number of countries to hold down spending. Rising costs of social security programs were attributable not only to liberalization of the programs but also to the maturing of programs, which meant that increasing numbers were eligible for benefits, and, in addition, to the aging of the population in most industrial countries.

For purposes of international comparisons of expenditures, the most satisfactory data are those compiled by the ILO and published in its reports on *The Cost of Social Security* which are issued every three or four years. Unfortunately, the last year for which they are available is 1980. Other useful comparative data are available for more recent years from the Organization for Economic Cooperation and Development (OECD) and from the European Economic Community (EEC).

Interestingly, although social security expenditures in Eastern Europe (as indicated by data for four Soviet bloc countries) were somewhat higher in relation to GDP in the early 1960s than elsewhere, they rose less rapidly during the 1960s and most of the 1970s than in most other industrial countries, and, by 1980, continued to be somewhat lower as a percentage of GDP than in Western Europe (Figure 1.1).[4] An important reason for these differing trends was the fact that prices were stable in most countries of Eastern Europe, and unemployment, at least according to official statistics, was nonexistent. Moreover, although the average annual rate of real economic growth declined in Eastern Europe between the late 1960s and the 1970s, it remained appreciably higher than elsewhere.

It is important to note that the decline in social security expenditures as a percentage of gross domestic product shown in Figure 1.1 between 1977 and 1978 was wholly or mainly a result of a change in the definition of social security expenditures in the ILO data. Before 1978, free hospital and medical services, as well as such usual public health measures as sanitation services, were included under "public health services." From 1978 on, however, all health care benefits provided to individuals were included under sickness and maternity benefits, whereas public health measures designed to protect the general public were excluded from the data.

Where social security benefits are indexed for rising prices or wages, an increase in the rate of inflation will not necessarily mean a rise in social security expenditures as a percentage of GDP, but it must be kept in mind that,

---

[4] In compiling the data for Figure 1.1 (and certain later tables), I have omitted public employee benefit expenditures because public employee benefits are not included in this study, except in passing. I have also omitted veterans' benefits, since their relative magnitude tends to reflect the extent of involvement in past wars, and, again, they are not included in this study. It should also be noted that the base for computation of percentages in the early years was gross national product (GNP) rather than gross domestic product (GDP). The 11 Western European countries included in the chart are Austria, Belgium, Denmark, Finland, France, Germany (Fed. Rep.), Italy, the Netherlands, Norway, Sweden, and Switzerland. The four British Commonwealth countries are Australia, Canada, New Zealand, and the United Kingdom, while the four Eastern European countries are Czechoslovakia, Hungary, Poland, and the USSR. Other countries are omitted because data were not available for the early years of the period.

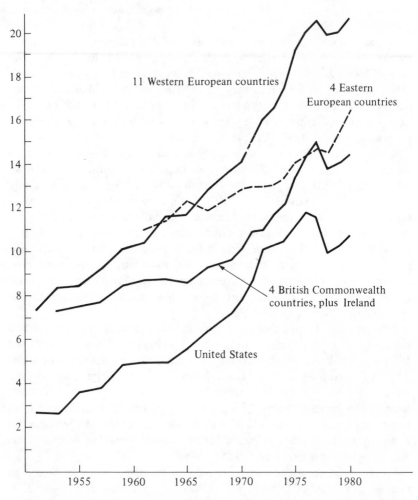

Figure 1.1. Average expenditures on social security as a percentage of gross domestic product, selected countries and groups of countries, biennially, 1951–69, and annually, 1970–80. (Data do not include public employees' and veterans' benefits.) (*Source:* ILO, *The Cost of Social Security,* selected issues.)

throughout the Western industrial world, medical care costs tended to rise more rapidly than the overall consumer price index and tended to account for a considerably larger percentage of social security expenditures than of consumer expenditures in general. Moreover, the combination of high inflation rates and an upward trend in the unemployment rate contributed to the upward trend in social security spending. The fact that benefits were indexed in most Western industrial countries tended to mean that the impact of rising prices on social security costs was felt fairly promptly, whereas in Eastern Europe only Hungary had an indexing provision calling for an automatic adjustment of old-age and invalidity pensions of 2 percent (or not less than 50 forints) a year.

The United Kingdom is widely regarded as a leading welfare state, but, in fact, British expenditures on social security have been appreciably lower in relation to GDP than those of most continental Western European countries throughout the postwar period, as we shall see in Chapter 2, when we analyze differences among countries in greater detail. Thus, it is not misleading to group Britain with other Commonwealth countries, as we have done in Figure 1.1. Ireland is also included with the British group because its original social security provisions were developed under British law, and Irish provisions have been strongly influenced by those of Britain since Ireland achieved independence.

Whereas expenditures in the British countries tend to be somewhat lower than those in Western Europe in relation to GDP, those in the United States have consistently been lower than in any of the groups of countries included in Figure 1.1. A major reason for this difference is the absence of a national health insurance or health service program in the United States, which has only the special health programs for the aged, the disabled, and the poor (Medicare and Medicaid). Nearly every other country included in this study has a comprehensive national health insurance or health service program. The United States is also unique in not having a children's allowance program, although expenditures for public assistance are probably somewhat higher than they would be if the United States had a children's allowance program.

What can be said about the trend in social security expenditures since 1980? In general, in spite of efforts to hold down spending, there has been an upward trend, to a considerable extent associated with the rise in unemployment rates. Thus, it is useful to consider the behavior of unemployment rates from 1960 to the third quarter of 1987 (Figures 1.2 and 1.3). Increases, generally beginning about the mid-1970s, were pronounced in the United States, Canada, France, West Germany, the United Kingdom, Australia, Belgium, the Netherlands, and Spain (data for Spain not shown). On the other hand, they were minimal or very slight in Japan, Austria, Norway, Sweden, and Switzerland (data for Switzerland not shown), whereas the increase was moderate in Italy (based on adjusted U.S. Bureau of Labor Statistics data[5]). Since 1983,

---

[5] Since the early 1960s, the U.S. Bureau of Labor Statistics has been adjusting unemployment data in selected other industrial countries to conform to American definitions. Its adjustments are somewhat more extensive than those of the OECD, but the differences are slight except in the case of Italy.

Percent

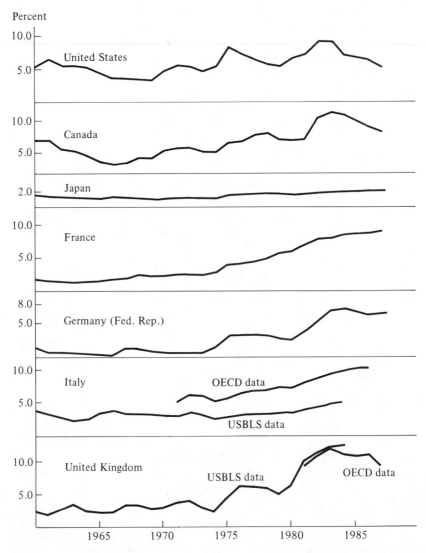

Figure 1.2. Adjusted unemployment rates, larger OECD countries, 1960–87. (Data for 1987, where available, refer to the third quarter of the year.) (*Source:* U.S. Bureau of Labor Statistics, 1978; Moy, 1985, 14; OECD, 1987d.)

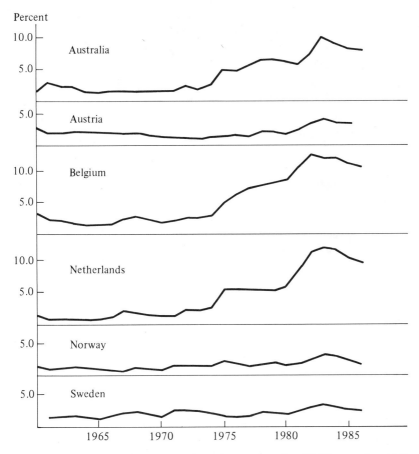

Figure 1.3. Adjusted unemployment rates, smaller OECD countries, 1960–87. (Data for 1987, where available, refer to the third quarter of the year.) (*Sources:* OECD, 1972, 1987d; U.S. Bureau of Labor Statistics, 1978.)

there has been a decline or leveling off in a number of countries, but the unemployment rate continues to be "stuck" at a very high rate (unprecedentedly high for the postwar period) in France and Spain, whereas in Belgium, the Netherlands, and the United Kingdom a decline has occurred but the rate continues to be very high. The rate also continues to be high (about 8 percent) in Australia.

For our present purposes, it is important to point out that, in general, increases in social security spending as a percentage of GDP occurred in all of the OECD countries included in our data (Table 1.1) as unemployment rose

Table 1.1. *Expenditures on social security as a percentage of gross domestic product, OECD countries, 1980, 1983, and 1985 (excluding expenditures on health care)*

Country	1980	1983	1985
Canada	10.2%	12.9%	12.3%
United States	10.1	11.0	10.1
Japan	10.2	11.3	11.0
Australia	8.4	9.9	9.7
Austria	15.2	16.0	16.0
Belgium	21.1	23.0	22.0
Denmark	16.6	17.8	16.4
Finland	6.9	8.3	8.8
France	21.4	23.9	24.3
Germany (Fed. Rep.)	14.7	15.2	14.4
Greece	9.2	13.4	15.0
Ireland	12.9	14.1	15.1
Italy	15.8	17.0	16.6
Netherlands	24.9	27.8	26.1
Norway	14.4	15.5	14.8
Spain	13.7		
Sweden	17.1	17.9	17.7
Switzerland	12.7	13.5	13.7
United Kingdom	10.4	14.6	14.7

Source: OECD (1987c).

from 1980 to 1983, and in many of them fell back somewhat between 1983 and 1985 as unemployment rates fell. The largest increases from 1980 to 1983 tended to occur in the countries with the sharpest increases in the unemployment rate, although there were some exceptions. Both the United States and West Germany experienced only slight increases, even though their unemployment rates were substantially higher in 1983 than in 1980. It should be kept in mind, however, that inclusion of spending on health care would change the pattern for some countries.[6]

What are the implications for social security policies? In my interviews with European social security experts, I have not encountered an expectation of fundamental changes. What most of them anticipate, rather, is a continuation of minor adjustments and adaptations like those of recent years. I am not so sure. Opposition to social security benefits flowing to middle- and higher-

[6] OECD data on social security expenditures, as published in the annual volumes on *National Accounts*, include only cash benefits and omit health care. Two recent OECD reports (1985a, 1987a), however, do include expenditures on health, but the most recent data on health expenditures are for 1984. See Table 10.3.

income persons is of significant proportions in the United States and Britain and in some conservative circles in West Germany, as is insistence that benefits should be more effectively targeted to the poor. These trends could eventually lead to reduced emphasis on both universal benefits and social insurance programs, despite the widespread evidence of support for both types of programs. We shall return to this central issue in future chapters. We turn now, in Chapter 2, to a discussion of the differences in rates of spending and in sources of revenue for social security programs.

Differences in social security spending

Rates of spending

What accounts for the wide differences in rates of social security spending among industrial countries, ranging all the way from 28.6 percent of gross domestic product (GDP) in Sweden to 7.8 percent in Japan in 1980? This is a question that has attracted the attention of a number of investigators, with results that are generally consistent from one study to another.

In Table 2.1, we have assembled data including a number of variables that have been found to be associated with social security expenditures as a percentage of GDP. The countries with the oldest social security programs have been found to be the largest social security spenders in several studies. In an analysis of data for 22 industrial countries, Aaron (1967, 25) found that the "maturity of the system" was the most important of any of the variables he tested in explaining the percentage of national income devoted to social security expenditures (see also Pechman, Aaron, and Taussig, 1968, appendix D). I had earlier developed a related finding, that the longer a country had had an old-age benefit program, the higher its average old-age benefit was likely to be in relation to per capita income and earnings levels (M. S. Gordon, 1963a, 455–6). In a more complex analysis, Wilensky (1975, 24) found that economic level and social security effort were strongly related, but that this relationship was "largely mediated through the proportion of the aged in the population . . . and, second, through both age of the population and age of the system . . . ." His study included both industrial and less developed countries, indicating that the low levels of social security spending in less developed countries are related to their extremely low per capita income levels. In a regression analysis, based on the variables included in Table 2.1, the percentage of the population aged 65 and older was particularly strongly related to the rate of social security spending, but the year of adoption of the first social security program and the percentage of elderly men in the labor force were also related to the level of social security spending in 1980.[1]

[1] In determining the date of the first program, I have excluded industrial injuries programs, which were adopted relatively early in most countries, because they were often followed by other programs only with a considerable lag, and because, in any case, they account for a very

TABLE 2.1. *Selected variables associated with social security expenditures, selected industrial countries, 1980*

Country	Social security expenditures as a percentage of GDP	Date of first program	Percentage of population aged 65 and older	Percentage of men aged 65 and older in labor force
Sweden	28.6%	1891	16.3%	14.2%
Denmark	25.0	1891	14.4	24.0
Netherlands	24.2	1913	11.5	4.8
France	22.7	1905	13.9	7.5
Belgium	20.6	1894	14.4	6.6
Germany (Fed. Rep.)	19.4	1883	15.5	7.0
Czechoslovakia	18.9	1888	12.4	19.5
Average, above countries	22.8	1895	14.1	11.9
Norway	18.8	1906	14.8	32.4
Ireland	18.4	1908	10.7	25.8
Hungary	18.1	1891	13.5	3.9
Germany (Dem. Rep.)	17.0	1883	16.0[a]	25.6[a]
Austria	16.7	1886	15.4	3.1
United Kingdom	15.3	1908	14.9	10.5
Finland	15.0	1917	12.0	17.0
Average, above countries	17.0	1899	13.9	16.9
Poland	14.9	1920	10.2	34.9
Italy	13.8	1912	12.9	12.6
USSR	13.8	1912	8.9[a]	10.6[a]
Spain	13.8	1919	10.9	12.3
New Zealand	13.0	1898	9.7	11.1
Canada	12.3	1927	9.5	14.7
Average, above countries	13.6	1915	10.4	16.0
Switzerland	12.0	1911	13.7	15.1
United States	10.0	1935	11.3	18.3
Australia	9.8	1908	9.6	11.1
Israel	9.6	1953	8.4	24.5
Greece	8.9	1922	13.1	30.6
Japan	7.8	1922	9.0	41.0
Average, above countries	9.7	1925	10.9	23.4

Note: Expenditures on public exployee benefits and verterans' benefits are not included in social security expenditures, as explained in Chapter 1, footnote 4; and dates of adoption of work injury programs are excluded from determination of the date of the first program, as explained in this chapter, footnote 1. *Sources:* ILO, *Year Book of Labor Statistics* (various issues); United Nations, *Demographic Yearbook* (various issues); ILO (1985b); OECD (1987b).
[a] 1975.

There are several reasons why the rate of social security spending might be expected to be high in the countries with the oldest programs. For one thing, social security programs become more costly as they mature and more people become eligible for benefits. For another, expenditures on government programs tend to rise in an incremental fashion because small increases from year to year are more likely to receive approval than sudden, large increases.

The influence of the percentage of elderly people in the population on the rate of social security spending is also easy to explain. Old-age pensions represent a large proportion of social security expenditures, as do health benefits, which flow in considerable measure to the elderly, with their relatively high medical costs. And, of course, the percentage of elderly people in the population tends to be relatively high in highly industrialized countries, which also tend to have adopted social security programs comparatively early.

The tendency for the percentage of elderly men in the labor force to be inversely related to the rate of social security spending must be viewed as both a cause and an effect of high levels of social security spending. Clearly, the larger the percentage of elderly men who are out of the labor force, the larger the proportion of older men who are receiving pensions. But it is also true that, where old-age pensions are comparatively high in relation to earnings levels, the incentive to retire is likely to be more pronounced. I found this to be the case in the early 1950s (M. S. Gordon, 1963a), and a later and more extensive analysis by Aaron produced similar results on the basis of 1960 data (Pechman, Aaron, and Taussig, 1968, 297–8). It would, however, be simplistic to interpret this finding to mean that social security *causes* retirement, as some writers have been inclined to do. When we take a closer look at the trend toward earlier retirement in Chapter 5, we shall find that ill health, reduced earning capacity, and adverse labor market conditions are very important among reasons for retirement, and the availability of reasonably adequate social security benefits simply makes the decision to retire under such circumstances more feasible.

The percentage of elderly women in the labor force is not a significant factor in explaining differences in rates of social security spending among industrial countries, because everywhere the percentage of women, at least among those aged 65 and older, in the labor force is low and has been so historically. Among women under about age 60, there has, of course, been a remarkable increase in labor force participation in many industrial countries, and we shall take a closer look at the impact of this increase on social security issues in Chapter 4.

What about the influence of per capita income on social security spending?

small percentage of expenditures in relation to GDP in comparison with health and pension programs. I had originally intended to present the regression results in an appendix, but discarded this plan in my effort to hold down the total length of the volume.

My regressions indicate that per capita income is only weakly, though significantly, related to social security spending as a percentage of GDP. This is somewhat surprising, in view of the fact that countries with high per capita incomes can afford to spend relatively generously on social security, but the weakness of the relationship indicates that other factors, such as the maturity of social security programs, cut across the influence of per capita income.

If, however, we measure relative social security expenditures, not as a percentage of GDP (the usual method) but in terms of social security expenditures per capita in U.S. dollars, we find a much closer association between levels of social security spending and per capita income (Table 2.2). This reflects the fact that some countries with comparatively high per capita incomes, such as Canada, the United States, and Switzerland, rank significantly higher in terms of social security expenditures per capita than in terms of the more usual measure, whereas others – for example, Italy, New Zealand, and Ireland – with low per capita incomes, rank lower in terms of social security expenditures per capita. Because social security benefit levels tend to be earnings-related in most countries, this is not particularly surprising. Even where benefits are predominantly flat-rate, their level is clearly influenced by income levels.

In Chapter 1, we found that increases in rates of social security spending from 1980 to 1983 were positively related, with a few exceptions, to increases in unemployment rates during those years.

I have also investigated several other possible influences on social security spending, with the following results: First, although it might be expected that social security expenditures would be inversely related to military expenditures, the pattern is far from consistent, although there is a slight tendency toward such a relationship. Second, in line with Wilensky's finding (1975, 52), highly centralized governments are likely to spend more on social security than less centralized governments. In particular, there are obstacles to expansion of social security in a federal system, where there are frequently constitutional problems to be overcome before the federal government can be involved in social programs. This has been true in Australia, Canada, Switzerland, and the United States, but not so clearly in the Federal Republic of Germany, where social insurance programs have been the province of the federal government since the 1880s. Where social insurance programs are financed in large part by the states, as in the case of unemployment insurance in the United States, moreover, employers tend to resist increases in payroll taxes which may raise their costs in relation to those of competitors in other states.

If the countries with the oldest programs are the largest spenders, we need to ask why some industrial countries were leaders and others were laggards in adopting social security programs. As a broad generalization, we know that

Table 2.2. *Selected variables associated with social security expenditures per capita, OECD countries, 1977*

Country	Social security expenditures per capita in U.S. dollars	Per capita income in U.S. dollars	Percentage of population aged 65 and older
Sweden	$2,652	$8,369	15.3%
Denmark	2,176	8,199	13.6
Netherlands	1,979	6,989	10.9
Belgium	1,939	7,449	13.9
Germany (Fed. Rep.)	1,797	7,465	14.7
Average, above countries	2,109	7,694	13.7
Switzerland	1,756	8,918	13.1
France	1,718	6,380	13.5
Norway	1,679	7,253	13.5
Austria	1,144	5,576	15.1
Finland	1,073	5,660	10.9
Average, above countries	1,474	6,757	13.2
Canada	1,069	7,485	8.5
United States	1,016	7,686	10.9
Australia	908	7,080	8.5
New Zealand	779	4,556	8.8
Italy	718	3,438	12.3
Average, above countries	898	6,049	9.8
United Kingdom	660	3,898	14.3
Ireland	526	2,711	10.9
Japan	488	5,761	8.1
Spain	386	2,896	9.8
Greece	258	2,701	12.3
Israel	236	3,460	7.8
Average, above countries	426	3,571	10.5

Note: Social security expenditures do not include public employee benefits and veterans' benefits, for reasons explained in Chapter 1, footnote 4.

Sources: Social security expenditures are from ILO (1981); per capita income in U.S. dollars is from United Nations (1978b); and percentage of population aged 65 and older is from United Nations (1978a).

industrialization and urbanization were the forces that led to the movement
for governments to protect workers from the economic risks associated with
illness, unemployment, and old age. During the nineteenth century, and especially in the latter half of that century, workers in Europe and to some
extent elsewhere sought to protect themselves from the risk of loss of wages
by forming sickness funds or mutual aid funds, but, although these funds
could provide protection against short periods of illness, it was difficult for
them to accumulate enough resources to protect their members against lengthy
periods of unemployment or disability, or to provide income over a long period to elderly members who could no longer work. Voluntary old-age insurance funds were also sponsored by some European governments, but typically those who joined up were relatively few and tended to be workers with
comparatively high wages.

Even so, although the role of industrialization was of overriding importance
in leading to the adoption of social security programs, it was not the most
advanced industrial countries that led the way. Germany, which was clearly
the leader in developing social insurance programs, was less industrialized
than England in the 1880s, although it was catching up. It also came later to
industrialization than Belgium. We must look to differences in political developments to explain why Germany preceded England by several decades in
the development of modern social security measures. Of predominant importance in the German case was the strength of the Socialist movement among
the working classes (Hazen, 1923, 280). Chancellor Bismarck, alarmed by
the growth of this movement, developed a two-pronged policy to crush it,
consisting of stern repression of Socialist agitation, on the one hand, and
amelioration of the harsh conditions of the working class, on the other.

Bismarck's program was enacted over the course of the decade, but not
the historic message of the Kaiser to the Reichstag in November 1881, which
stated:

The cure of social ills must be sought not exclusively in the repression of the Social
Democratic excesses, but simultaneously in the positive advancement in the welfare
of the working classes. . . . In order to realize these views a Bill for the insurance of
workmen against industrial accidents will first be laid before you, after which a supplementary measure will be submitted providing for a general organization of industrial sickness insurance. But likewise those who are disabled in consequence of old
age or invalidity possess a well-founded claim to a more ample relief on the part of
the State than they have hitherto enjoyed.

(quoted in Rimlinger, 1971, 114)

Bismarck's program was enacted over the course of the decade, but not
without intense controversy, with large employers generally supporting the
plans for compulsory social insurance and smaller employers opposing them.

Imbued with Marxist theory, and in marked contrast with the role the Social Democrats were to play in more recent times, the Social Democrats vigorously opposed the measures on the ground that it was impossible to improve the worker's economic position within the capitalist framework. They also argued that social insurance was nothing but another form of poor relief, except that the worker would have to pay for it.

In opting for earnings-related social insurance, rather than for replacing the poor laws with a more humane public assistance system, Bismarck was influenced in part by insurance schemes for the miners, and by the possibility of building onto the existing mutual funds that were already providing sickness benefits. Of perhaps dominant importance, however, according to Rimlinger (1971, 121), was Bismarck's view of social insurance as a means of binding the worker to the state, especially in the case of old-age and invalidity insurance, which would have the effect of increasing the worker's stake in the existing order.

In Britain, the movement toward modern social legislation did not develop much strength in Parliament until the first decade of the twentieth century, although a weak Workmen's Compensation Act was adopted in 1897. An important political difference between Britain and Germany was that the German Socialists began electing significant numbers of members to the Reichstag in the 1870s, but it was not until 1906 that a working class party – the Labor Party – was formed in England and began to elect members to Parliament. During the 1880s and 1890s, alternating Liberal and Conservative governments were preoccupied with the Irish Home Rule question and with such issues as extension of the franchise and the strengthening of imperialism. Moreover, the Boer War, which began in 1899, effectively stopped any serious consideration of social legislation for several years.

Nevertheless, the winds of change were stirring in Britain in the 1880s, especially during the recession of 1885–6. Union membership grew rapidly and labor began to display greater militancy (Fried and Elman, 1968, xi). Socialist ideas began to be accepted within the union movement, and to some extent among intellectuals and professionals, some of whom formed the Fabian Society in 1884. However, poverty continued to be viewed by the general public as a problem of the shiftless. A major influence in leading to more enlightened attitudes toward poverty was the publication in the late 1880s and 1890s of Charles Booth's meticulous studies of poverty in London, which eventually ran to 17 volumes. Booth showed that about one-third of Londoners were living in poverty, and that by far the most important causes of poverty were employment and health problems, whereas only about 15 percent of the cases could be attributed to idleness, drunkenness, or thriftlessness (Fried and Elman, 1986, xxiv; Booth, 1894).

A similar study was conducted in York by B. Seebohm Rowntree,[2] who identified six main immediate causes of "primary poverty" (income insufficient to obtain the minimum necessities) (Rowntree, 1922, 152–3):

> Death of the chief wage earner (15.6%)
> Incapacity of the chief wage earner through illness, accident, and old age (5.1%)
> Chief wage earner out of work (2.3%)
> Chronic irregularity of work (2.8%)
> Large size of family – more than four children (22.2%)
> Lowness of wages (52.0%)

By 1905, interest in more enlightened social legislation led Parliament to appoint the Royal Commission on the Poor Laws, which deliberated for four years and split into two factions, one of which issued a Majority Report favoring modernization of the poor relief system, and the other a Minority Report (strongly influenced by Beatrice Webb) which advocated the breaking up of the old Poor Law and the development of social services emphasizing prevention of poverty and dealing with each aspect of poverty according to its cause (Sidney and Beatrice Webb, 1910).

In 1908, after prolonged debate Parliament enacted the Old Age Pensions Act, in which the German old-age insurance model was rejected in favor of a flat-rate means-tested pension resembling the Danish provisions of 1891 (discussed in Chapter 3) and the old-age pension legislation enacted by New Zealand in 1898 and by Australia in 1908.

In general, the German social insurance model, with variations in detail, was adopted by most continental European countries in the late nineteenth and early twentieth centuries, whereas the flat-rate means-tested approach – at least in old-age pensions – was favored by the British Commonwealth and Scandinavian countries. How the two approaches converged to form what is now a two-tiered, or even a three-tiered or four-tiered, system of old-age, survivors, and disability pensions in many countries will be the subject of Chapter 3.

Political differences, of course, play a role in explaining differences in social security expenditures. In general, political parties with a working class orientation have tended to support liberalization and expansion of social security programs. And, as Wilensky (1981, 364) has shown, this often includes Catholic parties, partly because the rise of Catholic workers movements in a number of Western Europe countries have pushed Catholic politicians

---

[2] Rowntree's study in York was conducted around the turn of the century, but my citation is to a later edition of his book reporting his findings.

to the left. The strength of the Social Democratic parties in the Scandinavian countries helps to explain the Scandinavian pattern of relatively generous spending on social security, along with egalitarian tendencies.

The United States was a laggard in the development of social security among industrial countries, even though it was undergoing rapid industrialization in the latter part of the nineteenth century and the early part of the twentieth century. In part, this was attributable to the fact that until around 1910, the frontier was still expanding, and workers who were not "making it" in the cities could push West and acquire a farm. Another important factor was the failure of the labor movement under Samuel Gompers's leadership to support social legislation, in its emphasis on "bread and butter" unionism and concentration on concessions from employers (Bernstein, 1960; Rimlinger, 1971, chapter 6). It was not until 1929 that the American Federation of Labor Convention supported old-age pension laws in every state (though it had previously endorsed an Ohio referendum), and it was not until 1932 that the federation reversed its traditional opposition to unemployment insurance.

As Heidenheimer (with Layson, 1982) has pointed out, however, the United States led in the development of free public schools and access to higher education. The American view was that mass education would tend to equalize economic opportunities and, indeed, was a viable substitute for income maintenance and other social legislation.

Patterns of expenditures

Differences in rates of social security spending among industrial countries cannot be fully understood without giving some attention to variations in patterns of spending. We have earlier noted that health benefits and pension programs tend to account for the largest expenditures on social security, and this is uniformly true in the countries that are the largest spenders overall (see Appendix 1). Moreover, if we consider the seven top spenders in fiscal year 1980, they all had adopted some type of health benefit program at an early date (averaging 1898) and also had adopted some type of old-age pension program relatively early.

Unemployment benefits, important as they are, did not account for very substantial spending in relation to GDP in 1980, although a few countries – chiefly those experiencing comparatively high unemployment rates (e.g., Denmark, Belgium, Ireland, and Canada) – were spending substantial amounts on unemployment benefits in 1980. There is little question, however, that unemployment helped to explain the fact that in a number of countries, public assistance expenditures were large in relation to GDP in 1980, and much higher than they had been two decades earlier. Relatively high public assistance expenditures along with a comparatively high unemployment rate were found in Denmark, France, the Netherlands, the United Kingdom, Finland, Canada, and the United States. We have noted the influence of rising unemployment rates on social security spending from 1980 to 1983, and in Chapter 14, we shall be concerned with the relationship of unemployment to public assistance expenditures.

Like unemployment benefits, family allowances tend to account for relatively small amounts of social security expenditures in most countries, but there are exceptions. Historically, France and Belgium, in which these programs date from the 1930s, tended to be the largest spenders on family allowances; however, by 1980, spending on family allowances was comparatively high, also, in the Netherlands, Czechoslovakia (where it had been relatively high in 1960), Hungary, and Israel.

As we trace the development of social security programs, the similarity in patterns of development in countries with strong cultural ties and/or geographical proximity becomes apparent. Thus, the Austro-Hungarian Empire was strongly influenced by the German model, and a residue of this influence continues today in Czechoslovakia and Hungary, as well as in Austria. Both the Scandinavian and British Commonwealth countries show similar developments, as do Belgium and France, and France and Italy, whereas Greece and Spain tend to be low spenders on social security because they are relatively late comers to industrialization and have relatively low per capita incomes.

Sources of revenue

Wide as the variations in spending rates in industrial countries are, they are not as wide as differences in sources of revenue for their social security programs. Among Western industrial countries, New Zealand, at one extreme, derived 97 percent of its revenue for social security from general government revenues in 1979–80 and only 3 percent from contributory taxes. At the other extreme, Greece got only 9 percent from general government revenues, 74 percent from contributory taxes, and 18 percent from other sources (chiefly special taxes allocated to social security) (Table 2.3).

Perhaps the most striking aspect of the data is that the countries deriving 50 percent or more of social security funds from government revenues were all either British Commonwealth or Scandinavian countries (including Ireland among British countries for reasons mentioned earlier). Moreover, two other Scandinavian countries (Finland and Norway) derived large percentages of social security revenue from general government revenues. Once again, the influence of historical tradition shows up strongly. All of these countries (except Finland) began their old-age pension programs with means-tested flat-rate benefits financed from general government revenues or earmarked in-

Table 2.3. *Sources of revenue for social security programs, OECD countries, 1979–80*

| Country | Government revenues | Contributory taxes | | Other (including interest) |
		Insured persons	Employers	
New Zealand	96.8%	—	3.2%	—
Denmark	93.7	1.9	2.1	2.3
Australia	81.2	12.1	6.3	0.5
Canada	74.8	7.2	13.0	5.0
Ireland	68.5	11.0	19.6	1.1
United Kingdom	60.4	15.1	22.7	1.8
Finland	45.0	9.2	39.1	6.7
Norway	43.5	21.6	34.2	0.6
Belgium	36.3	19.3	39.9	4.4
Sweden	35.7	1.4	52.2	10.8
Italy	35.0	11.2	51.1	2.7
United States	32.3	27.9	38.0	1.9
Japan	31.5	28.1	25.3	15.1
Netherlands	28.5	37.4	29.3	4.7
Switzerland	27.0	45.0	23.5	4.5
France	24.2	21.9	50.3	3.7
Germany (Fed. Rep.)	23.3	40.4	34.9	1.4
Austria	17.9	36.6	41.3	4.2
Spain	17.0	12.4	69.1	1.6
Greece	8.7	36.8	37.0	18.1

Note: Sources of revenue for public employee and veterans' benefit programs are excluded, as are administrative expenses.
Source: Adapted from ILO (1985b, tables 5 and 7).

come taxes (though in Sweden part of the benefits were universal). Another important factor was the importance of free hospital and medical services, not only in Britain, with its National Health Service, but also in Ireland and to some extent in the Scandinavian countries. Historically, local government funds were important in the financing of public assistance and continue to play a significant role in Denmark, Finland, and Norway, whereas provincial funds play a significant role in Canada. (Data on funds from these sources are not shown separately in Table 2.3.)

On the other hand, the countries in the lower part of Table 2.3, deriving a very large proportion of their social security revenue from contributory taxes, were all continental Western European countries with primary emphasis on social insurance in their income maintenance programs. Moreover, in some of these countries – Italy, France, Spain, and Sweden – over 50 percent came from employer payroll taxes in 1979–80. In the 1950s and 1960s, under conditions of strong economic growth and moderate inflation rates, heavy reliance on employer payroll taxes was not regarded as a serious problem, and indeed, some countries that had originally provided for equal contributions from employers and employees had raised the employer contribution rate substantially above the employee rate. Even so, the issue of the incidence of employer contributory taxes attracted considerable attention among economists. J. A. Brittain's important study (1972), with its finding that the employer payroll tax tended to be shifted back to the worker in the form of slower wage increases was influential and was supported by the studies of other economists. A more recent analysis suggests that the issue is more complex, and that the capacity of the employer to shift the burden of the tax varies with the state of the economy, the firm's profit objectives, its degree of exposure to foreign competition, the supply and demand elasticities for its products, and other factors (Euzéby and Euzéby, 1984). Experts also argue that it is not the employer payroll tax per se but labor costs per unit of output that are critical in explaining the competitiveness of a firm's products. Nevertheless, it is not surprising that in the 1970s, under conditions of slower economic growth, the employer payroll tax came to be regarded with serious concern in countries where it was high, especially in relation to its effects on the competitiveness of export industries. In spite of much debate on the subject, there was relatively little change in the distribution of sources of revenue in countries with heavy reliance on employer payroll taxes between 1976–7 – the latest date for which data were available when I first began this analysis – and 1979–80. Perhaps the most significant change that occurred in some countries – Finland, Norway, Italy, the Netherlands, and France – was an increase in the percentage of funds coming from general government revenues, and this was at least partially explained by the rising public assistance burden associated with increasing unemployment.

In Eastern Europe, there are also wide variations in the relative importance of the various sources of revenue, with government revenues providing almost all of the funds in the USSR and Czechoslovakia, but somewhat smaller proportions in other countries (Table 2.4). However, contributory taxes on state-owned enterprises are the predominant source of funding of social security in all of these countries, but in some cases are incorporated into general government budgets.

Particularly prevalent in Eastern Europe is the absence of a contribution from insured persons, except in East Germany and Hungary, where the influence of early German provisions apparently continues to play a role. The absence of an employee contribution in the Soviet Union can be traced back

Table 2.4. *Sources of revenue for social security programs, selected Eastern European countries, 1979–80*

| Country | Government revenues | Contributory taxes | | Other (including interest) |
		Insured persons	Employers	
USSR	96.7%	—	—	3.3%
Czechoslovakia	95.1	—	3.7	1.2
Germany (Dem. Rep.)	49.7	21.9	28.3	0.1
Romania	45.6	—	54.4	—
Hungary	43.6	14.6	41.1	0.7
Poland	32.3	2.2	54.3	11.3

Note: Sources of revenue for public employee and veterans' benefit programs are excluded.
Source: Adapted from ILO (1985b, tables 5 and 7).

to the principles enunciated by the Bolshevik Government five days after its seizure of power, on November 12, 1917, and even earlier by Lenin at a conference of Social Democrats in Prague in 1912. These included (1) the coverage of all workers and all city and village poor, (2) the inclusion of all risks of income loss, (3) all the costs to be borne by employers, (4) unemployment and disability benefits to be at least equal to wages, and (5) the full control of administration in the hands of the insured. As Rimlinger (1971, 258) pointed out, however, the practical realization of these principles was a different matter, and it was not until a good many years later that there was an effective social security program in the Soviet Union. Even so, the principle of no employee contribution did prevail.

Another significant difference between social security financing in the Soviet Union and in Western social insurance schemes is the absence, in the Soviet system, of a contractual relationship between the insured person and the state. The right to benefits is granted by the state and is in no way dependent on the payment of contributions into social insurance funds. Social insurance programs are a manifestation of government benevolence, as Soviet official publications frequently point out (Rimlinger, 1971, 254).

In Western countries, another reason for growing concern about the role of high employer payroll taxes is the problem of an "underground economy," in which employers hire hidden workers whose earnings are not reported for contributory tax purposes or for income tax purposes. It seems reasonable to suppose that the higher the payroll tax, the greater is the likelihood that an underground economy will develop. In Sweden, where the payroll tax for all social security programs combined amounts to about 30 percent of payroll, and private employer benefits are provided in addition, it has been estimated that some 3–5 percent of employment is in the underground economy.[3] The problem is generally considered to be even more serious in France and Italy. In the latter country, underground workers are referred to as *lavoratori neri*, and a 1974 estimate put their number at about two million, or at 10 percent of the civilian labor force. Particularly in industries where unions have been able to negotiate substantial wage increases, high employer contributory taxes are said to create an inducement for employers to shift operations to small plants where the costs of social insurance can be more easily evaded (Moss and Rogers, 1980, 179, 185). A more recent study provides estimates of the relative importance of the underground economy in a number of Western industrial countries, as well as in the Soviet Union (Tanzi, 1982).[4]

Emphasis on financing through general government revenues, as in the British and Scandinavian countries, tends to result in greater redistribution of income than emphasis on contributory taxes, especially because these countries derive a substantial portion of revenue from progressive income taxes, and because benefits are targeted to a considerable extent, varying from country to country, to low-income groups.

At the same time, it might be expected that in such countries it would be more difficult to achieve increases in expenditures on social security, because supporters of increases would have to compete with supporters of every other government program for increased appropriations, whereas the revenue from contributory taxes tends to rise automatically and to facilitate increases in benefits in a period of rising wages. Aaron's study (1967) showed that heavy reliance on general revenues in the financing of social security was indeed likely to hold down spending. I also found evidence of such an effect on old-age pension programs in the 1950s (M. S. Gordon, 1963a). More recent data suggest that heavy reliance on general revenues in the financing of social security tends to be inversely related to the rate of spending, but only in a moderate degree.

As a recent ILO report (1984a) on the financing of social security pointed out, financial exigencies are likely to continue to suggest the need for changes. There has been considerable discussion of substituting a value added tax (VAT) for the employer payroll tax in Western Europe, on the ground that such a tax would be less likely to have an adverse effect on employment or to encourage an underground economy. As the ILO report by a group of experts pointed

---

[3] Interview with Karl-Olof Faxén, former chief economist of the Swedish Employers Federation, now retired, in October 1984.

[4] A recent report has indicated a sizable problem of underground work (*Schwarzarbeit*) in West Germany, involving an estimated million workers. Although some of these workers were officially unemployed, most were people moonlighting to supplement earnings from regular jobs (*The Economist,* April 19, 1986).

out, however, a value added tax would have effects on depreciation and profits and could discourage investment (ILO, 1984b, 88). A somewhat more favorable view is expressed by Perrin (1984b) in the recent ILO report on financing issues.

Social security and economic growth

Critics of social security frequently charge that rising social security expenditures are responsible for the slow economic growth in Western industrial economies in the years since about 1973. The charge takes a variety of forms. Heavy spending on social security, it is argued, contributes to inflation by stimulating consumption and exacerbating the problem of government deficits. Another line of criticism tends to emphasize the role of unemployment compensation, ''welfare,'' and social security benefits generally in reducing incentives to work. Still a third type of criticism stems from the charge made by Feldstein (1974) and some of his followers to the effect that the accumulation of rights to social security benefits in the future (social security wealth) reduces the incentive to save.

We shall consider the specific charges relating to government deficits, incentives to work, and incentives to save in later chapters. At this point, let us consider whether there is any relationship between the rate of social security spending and economic growth among the countries included in this study.

Before looking at the relevant data, it is important to recognize that the charge that social security spending has impeded growth does not come from economists who have undertaken serious studies of the reasons for slowing economic growth or its companion, slowing productivity growth, in recent years. We have summarized the findings of Maddison (1983), for example, in Chapter 1.

Maddison does point out, however, that a substantial portion of the rise in government expenditures that characterized the 1973–82 period was attributable to the built-in stabilizer role of social transfers in advanced welfare states and to the momentum that had been built up in earlier years to extend the coverage and generosity of benefits. He does not, however, explicitly consider the question of whether there was a clear relationship between ''welfare'' expenditures and the rate of growth, and, in fact, the number of countries included in his study was too small to provide a basis for such an inquiry. Other important recent studies, such as those dealing with the decline in productivity reported in the March 1983 issue of *The Economic Journal*, likewise do not consider the role of social security expenditures generally.

In the course of my study of the data relating to the countries included in this analysis, I have found a significant, though somewhat weak, negative relationship between the rate of social security spending and economic growth, but it is also clear that certain other variables – per capita income and the percentage of the labor force in agriculture in 1960 – were more consistently related to differences in rates of economic growth than were differences in rates of social security spending.

The countries that continued to have a relatively large percentage of the labor force in agriculture in the early postwar years had more to gain in terms of economic growth in the 1960s and early 1970s than the countries that were already highly developed and had relatively small percentages of the labor force in agriculture. This is consistent with Denison's finding (1967) that contraction of agricultural inputs was a very significant factor in explaining higher rates of growth in Western Europe than in the United States from 1950 to 1962. The countries that continued to have a relatively large proportion of the labor force in agriculture in 1960 also tended to have low per capita income and to experience relatively pronounced increases in per capita income as the percentage of the labor force in agriculture declined and they became more highly industrialized.

Moreover, the countries that were heavy spenders on social security in 1977 according to my analysis were by no means concentrated in the group with the slowest rates of growth. The countries with the slowest rates of growth included Sweden, with the highest rate of spending on social security, but also the United States, with one of the lowest rates of social security spending, and Switzerland and the United Kingdom, with moderate rates of social security spending. Scattered among countries with rates of growth exceeding 4.0 percent were such high social security spenders as the Netherlands, Belgium, and Denmark – countries that we have identified as having adopted social security programs relatively early (especially Denmark and Belgium).

In a study of 18 Western industrial countries that was specifically designed to test the hypothesis that the self-regulatory market mechanism fosters economic growth whereas strong social security programs sooner or later are inimical to growth, Korpi (1985) found no evidence to support this hypothesis in the period from 1950 to 1982. He also noted the relatively rapid rate of growth of countries with a large proportion of the labor force in agriculture at the beginning of the period.

If the association between social security spending and low economic growth is weak, that does not mean that there may not be particular situations in which social security policies may be retarding growth – the lack of emphasis on vigorous labor market policies, for example, in countries providing benefits over long periods for long-term unemployment. Some of these situations will be discussed in future chapters.

CHAPTER 3

National old-age pension programs: basic structure

The problem of poverty in old age

The forces responsible for poverty in old age in industrializing societies are demographic, economic, and social. The long-run decline in both death rates and birth rates results in a rising proportion of elderly persons in the population. Changes in technology and in the occupational structure of the labor force tend to place older people at a disadvantage in competing for available jobs, to bring on earlier retirement, and to render the transition from full-time work to retirement a more disrupting and abrupt process for the average worker. Finally, although it has frequently been suggested that the increase in geographical mobility and the process of urbanization have tended to weaken family ties, sociological studies have shown that, in fact, most elderly people live near to and have frequent contact with at least one adult child (e.g., Shanas et al., 1968).

Basic to an understanding of the problem of poverty in old age is the fact that it does not suddenly appear at age 65, or at some more or less arbitrarily determined age. Associated as it is with declining job opportunities, it may appear well before age 65, or not until some years later. Declining job opportunities tend to be attributable to chronic illness or disability, reluctance of employers to hire older job seekers, or the desire of employers to replace older workers with young people who have had more recent education or training.

Booth's (1894) study of poverty in old age in Great Britain showed that the proportion of paupers (persons having resort to poor relief) was about 5 percent of the total population, but, among the aging, rose from 10 percent for those aged 60 to 65 to 40 percent for those over 75. This pattern of increasing incidence of poverty with advancing age is found in all industrial countries and is, of course, associated with the rising incidence of disability and/or impaired earning capacity with advancing age.

One of the most illuminating studies of poverty in old age in the United States – conducted at a time when social security benefits were very low and the number of elderly persons receiving them was relatively small – was based on a nationwide survey of the population aged 65 and older conducted for the authors by the U.S. Bureau of the Census (Steiner and Dorfman,

1957).[1] The results indicated that about three-tenths of the elderly couples had income below a subsistence level, as did around one-third of the unrelated males and one-half of the unrelated females. In contrast with the situation today, sizable proportions of the unrelated men and women were living in households headed by an adult child, and many of these elderly people were living in a state of dependency on their adult children. This was much less true of the couples, who were more likely to be living in their own households.

Particularly significant findings related to the *causes* of poverty in old age. Contrary to the prevailing impression at the time that the essential core of the aged problem was the plight of elderly men who were forced into premature retirement by compulsory retirement provisions, the study showed that the main sources of economic distress in old age were widowhood, illness, and obsolescence of skills. Moreover, problems of illness and impaired earning capacity were much more frequent among men who had been manual workers than among those who had been engaged in sedentary occupations.

Early income maintenance legislation

The evolution of public income maintenance programs for the aged, disabled, and survivors is the story of the replacement of the punitive poor laws – as they applied to these groups – by more humane and less demeaning public income maintenance programs. We shall trace three main lines of development: (1) social insurance schemes, modeled after the pioneering German law of 1889; (2) benefits for the needy, based on a means test and resembling the provisions of a Danish law of 1891; and, evolving considerably later, (3) universal pensions paid to all persons attaining a specified age, without a means test.

Before tracing the development of these three approaches, we need to discuss the *rationale* for each of the three, recognizing that they can also be found in benefit programs for the ill, the disabled, and the unemployed, and that universal benefits may be found in children's allowance schemes, free health services, and free public schools.

Social insurance programs, though differing from other types of insurance in significant ways, do apply, along with insurance programs, the principle of sharing the risk. The risks that are shared are the main causes of loss of income in modern industrial societies: illness, prolonged disability, industrial accidents and diseases, unemployment, death of the breadwinner, and old age. No one can determine in advance with certainty which workers are likely

---

[1] The study was one of a group of interdisciplinary studies conducted by the Institute of Industrial Relations, University of California, Berkeley, with support from a Rockefeller Foundation grant.

to be affected by episodes of severe illness or unemployment, but the loss of income associated with such episodes can be a financial disaster for a low-income family. Through the pooling of resources in the development of an insurance fund, from which payments can be made that restore a portion of the lost income when disaster strikes, the affected families can be protected from severe financial hardship. The case of old age is somewhat different, because it can be predicted with certainty that all of those who do not experience premature death will reach "old age." However, the age of onset of impaired earning capacity cannot be predicted with certainty for all aging persons, and it can also be predicted that many workers will not be able to save enough through their own efforts alone to provide an adequate income throughout a prolonged period of retirement.

The principle of sharing the risk is familiar. Somewhat less familiar, and subject to neglect in much of the literature on social security, is the fact that social insurance programs are not designed to eliminate poverty at a given moment in time, but rather to contribute to stability of income over the life cycle. Some of their benefits flow to people who are not poor, but many of these persons would become poor if they were forced to exhaust their savings before becoming eligible for benefits, as in means-tested programs.

Another important characteristic of most, though not all, insurance programs, is that their benefits are related to previous earnings. This feature is regarded with favor in most countries and by most workers, but it is severely criticized by some analysts (e.g., Friedman, 1962), who believe that the only function of public income maintenance programs should be to provide a minimum income to the needy. Critics also argue that earnings differences among those at work should not be preserved in income maintenance programs for the retired. Most workers, however, strongly favor earnings-related benefits which tend to prevent an excessively sharp drop in income on retirement for the average worker and also give him or her the feeling of belonging to a comprehensive system that avoids the two-class orientation of a means-tested program in which the majority of the population is supporting a minority looked upon as poor.

An important aspect of social insurance programs is that they act as automatic stabilizers of the economy. This is especially true of unemployment insurance benefits, which begin to rise early in a downswing, helping to maintain purchasing power. It is also true of old-age and disability insurance programs because an increase in unemployment tends to lead to job loss on the part of some older workers, who may be able to qualify for social security retirement benefits, and on the part of some disabled workers, who may qualify for disability benefits.

Means-tested payments are limited to persons who have less than a specified income and also, historically, to persons possessing less than a very limited amount of property. In recent decades there has been some tendency toward income-tested, rather than means-tested programs, in which only the income received from property, and not its total value, is considered. Home ownership – the chief type of property owned by most elderly people – is often disregarded, at least up to a certain maximum value. Even so, though much less demeaning than nineteenth-century poor relief programs, means-tested or income-tested benefits are unpopular and have come to play only a residual role in most old-age pension programs.They are designed to protect those who, for one reason or another, are ineligible for adequate benefits under social insurance or universal pension programs.

Universal pensions are provided for all persons who have attained a specified age (usually 65) and who meet certain citizenship and/or residence requirements. They are found in six countries – all Scandinavian or British Commonwealth countries – and all of them (except Finland) countries that began with old-age assistance programs. Their history suggests that in most cases they were designed to appeal to a voting public that disliked means tests, but they were also expected to be less costly to administer than means-tested old-age benefits (Sweden) and likely to encourage rather than discourage saving (Denmark). Like means-tested benefits, they tend to be financed from general government revenues.

The objection can be made that universal pensions flow, to a certain extent, to persons who do not need them, but, in fact, upper-income elderly persons are likely to pay as much, or nearly as much, in taxes as they receive in benefits. Moreover, as we shall see, the evenhandedness of universal pensions has distinct advantages in relation to groups that can be bypassed under social insurance systems, such as divorced women.

The history of universal pensions, however, suggests certain problems. Nearly all of the countries with universal pensions now have income-tested supplements that bring the minimum income of the aged above the level of the universal pension if the universal pension no longer provides a subsistence level of income as a result of inflation. This is a considerably less costly way of providing a minimum income that is regarded as adequate than raising the universal pension of all recipients to that level. All of these countries except New Zealand also have supplementary earnings-related or employment-related insurance systems.

Clearly, however, the contention of some of the proponents of universal pensions – that they are more likely to encourage saving than income-tested programs – seems reasonable. The prospective retiree can always add to the expected income from the universal pension by saving, whereas the prospective recipient of an income-tested pension is likely to be inhibited from saving if his or her expected retirement income is approximately at the income limit above which the retiree would not be eligible for a pension or would have his or her pension reduced in amount. In fact, not only is a means test likely to discourage saving, but it may also provide an incentive for transferring property to adult children in advance of retirement. Some countries investigate and take into consideration the assets older persons may have passed onto their children in order to meet the means-test requirements (Horlick, 1973, 7).

Social insurance laws

Nearly a decade elapsed between the first announcement of Bismarck's proposals for social insurance and the enactment of the invalidity and old-age insurance law of 1889. A sickness insurance act had been adopted in 1883 and an accident insurance law (covering industrial injuries) in 1884. The final adoption of the invalidity and old-age act came after much debate and controversy, but as it turned out, the legislation was remarkably comprehensive for a pioneering measure. Particularly noteworthy were its provisions for invalidity, as well as old-age pensions, in contrast with other old-age pension laws, which often did not provide for invalidity benefits until some years after old-age pensions were adopted. The German experience with benefit funds had shown that many workers were forced to withdraw from the labor force long before old age because of permanent disabilities that would not be covered by the accident insurance program because they did not grow directly out of employment (U.S. Commissioner of Labor, 1911, 1354).

The German law of 1889 covered wage earners in most industries, including agriculture and domestic service, as well as salaried employees earning no more than 2,000 marks ($500) a year. The principle of excluding salaried workers with earnings above a certain level had been established in the sickness insurance legislation, presumably on the assumption that those earning more than the maximum amount could afford to pay for their own medical care or could purchase private insurance. It was followed in the health insurance laws of several other countries, and, also, less frequently, in old-age insurance laws. Such a provision is still included in the health insurance legislation of the Federal Republic of Germany and has become a matter of controversy in recent years under the impact of severe inflation in medical care costs, but it was discontinued in old-age insurance in 1968.

Contributions were earnings-related and were equal for employers and employees, while the Imperial Government provided a subsidy of 50 marks a year for each recipient of a pension and paid certain administrative expenses. In 1908, the government contribution amounted to 28 percent of the cost of benefit payments (U.S. Commissioner of Labor, 1911, 1413). With three sources of funds – employers, employees, and the government – the German provisions established the principle of tripartite financing which was followed by many other European countries in their social insurance schemes.

Old-age pensions were payable at age 70 to persons with a record of 1,200 contributory weeks (about 24 years), although elderly persons who could not meet the contribution requirements for a full pension were "blanketed in" during the early years of the system. Invalidity pensions were payable regardless of age to adults who became disabled to such an extent that they suffered a permanent loss of earning capacity. Eligibility was subject to a requirement for a certain number of weeks of contributions.

Old-age pensions were small, compared with those in most industrial countries today, varying from about 31 percent of earnings in the lowest wage class to about 20 percent in the highest. Thus, the benefit formula was somewhat tilted toward low earners – a result that mainly reflected the fact that the 50-mark contribution from the government added proportionately more to the pension of the low earner than to that of the high earner. Invalidity pensions were somewhat higher than old-age pensions for workers with long records of insurance, but lower for those with, say, only about 500 weeks of insurance (Dawson, 1912, 143–7).

Subsequent legislation added provisions for pensions to survivors and broadened coverage in certain respects. However, one of the unusual features of the German law was that it did not provide for a spouse's benefit. This continues to be true in the Federal Republic today, unlike the situation in most other countries.

Of interest were the provisions for administration by insurance institutions that were organized by the governments of the various German states; they were staffed by paid government officials, but also included representatives of employers and workers in equal numbers. This practice of decentralized administration with bipartite or tripartite representation is found in a number of European countries today, with a significant impact on the way in which decisions for policy changes are made.

Emphasis on medical care and rehabilitation for the disabled developed early within the German system and was oriented especially toward cases of chronic disability, nearly half of which were tuberculosis cases. Whenever recipients could be rehabilitated and return to work, the net result was likely to be a saving to the insurance institution (cf. Armstrong, 1932, 403).

One final feature of the German system in its early years that is worth mentioning is the fact that contributory rates were set well above current needs in order to accumulate a reserve to meet growing expenditures as more and more people became eligible for benefits. Thus, in 1908, the reserve amounted to 355 million marks, compared with expenditures in that year of 43 million and receipts of 68 million (U.S. Commissioner of Labor, 1911, 1409). Today most old-age insurance programs are financed on a pay-as-you-go basis (receipts equal estimated expenditures plus a modest reserve). There are many reasons for this, but not least among them is the impact of inflation on the value of reserves: The German experience with astronomical inflation following World War I resulted in the wiping out of its pension reserves. However, under 1983 amendments, as we shall see, a sizable and growing surplus is accumulating in the United States.

Although we noted in Chapter 2 that many continental European countries adopted German social insurance models, this was less true of old-age pensions in the period before World War I than of sickness and work injury programs. Early old-age security laws in Belgium, Italy, Spain, and France took the form of government subsidization of voluntary insurance. In 1910, the French Parliament enacted a compulsory old-age insurance measure, but, according to Rouast and Durand (1960, 10), the contributory taxes were too small and the pensions were seriously inadequate. Even in the Austro-Hungarian Empire, where the German example was especially influential, the first old-age insurance legislation of 1906 covered only salaried employees in Austria and Czechoslovakia.

Between the two world wars, however, most of the continental European countries (outside of Scandinavia, where flat-rate pensions prevailed) adopted earnings-related old-age pensions systems, although often less comprehensive than the German model. Thus, in the period immediately following World War II, when our more detailed analysis begins, the social insurance model predominated in continental Europe.

Old-age assistance laws

The Danish law of 1891 represented a modest attempt to remove the more offensive aspects of poor relief as they applied to the aged, but by modern standards it retained a punitive character. Its main effect was to remove the aged from the general public assistance regime and to provide them with aid on a less restrictive basis. The more important provisions, as modified by a law of 1908, included the following (Andersen, 1910, 25–60): (1) assistance to be available to needy persons over age 60 who were native citizens; and (2) who were not guilty of dishonorable conduct; and (3) who had lived in Denmark during the last ten years and had not been guilty of vagabondage or begging; and (4) who had not obtained public assistance during the last five years.

The law provided that aid could be given in cash or in kind (though it was apparently usually given in cash), but did not set up uniform standards for amounts of assistance. The amount of aid was determined by the communes on the basis of individual need, although in Copenhagen and Frederiksberg certain general rules were developed. Half of the expenses incurred by the communes were met from central government funds.

The early old-age pension laws that most resembled that of Denmark were those of New Zealand (1898), Australia (1908), and the United Kingdom (1908), although all of these laws provided for a uniform national pension amount. In all three countries, proposals for contributory insurance systems had been debated but rejected. In Britain (and also in Australia), opposition to a contributory system came especially from the friendly societies (mutual aid funds), which regarded any proposal for a government-sponsored insurance scheme as competitive with their solicitation of contributions from their members.[2] It should be added that with the passage of years there was a tendency to remove punitive features from the laws.

Universal pensions

The first country to adopt a universal pension program was New Zealand, in a major revision of its income maintenance laws in 1938, mentioned in Chapter 1. Benefits were intended to meet virtually any type of need and were all means-tested except for the modest universal pension provided for persons aged 65 and over, workers' compensation benefits, and substantial provision for free hospital care. There was to be a single social security fund which would provide the financing for most types of benefits, part of which was to be derived from an earmarked income tax levied on all adult residents and the remainder through a contribution from general government revenues. However, there was to be no direct connection between payment of the earmarked income tax and eligibility for benefits.

The act continued a means-tested old-age pension for those aged 60 or more (the original 1898 act had specified an age of 65 or more), while at the same time providing the universal pension for those aged 65 or more. Initially the universal pension was very small and was not available if the means-tested age benefit, which was considerably larger, was being received. In the course of time, though, the universal pension was very substantially increased, and, effective in 1977, the former means-tested and the universal pensions were replaced by a single universal ''superannuation'' benefit for persons aged 60 and older. It has amounted to 80 percent of average after-tax earnings for a couple (paid separately to each in the amount of 40 percent), whereas single

---

[2] For a detailed account of the debates in Britain, see Gilbert (1966) and de Schweinitz (1943). On New Zealand, see Sutch (1941) and Condliffe (1959), and on Australia, Kewley (1973). The Australian Commonwealth law superseded earlier old-age pension laws in New South Wales and Victoria.

persons have received 60 percent of the combined payment to a couple (Gourley, 1986, 203).[3] Benefits in New Zealand are now financed almost entirely from general government revenues, as we saw in Chapter 2, and the universal pension is taxable under the income tax.

Before leaving our discussion of early income maintenance programs for the aged (along with invalids and survivors), it is important to point out that, regardless of which of the three main types of benefits was provided, all three resulted not only in a movement away from the old poor laws but also in a shift from dependence on local taxation to the assumption of a substantial portion of the cost by the central government, sometimes along with contributory payments by employers and employees. Quite apart from the desire for national standards, an important reason for this trend was the growing perception of inequity in the old system of local financing of poor relief – inequity between those communities that had relatively little poverty and those that had a great deal.

Developments after World War II

Toward more complex systems

One of the outstanding changes during the period since World War II has been the development of income-maintenance programs for the aged, survivors, and disabled (OASD programs) that are more complex in basic structure than those that had developed earlier. Tracing this trend in the late 1960s, I referred to the development of two-tiered systems (M. S. Gordon, 1967). The countries that had begun with earnings-related social insurance systems eventually recognized the need for some type of minimum income guarantee to protect those that had never been covered by the social insurance system, or who, for one reason or another, had failed to develop rights to an adequate pension. On the other hand, the countries that initially developed old-age assistance systems in some cases replaced these with universal pensions and later in some cases enacted an earnings-related insurance system that provided benefits supplementing the basic flat-rate pension.

From the perspective of the 1980s, it is now more appropriate to refer to three-tiered systems in many cases, sometimes involving mandatory or nationwide collectively bargained employer pensions that supplement the public two-tiered system and sometimes consisting of complex combinations of universal, means-tested, and insurance benefits.

A major reason for these changes has been the postwar environment of rising prices and wages, in contrast with the prewar situation in which prices

---

[3] Initially somewhat lower percentages were reported (*ISSR*, 1977, *30* [1]: 80–91).

and wages tended to change slowly and, in recessions or depressions, to decline. With rising price and wage levels, old-age insurance benefits based on average lifetime earnings (which prewar programs usually provided) are inevitably inadequate in relation to current wages and prices at the time of retirement. This has led not only to the indexing of pensions, but also to benefit formulas based on either relatively recent or adjusted earnings. On the other hand, flat-rate benefits, whether income-tested or not, tend to be based on a subsistence–needs concept and, if not supplemented by an earnings-related pension, frequently involve a sharp drop in income for workers with average or above-average earnings at the time of retirement. Thus, labor organizations became a major force pressing for earnings-related supplements to flat-rate benefits.

The first country to adopt a universal old-age pension after the war was Sweden, which shifted from its previous partially means-tested system to universal pensions in 1946. According to Heclo (1974, 229), the Beveridge Report received a great deal of attention in Sweden, in an atmosphere of popular sentiment already committed to a better postwar life for all citizens. And, the universal pension scheme adopted in Sweden in 1946 did resemble the British flat-rate old-age insurance system enacted in the same year in that it was partially financed by contributions. In the Swedish case, however, the contributions took the form of an earmarked 2.5 percent income tax that was imposed for its "psychological value" in creating feelings of entitlement to benefits but was ignored as a condition of eligibility – like the New Zealand earmarked income tax.

In the usual Swedish tradition, the pension changes were debated at length by a special commission, and until almost the last moment it appeared that the commission would recommend substantially increased basic pensions, but subject to income-testing to hold down the total cost. However, as the commission was finishing its work, two civil servants brought forward a plan for equally high pensions but without an income test. They argued that, in spite of the higher cost of benefits under their proposal, the elimination of detailed investigations of income would save administrative costs.[4]

The earmarked portion of the income tax was gradually raised to 4 percent, but it met only about one-third of the cost; the national government met about one-half from general revenues, and local governments met the remaining one-sixth. Later, however, the major portion of the cost was shifted to the employer, through a payroll tax that in 1985 amounted to 9.45 percent; the national government's contribution was only 25 percent of the cost.

The next country to opt for a universal pension was Canada (1951), which

---

[4] One of the two civil servants was Karl Höjer, General Director of the Pension Board, whose book on Swedish social policy (in Swedish, 1952) was summarized for me by Victor Kayfelt, formerly a graduate student at Berkeley.

had had only a federal–provincial old-age assistance system for persons aged 70 and over, dating from 1927. The recommendation for a universal pension to be provided at age 70 was made by a Joint Committee of the Senate and the House of Commons, which presented a unanimous report, including the following (Clark, 1960, *I*, 233–4):

> All things considered, therefore, the Committee is of the opinion that the most suitable old age security plan for Canada under present circumstances consists of a two-fold program, as follows.:
>
> (a) A universal pay-as-you-go program applicable to all persons 70 years of age and over, based on the contributory principle and administered by the federal government. The benefit should be a flat, uniform amount of $40 a month for all eligible persons, and eligibility should be based solely on age and a suitable residence qualification.
>
> (b) For the age group 65 and over not eligible for the universal benefit, old-age assistance at the rate of $40 a month should be available.

Among the considerations influencing the committee was the fact that a large proportion of those aged 70 or more were retired from active employment and that two-fifths of them were receiving the means-tested pension. Although the committee considered the social insurance approach, and gave particular attention to the system that had been adopted by the United States in 1935, it noted that under an insurance system those entering the scheme late in life would earn only small benefits which would have to be supplemented by assistance programs.

It should be added that the complex system of contributory taxes initially adopted was later replaced by general revenue financing, the benefits were gradually increased and eventually indexed, and, as in Sweden, earnings-related supplementary benefits were later adopted, as we shall see.

Denmark's first move toward a universal pension was a very modest one. In 1956, Parliament passed a ''People's Pension'' law, under which the old-age assistance program would be retained, but a minimum amount, corresponding to 9 percent of average gross income of workers, would be paid to everyone 67 years of age and older, irrespective of income. The minimum amount was to be financed through a special income tax.

According to Friis (1969, 138), the minimum amount was looked upon as the first step toward full universal pensions. Proponents of the change argued that (1) the income test rules were too complicated and discriminated against persons who had saved but found the value of their savings eroded by inflation; and (2) the income test discouraged saving.

Although the minimum universal pension adopted in 1956 did prove to be the forerunner of a full universal pension, it was not until 1977 that the income test was abolished for the basic old-age pension payable at age 67; the invalidity and survivors' benefits continued to be income-tested. Then, in a reversal brought on by the need for economies, the income test was reinstated for persons aged 67 to 69 under legislation that became effective at the beginning of 1984.

Significantly, the movement toward universal pensions occurred at a time when there was a widespread belief that full employment and liberal income maintenance policies would eventually eliminate poverty. As time went on, the persistence of poverty in affluent countries led to the realization that the forces tending to perpetuate poverty – including immigration from low-income countries, unemployment, the growth of single-parent families, and others – were powerful. This induced a movement toward modifications that would target certain programs, especially those providing children's benefits, toward the poor, as we noted in Chapter 1. The thrust of the movement toward universal benefits was weakened as a result. However, before that happened, there developed a significant movement toward the adoption of earnings-related insurance programs to supplement flat-rate pensions, to which we now turn.

Earnings-related supplementary pensions

Between 1959 and the late 1960s, five countries with flat-rate pension programs – Sweden (1959), the United Kingdom (1959), Canada (1965), Finland (1961), and Norway (1966) – developed earnings-related social insurance programs to supplement their flat-rate benefits. Denmark acted in 1964 to adopt a program of supplementary benefits that were not earnings-related but accrued in the form of a flat amount for each year of service.

Much more recent is the two-tiered system adopted in Japan under legislation enacted in 1985, which provided for a flat-rate benefit payable under the national pension scheme (compulsory for adults not covered by the employee pension scheme), to be supplemented by an earnings-related benefit under the employee pension scheme. Although the national pension was not to be payable until age 65, the normal retirement ages under the employee pension scheme continued to be 60 for men and 55 for women; a "combined benefit," including the old-age pension provided by the national scheme, was to be paid by the employees' scheme (*S&LB*, 1986 [3–4]: 542–6).[5]

The story of the Swedish decision to adopt a supplementary earnings-related scheme in 1959 is particularly interesting, because it involved a prolonged political controversy. Pressure for earnings-related supplementary pensions began with some of the unions, particularly the metal and foundry workers' unions, in the 1930s and 1940s, initially taking the form of demands for employer pensions for manual workers similar to those enjoyed by salaried

---

[5] The retirement age for women under the employees' scheme was gradually to be raised to equal that for men.

employees.[6] The drive was taken over by LO (*Landsorganisationen,* the Swedish Federation of blue-collar unions) and later by the Social Democrats. Opposition came from the employers' federation and the so-called bourgeois parties. Whereas LO and the Social Democrats favored a mandatory state scheme of supplementary pensions on the ground that only in this manner would coverage extend to all employees, the employers and the bourgeois parties strongly supported nonobligatory pensions achieved through negotiations. The employers especially objected to public financing aimed at the accumulation of a large fund to meet growing pension rights, believing that this would discourage personal saving and weaken the private capital market.

Beginning with the appointment of a Parliamentary Committee on Pensions in 1950 (the first of a series of such committees which sat almost continuously from 1950 through 1959), the controversy included a referendum (with neither side getting a clear majority), the dissolution of Parliament in 1958, new elections the same year, a reshuffling of the Cabinet, and a narrowly averted parliamentary crisis in May 1959. Finally, the legislation sponsored by the Social Democrats was adopted by a substantial majority in the Upper House but by a majority of only one in the Lower House.

Available to all resident Swedish citizens (and aliens who met a residency requirement) reaching the age of 67 (more recently, 65) was the basic universal pension. The amount of the pension was made subject to automatic adjustment for price changes in 1950 and was designed to provide a modest but adequate level of living. This could be increased, on a means-tested basis, by various supplements to take account of certain needs, including a wife's supplement for wives aged 60 to 66 and rental supplements.

In the initial stage (the first 20 years of the program), the supplementary pension provided 3 percent of average annual earnings between the base amount (initially 4,000 kr. a year) and 7 1/2 times the base amount (initially 30,000 kr.) for each year of coverage. The average was based on the best 15 years of earnings and was calculated in terms of "pension points" – the ratio of actual earnings to the base amount. After the first 20 years, the pension was to be computed on the basis of 2 percent a year, with 30 years required for a full pension. The base amount, past earnings, and outstanding pensions were automatically adjusted for price changes. The basic pension and the supplementary pension combined were designed, when the supplementary scheme matured, to provide most workers with about two-thirds of their previous earnings up to the pension ceiling.

The pension could be claimed as early as age 63 with a reduction of 0.6 percent a month (an actuarial reduction) from the amount payable at age 67 and could be deferred beyond age 67 with an increment of the same amount

---

[6] On the controversy, see Heclo (1974), D. J. Wilson (1974), and Uhr (1966).

per month to age 70. (This was one of the first systems to provide for a flexible retirement age – to be adopted by a number of other countries subsequently, as we shall see in Chapter 5.) The provisions were changed somewhat when the normal retirement age was lowered to 65 in 1976.

An important feature of the Swedish supplementary scheme is that, unlike some of the similar systems that were to follow, it provides supplementary benefits for invalids and survivors.

Financing of the supplementary system was entirely through an employer payroll tax on earnings between the base amount and the ceiling – initially 3 percent, but gradually increased to 12.5 percent in 1981. In 1982, however, the tax was made payable on total earnings (not just the band between the base amount and the ceiling), and this revision made possible a reduction in the rate to 9.6 percent in 1983.

The supplementary benefit scheme adopted in Great Britain under a Conservative government in 1959 was a very different matter (*SSB*, 1959, *22* [September]: 4–9). For one thing, it was not indexed, nor were the flat-rate benefits to which the earnings-related supplement was to be added. For another, the band of earnings on which the supplementary benefit was based was very narrow, from £9 to £15 a week. Thus the ceiling was only 1.7 times the base amount, compared with 7.5 times in Sweden.[7]

Another highly significant feature of the British scheme was that it permitted employers to contract out of the earnings-related system if they had a pension plan that provided benefits comparable to those of the earnings-related scheme, and many did. Finally, the system did not provide supplementary benefits for invalids and survivors.

Over the years, the pension payable in Britain under the combined schemes increased at a very slow rate, even though flat-rate benefits were increased by statute from time to time. In fact, benefits were so low that a sizable proportion of pensioners applied for and received national assistance. During the 1960s, pressure built up within the unions and the Labor Party for a more adequate system, but changes in government interfered with the achievement of this, and it was not until 1978 that a modified earnings-related scheme, enacted under a Labor government in 1975, came into effect.

The new scheme retained the existing flat-rate pension, which was very substantially increased in 1975, and provided for an earnings-related supplement. Both components were to be indexed on the basis of changes in prices and earnings levels. Employers were again given the option of contracting out if they had a pension plan providing benefits equivalent to the national supplementary benefits, and by the time the law became effective, 20,000 employers had decided to exercise this option.

---

[7] In 1957, the opposition Labor Party had proposed a graduated benefit scheme much like the Swedish scheme.

The earnings-related pension was to be based on the best 20 years of earnings, but, under restrictive amendments adopted in 1986, it was to be based on revalued lifetime earnings and the rate of benefit was reduced from 25 to 20 percent. Contributions are fully earnings-related and are combined with contributions toward the other social insurance programs. The portion of the contribution that finances the supplementary pension scheme is reduced for employers and employees under schemes that have contracted out. The scheme provides for supplementary earnings-related benefits for invalids and survivors, unlike the 1959 provisions.

Another innovation under the 1986 amendments was a provision that individual employees could contract out of the state earnings-related scheme and opt for a personal pension on a defined-contribution rather than a defined-benefit basis. To encourage this, the state would contribute 2 percent of covered earnings (*ISSR*, 1986, *39* [4]: 466–9).

Canada's scheme of supplementary earnings-related pension benefits, adopted in 1965, is similar to the Swedish scheme in that it relates to a band of earnings, ranging initially from $600 to $5,000 a year, the maximum therefore representing 8.3 times the minimum. However, earnings-related plus flat-rate pensions under the Canadian system were not designed to provide as high a percentage of previous earnings as under the Swedish system. The Canadian plan would provide a supplementary pension of 2.5 percent of covered earnings a year for each year of service up to a total of 25 percent after ten years. There would be no additional credits after that. The scheme provided for automatic adjustment of the maximum earnings base to price changes until 1976 and to earnings changes thereafter. It also provided for adjustment of a worker's earnings at the time of retirement to reflect more recent earnings levels (i.e., during the last three years before retirement).

The supplementary scheme (in 1985) was financed by a contribution of 1.8 percent by employers and 1.8 percent by employees (3.6 percent for the self-employed).

The Norwegian supplementary pension scheme was similar to that of Sweden, whereas in Finland employers were required to provide uniform supplementary pensions but maintained their own separate pension funds. Denmark's employment-related supplementary pension scheme provided a flat-rate pension multiplied by years of coverage, amounting to 10,800 kr. a year (or about two-thirds of average earnings) after 40 years of coverage. In this respect, it resembled the Dutch pension scheme, which, however, was not a supplementary scheme.

Minimum income guarantees

Another important trend of the postwar period was toward the provision of a minimum income for the elderly, and in some cases for invalids and survivors, although the form taken by these provisions differed among countries.

A minimum insurance benefit was provided in some of the countries that relied primarily on social insurance programs, that is, a minimum benefit that exceeded the amount that some of the lowest paid workers would receive on the basis of their earnings records. The provision for a minimum had the effect of tilting the benefit formula toward the low earner, even though the formula might not otherwise be weighted toward the low earner.

The history of this type of minimum benefit in the United States is of special interest because it became a matter of controversy in the early 1980s and was abolished for future retirees under 1981 legislation.[8] A study of a sample of minimum benefit recipients who attained the early retirement age of 62 in November 1981 and applied for benefits indicated that the vast majority (78 percent) were housewives with very limited work experience and who in many cases would later receive a higher benefit as a spouse when the husband retired. On the other hand, some of the long-time recipients of the minimum benefit were elderly impoverished widows who would not be affected by its removal for new retirees. Moreover, the 1981 legislation did not affect another provision for a minimum benefit, enacted in 1972, that provided a pension of $8.50 a month multiplied by the number of years of coverage above ten, which was designed to assist low-paid workers with many years of service.

Somewhat similar in purpose to this latter American provision was a feature of the old-age insurance law in West Germany, enacted in 1972, which called for raising the average annual earnings of low-income workers with at least 25 years of coverage to 75 percent of national average covered wages for the years 1957–72, so that they would qualify for a higher retirement benefit. The German measure was aimed particularly at benefiting women with low earnings, who tended to qualify for a very small pension (*SSB*, 1973, *36* [July]: 36–9, 41).

Another common type of minimum income guarantee provided for a means-tested allowance or "social pension" for persons not eligible for a regular pension, or in some cases for those either not eligible or qualified only for a very low pension. This type of provision was found in Belgium, Czechoslovakia, France, Italy, Romania, Switzerland, and the United States in 1985. In the United Kingdom, a means-tested allowance was provided as part of the comprehensive supplementary benefits program.

A similar type of minimum income payment – found in Austria, France, Ireland, and Israel – took the form of a supplement to insurance benefits for those who qualified for a very low pension. In addition, four of the countries that had universal pension programs – Canada, Denmark, Finland, and New

---

[8] In fact, under the Omnibus Budget Reconciliation Act of 1981, the minimum benefit was abolished for all retirees, but it was restored for current retirees later that year (Schobel and McKay, 1982).

Zealand – provided for income-tested supplements to the universal pension, whereas Norway and Sweden provided supplements for those who did not qualify for an earnings-related pension.[9]

In Eastern Europe, the movement toward more complex provisions for the aged has been less pronounced than in other industrial countries, although, as we have seen, Czechoslovakia and Romania have provided for a means-tested minimum benefit. A distinctive feature of pension formulas in a number of the Soviet bloc countries takes the form of provisions particularly benefiting long-service workers.

A summing up

In 1985, as had been true in the late 1950s, the majority of countries included in this study relied primarily on social insurance programs to protect the income position of the elderly, but most of the schemes had been substantially liberalized, and they were also more likely to be associated with some type of guaranteed minimum income level for the elderly.

Only three countries continued to rely entirely on flat-rate pensions that did not vary with years of service. These were Australia, New Zealand, and Ireland – all countries that began with flat-rate old-age assistance schemes that were strongly influenced by British policies. Of the three, New Zealand had the most liberal system, with its universal pension for persons aged 60 or more and with a weekly pension which, when converted into U.S. dollars, compared favorably with those of the other two countries. However, Ireland has recently set up a National Pension Board to consider earnings-related supplements either through the public scheme or through monitoring and regulating occupational pension schemes (*S&LB*, 1987 [1]:159–60).

In addition to these countries with flat-rate benefits, there were three countries in which rights to old-age pensions could be earned on a flat-rate per annum basis and were not related to earnings. We have referred to some of these systems as employment-related schemes. They were found in the old-age insurance program of the Netherlands, in the employment-related supplementary scheme in Denmark, and in the lower tier of the revised pension program in Japan. Israel also provided a flat-rate benefit that amounted to 16 percent of the average wage, but with a supplement for each year of coverage beyond ten.

In all of the remaining countries, earnings-related pensions played an important role, either in the form of the main pension program or as supplements to basic flat-rate pensions. As we shall see in the next chapter, however, there

[9] For an illuminating account of supplementary means-tested benefits in five European countries, see Horlick (1973).

are substantial differences from country to country in the formulas determining earnings-related benefits, beyond those discussed in the present chapter, and in the flat-rate benefit amounts.

It is particularly interesting to note that all six countries that combined flat-rate universal pensions with either social insurance supplements or with assistance payments were either Scandinavian or members of the British Commonwealth, whereas Israel and Ireland, which had at one time been governed by Britain, provided flat-rate benefits through their insurance schemes. On the other hand, nearly all of the countries relying primarily on social insurance schemes had had such systems from the beginning.

These relationships suggest not only the power of tradition but also the fact that it is easier to build on schemes that have been well established than to replace them with an entirely different approach. It is probably also true that the evenhandedness of universal pensions has a particularly egalitarian appeal in British Commonwealth and Scandinavian countries.

Australia is of special interest as a country that has continued to rely almost entirely on income-tested programs, except for workers' compensation (state programs) and the basic family allowance system. True, New Zealand also relies largely on income-tested programs, but its universal pension system has been much more liberal than that of Australia. Australia's universal pension, dating from 1973, actually initially applied only to persons aged 75 or more, but then was extended in 1975 to people aged 70 or more. It had been the intention, supported by both political parties, to abolish the means test for those aged 65 to 69, but the heavy costs involved have been responsible for postponing this move, and, effective March of 1985, the universal pension was discontinued, except for the blind.

The Australian case is worthy of a closer look because a shift to greater reliance on social insurance has been recommended but not adopted on a number of occasions over the decades. The reasons for the resistance bear a resemblance to some of the criticisms of social insurance in the United States and elsewhere. According to Dixon (1983), the friendly societies (as in Britain) saw social insurance as a competitor which would challenge their very existence, and employers feared it would generate higher wage costs; likewise the states were hostile to it because they believed that it would extend Commonwealth power too far, and historically the Labor Party and many of the unions were opposed to social insurance.

A particularly strong statement against a shift to social insurance was included in the *First Main Report* of the Australian Government Commission on Inquiry into Poverty (1975, 33–4),[10] stressing the complexity of the cir-

[10] In the British manner, the only voting member of the commission was Professor Ronald F. Henderson, the chairman. My late husband and I had the privilege of attending a meeting of the commission when we were in Melbourne in 1973, where we heard a lively discussion of the pros and cons of greater reliance on social insurance in Australia.

cumstances giving rise to poverty and the undesirability of compulsion in social insurance programs. The commission recommended, instead, a guaranteed minimum income program. On the other hand, two other commissions presenting reports in the mid-1970s recommended earnings-related insurance schemes.

No basic change in Australia's income maintenance programs followed the recommendations of these commissions, although means-tested programs were liberalized in certain respects in the late 1970s and the 1980s. Yet Australia's reliance on income-tested programs continues to be exceptional. Despite the financial difficulties that some social insurance programs have encountered in recent years, there has been no serious move to abolish earnings-related old-age insurance programs, apart from the abortive move of the Thatcher government in Britain to phase out the earnings-related supplementary system. Even in the United States, where followers of Milton Friedman vigorously oppose compulsory social insurance, the threat that they might succeed or see it converted to an income-tested program was largely removed when the bipartisan National Commission on Social Security Reform came out with a vigorous statement against any such move (*National Commission. . .* , 1983, see the discussion in Chapter 4). Nevertheless, there continues to be a significant movement against benefits flowing to the middle class in several countries, including the United States, Britain, and West Germany. We shall return to this issue in Chapter 9 and in the concluding chapter.

A recent study of the impact of the means test in Australia (Goodin and Le Grand, 1987) provides striking evidence of a possible result of reliance on income-tested benefits. Although the ceiling on income above which eligibility for a pension disappears has remained relatively restrictive over the years and in fact has declined somewhat as a percentage of GDP per capita, the percentage of the population of pensionable age receiving the income-tested old-age benefit rose from 32 percent in 1911 to nearly 76 percent in 1981. The authors attributed this to behavioral responses in the form of rearrangement of assets of those approaching old age to ensure that the income produced had minimal effects on pension eligibility. Examples were investing in low-interest-bearing bank accounts or accounts bearing no interest, interest-free loans or gifts to children, and other similar moves.

Among social security experts, there is considerable support for a two-tiered system like those of Canada and Sweden, consisting of a basic universal pension and an earnings-related supplement (see, e.g., Bergmann, 1986). Such a system combines the principles of adequacy (assuming that the universal pension meets a reasonable standard of subsistence) and of equity (beneficiaries receive payments that are related to their contributions, if only loosely). The universal pension is evenhanded, unlikely to discourage saving, and flows to elderly persons without regard to marital status or contributions records.

The problem with this solution, however, is that adoption of an adequate universal pension in countries that do not have one, as Ball (1978) has pointed out with reference to the United States, would be extremely costly.

We turn now from a survey of the basic structure of pension programs to a more detailed discussion of their benefit and financing provisions.

CHAPTER 4

Other major features of old-age pension programs

Coverage

Unlike the early old-age pensions schemes, which were usually intended for wage earners, plus in some cases salaried employees, coverage under national old-age, survivors, and disability pension programs (OASD) now tends to be very broad, largely as a result of extension after World War II to all salaried employees, to the self-employed, and to farm workers.[1] The Soviet Union and other Eastern European countries tended to lag behind other industrial countries in covering agricultural workers, but they are now largely covered.

Extensive coverage does not necessarily mean that issues relating to coverage have disappeared. The existence of separate systems for such groups as miners and seamen in European countries can create financial problems where employment of these groups is declining and the ratio of covered workers to retirees declines. The situation is particularly complex in France, where there are separate systems for agricultural, mining, and railroad workers, public utility employees, public employees, seamen, agricultural self-employed workers, and nonagricultural self-employed workers. Because large disparities developed in the financial status of these separate systems, there is now a requirement that systems with a surplus must transfer funds to systems with deficits. Retirees may in some instances be eligible for pensions from several of these schemes, but the combined amounts are often inadequate (Mitton, Willmott, and Willmott, 1983).

The women's movement has also given rise to coverage issues, such as coverage of housewives and continued coverage during periods of pregnancy and childrearing. We shall consider these later in this chapter.

Most countries have separate systems for public employees, and many of these long predated general national systems. However, because governments have a special interest in adequate benefits for their employees, and because organizations representing these employees can often exert effective pressure, public employee systems tend to be more liberal than general systems.

---

[1] I shall use the initials OASD when referring to all types of old-age pension programs, and OASDI when referring to those that are insurance programs.

A long-standing controversy over whether federal government employees should be included in the OASDI system in the United States was finally settled when the 1983 amendments included a provision that all newly hired federal workers would be covered from 1984 on (Svahn and Ross, 1983). The decision was based largely on financial considerations: Contributions would be paid into the system for many years on behalf of these new largely relatively young employees before benefits would have to be paid in most cases, thus helping to improve the financial balance of the system.[2]

Among the complaints leading to the Solidarity movement in Poland was the existence of a wide disparity between retirement provisions of the general scheme and those for civil servants, which were far more generous. Solidarity demanded and won the removal of most of the special privileges for civil servants, only to see them largely reinstated after the imposition of martial law in December 1981 (Nagorski, 1981).

A good many countries exclude workers with very low earnings or, as in the United States, do not require contributions during quarters in which earnings are below a stipulated amount. Workers having casual employment, brief agricultural employment, or intermittent earnings are also excluded in some cases. The amount of minimum earnings can become a source of controversy in some instances. For example, in the United Kingdom, where coverage is optional for persons earning less than a minimum weekly amount, it has been argued that this excludes an undue proportion of women workers. In 1977, when the minimum amount was £15 a week, 22 percent of part-time female employees were earning less than that amount (David and Land, 1983).

Coverage of students, especially those enrolled in higher education, is considerably more common in Eastern Europe than elsewhere. Because social insurance is usually financed by the government and by state-owned enterprises in Eastern Europe, the students are not required to contribute, although in East Germany, where insured persons *are* required to contribute, there is a reduced contribution rate for students. Outside of Eastern Europe, only a few countries, such as Denmark, and the Netherlands (where all residents over age 18 are covered), include students.

Some countries provide for continued coverage during certain periods of interruption of employment. For example, a number of countries provide for coverage during the periods of compulsory military service, but coverage during periods of unemployment is relatively rare. An exception in this respect is the Federal Republic of Germany, which has particularly comprehensive provisions for coverage during periods of interrupted employment.

Equally broad provisions for periods of interrupted employment are found

---

[2] The amendments also provided that states could no longer terminate coverage of state and local government employees and that employees of private nonprofit organizations would be covered compulsorily (Svahn and Ross, 1983, 24–5).

in some of the Eastern European countries, including Czechoslovakia. The practice of continuing coverage during limited periods, typically two or three years, when a mother is out of the labor force caring for her children is quite common in Eastern Europe and in recent years, largely under the influence of the women's movement, has been spreading to Western Europe, including Belgium, Finland, and France.

Contribution or residence requirements

Old-age insurance systems almost invariably require a certain minimum number of years (or months, weeks, etc.) of contributions for full pensions, whereas universal pension plans and income-tested systems typically require a certain number of years of residence in the country and in some cases citizenship. There is a good deal of variation from country to country in these requirements. However, where a relatively lengthy period of contributions is required, there is a tendency to provide reduced pensions for persons who have not contributed the required period, typically in proportion to the duration of actual contributions, as in Belgium and the Netherlands.

Universal pension amounts sometimes vary with years of residence, as in Canada, where universal pension rights are earned at the rate of 1/40 of the maximum pension for each year of residence after age 18, up to a maximum of 40 years, and with a minimum of ten. Until recently, the Danish provisions were more lenient, requiring 40 years for a full pension, but only ten years if five of these years had been immediately prior to the normal retirement age of 67. Under legislation effective in 1984, however, the latter provision was dropped (*S&LB*, 1985 [2]: 297–8). Nevertheless, requirements calling for recent residence or recent contributions are fairly common.

Benefits

Decisions about benefit levels in old-age insurance are of basic importance, increasingly involving both an adequate minimum and an earnings-related feature. A basic problem facing most countries with earnings-related insurance systems in the 1950s was, as we have seen, the tendency for wages to rise steadily, with the result that benefits based on average lifetime earnings were inevitably inadequate in relation to current earnings at the time of retirement. West Germany was one of the leaders in facing this problem, in its important pension reform legislation of 1957. Average lifetime earnings still play a role in benefit determination, but the revaluation process involves computing the ratio of earnings of the individual retiree during the years he or she has worked, to the national average earnings level in each of those same years. The average ratio is then multiplied by national average earnings in the three years prior to the year preceding the retiree's application for benefits. For example, if the worker's earnings averaged 80 percent of national average earnings during his or her working years, the earnings on which the worker's pension would be based would amount to 80 percent of national average earnings in the three years preceding the year before he or she applies for a pension. After that, the pension is adjusted, not automatically, but on the basis of an annual recommendation of an advisory committee appointed by the government, which is expected to take into account wage changes and other economic factors.

The German benefit formula is more strictly related to earnings and years of insurance than those of most other old-age insurance systems, amounting to 1.5 percent of the individual's revalued earnings multiplied by his or her years of insurance. Thus, after 40 years of insurance, the pension will amount to 60 percent of adjusted earnings (actually somewhat less, because of the impact of inflation between the three years on which the worker's pension is based and the time when he or she begins to receive benefits). There is no spouse's benefit, but there are moderate flat-rate children's supplements.

The pension reform legislation of 1957 was preceded by extensive debate between representatives of the Christian Democrats, who controlled the government, and their major opponents, the Social Democrats.[3] The Christian Democrats favored the principles of a "social market" economy, associated with the name of Ludwig Erhard, in which social benefits should be provided in such a way as to minimize interference with private initiative and individual freedom, whereas the Social Democrats favored more intervention by the state to protect the individual from economic vicissitudes. The resulting legislation bore the mark of the Erhard view in, among other things, the strict link between benefits and previous earnings and the absence of a spouse's benefit.

Most closely resembling the German benefit formula are those of Austria, the German Democratic Republic, Japan (the employees' pension system), and Switzerland, but all of these countries provide a certain base amount before adding a percentage of earnings per year of service. For example, Switzerland provides a base amount of 80 percent of the minimum monthly pension (690 fr. in 1985) plus 1.67 percent of average revalued earnings per year of insurance, up to a maximum of 1,380 fr. per month (about $830 in U.S. dollars). The Swiss maximum benefit is relatively restrictive, amounting, as it does, to only twice the minimum benefit, although there is also a wife's benefit of 50 percent of the single pension if she is age 62 or if she is disabled. Moreover, there is no ceiling on earnings subject to contributory taxes, with the result that the Swiss scheme redistributes income from high to low earners relatively more than in most countries.

---

[3] For an extensive discussion of these debates and of the reasons for various provisions of the 1957 legislation, see Rimlinger (1971) and Liefmann-Keil (1961).

Another method of adjusting benefits to rising wages is to base the pension on earnings in a relatively recent period. This method is found in Greece, Italy, and Spain, and is also common in Eastern Europe, where revaluation of earnings has begun to appear only very recently. However, some countries recognize that many workers, especially manual workers, experience declining earning capacity in the later years of working life, and therefore base the pension on revalued earnings in the "best" years. France, for example, provides at age 60 a pension that amounts to 50 percent of average revalued earnings in the 10 highest years after 1947, whereas the Swedish supplementary earnings-related pension is based on the 15 best years.

Departing substantially from proportionality to wage levels are the countries that weight the benefit formula in favor of low earners. Such tilted benefit formulas are used in Greece, Poland, Romania, the USSR, and the United States. In Greece, for example, the pension amounts to a percentage of average earnings in the last two years which declines with increasing earnings. The American formula provided in 1985 a pension that amounted to 90 percent of the first $297 of average indexed monthly earnings (AIME), plus 32 percent of the AIME from $298 to $1,790, plus 15 percent of the AIME above $1,790 (up to a maximum determined by the adjusted earnings base in effect during the individual's years of coverage). The American formula, moreover, unlike most earnings-related formulas, does not vary the pension with years of insurance, but requires one-quarter of coverage for each year since 1950 or age 21 (if later), with a maximum of 40 quarters. The pension, then, is based on revalued average monthly earnings during the years of coverage, but with a provision for dropping out the five years of lowest earnings (*SSB*, 1986, *49* [January]: 14–15).

We have attempted to identify elements that go into the benefit formula, but it is also clear that these elements can be combined in various ways. One significant type of comparison of benefits from country to country is to compute the "replacement rate" – that is, the percentage of recent earnings received by average retired workers in the form of a pension. The U.S. Social Security Administration has been developing data on replacement rates for some years, by computing the benefit that would be received as a percentage of recent earnings by the average worker in manufacturing who had met the eligibility requirements for a full pension (Table 4.1). The results show that in 1965 the replacement rate for a single worker tended to be quite low outside of a few Western European countries with long-established earnings-related systems – Austria, France, the Federal Republic of Germany, and Italy. The lowest replacement rate, among the countries included, was that of Canada, where the supplementary earnings-related insurance system was just being adopted in 1965, and where the universal old-age pension amounted to $75 a month from age 70 on. Flat-rate pensions representing a small proportion of

Table 4.1. *Earnings replacement rate of social security old-age pensions for men with average earnings in manufacturing, selected countries, 1965–80*

Country	Single worker				Aged couple			
	1965	1969	1975	1980	1965	1969	1975	1980
Austria	67[a]	65	63	68	67	65	63	68
Canada	21	22	33	34	42	41	47	49
Denmark	35	31	29	29	51	45	44	52
France	49	41	60	66	65	56	74	75
Germany (Fed. Rep.)	48	55	51	49	48	55	51	49
Italy	60	62	61	69	60	62	61	69
Japan		26	37	54		27	39	61
Netherlands	35	43	43	44	50	61	61	63
Norway	25	34	41		38	49	55	
Sweden	31	42	57	68	44	56	73	83
Switzerland	28	28	40	37	45	45	60	55
United Kingdom	23	27	31	31	36	43	47	47
United States	29	30	38	44	44	44	58	66

[a] Pension as a percentage of earnings in the year before retirement.
Sources: Haanes-Olsen (1978, 4); Aldrich (1982, 5).

earnings were also the predominant element in the pension systems of Denmark, Norway, Sweden, and the United Kingdom at the time, as well as of the Netherlands. However, earnings-related benefits in Switzerland and the United States were also very low. Because most of the countries included in Table 4.1 provided either a wife's supplement or a universal pension for which women were eligible on the basis of age, the replacement rate for an aged couple tended to be considerably higher than for a single worker in 1965.

By 1980, the replacement rate for a single worker had risen substantially in Canada, France, Japan, Sweden, and the United States, and by more modest amounts in Italy, the Netherlands, Switzerland, and the United Kingdom. The increase in Sweden was especially spectacular, reflecting the maturing of the supplementary earnings-related system. Countries that experienced no increase, or even a slight decline, were Denmark, Austria, and West Germany, with systems that were essentially unchanged.

The couple's benefit had also tended to rise as a percentage of recent earnings in nearly all of these countries. The exceptions, again, were Austria, Denmark, and West Germany.

The limitations of these comparisons of replacement rates must be kept in mind, however. They apply to average workers who have met all of the requirements for eligibility for a full pension at the normal retirement age. But the elderly populations of most industrial countries include many persons who have had unsteady employment records or whose pensions date from a time when even revalued earnings were far below current levels. Widows, in particular, receive inadequate pensions in many cases, often because their late husbands retired some years ago. Cost-of-living increases help such widows but do not compensate for the low wages on which the pension is based. The high replacement rates shown for France and Italy, moreover, fail to convey an impression of the extent of poverty among the elderly populations of those countries. In recent years, there have been a number of studies of poverty, especially in the EEC countries, which will be discussed in Chapter 9 and which show that significant poverty persists among the elderly in most industrial countries, in spite of the liberalization of pension provisions.

Finally, data on replacement rates in national old-age pension schemes do not give us the complete picture, because they do not include income from employer pensions, which will be considered in Chapter 8.

Indexing provisions

Indexing provisions are designed to adjust pension benefits to changing wages, prices, or other economic variables. In practice, adjustments have been almost exclusively upward, given the inflationary trends of the period since the mid-1960s.

Automatic adjustment of universal pensions to changes in a cost-of-living index was adopted in Sweden in 1950 (Heclo, 1974, 231). Even earlier, in 1933, Denmark had legislated an automatic cost-of-living adjustment. In both of these cases, flat-rate pensions were involved, and increases to compensate for rising prices were needed to prevent the purchasing power of the pensions from declining. However, as we have seen in the German case, the problem in old-age insurance programs is more complex, because two types of adjustment are needed: (1) a way of relating the pensions granted at the time of retirement to current wage levels rather than actual lifetime earnings, and (2) a way of preventing the value of outstanding pensions from declining, either in relation to the cost of living or to prevailing wage levels or both.

Gradually various countries followed the German example in providing for both types of adjustment, but criteria for revaluing past earnings records or for adjusting outstanding pensions were not always identical with those adopted by the Federal Republic. By 1985, nine of our countries revalued past earnings in accordance with wage changes in their old-age insurance or supplementary earnings-related insurance systems. Italy, however, revalued recorded earnings according to changes in the cost of living, Belgium according to wage and price changes, Norway according to changes in prices and income levels, and Sweden according to price changes.

In the adjustment of outstanding pensions, changes in prices or in a cost-of-living index were considerably more likely to be the criteria than were wage changes. Whereas only four of our countries provided for adjustment in accordance with wage changes, ten based adjustments on price changes. Elsewhere a combination of criteria was used. In the Federal Republic, as we have seen, the advisory body appointed to recommend adjustments was to consider both wages and other economic factors. In Italy and Switzerland, both price and wage indexes were to considered, whereas in Spain, price, wage and other economic changes were to be considered.

When automatic adjustment is called for in the legislation, as it is in a number of countries, problems arise in periods of budgetary stringency. Special legislation providing for delays has been a frequent reaction to this type of problem in recent years, as in the American Social Security Amendments of 1983, which postponed an automatic cost-of-living increase that would have been effective July 1, 1983 to January 1, 1984.

Another significant difference in indexing provisions has to do with the frequency of adjustments. Annual adjustments are either automatic or anticipated in a number of countries, but there are several countries, including Israel and Canada (in its universal program), where quarterly adjustments are automatic. The more frequent the adjustments, the more favorable to the beneficiary and the more costly to the system.

Clearly the long-term impact of indexing provisions relating to outstanding pensions will differ, depending on whether wage changes or price changes are used as criteria. The long-run trend in industrial countries has been for real wages to rise – that is, for the rate of wage increases to exceed the rate of price increases. Adjusting pensions to wage changes enables pensioners to benefit from a rise in real wages, along with employed persons. Indexing on the basis of price changes means that the real incomes of pensioners gradually decline in relation to those of employed workers.

There were times in the 1970s and early 1980s, on the other hand, when prices were rising more rapidly than wages. This meant that pensioners were faring better than employed workers in maintaining the real value of their incomes in countries with automatic adjustment of pensions to price changes. It also meant, in countries with contributory taxes based on earnings, that the increase in revenues to the pension system tended to fall behind increases in pension expenditures, which rose with rising prices.

It is sometimes argued that pensions should be indexed on the basis of a special consumer price index for the elderly rather than a general consumer price index, on the ground that the elderly tend to spend relatively more of their incomes on food, medical care, and utilities than do younger people. On the other hand, it is argued that the elderly are less affected by inflation in home purchase costs and mortgage interest rates because they frequently own their homes free and clear.

The U.S. National Commission on Social Security, in its final report (1981), recommended continuing research on the issue. In Britain, two special indexes of the impact of inflation on the purchasing power of one- and two-person households have been developed. They are not used for adjustment of social security benefits, but they did rise slightly more rapidly from 1970 to 1980 than the general consumer price index, reflecting sharp price increases for food and utilities, on which pensioners spend proportionally more than does the general population. The British situation, however, is very different from that in the United States because health care expenditures are not included in any of the indexes since they are covered by the National Health Service; furthermore, housing costs are also excluded from the special pensioner indexes because many of the elderly receive housing subsidies (*SSB*, 1982, *45* [January]: 11–15).

There is much to be said for pension adjustments that are judgmental, as in West Germany, and are based on a combination of economic criteria. On the other hand, many would argue that pensioners are more effectively prevented from erosion of the purchasing power of their pensions by automatic indexing provisions. The practical results do not seem to differ greatly from one country to another, largely because legislatures find it undesirable politically to deny adjustments in pensions. Not only are the elderly viewed as an important voting bloc, but also their adult children have an important stake in adequate pensions for their parents whom they might otherwise have to support.

Provisions for women

Profound changes have occurred in the status of women in industrial societies since early national old-age pension laws were enacted. In the late nineteenth and early twentieth centuries, most married women were not in the labor force, except as they were employed as family workers on farms or in small business firms. The spectacular increase in labor force participation of women since World War II has led to a situation in which wives are increasingly acquiring rights to benefits on their own, giving rise to questions about the need for spouses' or widows' benefits for women who have no children in their care and are well below retirement age. The rise in the divorce rate has also created complications, leading to pressure to provide divorced women with rights to benefits based on their ex-husbands' insurance credits. Similarly, the increasing frequency of cohabitation of couples who are not legally married has created complex questions about eligibility for benefits based on earnings of one of the couples.

The issues surrounding the status of women under social security programs have been debated with increased intensity in the past two decades. However, they have been somewhat less central to concerns of the women's movement than, for example, terms and conditions of employment. Many of the countries included in this study have enacted legislation providing for equality of opportunity in employment in the past few decades – matters that are beyond the scope of this volume. Another important concern of the women's movement has been family policy, including such issues as the duration of maternity leave and the provision of child care centers, to be discussed in Chapter 13.[4]

Nevertheless, a number of changes for which women have pressed have been made in OASD programs. Among the more frequent complaints leading to changes have been (1) the lack of protection for housewives in case of disability; (2) the failure to preserve spouses' rights in the case of divorce or separation; (3) the poor return of many women from their social security contributions in view of their irregular earnings and the likelihood in many cases that they will be eligible for more in the form of spouses' benefits than of retired workers' benefits; and (4) the failure to provide for equal treatment of spouses, regardless of sex, and of widows and widowers. Somewhat ironically, one of the results of the drive for equal treatment has been to improve the rights of husbands and widowers.

The role of labor force participation

As we review provisions for women in social security legislation, we can discern a fairly clear pattern of differences among countries that is related to differences in the percentage of women in the labor force. In spite of the sharp upward trend in the propensity of women to work in industrial countries, wide differences remain, and in some countries – including a number in which there has been a sizable movement out of agriculture in recent decades – the labor force participation rate of women actually declined for a time (Table 4.2). In 1985, the percentage of women in the labor force in Western industrial countries ranged from 33.6 percent in Spain to 78.2 percent in Sweden. The rate has tended to be very high in the Soviet Union, and elsewhere in Eastern Europe was about 60 percent in Czechoslovakia, Poland, and Romania around 1980, and somewhat lower elsewhere (data not shown).

These differences in labor force participation tend to play a role in explain-

---

[4] For a comprehensive recent discussion of these issues, see Bergmann (1986).

Table 4.2. *Percentage of adult women in the labor force,*
OECD countries, years around 1964, 1970, and 1985

Country[a]	1964	1970	1985
Sweden	54.0%	59.4%	78.2%
Denmark	49.3	58.0	74.5
Finland	62.9	61.4	73.5
Norway	37.0	38.8	68.3
United States	43.7	48.9	63.9
Canada	39.7	43.2	62.4
United Kingdom	48.2	50.7	60.1
Japan	56.3	55.4	57.2
France		48.3	55.0
Australia	38.5	46.5	54.1
Switzerland	52.7	52.3	53.2
Austria		48.7	51.0
Belgium	38.0	40.2	50.5
Germany (Fed. Rep.)	49.0	48.1	50.4
New Zealand	33.0	37.5	47.6
Greece		31.2	41.5
Netherlands		31.0[b]	41.2
Italy	35.5	33.5	40.8
Ireland	35.2	34.3	36.6
Spain		29.2	33.6

Note: Data represent the total number of women in the labor force divided by
the female population aged 15 to 64.
[a] Countries are ranked by percentage in 1985.
[b] 1975.
Source: OECD (1987b). 1964 data are from an earlier issue of the same publication.

ing differences in social security provisions relating to women. The higher
the labor force participation rate, the less likely are benefits for wives or
widows without children in their care (and not disabled) to be available before, say, 50 years of age, whereas in countries with low female labor force
participation rates, such benefits are sometimes available regardless of age or
at least at a relatively early age. On the other hand, although roughly one-half
of our countries provide for a lower pensionable age for women than for men,
there is no consistent relationship between this practice and the labor force
participation rate of women (Table 4.3).

The differences can be better understood if we consider the fact that in
countries with high female labor force participation rates, women tend to
remain in the labor force until their late 50s or even into their 60s, whereas in

Table 4.3. *Normal pensionable age under national old-age insurance or pension programs by sex, 27 industrial countries, selected dates, 1914–85*

Country (and date of first law)	1914		1931		1961		1985	
	Men	Women	Men	Women	Men	Women	Men	Women
Australia (1909)	65	65	65	65	65	60	65	60
Austria (1906)	65	60	65	65	65	60	65	60
Belgium (1924)			65	65	65	60	65	60
Canada (1927)			70	70	70[a]	70[a]	65	65
Czechoslovakia (1906)	65	65	65	65	60	55	60	53–57[b]
Denmark (1891)	60	60	65	65	67	62	67	67[c]
Finland (1937)			65	65	65	65	65	65
France (1910)			65	65	65	65	60	60
Germany (Dem. Rep.) (1889)	70	70	65	65	65	60	65	60
Germany (Fed. Rep.) (1889)	70	70	65	65	65	65	65	65[d]
Greece (1934)					65	60	65	60
Hungary (1928)			65	65	60	55	60	55
Ireland (1908)	70	70	70	70	70	70	66	66
Israel (1953)					65	60	65	60
Italy (1919)			65	65	60	55	60	55
Japan (1941)					60[e]	55[e]	60[e]	55[e]
Netherlands (1913)	65	65	65	65	65	65	65	65
New Zealand (1898)	65	60	65	60	65[f]	65[f]	60	60
Norway (1936)					70	70	67	67
Poland (1927)					65	60	65	60
Spain (1919)			65	65	65	65	65	65
Sweden (1913)	67	67	67	67	67	67	65	65
Switzerland (1946)					65	63	65	62
USSR (1922)			60	60	60	55	60	55
United Kingdom (1908)	70	70	65[g]	65[g]	65	60	65	60
United States (1935)					65	65	65	65
Yugoslavia (1922)					55	50	60	55

[a] Old-age assistance was available for persons aged 65 to 69.

[b] The age for women varies from 53 to 57 according to the number of children raised.

[c] Until January 1, 1984, the age was 62 for single women.

[d] A woman could apply for an old-age pension from age 60 on with 20 years of insurance.

[e] These ages are under the employees' pension program. Under the national pension program, the pensionable age is 65.

[f] The superannuation (or universal) pension was payable at age 65; the old-age pension, which was subject to an income test, was payable at age 60.

[g] Age 65 applied to the contributory scheme; the pensionable age under the noncontributory schemes was 70.

Sources: Armstrong (1932, chart VIII); USSSA, *Social Security Programs Throughout the World* (1949, 1961, 1986); Tracy (1978); ISSA (1985).

countries with fewer women in the labor force, continued labor force participation by middle-aged and older women is relatively uncommon. Thus, it appears that in the latter group of countries, women are not *expected* to work in lieu of receiving social security benefits when a spouse retires, dies, or becomes disabled.

Among market-oriented industrial countries, Sweden had the highest female labor force participation rate in 1985 and a pattern of persistent labor force participation by more than 80 percent of women through most of the adult years, dropping significantly only when women reached their late 50s. The normal pensionable age for men and women under both the universal pension plan and the supplementary earnings-related system was 65, although reduced benefits were available from age 60 under several different provisions. There was also a means-tested supplement for wives aged 60 to 64. Widows were eligible for a universal pension if aged 50 or with a dependent child, and for amounts reduced by 1/15 a year below age 50 down to age 36. The earnings-related supplementary plan provided benefits for widows regardless of age, and, of course, for women who had earned supplementary benefits in their own right, but not for spouses.

Significantly, it is being recognized that some of these provisions for survivors are somewhat inconsistent with the high propensity of women to work. A special committee on pensions recommended in the early 1980s that widows' pensions in their present form for those under retirement age should be abolished and replaced by means-tested rehabilitation grants to be payable for limited periods to facilitate adjustment of the widow to the changed situation. The recommendations called for a gradual change, so that women who had reached age 45 before the new legislation came into effect would be eligible for pensions under the former regulations (*ISSR*, 1982, *35* [2]: 231–3). However, the proposals have been controversial, particularly with respect to the transitional provisions, and I learned in Stockholm in 1986 that they had narrowly missed adoption.

In this connection, it should be pointed out that Sweden is noted for its vigorous labor market policies, and these must be taken into account in considering policies toward women. Married women wishing to reenter the labor force when their children are grown are encouraged to enter one of the numerous government-sponsored training programs and receive a training allowance subject to a liberal means test. Such training is also available for widows.

The United States is an example of a country with a female labor force participation rate in 1985 that was relatively high, but well below Sweden's, and with a life cycle pattern that was similar to Sweden's. As in Sweden, the normal pensionable age was 65 for both men and women, but actuarially reduced benefits were available from age 62 for retired workers and spouses, and from age 60 for widows and widowers. We shall find in Chapter 5 that very large percentages of both men and women take advantage of the provisions for reduced early retirement benefits. As elsewhere, the age requirement for widows did not apply to women who had children in their care, and a reduced pension was available for a disabled widow or widower aged 50 to 59.

The case of the Netherlands is particularly interesting because the labor force participation rate of women in 1985 was relatively low for a highly industrialized country and more like those of less industrialized countries such as Spain and Greece, even though it has begun to rise in recent years. An unusual feature of the Dutch pension provisions has been that a married woman was not entitled to a pension in her own right (as a retired worker) unless (1) her husband had reached the age of 65 and was not entitled to a pension; or (2) she was married after she and her husband had acquired rights to a pension; or (3) she was regarded as the breadwinner and her husband had not yet reached age 65. However, as a result of an EEC directive on equality of the sexes in social security (to be discussed later), the Dutch law has been changed, and each spouse, on reaching age 65, will be entitled to a pension equal to half the net minimum wage as long as the contribution period has been met, whereas previously the pension for a couple amounted to the entire net minimum wage. There were other changes as well (*S&LB*, 1985 [3–4]: 563–5).

In Eastern Europe, labor force participation rates of women (not shown) tend to be high, and, in the Swedish pattern, remain high among middle-aged and older women. Even so, in 1985 the Soviet bloc countries all provided for an earlier normal pensionable age for women than for men, and in Czechoslovakia, the pensionable age ranged from 53 for women who had had five or more children to 57 for women with no children. In the Soviet Union, a woman who had had five or more children and reared them to the age of eight was eligible for a pension at age 50 on completion of 15 years of employment. Benefits for wives, on the other hand, tend to be restrictive as to age requirements, or, as in Poland and Romania, nonexistent.

Thus, the provisions in Eastern Europe tend to be designed to encourage wives and widows to work, but also, evidently in the interest of maintaining population growth, to reward women who have raised many children.

Although continued increases in labor force participation rates of women might seem to call for more restrictive age requirements for spouses' and widows' benefits in some countries, such changes are not easily achieved, because it is politically difficult to remove privileges that have been embodied in the legislation. Most of the changes have been in the direction of liberalization, although Britain tightened its provisions for widows under its 1986 amendments. Provisions for spouses were uncommon in early old-age pension programs but were added between the two world wars and have become more complex. In the early 1930s, widows' pensions were rarely available to women under age 65 with no children and not disabled (Armstrong, 1932, chart X). The tendency has been to lower age limits but at the same time in some cases to vary pension amounts according to the age of widows. Table 4.3 shows also that lower pensionable ages for women than for men are much more common than they were in the early 1930s. In 1931, New Zealand was the only country with a lower pensionable age for women than for men, but by 1961, there were 16 countries with a lower age for women. Since then, there has been no net increase in the number of such countries, and Denmark has changed its law to remove the normal retirement age of 62 for single women, so that all women and men now reach the age of eligibility for a retirement pension at age 67, with provisions for early retirement in cases of impaired earnings capacity.

Elsewhere, notably in the United Kingdom, there is agitation for the same retirement age for men and women, but disagreement exists over whether this should be accomplished by adopting a compromise age of 63, or reducing the normal pensionable age for men to 60, the age that prevails for women. We shall consider early retirement provisions for women in greater detail in Chapter 5.

Although the age of eligibility for a spouse's benefit tends to be related to patterns of female labor force participation, this is not so true of amounts of spouses' benefits, which vary considerably from country to country. We noted in Chapter 3 that there was no provision for a spouse's benefit in the original German old-age insurance law, and this continued to be true in 1985 in six countries, several of which were strongly influenced by German legislation – the Federal Republic itself, Austria, Italy, Poland, Romania, and Yugoslavia. All of the other countries included in this study did provide for a spouse's benefit which in some cases became available when the insured worker qualified for an old-age pension, but in a number of cases was provided only for wives who had reached a certain age (often 60). In Canada and Sweden, a spouse's benefit was available on an income-tested basis under the universal pension system for wives aged 60 to 64, whereas in New Zealand an income-tested benefit was available for a spouse under age 60. In the United States, a spouse could qualify for a full benefit at age 65 or for a reduced benefit at ages 62 to 64.

Spouses' benefits are usually not provided under supplementary earnings-related schemes because the spouse's need is presumed to be met by the universal pension or flat-rate insurance pension that provides the first tier of protection.

Another type of deviation from the usual pattern is found in some earnings-related systems that, nevertheless, provide for a flat-rate pension for the spouse.

This was the case in 1985 in Czechoslovakia, France, East Germany, Greece, Hungary, and Japan (employees' system). France went even farther by income-testing the spouse's pension, whereas Hungary accomplished much the same purpose by imposing a version of an income test that was defined in terms of the amount of the insured worker's pension.

Children's benefits were provided under most old-age pension schemes, but relatively few recipients of old-age pensions have minor dependent children; children's benefits are much more significant in provisions for survivors and the disabled.

One of the results of the drive for sexual equality has been to extend spouses' benefits to husbands as well as to wives on the same eligibility conditions. By 1985, this was the case in 11 of our countries, sometimes as a result of high court decisions.

Although women who have been housewives during all or most of their adult lives tend to be eligible for social security benefits only on the basis of their husbands' insurance, there are important exceptions. In countries with universal old-age pensions, a woman's right to receive her pension cannot be disturbed by divorce or separation, and three of these countries – Finland, Norway, and Sweden – provide universal pensions in cases of invalidity and also, on a more restrictive basis, in cases of survivorship.

Voluntary participation of housewives in social insurance has been permitted for some time in Belgium, West Germany, and Italy. In West Germany the provisions have been liberalized several times: in 1972 to permit housewives who had not previously been compulsorily covered to participate on a voluntary basis, and in 1982 to allow women who had withdrawn their accumulated contributions at the time of marriage to reinstate their insured status by making new contributions; however, there were restrictions on the benefits they could receive.

For the most part, in fact, relatively few women have participated on a voluntary basis, probably because the contributions impose an economic burden that is difficult except for relatively well-to-do families. In Canada, where voluntary contributions were seriously considered, the proposal was ultimately rejected on the ground that it was unlikely to benefit women in low-income families. A government survey had shown that, whereas about 75 percent of the respondents thought the proposal was a good idea, around 60 percent had some doubts about contributing. This appeared to confirm what some critics had been arguing, that a voluntary contribution scheme would benefit only those who could afford it (Paltiel, 1982). Canada has opted, instead, for a credit-splitting plan in the case of dissolution of a marriage.

In fact, probably the most innovative, and controversial, proposal that has come out of the debates over sexual equality has been the splitting of insurance credits of spouses. Some version of this is found in Belgium, Canada, France, and West Germany; similar proposals have been debated in the United States, and the recent Dutch provisions are a version of credit splitting.

In France, an amendment adopted in 1974 permits a widow to combine her own earned pension with a survivor's benefit based on her husband's insurance credits, but the limit for such a combined pension is one-half of the insured person's pension plus one-half of the survivor benefit (*SSB* 1976, *39* [September]: 37–44). Belgium's credit-splitting provision applies in the case of a divorced woman. Under a 1956 law, a woman aged 60 or over who has been separated from her husband and has not remarried has the right to receive one-half of his pension if she is not employed and not receiving a retirement or invalidity pension in her own right.

After considerable debate, the Canada Pension Plan (the supplementary earnings-related system) was amended to provide that on the dissolution of a marriage, the pension credits of both spouses accumulated during the marriage, upon application of one of the spouses, could be totaled and then split equally between husband and wife, provided that the marriage had lasted at least three years and the spouses cohabited for at least three consecutive years. The measure was designed particularly to benefit housewives, who in this manner might become eligible for earnings-related invalidity or survivor benefits, as well as retirement benefits. During the early years after adoption of this provision, very few people took advantage of it, despite efforts to publicize it (Paltiel, 1982). However, more recently the law has been amended to provide for automatic splitting of pension credits, provided continuous cohabitation had lasted for at least 12 consecutive months (Canada, Health and Welfare, 1986, 7–8).

In West Germany, credit splitting in the case of divorce is compulsory, although the spouses can preclude the sharing of rights by an explicit agreement in the marriage contract (Solcher, 1978). Moreover, if one spouse dies, the surviving spouse is awarded a pension based on the total pension rights acquired by both husband and wife (for the detailed provisions, see Fuchs, 1982).

There are many arguments in favor of credit splitting, but there are also potent arguments against it.[5] As former U.S. Commissioner of Social Security, Robert Ball (1978), has pointed out, a voluntary credit-splitting plan involves a problem of adverse selection: Those who stand to benefit from the option will choose it, whereas others will avoid it. However, he also questioned the feasibility of a compulsory plan, on the ground that many married workers, both male and female, do not regard their earnings as belonging equally to a spouse.

---

[5] See the extensive discussion in Jones, ed. (1983).

Clearly, more experience is needed under the various plans that have been adopted before it will be possible to weigh their advantages and disadvantages fully. Meanwhile, the ILO committee of experts mentioned in Chapter 2 recommended that persons living together should each have benefits in their own right, whether married or not, and their partners should, where necessary, pay contributions to secure those rights out of their incomes (ILO, 1984b, 39–46).

Thus far, we have referred to several provisions for credit splitting in the case of divorce, but what about the rights of divorcees more generally? Although social security has not normally covered the risk of divorce, the situation is changing, and there are now a number of laws that preserve the rights of divorced persons, at least until they remarry, and rights may even be recovered if the later marriage ends in death of the spouse or in another divorce. Along with these changes has come a tendency to grant a man and woman who have been living together the same rights as those who have been legally married, provided the relationship has lasted for some time, and particularly if they have children.

In Sweden, for example, "an unmarried or divorced woman or widow who was living permanently with an unmarried or divorced man or widower at the time of his death and who had been married to him or has had children by him shall be treated in the same way as a widow for the purposes of entitlement to the widow's pension" (ILO, 1973 – Swe. 3). Provisions relating to divorced persons have been liberalized in a number of other countries, including the United States and the Netherlands.

Divorce is not mentioned in some of the laws in Eastern Europe, but Czechoslovakia has a provision under which a widow's pension is payable to a divorcee if she has been receiving a maintenance allowance at the time of her husband's death (for the details, see ILO, 1975 – Cz. 3).

Another result of the drive for sexual equality has been the equalization of rights of widows and widowers. High court decisions in Austria (1980), the Federal Republic of Germany (1975), and the United States (1977) have declared differences in qualifying for widows and widowers unconstitutional and have led to legislation to correct the situation, whereas in Denmark equal treatment of widows and widowers under the supplementary employment-related scheme was provided in 1978 legislation and in Canada under 1974 legislation (*ISSR*, 1980, *33* [3–4]: 267–336; Paltiel, 1982; USSSA, 1982).

Equal survivorship rights need not be very costly to the system in practice, as an analysis by the U.S. Social Security Administration (1982) showed. The number of widower beneficiaries in the period studied was only about 0.5 percent of the number of widow beneficiaries. Similarly, male spouses accounted for a very small percentage of those receiving spouses' benefits.

The main reason for this was that most men were entitled to higher benefits based on their own earnings records than as widowers or spouses.

What about amounts of benefits for widows and widowers? In earnings-related systems, they are usually expressed in terms of a percentage of the insured worker's benefit or of the insured's earnings. They tend to exceed spouses' benefits by a substantial margin, in recognition of the greater needs of an individual living alone. The percentages vary a good deal from country to country, but the adequacy of the benefits will depend on the basic formula for the retired worker's benefit as well as on the percentage of that benefit received by the survivor.

Normally a widow or widower cannot receive both a widow's or widower's benefit and a retired worker's benefit simultaneously, but only the higher of the two rates for which the individual qualifies.

The EEC directive

This discussion of equality in pension rights would not be complete without reference to the directive of the Council of European Communities of November 1978, which called for elimination of certain discriminatory practices in social security programs and gave the member states six years (or until December 22, 1984) to comply. It applies to all social security programs except survivors' and family benefits (chiefly family allowances), but it is further limited by certain permissible exclusions from its scope, including (1) the determination of pensionable age, (2) advantages granted to persons who have brought up children, (3) the acquisition of benefit entitlements following periods of interruption of employment due to the bringing up of children, and several others (*ISSR*, 1978, *31* [4]: 494–5).

In spite of the exclusions, there were changes that needed to be made in a number of countries to conform with the directive. According to Laurent (1982), the United Kingdom, Ireland, and the Netherlands, in particular, had provisions that needed to be altered. Changes in the Netherlands have already been mentioned.

Financing

Financing provisions have been under special scrutiny in the recent period of rapidly rising costs of social security programs. Employers have protested the increasing burden, governments facing budgetary deficits have resisted increasing allocations to social programs, and increasing attention has been given to the impact of rising employee contribution rates on low earners.

Sources of revenue

Differences in sources of revenue for OASD programs are wide, as are those in the financing of social security in general, but they follow a somewhat similar pattern. The ILO does not publish data on the financing of OASD programs separately but does provide data on sources of revenue for social insurance and allied programs, including family allowances. The data differ very little from those shown in Tables 2.3 and 2.4 because the only difference is attributable to the inclusion of public assistance in those tables and not in the data relating to social insurance and allied programs. Since public assistance is financed from general government revenues, the effect of excluding it is to reduce the share from government revenues slightly. Otherwise, the percentages from government revenues are not affected, and the rank order of OECD countries differs hardly at all from that in Table 2.3; Table 2.4 is not affected because public assistance expenditures are very limited in Eastern Europe.

The USSSA (e.g., biennial, 1986) does provide data on financing of OASD programs, not in the form of proportional shares, but indicating rates of contributory taxes for employers and employees and providing information on allocations from general government revenues. Perhaps the most significant point that can be made about financing of OASD programs is that the general pattern of relatively substantial contributions from general government revenues in the British Commonwealth and Scandinavian countries, contrasted with heavy reliance on contributory employer and employee taxes in many of the Western European countries and the United States, prevails, as it does in the financing of social security programs in general. This largely reflects the more substantial role of universal pensions and income-tested benefits, which are usually financed from general revenues in the British and Scandinavian countries, and the much greater reliance on earnings-related social insurance programs in many of the continental countries and the United States. At one extreme are Australia and New Zealand, where pension programs are flat-rate and financed entirely from general government revenues, and at the other extreme are France and the United States, where pension programs are financed entirely, or almost entirely, by contributory taxes.

The absence of a significant contribution from general government revenues in France and the United States is not typical. Most of the countries relying mainly on social insurance do provide for a contribution from general government revenues, as did the original German old-age and invalidity insurance law of 1889. However, in recent years there has been resistance to increases in the contributions from general revenues under conditions of budgetary stringency, but there has also been resistance to increases in employer payroll taxes as a way of meeting rising costs, particularly in view of the problem of maintaining a competitive position in international trade that has been crucial for many countries since the 1970s. The resistance of employers to increased payroll taxes must also be viewed in the context of a tendency, mentioned in Chapter 2, to increase the employer tax more than the employee tax, so that, although in many countries they were originally equal, the employer tax rates are now usually higher than those imposed on employees. The result has been some tendency to impose more costs on the beneficiary, either through delays in cost-of-living adjustments or through increases in charges paid by insured persons for prescriptions and office visits under health insurance programs.

The prevalence of a contribution from general government revenues is explained by a desire to hold down the contributory taxes and also, at least in some cases, by a recognition of the fact that the regressive incidence of the contributory taxes should be at least partially offset by the more progressive sources of general government revenues, which usually are derived in large part from a progressive income tax. The lower the ceiling on earnings subject to contributory taxes, the more regressive the contributory taxes are likely to be, because the tax tends to be proportional to earnings up to the ceiling and regressive from that point on, as more and more of the earnings of high earners are subject to the tax. Table 4.4 shows that the ratio of the ceiling (maximum earnings subject to the tax) to average manufacturing earnings in 1985 tended to vary from 1.50 to 2.00 in most countries, but was considerably higher than this in Greece and Norway, and much lower in Canada (where it applied only to the supplementary earnings-related scheme).

Several countries have had provisions designed to make contributory taxes less regressive. In West Germany, for example, the insured person was exempted from the employee tax in 1985 if that person's earnings were below 10 percent of the earnings ceiling; the employer had to pay 18.7 percent instead of 9.35 percent for such workers. There has, however, recently been a proposal to discontinue this feature. The Netherlands went much farther and levied no payroll tax on the employer (except for invalidity insurance) and financed the old-age insurance program primarily by a 29.1 percent earmarked income tax, from which lower-income persons were exempted. The cost of covering lower-income persons was met from general government revenues, which also covered any deficit. Furthermore, as noted earlier, the Dutch pensions were flat-rate, varying with years of insurance but not with wages. This combination of financing and benefit provisions resulted in a system that tended to redistribute income from higher- to lower-income persons to a greater extent than in most social insurance systems, while at the same time providing benefits that represented a moderately favorable replacement of previous income (Table 4.1; see also Menzies, 1974b). Interestingly,

Table 4.4. *Ratio of maximum earnings subject to contributory taxes to average earnings in manufacturing, selected industrial countries, 1985*

Austria	1.54
Belgium	No ceiling for contribution purposes
Canada	1.00
France	1.26
Germany (Fed. Rep.)	1.72
Greece	2.80
Ireland	1.53
Italy	No ceiling for contribution purposes
Japan	1.59
Netherlands	1.66
Norway	2.47
Sweden	No ceiling for contribution purposes
Switzerland	No ceiling for contribution purposes
United Kingdom	1.62
United States	1.98

Sources: USSSA (biennial 1986); OECD (1986).

it was the desire of both workers and employers to reserve earnings-related pension programs for the private sector which was highly influential in the decision of the government shortly after World War II to provide for flat-rate benefits and financing largely by a tax on insured persons in the national system. The result was a very substantial development of employer pensions, as we shall find in Chapter 8.

Another approach that results in proportional rather than regressive contributory taxes is removal of the ceiling on earnings subject to the tax. In Belgium, Italy, and Switzerland there was no ceiling on earnings subject to contributions in 1985, and in Sweden there was no employee tax and no ceiling on wages subject to employer taxes.

In the United States, the resistance to a contribution from general government revenues in the financing of the OASDI program has been very strong, even on the part of key members of Congress and administration officials who have guided liberalization of the program over the years. The emphasis has been on maintaining the ''self-supporting'' character of the system, and relying on the increases in revenue from contributory taxes that resulted from rising wages and employment to finance increases in benefits. Reliance on general government revenues for a portion of the costs would, it has been argued, make it more difficult to achieve increases in benefits because of opposition to the increased income tax burden that would be involved. To a considerable degree, this attitude reflects awareness of continued conservative opposition to the OASDI program, which has undoubtedly been stronger in this country than in European countries with much older pension programs.[6] It should be noted, however, that general revenues do play a role in the financing of Medicare.

The Reagan administration came into office in 1981 at a time when the old-age and survivors fund was facing an impending deficit resulting from the impact of high inflation rates on the burden of cost-of-living adjustments and from the adverse effect of rising unemployment on revenue to the system. The administration promptly proposed a package of cuts in benefits, some of which were adopted. The more controversial cuts, however, especially a reduction in benefits for persons retiring at age 62 from 80 percent to 55 percent of full benefits, were strongly resisted in Congress. When it became clear by September that Congress would resist major reductions, the president announced his intention to authorize appointment of a ''blue ribbon'' commission to develop a plan that would ensure the fiscal integrity of the system (Svahn and Ross, 1983, 6). The members were appointed by the president and by the leaders of the two houses of Congress, resulting in a commission with a Republican majority. After deliberating for a year, the commission reached a tightly negotiated compromise, under which tax increases that had been scheduled for the 1980s were to be speeded up, the self-employment contributory tax was to be increased, and other measures to ensure the financial soundness of the system were to be recommended. Among these the most important were the coverage of new federal employees, discussed earlier, the taxation of 50 percent of the social security benefits of higher-income beneficiaries,[7] and the shift in the date for indexing from July 1 to January 1 (*National Commission . . . ,* 1983). At the same time, while recommending these changes, the commission declared itself opposed to any changes that would fundamentally alter the structure of the social security program, thereby quieting fears that the system would be made voluntary, benefits subjected to an income test, or other drastic changes adopted. The commission's recommendations were included, with only minor modifications, in the 1983 Amendments to the Social Security Act.[8]

---

[6] In 1964, Senator Barry Goldwater, as a candidate for the presidency, called for replacing OASDI with a voluntary program. Opinion surveys following the election showed that this was a major factor in his defeat, and, in general, surveys have shown widespread support for the social security program.

[7] The reason behind taxing half of the benefits was that, although an employee had paid a tax on his or her own contributions, he or she had paid no tax on the employer contributions to OASDI.

[8] A majority of the commission also recommended raising the retirement age under social security. See Chapter 5.

Contributory taxes and income taxes

In recent years, as the burden of financing social security has increased in country after country, there has been growing interest in the relationship between social security contributory taxes and income taxes. In an analysis of the situation in five countries – Australia, Canada, the Federal Republic of Germany, the Netherlands, and Sweden – Haanes-Olsen (1979) found that pension benefits were usually taxable and that contributions were usually deductible from taxable income, but because of personal exemptions and other reliefs for the aged, a pensioner who had been an average worker in manufacturing would not be liable for an income tax in the Netherlands and Canada, and would have a limited amount of taxable income in the Federal Republic and possibly also in Sweden. In Australia, although the old-age pension is considered to be taxable income, tax exemption limits usually exceed benefit levels.

Taxation of social security benefits in the United States had been strongly resisted before 1983, but the decision to tax half of the benefits received by relatively high-income beneficiaries (with the proceeds flowing into the social security funds) helped to make the financing of the system less regressive. Another change, adopted in 1975, that helped to offset the burden of the contributory tax on low earners, was the earned income credit, discussed in Chapter 13.

There is another aspect of OASD financing that merits comment. In the United States, social security income and spending were at one time not included in the federal budget, but rather were maintained in a completely separate fund. This is the practice in a number of other countries. Inclusion of social security in the budget, as is now the practice in the United States, makes social security expenditures vulnerable to cuts at a time of great concern about the budget deficit, even though the social security system is self-supporting and is actually producing a sizable surplus at present. One of the provisions of the 1983 amendments was to remove the social security system from the budget "to insulate the program from pressures caused by unrelated budgetary considerations," but this was not to be effective until 1993 (Svahn and Ross, 1983, 30).

At an international symposium in 1982, Guy Perrin of the Social Security Department of the ILO expressed the view that it was preferable to create a separate social security budget, financed not only by contributory taxes but also from especially earmarked subsidies from the national budget (*ISSR*, 1983, *35* [2]: 236–7).

Pay-as-you-go

Although early old-age insurance programs tended to follow the private insurance practice of accumulating a fund that would be adequate to meet future
benefit costs, as we saw in the German case, most OASDI programs are now
on a pay-as-you-go basis, limiting reserves to amounts that will be adequate
to cover benefit costs for a short period in the future – for example, a year.
One of the reasons for this change, as we commented in Chapter 3, was the
adverse impact of inflation on the value of reserves, and indeed, the entire
array of uncertainties surrounding estimates of future benefits and costs in an
unstable economic environment. Another important factor has been reluctance to impose on the present generation of workers tax burdens high enough
to meet much larger costs in the future as the aged population increases and
systems mature.

   The result of pay-as-you-go financing is to bring about intergenerational
transfers from present workers to retired, disabled, and survivor beneficiaries.
It implies a pact between generations: Present-day workers pay their contributory taxes on the understanding that a future generation of workers will in
turn pay taxes to finance the benefits that will accrue to them in the future.
The result of these transfers is a reduction in income inequality because although the contributory taxes are regressive, the benefits flow in large part to
persons who have little other income. However, in most social insurance systems the transfers are from persons with average earnings to low-income recipients, not from high-income to low-income persons (see, for example, Carroll, 1960). Where there is no ceiling on contributions, as in Switzerland, a
larger proportion of the transfers come from high-income persons.

   For a considerable period of time, while it was in the process of maturing,
the Swedish supplementary earnings-related system was an exception to the
widespread use of pay-as-you-go financing. Partly because it was anticipated
that private savings would be adversely affected by the adoption of this government program, as employers reduced their contributions to private schemes
in order to meet their obligations to the public system, employer contributory
taxes were set high enough to bring about the accumulation of a sizable fund.
In fact, the pension fund became the dominant credit source in the capital
market, with an annual lending capacity roughly twice that of all insurance
companies together (Eriksen, 1981; see also Heclo, 1974). The fund also
created controversy for a time over the power it gave the government to guide
investments, but gradually the accumulation of funds diminished in importance as pension disbursements rose sharply with the maturing of the system.

   Pay-as-you-go financing in the United States has been attacked by conservatives on several grounds. In the first place, it is argued that OASDI is not
an insurance system, because contributions meet only the cost of benefits to

present beneficiaries, and the notion that the system is accumulating funds to cover the worker's rights to benefits in the future is illusory. In fact, many workers believe that their contributions do provide the funds that will flow to them as benefits in the future. In a world of rising wages, indexing of benefits, and very little accumulation of interest in a fund, however, the individual's contributions are unlikely to equal his or her future benefits, quite apart from the fact that in immature systems, benefits are often paid to persons who have not met the full requirements for contributions. Moreover, social insurance systems need not be fully funded in the private insurance sense because the payment of future benefits depends on the integrity of the government in carrying out its obligations, not on the financial capacity of a private fund.

It should be emphasized in this connection that the OASDI tax in the United States is currently producing a surplus, as we have seen – a surplus that will continue to accumulate an increasing unspent balance until well into the twenty-first century and that will go far toward meeting the much higher expenditures that will be required when the baby boom generation reaches retirement age. It is important that the surplus be allowed to accumulate and not diverted to finance liberalizing amendments, as some observers fear will happen. At the same time, it must be recognized that it is the combined balance of the social security system and the rest of the budget that determines the impact of government receipts and expenditures on the economy. Should there come a time when not only social security but also all other government revenue and expenditures are generating a combined surplus, there might have to be adjustments to prevent a deflationary impact on the economy. We shall return to this issue in the concluding chapter.

The future

There is little question that OASD programs are facing the most serious problems they have encountered since the end of World War II. Continuation of high unemployment rates, particularly in Western Europe, and of generally slow economic growth may conceivably lead to more profound changes than we have yet witnessed.

Clearly there will be continuing debates over financing, particularly in countries with heavy emphasis on contributory employer taxes. In France, certain critics have called for the abolition of the ceiling on contributory taxes as a means of making financing of the system less regressive and as a way of protecting labor-intensive industries from an alleged disproportionate burden (e.g., Mills, 1983). The ILO committee of experts, while recommending no pronounced changes in financing, did maintain that a relatively low ceiling on employers' contributions might have adverse effects on employment, discouraging the use of part-time workers and encouraging firms to lengthen working hours and to prefer overtime use of present workers rather than hiring additional workers (ILO, 1984b, 88).

Another proposal that has been discussed to a certain extent in Western Europe, as we noted in Chapter 2, is replacement of the employer contributory tax by a value added tax, but there are problems with such a shift, as we suggested. A study conducted at the University of Bonn concluded that such a change would not be desirable for West Germany.[9] All things considered, there is much to be said for a reasonable balance in the contributions of employers, employees, and the government, rather than the imposition of a particularly heavy burden on the employer.[10]

An encouraging movement in relation to financing is the trend toward scrutinizing the relationship between social security financing and the income tax. To the extent that countries find ways of relieving the burden of contributory taxes on low earners and of taxing the benefits of pensioners with relatively high incomes, the financing of social security will become less regressive. Moreover, a frequent complaint about social security in the United States, and to some extent elsewhere, is that there is no reason for high-income persons to receive social security benefits. It is far better to combat this argument by taxing the benefits of such persons than by making the receipt of benefits subject to an income test. If benefits were income-tested, high earners would want to opt out of the system rather than pay social security taxes, and the result would be a two-class system. Furthermore, high-salaried workers could well find themselves and their families inadequately protected in the event of disability or death. A tax on benefits, on the other hand, affects primarily those with relatively adequate incomes.

We can also expect to see continued changes in the status of women under social security. Increased protection for housewives, especially in the case of disability, is likely to receive greater attention whereas, on the other hand, benefits for spouses and widows under retirement age, and neither disabled nor with children in their care, are likely to be viewed with increasing skepticism, as in Sweden.

Finally, the most serious problem facing many countries is a continued rise in the percentage of the aged in the population. For many countries, the problem will become particularly serious around the year 2010, when the huge cohorts of postwar babies begin to reach retirement age. For other countries, a substantial increase in the percentage of elderly in the population is projected between 1980 and 2000.

In 1980, the percentage of persons aged 65 and older in the population (arranged from highest to lowest in Table 4.5) was especially high in certain

[9] Interview with Professor Wilhelm Krelle, University of Bonn, September 1986.
[10] On financing issues, see also ILO (1984a) and Skidmore, ed. (1981).

Table 4.5. *Percentage of the population aged 65 and older, OECD countries, 1980–2030*

Country	1980	2000	2010	2030
Sweden	16.3%	16.6%	17.5%	21.7%
Austria	15.5	14.9	17.5	22.8
Germany (Fed. Rep.)	15.5	17.1	20.4	25.8
United Kingdom	14.9	14.5	14.6	19.2
Norway	14.8	15.2	15.1	20.7
Belgium	14.4	14.7	15.9	20.8
Denmark	14.4	14.9	16.7	22.6
France	14.0	15.3	16.3	21.8
Switzerland	13.8	16.7	20.5	27.3
Italy	13.5	15.3	17.3	21.9
Greece	13.1	15.0	16.8	19.5
Finland	12.0	14.4	16.8	23.8
Netherlands	11.5	13.5	15.1	23.0
Spain	10.9	14.4	15.5	19.6
Ireland	10.7	11.1	11.1	14.7
New Zealand	9.7	11.1	12.0	19.4
Australia	9.6	11.7	12.6	18.2
Canada	9.5	12.8	14.6	22.4
Japan	9.1	15.2	18.6	20.0
OECD average	12.2	13.9	15.3	20.5

Source: Maguire (1987).

Western European countries, most of them countries with relatively high rates of social security spending in 1980. However, the greatest increases between 1980 and 2000 are projected to occur in such countries as Italy, Spain, Yugoslavia, and Japan – countries that as recently as 1960 had high percentages of their labor forces in agriculture and have experienced sharp declines in the birthrate as the population became more urbanized.

Suggesting large increases in the cost of social security, especially for medical care, is a projected rise in the percentage of the population in the 75 and older bracket (data not shown).

Most of the countries included in Table 4.5 will experience a rise in the percentage of elderly in the population from the year 2000 to 2010, but the sharpest increases will occur from 2010 to 2030, according to these projections. It is important to recognize, however, that although the numbers of elderly persons in the population are certain to rise rapidly, at rates that cannot be predicted with great accuracy because of possible future changes in mortality and morbidity rates, projections of the *percentages* of elderly in the population must be viewed with recognition of the fact that the projections involve numerous assumptions that may not prove reliable. A pronounced rise in the birth rate in the near future could lead to an increase in the number of young people entering the labor market in the first decade of the twenty-first century. Although this appears unlikely, in the light of recent trends in birth rates, predictions of long-run trends in birth rates are notoriously unreliable. The demographers who predicted a continued rise in the percentage of aged in the population in the 1930s can scarcely be blamed for failing to foresee the sharp rise in the birth rate after World War II.

Since 1960 or 1965, the birth rate has tended to decline in nearly all industrial countries. Noteworthy, also, is the fact that by 1982 it was much lower in a number of countries of Western Europe than in the United States, the British Commonwealth countries, or in some of the countries of Eastern Europe. Unless there is a decided change in this situation, the percentage of elderly persons in the population, as well as their numbers, will rise appreciably in the early decades of the twenty-first century. There is serious concern over the probable decline in the ratio of people in the working age population to the retired and the accompanying burden of social security expenditures that will be involved. In my conversations with experts in various countries, I found that this was a matter of special concern in West Germany, where the proportion of aged in the population is even now very high and expenditures on pensions in relation to GDP are exceptionally high.

It is important to recognize, however, that a great deal will depend on the rate of economic growth, which cannot be reliably predicted as far ahead as the first few decades of the twenty-first century. Should there be a high rate of economic growth, it is likely that there would be increased immigration of foreign workers into many Western industrial countries and that this would help to maintain the ratio of workers to retirees. A high rate of economic growth would also encourage a continued increase in the proportion of women in the labor force, another factor that would help to maintain the ratio of workers to retirees.

Another consideration is that a decline in the proportion of children in the population will reduce the need for expenditures on education and other childhood needs (for a thoughtful discussion of these issues, see Aaron, 1986). Even so, there are economies in old-age pensions that are worthy of consideration and that will be discussed in the concluding chapter.

There is also the critical question as to whether there is any likelihood that the trend toward earlier retirement of elderly men can be reversed. We turn to this issue in the next chapter.

CHAPTER 5

The age of retirement

One of the most important dilemmas in relation to income security for the aged stems from the conflict between demographic trends, which suggest the desirability of gradually raising the conventional age of retirement, and economic forces, which tend to exert pressure toward earlier retirement. There has been a pronounced trend toward earlier retirement of elderly men in industrial countries throughout the period since the latter part of the nineteenth century, whereas in the case of women the proportion in the labor force at advanced ages has been small during the entire period.

Since the 1960s, the trend toward earlier retirement of men has continued in industrial countries, whereas the labor force participation rates of elderly women have not changed greatly, at least for those aged 65 or more. Moreover, numerous measures have been adopted to facilitate early retirement, and, at the same time, the concept of a more flexible retirement age in both directions has been encouraged through the provision not only of early retirement measures but also of incentives for postponing retirement under national social security policies.

Although the long-term trend toward increased life expectancy has chiefly reflected the increase in life expectancy at birth, there has been some tendency in the past few decades for life expectancy at age 65 to increase at a more pronounced rate than life expectancy at birth, at least in some of the industrial countries. If we compare measures of life expectancy in the early 1980s with those in 1950, on the basis of data in a recent OECD report (OECD, 1987a tables 9 and 11), we find life expectancy at age 65 to have been increasing at a greater rate than life expectancy at birth in a number of OECD countries, but not in all of them. Moreover, the tendency was much more pronounced for women than for men, and everywhere female life expectancy at age 65 was considerably higher than male life expectancy, averaging 17.9 years for women and 14.0 years for men in the early 1980s in the 24 countries included in the table. Although the change reflects a decline in mortality rates for those aged 65 and older, there is little agreement as to whether the health status and capacity to work among older people have improved as a result. Some argue that those who live to more advanced ages are more susceptible to the killer diseases – cancer, heart attacks, and strokes – whereas others maintain that

Table 5.1. *Percentage of older men in the labor force, by age group, OECD countries, years around 1960, 1970, and 1985*

Country	Men aged 60 to 64			Men aged 65 and older		
	1960	1970	1985	1960	1970	1985
Australia	79.6%	77.4%	42.7%	26.4%	22.2%	8.9%
Austria	66.0	44.9	21.5	15.1	8.0	3.0
Canada	75.8	74.1	67.9[a]	28.5	22.6	12.3
Denmark	87.5	78.3	49.5	34.5	22.2	12.7
Finland	79.1	65.0	43.3	39.7	19.0	10.6
France	71.1	68.0	30.8	27.2	19.3	5.3
Germany (Fed. Rep.)	72.5	74.9	33.2	22.8	19.9	5.2
Ireland	85.5[b]	87.6	70.4	51.5[b]	44.0	19.0
Italy	53.6	48.2	38.2	23.6	12.9	8.9
Japan	81.9	81.5	72.5	59.5	49.4	37.0
Netherlands	80.8	73.8	36.2	19.9	11.4	4.0
New Zealand	69.0	71.9[c]	45.7	22.0	23.6[c]	10.9
Norway	88.1	79.0	72.2	37.7	25.7	30.3
Sweden	82.5	75.7	65.7	27.1	28.9	11.0
Switzerland	88.8	87.3	82.7[d]	41.9	32.2	15.1
United Kingdom		87.0	52.0		20.2	7.6
United States	77.1	71.7	48.0	29.7	25.7	10.3

[a] 1981.
[b] 1966.
[c] 1976.
[d] 1980.
Sources: OECD (1987b); ILO, *Yearbook of Labor Statistics* (various issues).

the change reflects a genuine improvement in health among the elderly. Moreover, rapid technological change tends to enhance the problem of occupational obsolescence among aging workers.

In any event, the trend toward earlier retirement among men was even more pronounced in the 1970s and early 1980s than it had been in the 1960s. By 1985, the proportion of men aged 65 and older in the labor force was less than 10 percent in seven of the OECD countries for which data were available (Table 5.1). It was also less than 10 percent in 1980 in Hungary (Table 5.2). It was less than 20 percent in another eight OECD countries in 1985, and in Czechoslovakia in 1980. Clearly, also, the usual retirement age had moved down to the early 60s in a number of countries. Less than 50 percent of men aged 60 to 64 were in the labor force in 1985 in Australia, Austria, Denmark, Finland, France, West Germany, Italy, the Netherlands, New Zealand, and the United States. In Eastern Europe, around 1980, the percentage of men

Table 5.2. *Percentage of older men in the labor force, by age group, Eastern European countries, 1960, 1970, and years around 1980*

Country	Men aged 60 to 64			Men aged 65 and older		
	1960	1970	1980	1960	1970	1980
Czechoslovakia	51.1%	32.7%	46.3%		14.3%	19.5%
Germany (Dem. Rep.)	85.5	83.4		31.6	27.2	
Hungary	69.6	43.8	13.2	57.0	40.9	4.0
Poland	81.9	83.0	62.4	55.5	56.4	34.9
Yugoslavia	75.4	62.7	47.9	50.9	40.9	35.7

Source: ILO, *Yearbook of Labor Statistics* (selected issues). (The ILO has not published more recent data for these countries.)

aged 60 to 64 in the labor force was extremely low in Hungary and below 50 percent in Czechoslovakia and Yugoslavia.

The influence of changing retirement policies in explaining these trends will become clear as we consider policy developments in recent decades. Meanwhile, it will be useful to consider first the findings of research relating to the reasons for retirement, because we need to recognize the interaction of health status, prospective retirement income, and occupation on the decision to retire, as well as national policies relating specifically to the age of retirement.

Research in the 1950s

It is useful to begin with a discussion of research findings in the 1950s, because those findings tended to discredit the popular belief at the time that compulsory employer retirement policies were the major factor in leading elderly men to retire, as we noted in Chapter 3. Compulsory retirement policies had proliferated with the spread of employer pension plans, but results of surveys in both the United States and Great Britain indicated that such policies were by no means the major factor leading to decisions to retire.

Historically, industrialization and urbanization have tended to be accompanied by a reduction in the usual age of retirement. Aging farmers, especially those who are self-employed, can gradually turn the responsibility for managing the farm over to adult children without leaving the labor force completely. Thus, the percentage of elderly men in the labor force tends to be relatively high in countries with a large proportion of the labor force in agriculture. This helps to explain the relatively large proportions of elderly men in the labor force in Ireland, Japan, Norway, Poland, and Yugoslavia indicated in Tables 5.1 and 5.2. Similarly, the self-employed in nonagricultural pursuits can often retire gradually, and thus the decline in the percentage of the population in nonagricultural self-employment has been a factor in bringing on earlier retirement.

The forces playing an important role in decisions to retire showed up consistently in a number of the studies conducted in the 1950s (United Kingdom, Ministry of Pensions and National Insurance, 1954; Stecker, 1955; Steiner and Dorfman, 1957; Thompson and Streib, 1958):

1. By far the most frequent reason given by elderly men for their decisions to retire was ill health. Significantly, this reason was given much more often by men in occupations that made heavy physical demands than by those who had been engaged in sedentary occupations (Steiner and Dorfman, 1957, 47).

2. Although job security tended to increase with advancing age, elderly men who lost their jobs frequently had great difficulty in finding another one. Thus a decision to retire often followed a period of prolonged unemployment – the "discouraged worker" reaction.

3. Although ill health was the most prevalent reason given for retirement, it clearly interacted with other variables (expected retirement income, age, occupation, the state of the labor market, etc.) in determining the timing of the decision to retire. An individual might experience deteriorating health and yet go on working if expected retirement income was inadequate. Moreover, among those who retired voluntarily, it was persons in comparatively good health who were most likely to return to work. Thus "the retired population reflects the net effects of a sifting process which tends to leave those who are suffering from some type of physical or mental disability in the permanently retired group" (M. S. Gordon, 1963a, 437).

4. In an analysis of the relationship of the replacement rate (the ratio of average benefits under national old-age pension systems to average earnings) to the percentage of men aged 65 and older in the labor force in 14 industrial countries in 1950, I found a highly significant inverse relationship (M. S. Gordon, 1963a, 443–50). In other words, the more favorable the replacement rate, the more likely were elderly men to retire. In a later analysis for 19 countries in 1960, Aaron arrived at similar results (Pechman, Aaron, and Taussig, 1968, 130, 296–304).

Early retirement in the United States

In 1961, Congress amended the Social Security Act to permit men aged 62 to 64 to qualify for actuarially reduced early retirement benefits. The reduction was about 6.7 percent for each year in advance of 65, or about 20 percent for men retiring at age 62 (Hart, 1961, 4–13). The change was enacted at a time of relatively high unemployment and was designed to "alleviate the hardships" faced by men who found it impossible to continue working because of ill health, technological unemployment, or for other reasons (Hart, 1961, 4).

Women workers had been permitted to retire with reduced benefits at ages 62 to 64 since 1956.

The response to the new measure was pronounced, and, in view of the evidence that the replacement rate had an important bearing on decisions to retire, was somewhat surprising. In 1962, the first full year under the new provision, reduced benefit awards accounted for slightly more than half of all retirement awards to men. By 1981, reduced awards accounted for 61 percent of male retirement awards and 89 percent of currently payable awards (*SSB: Annual Statistical Supplement, 1983*, 102).[1] Why were so many men willing to accept reduced benefits at a time when benefits were low and the reduction would apply for the rest of their lives in most cases? Answers to this question began to emerge when the results of the 1963 Survey of the Aged became available. The data showed that "most beneficiary men aged 62 to 64 were in economically distressed circumstances" (Epstein and Murray, 1967, 106). They suffered from ill health, or had been laid off, and a large proportion had not held a full-time job since before 1960. They tended to have low educational and occupational levels and included a relatively large proportion of minority group workers.

Later surveys provided more details on the characteristics of early retirees. An analysis of newly entitled beneficiaries in 1968 showed that men who retired at age 62 and stopped working were especially likely to be in economic distress; the proportion who left their jobs for health reasons was even higher than among those filing at ages 63 and 64, and much higher than for those aged 65 (Table 5.3). They were also more likely to be completely incapacitated for work; in other words, they felt impelled to seize the earliest opportunity to receive benefits.

Not all of those who retired early were economically distressed, however, especially among men who qualified for early retirement public or private employer pensions. Almost one-third of early male retirement beneficiaries in the late 1960s received or expected to receive an employer pension (USSSA, 1976, 149). Those who had retired on their own initiative were especially likely to have an employer pension.

Very significantly, also, eligibility for an employer pension was highly correlated with earnings (Beller, 1981). In fact, positive attitudes toward re-

---

[1] A large proportion of awards not currently payable are to persons aged 65 and older who are continuing to work but are receiving Medicare benefits.

Table 5.3. *Most important reason for leaving last job reported by nonworking men initially entitled to retired-worker benefits, July–December 1968, by age at entitlement*

Categories of responses	Total	Aged 62–64			Aged 65
		Total	62	63–64	
Number reporting on reasons (in thousands)	133	96	58	39	37
Percent	100	100	100	100	100
Health	45	54	57	48	23
Specific illness or disability	29	34	38	30	14
Accident, injury	2	3	3	2	1
General poor health	14	16	16	16	8
Job-related	27	20	19	22	44
Compulsory retirement	12	3	1	7	36
Job discontinued, laid off	11	13	14	12	6
Dissatisfied	4	4	4	4	2
General retirement age	7	5	4	6	14
Eligibility for social security benefit or pension	2	2	2	2	1
Age for retirement	6	3	2	4	13
Retirement, wanted to retire	17	17	15	19	16
Changed jobs	1	—[a]	1	1	1
Family or personal	3	3	3	4	1
Miscellaneous	1	1	1		

[a] Less than 0.5 percent.
Source: Reno (1971, 5).

tirement varied directly with total retirement benefit income (Reno, 1971, 11), and the men who anticipated relatively high total retirement benefit incomes were necessarily those who expected to receive an employer pension in addition to social security, given the low level of social security benefits at the time.

One may conclude, on the basis of these 1968 data, that early male retirees could usefully, and without too much simplification, be classified into two quite different groups: a majority consisting of low-income men who suffer from reduced earning capacity, and a minority with more positive attitudes toward retirement and a superior retirement income prospect resulting from entitlement to an employer pension on top of social security benefits.

That situation, however, is changing in a highly significant way. The proportion of new social security retirement beneficiaries covered by private or public employee pension systems has been increasing; and, along with that increase, the proportion of men who have been retiring early because they wanted to retire, and not because they felt impelled to retire as a result of impaired earnings capacity, has been increasing. The survey of new beneficiaries receiving retirement benefits in the period June 1980 to May 1981 showed that about 68 percent of the men who had been wage and salary workers, compared with 52 percent in 1968, were covered by an employer pension system. Among those retiring at age 62 or at age 65, 70 percent were covered, whereas the percentage was somewhat lower among those seeking benefits at ages 63 to 64 (Iams, 1985). Moreover, among these wage and salary workers in the 62 to 64 age group, in contrast with the 1968 findings, 38 percent had retired on an employee-initiated basis – that is, because they wanted to retire – compared with 17 percent in the 1968 survey (Sherman, 1985, 29). It remained true, however, that the early retirees were more likely to be in blue-collar and service occupations than those who waited until age 65 or older to retire.

A recent study, based on sophisticated regression analysis, has concluded that choices based on economic factors are of primary importance in determining the age of retirement for most older workers (Fields and Mitchell, 1984). Even so, it is important to keep occupational differences, which Steiner and Dorfman found to be crucial, in mind.

A French study has also indicated important occupational differences in attitudes toward retirement and in the role of ill health in inducing retirement (Boullot et al., 1976). Only the higher staff members and those in the liberal professions prolonged their work because of interest in it. Decisions to apply for a retirement pension before the age of 65 were strongly influenced by physical problems. Moreover, differences in life expectancy at age 60 were related to occupation: The life expectancy of a teacher, for example (18.6 years), was similar to that of an upper staff member (18.1) but much greater than that of an unskilled worker (14.7). Furthermore, differences in retirement income by occupational level were also pronounced.

Retirement policies in industrial countries

There are few industrial countries that have not been affected by the movement to combat unemployment by inducing early retirement, whether or not accompanied by commitments to hire unemployed workers, in relatively recent years. As a report of the ISSA (1985) pointed out, it may seem paradoxical that, in a period in which high unemployment rates have had a significant impact on the financial stability of social security pension systems, these systems have been burdened by steps to induce earlier retirement.

Before we consider in detail the policy changes that have occurred, it is important to recognize that there has been a pronounced difference between

Western and Eastern Europe in retirement policies. It has been in Western Europe that the adoption of provisions aimed at encouraging early retirement has been particularly prevalent, whereas in Eastern Europe (where, except for Yugoslavia and possibly Hungary, there has been, at least until recently, no recognized unemployment) manpower policies have been aimed, among other things, at inducing older persons to continue working beyond the normal pensionable age. Even so, except for Czechoslovakia from 1970 to 1980 and Poland from 1960 to 1970, labor force participation rates of old men in Eastern European countries included in Table 5.2 have tended to decline, as the shift out of agriculture has continued and as pension levels have been increased.

Changes in retirement policies in Western Europe have led to greater complexity. Not only has the normal retirement age been lowered in a number of countries, but there have also been provisions for reduced benefits for early retirees, early retirement benefits for long-service workers, special prepension benefits financed through unemployment funds, early retirement contingent on disability, and several others. Moreover, in a number of countries in Western Europe, three or four different early retirement options are in effect simultaneously.

It would be a mistake, however, to imply that the trend toward early retirement provisions did not begin until the 1970s. By the early 1960s, there were a number of countries, in addition to the United States, that permitted early retirement on a reduced pension; Austria and West Germany permitted retirement as early as five years before the normal retirement age for persons who had been unemployed at least a year, and Austria also permitted early retirement for workers with many years of insurance coverage.

The normal pensionable age

One of the most important aspects of the trend toward earlier retirement has been a downward trend in the normal pensionable age. In Chapter 4, we called attention to the lower pensionable age for women than for men in a number of countries, and it is also true that, for the most part, the trend has been downward for both sexes (Table 4.3).

Reductions in the normal pensionable age in the early history of old-age pension programs had a somewhat different explanation from those that occurred later. Age 70 had been selected for some of the early programs in order to hold down the cost of a new, and often controversial, program. Later, when the scheme was established and accepted, it became politically feasible to reduce the pensionable age to 65, which was often the age for private pension plans and for plans for public employees. Another factor that influenced the choice of the original pensionable age was life expectancy. The fact that life expectancy has tended to be high in the Scandinavian countries helps to explain the choice of age 70 in Norway and 67 in Sweden. On the other hand, the selection of pensionable ages below 65 in some of the Eastern European countries, and also in Italy and Japan, was probably influenced by relatively low life expectancy.

Between 1961 and 1985, noteworthy decisions to lower the pensionable age were made in Canada, France, Ireland, New Zealand, Norway, and Sweden. The New Zealand decision was discussed at some length in Chapter 3; in Canada, the change was made in conjunction with the adoption of the earnings-related supplementary system in 1965, was implemented gradually, and was clearly influenced by the fact that 65 was normal pensionable age in the United States. In all of the other countries, the change did not occur until the 1970s and was at least partially influenced by rising unemployment.

In France, until 1972, a worker could retire at any time between ages 60 and 70, but at age 60 the pension was only 20 percent of base earnings, rising by increments of 4 percent a year to 40 percent at age 65. This was unsatisfactory, especially in view of the fact that workers in certain special systems could receive full benefits at age 55 or 60 (ISSA, 1985). A report prepared for the government by Laroque (1962) had recommended improvements, but it was not until 1972 that the law was amended to provide for a gradual increase in the pension payable at age 60 to 25 percent and in the increment for deferring retirement to 5 percent a year. As the problem of unemployment increased from 1974 to 1976, the employment problems of aging workers became more serious, and in 1976 the government adopted a provision under which manual workers with 43 years of employment in arduous labor – including five of the last 15 years before retirement – could retire at age 60 with a pension equal to that usually payable at age 65. This was extended in 1982 to all wage and salary workers with a record of 37.5 years of insurance, and in 1984 to the self-employed in handicrafts, industry, and commerce.

Norway's decision to reduce the normal pensionable age from 70 to 67 was reached in 1972, while at the same time, an innovative provision was adopted calling for a partial pension payable to persons aged 67 to 69 who shifted to part-time work. Sweden followed in 1976 with a decision to reduce the normal pensionable age from 67 to 65. Its move was partially motivated by a desire to improve job opportunities for younger workers, but it was also facilitated by the surplus in Sweden's social security funds, mentioned in Chapter 4. At the same time, Sweden adopted a partial pension provision, which differed from Norway's in that it applied to the preretirement years of 60 to 64.

To the best of my knowledge, the only industrial country that has recently adopted legislation providing for an increase in the normal pensionable age is the United States,[2] although Japan and Spain have recently enacted legislation lengthening the number of years of insurance required to qualify for a pension (Dumont, 1987). The 1983 amendments to the Social Security Act, following a recommendation by most of the members of the National Commission on Social Security Reform, provided for a gradual increase in the normal pensionable age from 65 to 67, beginning in the year 2000 and culminating with a retirement age of 67 in 2022. Early retirement would still be permitted from age 62, but benefits would be reduced by 30 percent of full benefits, instead of 20 percent. As an added inducement to delaying retirement, the legislation also provided for a gradual increase, beginning in 1990, in the bonus of 3 percent of retirement benefits now received by beneficiaries for each year in which retirement is delayed after age 65, to 8 percent by 2007 (Svahn and Ross, 1983, 26, 30).

Proponents of the increase in the normal retirement age among members of the commission were concerned about the future solvency of the system and pointed to the gradual rise in life expectancy, as well as the likelihood that older workers would be in greater demand in the future as a result of the decline in the youthful population now under way. The fact that the change would not begin until 2000 was designed to give workers who would be affected ample time to prepare for the change (*National Commission . . . ,* 1983, statement 1).

In a vigorous statement in opposition to the increase in the normal retirement age, five Democratic members of the commission argued that the change would mean a reduction in benefits. They cited evidence to the effect that the increase in life expectancy had not been accompanied by an increase in the health of those who were living longer – on the contrary, these persons tended to experience "more chronic illness and impairments." Instead of a change in the retirement age, the minority proposed a modest increase in the contributory taxes to meet the projected short-fall (*National Commission . . . ,* 1983, statement 2).

Provisions for early retirement

In a complex and rapidly changing situation, it is all but impossible to obtain complete information on all of the early retirement provisions in industrial countries, and in some cases information from different sources is conflicting, but an attempt has been made to summarize these provisions in 1985 in Appendix 2.

---

[2] There have been a few instances, however, in which the normal retirement age for women has been raised, as in the case of Denmark, where the retirement age for single women was raised from 62 to 67.

Early retirement with a reduced pension: In addition to the United States seven of our countries provided for early retirement with a reduced pension, although in Canada the provision applied only in Quebec before 1987. In all cases, however, the earliest retirement age under these provisions was lower than in this country – that is, 60 for the most part, except for the early retirement age of 55 for women in Belgium and Greece.

Where the reduction is actuarially determined – that is, based on average life expectancy – the long-run costs to the pension system are theoretically not increased because the longer period over which pensions are paid to early retirees is offset by the lower pensions they receive. However, if many persons opt for early retirement, the result will be substantially increased pension costs for a considerable period because of the sharp rise in the number of persons receiving pensions. Moreover, estimates of life expectancy may not be entirely accurate.

Early retirement contingent on long service: Where early retirement was available for those with many years of coverage under an old-age insurance system, an option in seven of our countries (though only for men in Belgium), the typical provision called for 35 years of insurance, but the age at which the option became effective varied considerably.

As Tracy (1979) has shown, the introduction of this option in Austria and West Germany radically altered patterns of retirement. Austria amended its social security provisions in 1961 to permit early retirement with 35 years of insurance coverage from age 60 for men and 55 for women.[3] As a result, the proportion of men receiving new pension awards before the normal retirement age rose from a very small percentage in 1960 to about 50 percent in 1966. (A small part of the increase was attributable to a provision under which a pension could be received early after a year of unemployment.) There was also an increase for women to about 30 percent; the lower normal retirement age for women probably accounted for the smaller percentage of early retirements among women.

In West Germany, 80 to 90 percent of new pension awards occurred at age 65 until 1973, when amendments permitted retirement from age 63 with 35 years of insurance and from age 62 for partially disabled persons who did not qualify for a full disability pension (later reduced to age 60). The long-service provision accounted for most of the dramatic change that occurred – from relatively few men retiring early before 1973 to 61 percent in 1976. The change for women was less decisive, because many women had been taking advantage of an existing early retirement provision which allowed retirement

---

[3] The age at which benefits were available for long-service workers was actually reduced gradually, a year at a time, over a period of five years.

up to five years early for women with at least 15 years of contributions, 10 of which were earned in the last 20 years before retirement.

A point worth emphasizing here is that, under the German benefit formula, a worker retiring at age 63 may very well receive a benefit that is only slightly lower than he or she would receive at age 65. Suppose the worker has had 35 years of service and retires at age 63; the worker's benefit will be 1.5 percent of his or her adjusted base wage for each year of service, or 52.5 percent. If that same worker continues in employment to age 65, he or she will receive 3 percentage points more, or 55.5 percent. Thus the penalty is substantially less severe than for a worker opting for early retirement at age 63 in the United States, where the actuarial reduction would amount to 13.4 percent of the full benefit available at age 65. The situation in other countries with benefit formulas similar to that of Germany would be comparable.

Early retirement contingent on prolonged unemployment: The oldest provisions of this type, permitting retirement as early as five years before the normal pensionable age for those unemployed at least a year, are found in Austria and West Germany, but similar provisions have spread to a number of other countries in recent years. By 1985, six countries had such provisions. German data indicated that the number of persons drawing benefits under this provision rose substantially during the higher unemployment years of the 1970s.

Prepension payments: Closely related to early retirement for the long-term unemployed is a newer type of scheme, usually operating through the unemployment insurance system, which provides prepension payments to older unemployed workers or workers who voluntarily retire, until they reach the normal pensionable age. Typically, these arrangements have been reached through the centralized collectively bargained agreements that are prevalent in a number of Western European countries, and later have been ratified by legislatures, giving them the force of law.

France led the way in this development with an agreement between the major employer organizations and the principal trade union federations, concluded in March 1972, under which unemployed workers aged 60 or over were guaranteed an allowance payable until age 65 and 3 months. The allowance supplemented normal unemployment benefits to provide a guaranteed income equal to 70 percent of the individual's recent earnings (*ISSR*, 1973, *26* [3]: 318–20; Boullot et al., 1976).

The agreement took the form of a rider to a collective agreement of December 31, 1958, that had inaugurated unemployment insurance in France. It was clearly designed to enable an unemployed older worker to delay applying for an old-age pension in order to qualify for the substantially higher pension he or she would receive by waiting until age 65. The prepension system continued the worker's old-age insurance coverage and accumulation of years of service.

The initial agreement was liberalized over the years, among other things, to extend the guaranteed payment to workers aged 60 or more who voluntarily left their jobs, and to provide a similar payment (financed somewhat differently) to workers dismissed for economic reasons from age 56 and 2 months (*ISSR*, 1980, *33* [3–4]: 395–6).

The Socialist Government, which came into office in 1981, originally adopted policies liberalizing social benefits, but later found it necessary to impose restrictions because of adverse trends in employment and in the balance of payments. Meanwhile, as a result of the increase in the retirement pension payable at age 60, the prepension benefit was no longer paid to workers who qualified for this higher pension.

Developments in Belgium rather closely followed those in France, but a new feature was added in 1976 legislation aimed at promoting employment of youth by providing special prepension benefits for older workers who voluntarily withdrew from employment, *provided* the employer hired a worker under age 30 as a replacement, not necessarily in the same job (Tracy, 1978). A follow-up study in 1977 showed that, under conditions of rising unemployment, the number of persons applying for prepensions was substantial, especially among men, who were more likely than women to be covered by the provisions, and who found that the income available from the prepension scheme was generally superior to the reduced old-age pension for early retirement under the old-age insurance system (Dupriez, 1977). However, the program tended to work to the disadvantage of workers in small firms, who were not automatically covered by the provisions. Accordingly, provision was made on a temporary basis in 1982 for a preretirement pension scheme, contingent on the replacement of the retiring worker by a younger jobseeker, financed entirely by the state, to exist alongside the collectively bargained scheme. Apparently, however, the program has not been very effective in promoting employment of younger unemployed persons.[4]

Somewhat similar was a "job release" plan adopted in the United Kingdom in 1977, under which workers within one year of the normal pensionable age who voluntarily left their jobs would receive a special flat-rate allowance, provided the employer agreed to recruit a replacement from the unemployment register. The scheme has been expanded over the years, and in 1983–4 applied to men aged 62 to 64, to women aged 59, and to disabled men aged 60 to 61. Under provisions in effect in 1983, the program was voluntary, and to be eligible for the special allowance payable to the worker who retired, he

---

[4] Interview in June 1985 with J. Goosse, director of the ILO branch office in Brussels and with Edouard Wuilgoot of the Belgian Office National de l'Emploi.

or she had to be leaving full-time employment. Participation of the employers was also voluntary, and they were obliged to submit evidence that the retiring worker was being replaced by an unemployed worker in a full-time job on a permanent basis, not necessarily in the same position held by the retiring worker. The special allowance was taxable and in 1983 amounted to considerably more than the old-age pension without an earnings-related supplement.[5]

A relatively recent addition to the countries with schemes of this sort is West Germany, in which a program of voluntary early retirement at age 58 came into effect in 1984. Its application at the sectoral or enterprise level is left to agreements between employer and employee representatives (*ISSR*, 1984, *37* [3–4]: 553–4).

Early retirement contingent on disability: Disability benefits often make possible early retirement for persons who are permanently disabled and can meet the eligibility conditions with respect to severity of the disability and (in insurance schemes) contribution requirements (to be discussed in Chapter 6). As Appendix 2 shows, eight of our countries had special provisions for early retirement contingent on disability in 1985, and in some cases the definition of disability was more liberal than under the disability scheme.

Partial pensions: Perhaps the most interesting scheme for early eligibility for an old-age pension–and possibly the "wave of the future"–is the Swedish provision for partial pensions, adopted in its 1976 legislation. Under this plan, persons aged 60 to 64 may reduce their working hours and combine part-time employment with receipt of a partial pension. The working hours must be reduced by at least five hours a week, but must amount to at least 17 hours. The partial pension covered 65 percent of the loss of earnings resulting from shifting to a part-time schedule until 1981, when the percentage was reduced to 50. The scheme has proved to be popular, with about 20 percent of eligible employees and 7 percent of eligible self-employed receiving a partial pension in 1983. Employers have been reported to be cooperative, and partial pensioners have valued their increased leisure. Many of them stayed on in their regular jobs, and firms with declining employment and a large proportion of older employees have tended to be strongly represented among companies making use of this scheme (Ginsburg, 1985).

The British part-time job release scheme in effect in 1983 was more restrictive than the Swedish scheme, because it was linked with the full-time job release scheme in that its purpose was to open up part-time jobs for the unemployed. A worker who applied for participation must have been employed

---

[5] A Department of Employment report in 1983 indicated that a total of about 195,000 men entered the job release scheme between 1977 and June 1983 (*Employment Gazette*, 1983, *91* [9]: 407).

full time and must have been shifted to a part-time assignment by the employer. The employer, in turn, had to agree to hire an unemployed person for at least as many hours a week as those relinquished by the employee who has been shifted to part-time work. Thus it could not be used by an employer in a declining industry as a means of reducing total hours worked. The age and eligibility conditions were the same as for workers applying for participation in the full-time job release scheme (United Kingdom, Department of Employment, 1983b).

Spain and Denmark have recently adopted partial pension schemes, and Finland was expected to adopt one in 1986. There is reason to believe that other countries may follow suit.

Early retirement for workers in arduous or unhealthy occupations: This type of provision is particularly prevalent in Eastern Europe, where other early retirement options are generally not available, but it is found also in a few Western European countries and Japan. In a number of cases it is an outgrowth of special retirement systems for miners. Because employment in mining and in some other relatively unhealthy industries or arduous occupations tends to be declining, provisions for early retirement are particularly appropriate.

Early retirement provisions for women: Apart from the numerous countries that had a lower normal pensionable age for women than for men, and those that required fewer years of contributions for women in 1985, there were several countries that had special early retirement provisions for women or for women who had raised children. The Czech provisions have been mentioned in Chapter 4. In Greece, a woman with dependent children could retire from age 55 with 5,500 days of contributions, whereas in the Soviet Union, age and years of employment requirements were reduced for mothers of five or more children.

Countries with no early retirement provisions: Six of our countries – Australia, Ireland, Israel, New Zealand, Romania, and Switzerland – had no provisions for early retirement in 1985. Canada had only the possibility under redundancy provisions in certain industries, until legislation was enacted in 1986, effective at the beginning of 1987, allowing retirement from age 60 with reduced benefits and delayed retirement beyond age 65 with increased benefits to age 70 (*ISSR,* 1987, *40* [1]: 103–4). Several of the countries with no provisions for early retirement had flat-rate benefits, and it is more difficult to incorporate early retirement provisions in such schemes, because the level of flat-rate benefits tends to be determined on the basis of subsistence needs, and a lower benefit for early retirees is therefore difficult to justify. In New

Zealand, with a universal pension available at age 60, there is little need for special early retirement provisions.

The retirement situation in Japan is unique among the countries included in this study. The fact that employment is "permanent" in Japan is well known in this era when Japanese management practices are everywhere being studied to shed light on the secrets of Japanese efficiency. Perhaps less well known is the fact that permanent employees in large firms have traditionally been required to retire from their regular jobs at age 55 (50 for women), five years before the normal retirement age under the employees' pension insurance plan. To be sure, they have been granted sizable lump-sum payments at the time of retirement, but these have not generally been large enough to tide them over to age 60, and most workers have tended to continue employment at lower-paid jobs, often in the same firms, until age 62 or 63 (Fisher, 1973; Tracy, 1978).

Japanese unions have complained about this situation and about the inadequacy of retirement benefits, but large firms have resisted changing compulsory retirement policies and have been able to achieve economies by replacing older workers with younger employees. Smaller firms have been more willing to raise the retirement age because of their difficulties in recruiting younger workers. Recently, however, there have been signs that this situation is changing. A survey of 1,000 large companies indicated that a large proportion were changing their retirement allowance systems to restrain increases in their personnel costs, and more than half of the firms have sought to improve employment conditions of older workers through such measures as extending mandatory retirement ages (S&LB, 1983 [4]: 595). The changes in national pension provisions mentioned in Chapter 4 did not affect the normal age of retirement, except that the retirement age of 55 for women under the employees' pension plan was gradually to be raised.

Inducing later retirement

As the concept of flexible retirement policies has gained ground in recent decades, policies providing increments for postponing receipt of retirement benefits beyond the normal pensionable age have become increasingly common. By 1985, 14 of our countries provided for such increments, and the number had been increasing. A number of the annual increments were in the neighborhood of 7 percent, suggesting that they were determined largely on an actuarial basis. In Denmark, Finland, Norway, and Switzerland, however, they were substantially higher than 7 percent.

As Tracy (1978, 79) pointed out, and as the labor force data in Table 5.1 indicate, there is thus far little evidence that these provisions have had any effect in halting the downward trend in the labor force participation rates of elderly men. One possible exception is Norway, which in 1972 adopted a partial pension plan for persons aged 67 to 70 and also provided an increment of 9 percent in the amount of the individual's pension for each year receipt of the pension was postponed from age 67 to 70. Table 5.1 indicates that the percentage of men aged 65 and older in the labor force in Norway rose between 1970 and 1985.

Another country in which the proportion of elderly men in the labor force—both among those aged 60 to 64 and those aged 65 and older—rose from 1970 to 1980 was Czechoslovakia, where an increment of 7 percent of the pension is provided for those postponing retirement beyond the normal pensionable age (60 for men) and where the government has taken other steps to induce later retirement, including simultaneous receipt of a pension and earnings for persons in selected occupations.

The retirement test

In the United States, the retirement test (i.e., the limitation on earnings that a social security recipient may receive without loss of benefits) has long been a matter of controversy, with some organizations representing the aged arguing that it discourages work effort and social security experts arguing that removal of the test would be costly, would chiefly benefit persons who go on working full-time at relatively high salaries beyond age 65, and would therefore provide benefits for persons who do not need them.[6]

Most countries do impose a limitation on earnings that can be received by a pension recipient. In 1985, this was true of the great majority of countries included in this study. The exceptions were Canada, East Germany, the Netherlands, New Zealand, Romania, Sweden, and Switzerland, whereas Czechoslovakia and the USSR imposed no limitation on earnings for those in certain occupations. In West Germany, the limitation applied only to those who retired before age 65 and had been imposed when the law was amended to permit retirement at age 63 with 35 years of insurance. In France, a pension recipient could not work in his preretirement firm and was subject to a tax on earnings in other work.

Labor force data (Table 5.1) do not suggest that the absence of a retirement test stimulates work after retirement. In fact, most of the countries that have no retirement test tend to have relatively few men in the 65 or older group in the labor force. Other factors appear to be more important in explaining variations in labor force participation in the 65 and older group.

---

[6] An analysis by the USSSA showed that elimination of the retirement test for the entire population aged 65 to 69 would increase benefits by about $1.8 billion (on the basis of 1975 data) and that two-thirds of this increase would go to middle or high earners (Esposito, Mallan, and Podoff, 1980).

Factors associated with early retirement

The drop in the labor force participation rate of men aged 65 and older has been persistent, but there continue to be variations that are associated less with policy differences than with factors that we found to be important in explaining differences in rates of spending on social security among industrial countries, such as the age of the system and the percentage of the labor force in agriculture. In fact, if we line up these factors in a manner similar to that used in Table 2.1, we find that the year of adoption of the first old-age pension system is inversely related, fairly consistently, to the percentage of elderly men in the labor force. That is, the countries with the oldest old-age pension programs tend to have relatively few elderly men in the labor force. This is consistent with other data for Austria and West Germany, for example, showing that very few men delay applying for an old-age pension beyond the normal pensionable age. There is also some tendency for countries with comparatively high percentages of the labor force in agriculture to have high percentages of elderly men in the labor force, although there are important exceptions, such as Italy and Finland. And finally, although we do not have the relevant data for all of our countries, there is a tendency toward an inverse relationship between the income replacement rate (as shown in Table 4.1) and the percentage of elderly men in the labor force – a finding that has been revealed in several studies, as we noted earlier.

Among men in the 60 to 64 age group, however, the influence of retirement policies tends to be important. The countries with relatively small percentages of men in this age group in the labor force tend, on the average, to have several different types of early retirement options available, whereas those with comparatively large percentages in the labor force have few or no early retirement options. Notable among those with no early retirement provisions or very limited provisions in 1985 and relatively high labor force participation rates of men in the 60 to 64 age group were Switzerland, Ireland, and Norway. At the other end of the spectrum were Austria and West Germany, with four or five early retirement options and low percentages of men aged 60 to 64 in the labor force, along with Finland, France, and Italy, with at least two early retirement options.

Women and retirement

We turn now to patterns of retirement among women – a subject that has been relatively neglected in the literature. What has been happening to the labor force participation rates of older women? In Tables 5.4 and 5.5, we include data for the 55 to 59 and 60 to 64 age groups. Those 65 and older are not

Table 5.4. *Percentage of older women in the labor force, by age group, OECD countries, years around 1960, 1970, and 1985*

Country	Women aged 55 to 59			Women aged 60 to 64		
	1960	1970	1985	1960	1970	1985
Australia	22.3%	29.1%	27.1%	13.3%	16.3%	11.2%
Austria	40.1	35.8	25.9	19.8	13.2	7.6
Canada	27.9	38.7	41.9	20.3	29.1	28.3
Denmark	34.3	49.1	57.3	22.7	33.5	25.6
Finland	50.6	56.1	66.7	36.0	35.9	38.8
France	42.2	46.0	41.4	33.9	34.3	18.0
Germany (Fed. Rep.)	32.3	37.2	40.2	21.0	22.5	11.8
Ireland	22.4[a]	21.8	21.1	21.2[a]	20.7	15.3
Italy	16.8	16.9	20.8	12.8	10.6	10.2
Japan	45.8	48.7	51.0	39.1	39.1	38.5
Netherlands	13.9	18.4	20.7	9.5	12.7	8.9
New Zealand	22.1	29.3[b]	30.9	12.7	13.7[b]	11.7
Norway	27.0	32.0	60.0	23.1	24.5	46.2
Sweden	31.8	41.1	74.4	21.5	25.7	46.4
Switzerland	30.3	39.8	41.1	25.4	30.3	24.4
United Kingdom		50.7	51.9		28.0	22.4
United States	40.7	48.8	50.1	29.4	34.8	33.2

[a] 1966.
[b] 1976.
Source: ILO, *Yearbook of Labor Statistics* (selected issues); OECD (1987b).

included, because, on the whole, relatively few women in this age group are in the labor force.

Among women aged 60 to 64, the proportion of women in the labor force varied a good deal, tending to be relatively high in countries with large percentages of the labor force in agriculture, such as Finland, Japan, and Poland, and very small in Ireland, Italy, and the Netherlands, with their cultural traditions favoring women remaining at home. The proportion also tended to be low in New Zealand, with its universal pension payable at age 60.

Since 1960, there has been no consistency in the changes that have occurred from country to country. A few countries, such as Norway and Sweden, show a very strong upward thrust in the percentages of women in this preretirement age group in the labor force, probably reflecting the influence of the strong upward trend in the tendency of women to work in these countries, shown in Table 4.2. As a society becomes accustomed to a situation in which work on the part of married women is taken for granted, continued

Table 5.5. *Percentage of older women in the labor force, by age group, Eastern European countries, years around 1960, 1970, and 1980*

Country	Women aged 55 to 59			Women aged 60 to 64		
	1960	1970	1980	1960	1970	1980
Czechoslovakia	43.1%	36.5%	40.8%	30.3%	18.2%	21.5%
Germany (Dem. Rep.)	53.6	62.5		28.6	31.5	
Hungary	30.6	29.2	18.8	26.1		8.7
Poland	60.2		57.9	48.9		37.4
Yugoslavia	27.4	27.4	27.8	22.2	23.5	22.1

Source: ILO, *Yearbook of Labor Statistics* (selected issues).

labor force participation on the part of older women is likely to be welcomed.

In a number of other countries, the proportion of women aged 60 to 64 in the labor force rose from 1960 to 1970, but then declined from 1970 to 1985, probably reflecting less favorable employment opportunities during this period. This group included Australia, Canada, Denmark, France, West Germany, the Netherlands, New Zealand, Switzerland, the United States, and Yugoslavia, although in some cases the changes were very slight. The increased availability of early retirement options for both men and women probably also played a role in some of the countries in explaining the drop between 1970 and 1985.

The data on women aged 55 to 59 are particularly interesting because here the influence of the upward trend in the overall labor force participation of women shows up very strongly, most spectacularly in the Scandinavian countries, where by 1985 the proportion of women in this age group in the labor force ranged from 57.3 percent in Denmark to 74.4 percent in Sweden. A second group of countries, with a substantial upward trend in the labor force participation rate of women in this age group and a rate that amounted to 40 percent or more in 1985, included Canada, West Germany, Switzerland, the United Kingdom, and the United States. Rates were also high in Japan and Poland, but probably reflected in considerable part a large percentage of older persons in agriculture. Sharing in the upward trend but with considerably lower percentages in 1985 were New Zealand and the Netherlands. In Austria, where women could retire at age 55 after 35 years of contributions or after a year of sickness or unemployment, the rate showed a declining trend, while in Hungary, also, the rate tended to decline. Elsewhere in Eastern Europe, the rates differed from country to country but showed no pronounced trend over the period.

If the experience in the Scandinavian countries is indicative of future trends in the labor force participation of women in their late 50s and early 60s, the implications for the income status of older people may be important. With both spouses working in this stage of life when children have become independent, aging couples are likely to be able to save more than if only one of the spouses is earning. Moreover, both are likely to be accumulating rights under national pension programs, and one or both may be accumulating rights to employer pension plans, public or private. Add to this the fact that the proportion of women employed in professional and managerial occupations is increasing in many industrial countries, though at varying rates (see, for example, Galenson, 1973), and that men and women in these occupations tend to retire later than those in other occupations, one may conclude that the percentage of couples retiring with substantial incomes is likely to be considerably higher than in the past, despite the trend toward early retirement among men.

So much for labor force statistics. What can we learn about patterns of retirement and the reasons for retirement among women?

Recent American data show that retirement patterns of married women workers differ markedly from those of unmarried women. Among workers receiving their first retirement benefits in 1982, married women were much more likely to receive benefits at age 62 than unmarried women or married or unmarried men (Table 5.6). In fact, virtually three-fourths of the married women received their benefits at age 62. (It is important to keep in mind the fact that the data relate only to married women who apply for retired worker benefits; married women who apply for wives' benefits are not included in the data.) Most of the remaining married women received their benefits at ages 63 or 64. Very few went on working until age 65. Unmarried women, on the other hand, were less likely to receive their first benefits at age 62 than either married or unmarried men, but somewhat more likely to receive them at age 63 or 64. However, the percentage of unmarried women who received their first benefits at age 65 was higher than for any of the other sex and marital status groups.

Not only did most married women receive their first benefits at age 62, but about half of them had stopped working before receiving benefits. In fact, more detailed data (not shown) indicate that among those receiving their benefits at age 62, about 70 percent had stopped work before receiving benefits, and 43 percent had stopped work more than three years before. Thus, many married women stopped work despite the fact that retirement benefits would not be available for a considerable period. Because married women are often younger than their husbands, some of these women may have been married to men who had begun to receive retirement benefits, whereas others may

Table 5.6. *Age at receipt of first benefit and time interval between leaving last job and receipt of first benefit, new retired-worker beneficiaries, by sex and marital status, United States, 1982*

	Men		Women	
	Married	Unmarried	Married	Unmarried
Age at receipt of first benefit				
62	47%	53%	74%	40%
63–64	28	25	18	30
65	15	12	6	21
66 or older	9	10	2	9
Total percent	100	100	100	100
Time interval between work stoppage and receipt Stopped work				
More than 6 mo. before receipt	25	34	51	30
Within 6 mo. of receipt	41	38	22	30
More than 6 mo. after receipt	8	7	7	11
Still at work	26	20	19	29
Total percent	100	100	100	100

Source: Sherman (1985, 24).

have been married to men whose earnings were reasonably adequate. They were less likely than unmarried women to be dependent on their own earnings.

Another interesting feature of the 1982 data was a decided improvement in the retirement income status of new female beneficiaries compared with the results of a 1970 survey. Not only had social security benefits become more adequate for these retirees, but also, among all sex and marital status groups, the proportion who were receiving employer pension income – public or private – was decidedly higher than in the earlier survey (*SSB*, 1985, *48* [February]: 17–26).

Data for other countries – relating chiefly to ages at which women apply for retirement pensions, rather than to results of surveys – indicate that women tended to take advantage of early retirement options, including a lower normal pensionable age for women than for men. In West Germany, for example, where 1972 legislation provided for retirement from age 60 for women with sufficient contributions, there has been a tendency for the proportion of women retiring before age 65 to increase. By 1984, according to *The Economist* (February 4, 1984), nearly two-thirds of all women drew their pensions early.

In the United Kingdom, the great majority of women workers have tended to take advantage of the right to receive a retirement pension at age 60. Throughout the period from 1960 to 1970, according to Tracy (1979), some 70 percent of female workers opted to retire at age 60. Those who went on working beyond age 60, however, benefited from the increment of 6.5 percent for each year that retirement was deferred.

The situation in France was, at least until recently, when pensions for those retiring at age 60 became much more adequate, something of an exception. There Tracy found that the percentages of women going on working until age 65 (slightly more than 40 percent) were about equal to those for men throughout the period from 1963 to 1976. The percentages opting for deferred retirement beyond age 65 were also similar for men and women, rising, in the case of women, from 17 percent in 1963 to 22 percent in 1976.

In Eastern Europe, attempts to induce working beyond the normal retirement age appear to have had some results, at least in the Soviet Union and in Czechoslovakia. According to a report prepared by the ISSA (1982), in the Soviet Union about 65 percent of the men and 52 percent of the women received their retirement pensions at the normal pensionable ages of 60 and 55, respectively, whereas 16 percent of the men and 27 percent of the women were found to continue to work beyond the ages of 65 for men and 60 for women. In Czechoslovakia, the proportions of older men in the labor force rose substantially between 1970 and 1980, both for those aged 60 to 64 and those aged 65 and older (Table 5.2), while the labor force participation rates of older women have also increased (Table 5.5).

The outlook for the future

Changes in the age of retirement have clearly been very significant for both men and women, with men tending to retire in their early 60s in a number of industrial countries and women increasingly going on working until around age 60 or slightly later.

It has sometimes been argued that the departure of elderly men from the labor force, or their tendency to shift to part-time work, results in a reduction in gross national product. This argument clearly carries more weight in a period of very tight labor market conditions, when replacements cannot be recruited, than in a period of substantial unemployment. Historically, the decline in labor force participation of elderly men has tended to be offset by an increase in the labor force participation of women and, at least in some countries, of young people who seek part-time work while completing their education. These changes have been encouraged by the relative growth in the service industries, which provide job opportunities for women and youth.

The cost to the economy of early retirement of men takes the form of the increase in the cost of income maintenance involved. As I have suggested earlier, even where the early retiree receives an actuarially reduced pension, which does not increase long-run costs to the pension system, the immediate effect of an increase in early retirement is a sizable cost. The cost to the individual man will depend on the terms of the early retirement option, but also, from a psychological point of view, on his attitude toward early retirement.

What are the prospects for a reversal in the trend toward earlier retirement of men? Clearly it cannot be expected as long as severe unemployment continues, especially in Western Europe. The longer-term prospect is difficult to predict. Developments that would encourage a reversal of the trend would be (1) a decided increase in the rate of economic growth, (2) a shortage of younger workers resulting from the falling birth rate in most industrial countries in the last 15 to 20 years, and (3) strong efforts by employers and unions to encourage the development of part-time employment opportunities for aging men within the firms in which they have been employed. On the other hand, a rapid rate of technological change would probably have an adverse effect on the employment of older men, who suffer from occupational obsolescence as a result of technological change, as employers seek to replace them by recently educated young persons with appropriate training.

Long-run economic predictions are notoriously unreliable, but there is at least a possibility that the outlook is for moderate economic growth accompanied by rapid technological change. In such an environment, a reversal of the trend toward earlier retirement among men would be unlikely. In fact, if this type of prediction held for the United States, Congress might eventually repeal the legislation providing for raising the normal retirement age before it became effective, or postpone its effectiveness.

The outlook for women is somewhat different. The upward trend in the propensity of women to work is affecting most age groups, at least through the middle and late 50s, and is being encouraged by the shift in employment to the service industries. It appears likely that the age at which most women will retire will stabilize in the 60 to 64 group, although the increase in the proportion of women in such professions as law and medicine may mean that some will go on working to age 65 or beyond.

The effects of these trends on the economic status of the aged population, as suggested earlier, may not be altogether unfavorable, although the large proportion of women who work part-time must be kept in mind in assessing these prospects.

Before leaving the subject of future prospects, reference should be made to a survey of attitudes toward retirement conducted by the Commission of the European Communities among the working population of member countries (*SSB*, 1980, *40* [June], 26–8). The results showed that the majority (57 percent) intended to stop working at retirement age or earlier, whereas 25 percent planned to continue in paid work after receiving their pension. About one-third intended to retire early with a reduced pension (one out of two to get more leisure time, and one in five because of poor health). Moreover, a large majority (72 percent) supported the idea of a gradual transition from work to retirement. Interestingly, also, the results showed that the proportion of persons wishing to continue in paid employment (presumably part-time) was relatively high in countries with low earnings-replacement rates, such as Denmark, Ireland, and the United Kingdom.

Finally, let me suggest certain policy changes that may be desirable as countries adapt their policies to the changing labor force patterns of older men and women: First, the provision of partial pensions to persons who shift to part-time work, both before normal retirement age, as in Sweden, and after that age, as in Norway, should be considered, along with efforts to encourage employers to shift such workers to part-time assignments within the firms in which they have been working. Such provisions have certain advantages over a retirement test, although their adoption would not necessarily mean that the retirement test would have to be discontinued. They encourage a gradual transition from work to retirement. They would also be less likely to induce concealment of part-time earnings than the retirement test, which penalizes a beneficiary with earnings above a certain amount.

Second, the link between disability and early retirement benefits needs to be given more careful consideration in some countries. Partial disability benefits are unavailable in some cases and have probably been too lenient in others, such as the Netherlands. A very interesting suggestion was made by Staples (1978), who noted that among 28 countries, "earnings loss due to old age, disability, or unemployment is the common factor running through conditions [for early retirement] as they are presently applied." He proposed a concept of a more generalized risk, such as "earnings loss due to advancing age," that might be based on a combination of criteria involving age, earnings impairment, and current employment status. Under such a system, early retirement benefits would be available only to those who could demonstrate impaired earning capacity. Such an approach would deny social security benefits before the normal retirement age to those who were not experiencing impaired earning capacity but were eligible for an employer pension and wished to retire voluntarily.

This chapter should not be concluded without mention of laws banning mandatory retirement, or mandatory retirement before age 70, found in one version or another in the United States, the province of Quebec, Norway, and possibly a few other countries. These laws are unlikely to have a significant effect on prevailing trends, though they may have an influence in individual cases. The forces that have led to the proliferation of provisions making early retirement more attractive are simply too powerful, including the many moves by employers to ease older employees out of the work force through attractive early retirement provisions (sometimes called the "golden handshake"). The role of employer pensions in encouraging early retirement will be discussed in Chapter 8.[7]

[7] Not discussed in this chapter have been the numerous "redundancy" laws in Western Europe that impose restrictions on the dismissal of workers in redundancy situations. They will be discussed in Chapter 12.

CHAPTER 6

Long-term invalidity programs

Disability is a social problem of major dimensions, affecting more than one-sixth of
the noninstitutionalized working age population, producing a major part of the manpower wastage, creating loss of earnings and family income, and requiring a substantial investment of public resources in income maintenance programs.

(Haber, 1967)

Incidence of long-term disability

Provisions for long-term disability are important not only in their own right,
but also because they have played an important role in relation to the trend
toward earlier retirement. Many of those who seek early retirement are disabled, and long-term disability pensions facilitate early retirement for older
persons who are disabled but are not yet eligible for early retirement benefits.
Moreover, disability increases sharply with advancing age and reaches a substantial percentage of the population in the early-60s age group – that is, in
the years preceding age 65 (still the most prevalent normal retirement age).

Unusually detailed data relating to the disabled are available for the United
States, where a number of surveys have been conducted by the Social Security
Administration. I shall start by discussing these data because it is important
to have an understanding of the incidence and nature of long-term disability
before considering the policies relating to disability benefits. To the extent
that I have seen data for other countries, they are very similar to the American
data (see, for example, Townsend, 1979, on Britain; Koch-Nielsen, 1980, on
Denmark; and Wadensjö, 1984b, on Sweden).

A large-scale survey conducted in 1972 indicated that 15.6 million persons,
or nearly 15 percent of the population aged 20 to 64, were disabled. They
tended to be "older, poorer, with fewer years of schooling, and somewhat
more likely to be black, to live in the South, and to have a rural residence;
and more likely to be divorced, separated, or widowed – even at the younger
ages" than the nondisabled (Allan, 1976, 18). Interestingly, women were
slightly more likely to be disabled than men, but, for both sexes, the percentage who were disabled rose with advancing age and reached a high point of
about 35 percent in the 60 to 64 age group. The incidence of disability would

111

Table 6.1. *Percentage of population disabled, by sex, age, and severity of disability, United States, 1972*

	Total	Severely disabled	Occupationally disabled	Secondary work limitation
Men				
Average, aged 20–64	14.0%	5.9%	3.8%	4.3%
20–24	8.9	1.5	2.2	5.2
25–34	6.5	1.4	1.9	3.2
35–44	9.5	3.7	2.5	3.3
45–49	19.4	6.5	7.7	5.2
50–54	15.7	7.0	4.4	4.3
55–59	24.3	11.0	7.4	5.9
60–64	34.6	23.7	5.4	5.5
Women				
Average, aged 20–64	15.2	8.4	2.8	4.0
20–24	5.4	2.0	0.4	3.0
25–34	8.1	3.5	1.9	2.8
35–44	12.2	6.0	2.2	4.0
45–49	18.9	9.0	4.2	5.7
50–54	23.0	12.4	4.3	6.3
55–59	25.7	17.7	4.3	3.8
60–64	35.0	25.0	5.7	4.3

Source: Allan (1976).

be even higher among those aged 65 and older, but they were not included in the survey because from age 65 on, people receive old-age rather than disability benefits (Table 6.1).

The survey distinguished among (1) the "severely disabled" – unable to work altogether or unable to work regularly; (2) the "occupationally disabled" – able to work regularly but unable to do the same work as before the onset of disability or unable to work full time; and (3) those with "secondary work limitations" – able to work full time, regularly, at the same work, but with limitations in the kind or amount of work that can be performed. Women who had limitations in keeping house but not with respect to paid work were classified as having secondary work limitations. It was the incidence of severe disability that rose most sharply with advancing age, but there was also a tendency for the percentage who were occupationally disabled to rise with increasing age. The percentage of those with secondary work limitations was less closely related to age.

Among men, more than three-fifths had job-related disabilities, whereas among women, moving vehicle accidents were the most frequent cause of disability. The higher incidence of job-related disabilities among men reflects the fact that they are more likely to be employed in hazardous or arduous occupations. Women were also more likely to have been the victims of accidents or chronic conditions developing in the home. The proportion with job-related disabilities tended to rise somewhat with advancing age, whereas, as would be expected, the percentage with disabilities resulting from automobile accidents tended to decline with increasing age.

Of particular interest are the types of conditions reported by severely disabled persons in the 55 to 64 age group, among whom the greatest incidence of long-term disability occurs. The most frequent type of condition was cardiovascular (including heart attacks, heart trouble, and high blood pressure), from which 13 percent of persons in this age group suffered. Following very closely in frequency were musculoskeletal conditions (including arthritis or rheumatism, trouble with the back or spine, and others). Other relatively prevalent conditions included respiratory ailments such as chronic bronchitis and emphysema, miscellaneous arterial/vascular diseases such as hardening of the arteries, digestive problems, and mental problems (Krute and Burdette, 1978).

Analysis of the income status of household units with a disabled person showed striking differences between units in which a married man or woman was disabled and those in which an unmarried person (presumably in most cases the only member of the household) was disabled. Earnings accounted for a much larger percentage of the income of the married couples, and spouse's earnings played a significant role, accounting for about one-fourth of the income of units including a disabled married man and almost three-fourths of that of units including a disabled married woman. Public income maintenance payments, on the other hand, played a major role in supporting disabled unmarried persons, with a particularly large percentage of the income of disabled unmarried women coming from public assistance.

Of special interest was the finding that, among persons who could meet the eligibility conditions and were so severely disabled that they could not work at all, 54 percent of the men and 86 percent of the women were not receiving disability benefits (Lando, Coate, and Krause, 1979, 7–8).

There was a pronounced rise in the number of persons receiving disability benefits in the United States and in certain other industrial countries during the 1970s – an increase that was at least partly explained by the rise in unemployment. During periods of high unemployment, it is more difficult for the disabled to retain their jobs or to find new jobs if displaced. Moreover, once receiving disability benefits, they are likely to continue to be dependent on them, especially if they are in older age brackets and thus suffer the dual disadvantage of being old and disabled in the job market. As one study indicated "a ratchet effect may result, as more people are pushed on the rolls by a deteriorating labor market than are pulled off by improving labor market conditions" (Lando et al., 1979, 6).

In our discussion of disability programs, we shall consider first those relating to nonoccupational disability, or "invalidity" (the usual European term), because they are usually integrally related to old-age and survivors programs, which we have been considering, although in some European countries they are linked to sickness programs. Occupational disability will be considered in Chapter 7.

One of the major differences among countries is in their degree of emphasis on vocational rehabilitation of the disabled, but because the most successful vocational rehabilitation programs tend to be closely linked to labor market programs, they will be considered in Chapter 12.

Major features of programs

Coverage

There is little need to consider the coverage provisions of invalidity programs because the history of coverage provisions in these programs is very similar to that of coverage provisions of old-age pension programs, although adoption of invalidity programs often lagged behind enactment of old-age pension legislation.

Eligibility: degree of disability

Determination of the degree of disability required for eligibility for an invalidity pension in early legislation was strongly influenced by the German law of 1889, which provided invalidity pensions for adults who had lost at least two-thirds of the earning capacity of persons similarly situated and not incapacitated in the same region.

By the early 1930s, 16 of the countries included in this study had invalidity pension programs, and most of them required loss of two-thirds or more of earning capacity (Armstrong, 1932, chart VIII). In many of the European countries, a disabled person was not eligible for an invalidity pension until having exhausted rights to sickness benefits, which were intended to provide for short-term illness or disability.

Gradually a movement developed to distinguish between persons who had experienced total or almost total loss of earning capacity and those who were capable of doing some work, though not always in their usual occupation. However, this movement did not become significant until after World War II. By 1958, 24 of our countries had invalidity pension programs, and 10 of these provided for partial as well as for total disability. The countries that had not yet adopted programs were Canada, Israel, and the United Kingdom, although the British provisions permitted payment of sickness benefits for an indefinite period for persons with permanent incapacity for work.

The United States did not provide for nonoccupational disability under its social security program until 1956, and the original law applied only to persons aged 50 to 64 who were unable to "engage in substantial gainful activity because of any medically determined permanent physical or mental impairment which can be expected to result in death or be of long-continued and indefinite duration." Later the law was amended to provide for disabled adults under age 50, and, in 1965, the provision relating to duration was amended to provide for disabilities lasting "at least 12 months." Advisory commissions and councils have on several occasions recommended that provision for partial disability be considered, but thus far the recommendations have not been adopted.

By 1985, all of the countries included in this study had invalidity pension programs and 14 of them provided for partial as well as for total or severe invalidity. Where there was some provision for partial disability, the degree of disability required for a full invalidity pension tended to be high – loss of 100 percent or at least two-thirds of earning capacity. Definitions of partial disability differed greatly. The stiffest provisions were in Denmark, France, Hungary, and Japan, where loss of two-thirds or more of earning capacity was required (although Japan provided a lump-sum payment under its employees' pension program if loss of earning capacity ranged from 30 to 69 percent). In Sweden and Switzerland, there were requirements for loss of at least 50 percent of earning capacity. The actual amount of the pension varied with degree of disability in some countries. For example, Sweden provided two-thirds of a basic pension for loss of 67 to 83 percent of earning capacity, and one-half of a basic pension for loss of 50 to 66 percent, but many of the disabled were also entitled to earnings-related supplements or to special supplements if not eligible for earnings-related payments (Haveman, Halberstadt, and Burkhauser, 1984, 61).

Unlike the practices that had developed in some occupational disability programs, in which the degree of disability was determined on the basis of a schedule of types of physical impairments – such and such a percentage of total disability for loss of a limb, for example – ratings of disability in nonoccupational programs tend, for the most part, to be based on estimates of earning capacity. In a review of provisions in EEC countries, Bouquet (1979) indicated that disability ratings were based on loss of earning capacity in the six founding members of the EEC, as well as in Denmark. In the United Kingdom and Ireland, on the other hand, temporary incapacity for work lasting more than a certain length of time would entitle the disabled person to an invalidity pension, but the incapacity had to be total.

In general, the laws provide for a considerable delay before a determination of incapacity is reached, in order to encourage completion of a physical and vocational rehabilitation program before establishing the degree of residual incapacity, if any. This has been accomplished in a number of countries by prolonging the maximum period for which sickness benefits can be paid. Thus, in countries with emphasis on both physical and vocational rehabilitation, temporary disability (sickness) benefits are payable either until recovery or a permanent disability rating has been established, or for a fairly lengthy maximum period (in 1985, it was up to 78 weeks in West Germany, following a period of six weeks of employer sickness leave, whereas it was up to 52 weeks in the Netherlands).

On the other hand, sickness benefits were available only for relatively short periods in certain other countries. In Canada, where sickness benefits were adopted only rather recently and are part of the unemployment insurance system, duration was limited to 15 weeks. Maximum duration was approximately half a year in Greece (except for tuberculosis cases), in Italy, and in the five American states (plus Puerto Rico) that had temporary disability insurance programs. Workers in states with no temporary disability program might be entitled to employer sick leave, but only for a short period.

Disability ratings took age into account in some countries, recognizing that an older disabled person was likely to encounter barriers to reemployment and that young people were more likely to recover completely. In the United States, social security regulations provided that age, education, and work experience were important in deciding whether a person was able to engage in other types of substantial gainful activity when there was an impairment that prevented working in the previous occupation. At the same time, the regulations made it clear that there had to be medical evidence of an impairment and that unemployment associated with advancing age did not by itself establish eligibility for a disability pension.

In some countries, moreover, the state of the labor market was taken into account in determining the extent of loss of earning capacity. We shall find that a pronounced increase in the percentage of insured persons receiving disability benefits in several European countries in the 1970s under conditions of rising unemployment was at least partly explained by changes in policies that gave greater weight to the likelihood that an individual would be reemployed.

In the Soviet Union, where policies were strongly influenced by manpower objectives, great emphasis was placed, as in Sweden and West Germany, on early assessment of the work capacity of a disabled person – in the Soviet case, by a team of specialists in three branches of medicine (a therapist, a neuropathologist, and a surgeon). The individual was classified in one of three invalidity groups: (1) severely disabled persons who needed constant attendance, (2) seriously disabled persons who did not need constant attendance, and (3) persons whose work capacity was reduced and who were in some cases unable to work in their former occupation. For those in the third group, in particular, rehabilitation and/or retraining was emphasized. Moreover, legislation provided that a disabled person normally had to be employed at the enterprise where he or she had worked before becoming disabled (Makkaveyskiy, 1981).

Contribution or residence requirements

Where invalidity pensions are part of a social insurance program, as in most industrial countries, there are usually requirements that the individual must have been insured for a certain minimum period of time, unlike the situation in industrial injuries insurance, where there is usually no length-of-work requirement. However, in invalidity programs, the requirements tend to be more lenient than in old-age pension programs. For example, in Austria, in 1985, where 180 months of contributions were required for an old-age pension, including 12 months in the last three years, only 60 months were required for an invalidity pension (including 12 in the last three years). The provision for 12 months in the last three years was designed to call for recent attachment to the labor force and resembled provisions in nearly all countries calling for a record of recent attachment.

Young people tend to be at a disadvantage if they become disabled within a short time after beginning to work, and thus some countries granted them access to a pension on somewhat more lenient terms. In the United States, for example, where the contribution requirements were particularly lengthy, the required period of coverage was reduced for persons under age 31.

A particularly striking aspect of contribution requirements was that they varied greatly from country to country. In the Netherlands, current employment at the onset of disability was sufficient before 1979, when the law was amended to require employment in the previous year. A more common requirement in European countries was five years of insurance. In Switzerland, however, eligibility for a full disability pension called for contributions in all years since 1948, or since age 21 if later, but eligibility for a partial pension required only one year of contributions (the size of the partial pension varying with years of contributions). The provisions in the United States were somewhat similar to those for a full disability pension in Switzerland, calling for one quarter of coverage for each year since 1950 (or age 21 if later), up to the year the disability began, with a maximum of 40 quarters for fully insured status and a requirement for 20 quarters of coverage in the last ten years before the onset of disability.

In Australia and New Zealand, with their income-tested invalidity pensions, and in the countries with universal basic invalidity pensions, there were residence requirements, which were similar to and sometimes identical with those for old-age pensions. In Canada, however, there was no universal invalidity pension, but invalidity pensions were provided under the supplementary earnings-related system, and there were also means-tested benefits.

In almost all industrial countries, an individual who had reached the normal retirement age and had been receiving an invalidity pension began to receive an old-age pension with little formality. Relaxed requirements for invalidity pensions for persons nearing retirement age have also been adopted in several countries recently as part of the trend toward encouraging early retirement, as we saw in Chapter 5.

Benefit amounts

In most of the countries with earnings-related invalidity insurance programs, the formula for invalidity benefits was the same, or nearly the same, as for old-age pensions. The actual benefit received, however, might be lower in countries where benefit amounts were directly related to years of insurance, because persons qualifying for disability benefits were under the age of retirement and were likely to have had fewer years of insurance than those awarded retirement benefits. Some countries sought to compensate to some degree for this effect. In West Germany, for example, if the invalidity occurred before age 55, the pension would be computed as if the worker had been insured up to age 55, so long as contributions had been paid for 36 months in the last five years, or at least for half of the months since the individual entered the scheme. East Germany had a somewhat similar provision.

In the Soviet Union, a full invalidity pension was 90 percent of the old-age pension, but 100 percent if the disabled worker had worked the minimum number of years required for an old-age pension. This was consistent with a tendency in Eastern Europe to reward long-service workers in various ways.

In Australia, flat-rate income-tested invalidity benefits were equal to income-tested old-age benefits, whereas in New Zealand they were somewhat lower than universal old-age pensions. In the United Kingdom, the situation was more complex. The basic flat-rate insurance benefit for an invalid (£34.25 a week or about one-fourth of average wages in 1985) was slightly below the basic old-age benefit, but the amount received by the invalid turned out to be a little higher because it was supplemented by an amount varying from £2.40 to £7.50 a week, inversely with age at incapacity. However, since 1975, Britain has provided for a noncontributory invalidity pension or severe disablement allowance, which in 1985 amounted to £21.50 a week for persons who could not meet the insurance requirements for the regular invalidity pension. This was designed to prevent such individuals from becoming wholly dependent on supplementary benefits (public assistance). I have not found a comparable provision elsewhere. Britain also provided earnings-related supplementary benefits, but they had not been in effect long enough to add appreciably to the basic benefit.

Benefit amounts for partial pensions were invariably lower than for full pensions, but again, there were wide variations from country to country. Understandably, the relationships between benefit provisions for partial pensions and those for full pensions were related to differences in degree-of-disability requirements. For example, in Hungary, where a worker must have lost 67 percent of earning capacity to qualify for a partial pension, the partial pension was only 5 percent below the full pension. In neighboring Czechoslovakia, where an individual could qualify for a partial pension with a one-third loss of earning capacity, the partial pension was 50 percent of the full pension.

There were also, as already suggested, a number of countries in which the partial pension amount could vary considerably, depending on the actual degree of disability. This was the case in Sweden (discussed earlier) and decidedly so in the Netherlands, where the pension varied from 9 to 65 percent of the basic full pension for disabilities ranging from 15 to 80 percent under the scheme for residents, whereas under the scheme for employed persons the pension varied from 9 to 70 percent of earnings for disabilities ranging from 15 to 80 percent (or slightly higher for a person over age 50 and disabled for more than two years).

Supplements

Invalidity pension programs provided for a variety of supplements, not only for dependents of the disabled worker but also for the cost of constant attendance where needed, and in some cases for housing subsidies, rehabilitation allowances, and special allowances for single pensioners with children. These complex provisions have evolved over the years and did not characterize the early invalidity programs, although constant attendance allowances have a long history.

Most disability programs provided for supplements for dependents, but the provisions varied a good deal. There was some tendency for provisions for spouses to be more restrictive than in the case of old-age benefits, especially in countries where female labor force participation rates were high. Thus in East Germany and the United States, a spouse was not eligible for a benefit if she was below the minimum retirement age for women, but she could qualify if she was caring for a child or was disabled. In Norway and Sweden, she had to be aged 60 or more to be eligible. In the Soviet Union, the supplement for one dependent was kept at a very low level, with the apparent intention of providing an incentive for the spouse to work, although the supplement for two or more dependents was also very low.

Spouses' benefits in Australia and New Zealand, like the invalid's own benefit, were income-tested, but the spouse's benefit was also income-tested in some countries where the invalid's benefit was on an insurance basis, including Israel and the Netherlands.

Benefits for children played a more significant role in disability programs than in old-age programs, simply because there are more likely to be dependent children in families of disabled workers. They were provided in the majority of our countries, varying considerably in amount, but about eight countries provided only those children's benefits that were available through the family allowance system, and these tended to be countries where family allowances were comparatively generous.

Children's benefits were usually available until the school-leaving age, but in a number of countries – including Australia, Austria, Canada, and Switzerland – they were provided until age 25 or 26 for a young person enrolled in school or higher education. The countries that did not extend children's dependency benefits beyond the school-leaving age frequently had extensive student aid and/or loan programs for students enrolled in higher education. This was true, for example, in the United Kingdom and some of the Scandinavian countries. The Soviet Union had a comprehensive policy of student stipends, related to manpower objectives and varying in amount per student among fields of study according to manpower planning priorities. Extensive programs of aid for students in higher education also existed in some of the other Eastern European countries (see Liberska, 1979, for example, on Poland).

In the United States, Congress extended the age of eligibility for children's benefits under the OASDI program to 21 in 1965 for young persons enrolled in school or in higher education, but this program was phased out (except for elementary and secondary students under age 19) under amendments adopted in 1981 at a time when cuts in social security were being sought because of concern about the budget deficit. The situation had changed since 1965 because, under legislation adopted in 1972 and later, an extensive program of grants for low-income students in higher education had been adopted, and student loans were also available on a substantial scale. Dependents of social security beneficiaries in low-income families would have access to aid from these more general programs, but total student aid declined somewhat in constant dollars from 1980 to 1986–7 (The College Board, 1987, 7).

Constant attendance allowances and other similar benefits: Constant attendance allowances date from the early part of this century in industrial injuries programs but did not begin to be provided under nonoccupational disability programs until the 1930s. They are cash benefits paid on behalf of permanently disabled persons with disability pensions who require care by another person in the home. Since World War II, the number of countries providing such benefits in nonoccupational disability programs has increased substantially. In 1958, 12 of our countries, primarily in Europe, had such provisions, and by 1985, the number had increased to 21, still primarily in Europe. Outside of Europe, only Israel and Japan had provisions for constant attendance allowances.

One of the reasons for the spread of these provisions has been the increase in the labor force participation of women, which has meant that they are often not available to care for a disabled spouse or other relative. Another reason has been the pronounced rise in the cost of institutional care, with the result that significant economies can sometimes be achieved by providing for care in the home rather than in institutions (*SSB*, 1974, *37* [November]: 32–7).

A common requirement is that the disabled person is incapacitated to such an extent that he or she needs help with eating, dressing, and bodily functions. In some programs, however, a disabled person who needs only part-time care may qualify for an allowance. The benefit is used to hire a nurse or a practical nurse or to reimburse family members for their costs in caring for a relative.

These allowances varied greatly in amount in 1985. In 11 of our countries, they were defined as a percentage of the invalidity pension for a single person, but the percentages varied all the way from 20 percent in the Netherlands to a range of 60 to 150 percent in Israel. In most of the other countries, the allowance was on a flat-rate basis, presumably determined on the basis of estimated need. In Eastern Europe, there has been a tendency to shift away from a percentage of earnings to a flat-rate amount. In Switzerland, the allowance was subject to an income test, whereas in Belgium and East Germany, the family's needs were taken into consideration in determining the amount of the allowance.

In a number of the countries that provided constant attendance allowances for disabled pensioners, the allowance could be continued after the beneficiary shifted to an old-age pension. There were cases, however, in which constant attendance allowances or other special benefits were not provided for disabled persons on old-age pensions, with the result that a loss of income might be experienced when the beneficiary shifted to an old-age pension.

In addition to constant attendance allowances, and sometimes in their absence, most industrial countries had provisions for home-help services. However, these services varied greatly in their extent and in their financing. They might be performed through charitable organizations or as municipal programs, sometimes partly funded by national assistance funds. In the Scandinavian countries, pensioners might receive a means-tested benefit to enable them to hire an attendant when nurses, who were usually provided free of charge to needy persons, were not otherwise available (*SSB*, 1974, *37* [November]: 32–7).

In the United States, where there were no provisions for constant attendance allowances (except under industrial injuries programs in a few states and under Veterans Administration programs), there has been a trend recently toward expanding noninstitutional long-term care services. The chief public programs through which such services are provided are the Older Americans Act, the Social Services Block Grant program, and Medicaid (the medical assistance program for the poor). Medicaid provisions have recently been broadened to encourage states to provide home care services, whereas formerly they were limited to providing nursing services. Under Medicare (the health insurance program for the aged), however, home nursing services may be provided only in acute, not in chronic, cases.

As Grana (1983) has pointed out, benefits in most public home-help programs in the United States, except for those of the Veterans Administration, are provided in kind, not in cash. In other words, the client is usually provided with a fixed amount of services, rather than a cash payment, by the administering agency. Services may be provided by salaried personnel of the local public authority, or purchased on the private market by the authority. This practice probably has its roots in historical procedures of public health authorities, but it continues at least partly on the assumption that those elderly in need of services are likely to be confused and incapable of making sound decisions. Grana argues that, in fact, a large proportion of the elderly are quite capable of making sensible decisions, or have access to assistance from close relatives or friends, and that providing benefits in cash rather than in kind would make it possible for them to arrive at more flexible uses of the funds to meet their specific needs.

The situation in the United Kingdom is of particular interest because there was no invalidity pension as such until 1971, when new benefits were introduced for the disabled, including invalidity pensions and attendance allowances. Then in 1975 the noncontributory allowance mentioned earlier was introduced, in 1976 an invalid care allowance, and, at about the same time, a mobility allowance for disabled persons with difficulty in walking (Townsend, 1979, 907). These allowances were all flat-rate and noncontributory, except for the regular invalidity pension, which was contributory and provided an earnings-related supplement to a flat-rate pension.

The attendance allowance was provided for severely disabled persons (including children over the age of two) who had needed a great deal of care for at least six months. The amount, in 1982, was higher for those needing both day and night attendance than for those needing only day *or* night attendance. The invalid care allowance was provided for men and single women of working age who were unable too work because they had to stay at home to look after a severely disabled person who was getting an attendance allowance. Dependents' allowances were also available for such persons, and they also benefited from protection of their pension rights for periods out of the labor force. The mobility allowance was provided to persons between the ages of five and 65 who were unable, or almost unable, to walk. Recipients who were receiving this allowance before age 65 were entitled to continue receiving it until age 75 (but the benefit ceased for disabled married women at age 65). There was also an allowance for assistance with fares to and from work (United Kingdom, Department of Health and Social Security, 1982b, 21).

Thus, Britain had an exceptionally comprehensive group of allowances to meet the needs of the disabled. How many people receive these allowances? In 1981, 746,000 persons, or 2 percent of the population aged 15 to 64, were receiving either regular contributory invalidity pensions or noncontributory allowances, of whom about 18 percent were receiving the noncontributory benefit. Of those receiving the regular pension, 82 percent were men, whereas among noncontributory recipients, only 48 percent were men. Thus, the noncontributory allowance was of special importance to women, who were less likely to have worked long enough to be eligible for a contributory benefit.

Of particular interest are data relating to the sex and age of persons receiving the attendance allowance. In 1981, there were 351,000 recipients of these allowances, including persons of all ages from children of two on up. Three-fifths of the recipients were women, and among the women receiving the allowance, 37 percent were aged 80 or more, whereas among the male recipients, only 13 percent were in this elderly age bracket. Thus, it is clear that an important explanation of the high proportion of women among recipients of the attendance allowance is the greater life expectancy of women and the fact that at advanced ages they are increasingly likely to need attendance (data computed from United Kingdom, Department of Health and Society Security, 1982a, 96–7).

Disabled housewives: An issue that has received increasing attention in a number of countries, stimulated at least in part by the women's movement, is the problem of the disabled housewife, who has not worked enough to qualify for a disability pension.

Britain was one of the few countries in recent years in which a disabled housewife could qualify for a pension in her own right – through the noncontributory system. Even so, proponents of sexual equality have complained about the fact that she could qualify only if her disability was such that she could not perform "normal household duties," whereas a man or a single woman could qualify on the basis of loss of earning capacity at work. Critics also have complained that the invalid care allowance was not available for a married or cohabiting woman, even though many of them provided substantial care for the sick and elderly and thus could not work or could work only on a reduced basis (David and Land, 1983). One of the changes adopted under the 1986 amendments was extension of the invalid care allowance to married women. (*S&LB,* 1987 [1]: 163–4).

There were several other countries in which a housewife could qualify for an invalidity pension in her own right and not on the basis of her husband's insurance or pension status. One of these was Denmark, where a disabled housewife could receive a flat-rate benefit in her own right, amounting to about 121 percent of average male industrial earnings (Abel-Smith, 1981). Israel had an unusual provision, under which no qualifying period was required for a disabled housewife. She had to be an Israeli resident aged 18 or more who was unable to carry out her role as a housewife or whose capacity to carry out her role was immediately or gradually reduced by 50 percent or more owing to her disability (*ISSR,* 1977, 30 [1]: 88–90).

In Switzerland, adult insured persons who were not gainfully employed before their physical or mental health was affected were considered to be invalid when their state of health prevented them from coping with their usual tasks. According to Villars (1979), this provision was aimed particularly at housewives. Granted that they must be insured, but a person could qualify for invalidity benefits after one year of insurance.

Apart from these provisions designed particularly for housewives, we must keep in mind the fact that there were a number of situations in which a disabled housewife could qualify for a pension based on her husband's insurance. The most common of these was the case of a disabled widow, who was entitled to a widow's benefit regardless of her age in about 16 of our countries. Then there were the countries, mentioned in Chapter 4, that had no age limit for receipt of a wife's or in some cases for a widow's benefit, where presumably the benefit was available whether or not the woman was disabled. There were also a few countries – Czechoslovakia, East Germany, Switzerland, and the United States – where there was no age limit for a wife's benefit if she was disabled. However, these provisions benefited only the wives of persons receiving retirement or disability benefits. Much more comprehensive in their scope were the universal invalidity pensions in Finland, Norway, and Sweden, for which a disabled woman could qualify if she met the residence requirements (and, in Norway, a minimal insurance requirement). It should also be kept in mind that disabled housewives may be able to qualify for public assistance on a means-tested basis in some countries.

Persons disabled from childhood: Another group that has benefited from liberalization of social security programs in relatively recent years consists of disabled children and persons disabled from childhood, who have no opportunity to meet insurance requirements. Once a child has passed age 16 or thereabouts, dependents' benefits are no longer available unless, in some countries, the young person is enrolled in higher education or training programs.

Here again, a movement to provide benefits for disabled children or for young persons disabled from childhood has undoubtedly been influenced by the increased labor force participation of women. Such children in a former era would have been cared for by the mother and no special need for benefits would have been perceived.

Especially in Eastern Europe, where policies are so strongly oriented to encouraging women to work, there have been a number of instances of legislative changes in recent years aimed at extending or improving benefits for disabled children or adults who have been handicapped from childhood. In Czechoslovakia, the benefit for a disabled child was raised substantially in 1982, and provision was made for young disabled persons aged 18 to 28 to qualify for a disability pension without meeting the normal work requirement (*ISSR*, 1982, *35* [4]: 573–4). In the same year, legislation was enacted in Poland to extend the scope of protection of persons handicapped from birth or during their childhood (*S&LB*, 1983 [2]: 274–6).

In the Soviet Union, persons disabled from childhood have been characterized as a special group, qualifying for benefits that are universal in character in the sense that they are not subject to work requirements or to an income test applied to their families. Moreover, since 1980, a new benefit amounting to 20 rubles a month has been available for invalid children up to the age of 16, whereas formerly it had been expected that parents would meet the expenses of such children (*ISSR*, 1980, *33* [3–4]: 206).

According to Bouquet (1979), most of the EEC countries provided benefits that were midway between assistance and insurance for persons with congenital handicaps. In Denmark and the Netherlands, however, benefits for such persons were universal. In the Netherlands, this meant that persons who were handicapped from an early age were not required to meet the eligibility requirement of previous employment (*ISSR*, 1980, *33* [2]: 206).

In the United States, a disabled child's dependent's benefit could be continued into adulthood, but this provision protected only those disabled young persons who were children of old-age, survivors', or invalidity beneficiaries. In Britain, a person disabled from childhood would be eligible for the non-contributory disability benefit, and both attendance allowances and mobility allowances were provided for disabled children where needed.

One of the most liberal provisions for disabled children (as for disabled housewives) was in Israel, where a disabled child was eligible for a benefit that amounted to 30 to 120 percent of an invalidity pension, a benefit that could be carried forward into adulthood.

Just as we can expect to see a growing movement to make special provisions for disabled housewives, the movement to provide for persons disabled from childhood is likely to continue.

Comparisons of benefit levels

A very useful study of comparative disability benefit levels in EEC countries was conducted for the EEC under the direction of Abel-Smith (1981). Benefits for a number of carefully defined types of cases of disability were computed as a percentage of average earnings of industrial workers (including children's allowances, which are available whether or not the parent is employed, and excluding income taxes and social security taxes).

The results indicate, as would be expected, that benefits were highest for cases of permanent total occupational disability, needing constant care (Table 6.2). In fact, in the case of a male aged 28 with a disability of this category, total benefits exceeded earnings (as defined above) by a substantial margin in four of the countries and by a considerably smaller margin in Italy and the Netherlands. Of interest, also, is the fact that the percentages for this type of case did not vary widely by marital and parental status. This reflects the fact that there is no spouse's benefit in most of these countries, that special children's benefits (other than children's allowances) are provided on a rather small scale in only about half of the countries, and that the inclusion of children's allowances in the earnings measure reduces the percentage of earnings replaced for the man with two children. Because this is a case of 100 percent disability, the fact that benefits exceeded earnings presumably was not a matter of concern in relation to willingness to return to work.

Benefits for the second type of case included in Table 6.2 were substantially lower than those for the first type, reflecting the general tendency for occupational disability benefits to be higher than those for nonoccupational disability. The Netherlands, which merged its occupational and nonoccupational disability programs in 1967, is an exception. In Italy, the lower benefits for the nonoccupationally disabled man were partly attributable to the fact that a constant attendance allowance was provided when needed in occupational, but not in nonoccupational, disability cases. However, 1984 amendments provided for an attendance allowance in nonoccupational cases (S&LB, 1986 [3–4]: 561).

The data for the third type of case – a nonoccupationally disabled male who could not meet the insurance requirements and therefore had to rely on public assistance and such other noncontributory benefits as might be available to him – are of special interest because they shed light on the relative generosity of public assistance programs in these countries, to which we shall be turning our attention in Chapter 14.

Table 6.2. *Benefits provided for severely disabled persons as a percentage of earnings, six EEC countries, 1976*

Marital status	Belgium	Germany	Denmark	Italy	Nether-lands	United Kingdom
100% disabled, needs constant attendance, male aged 28, occupational disability						
Single	152.9%	208.8%	132.2%	106.7%	103.3%	171.4%
Married	153.5	189.7	124.5	108.4	104.4	180.3
Married, two						
children[a]	150.6	186.4	136.5	112.8	105.8	186.7
100% disabled, needs constant attendance, male aged 28, nonoccupational disability						
Single	86.5	110.1	110.0	24.2	103.8	79.8
Married	85.7	100.0	100.6	26.6	104.4	92.9
Married, two						
children	89.2	118.3	114.1	31.2	105.8	109.2
100% disabled, needs constant attendance, male age 28, nonoccupationally disabled, not insured						
Single	52.8	102.6	115.7	31.8	60.8	89.1
Married	53.1	102.6	106.1	30.4	83.5	102.5
Married, two						
children	61.6	118.7	121.2	28.4	86.7	103.6
100% disabled, needs constant attendance, male aged 18, disabled from birth						
	52.8	102.6	115.9	31.8	32.3	89.1
100% disabled, needs constant attendance, male aged 68						
Single	(b)	98.4	79.7	56.5	58.8	60.9
Married	(b)	89.4	88.0	57.5	79.3	76.0
100% disabled, does not need attendance, male aged 28, nonoccupationally disabled						
Single	58.1	74.9	92.3	24.2	85.2	40.0
Married	85.7	68.0	84.7	26.6	85.7	54.9
Married, two						
children	89.2	89.2	99.3	31.1	89.1	76.8

Note: Average earnings are average net earnings of a manual industrial worker, including children's allowances, where applicable, and after tax and social security deductions.
[a] The two children are defined as under five years of age in all cases.
[b] A single person receives 60 percent of average revalued lifetime earnings, and a married person 75 percent.
Source: Abel-Smith (1981).

The fourth type of case – a male aged 18, disabled from birth – fared much the same as the third type in all of these countries except for the Netherlands, where his benefits were much lower in relation to earnings than those for case 3. The explanation is the dual system of invalidity benefits in the Netherlands, which includes a scheme that covers all residents over age 18 (including persons disabled from childhood), but also a parallel system of *additional* benefits for employed persons.

The fifth case, that of a male aged 68, receives old-age rather than disability benefits, but the data are of interest because they shed light on the relative replacement rates of old-age and invalidity benefits in these countries, as well as on the relative replacement rates of elderly and youthful severely disabled men. Because case 5 involves nonoccupational disability, its replacement rates should be compared with those of case 2. In all of the countries except Italy, the replacement rates for elderly single and married men were considerably below those for the male aged 28. Part of the explanation was the fact that, as Abel-Smith pointed out, some of the schemes for old-age or retirement pensions offered benefits that were inferior to invalidity benefits, presumably because of lower assumed need.

These comparisons involve issues that in some countries have become controversial. We shall find, for example, that the unusually pronounced rise in the number of disability beneficiaries in the Netherlands has led to recommendations that invalidity benefits be made less favorable in relation to old-age benefits.

Finally, we come to the sixth case, a severely disabled man aged 28 who is not in need of constant attendance. Comparison of replacement rates for this group with those of group 2 provides an indication of the contribution of constant attendance allowances and other special supplements to the total benefits of those in group 2. The contribution was substantial, except in the case of Italy, where there was no constant attendance allowance, and in the case of married men in Belgium, where the provisions called for an invalidity pension of 43.5 percent of earnings for a single person and 65 percent for a person with dependents *or* if constant attendance was required.

Disability beneficiaries

During the 1970s, sharp increases in the number of disability pensioners gave rise to concern in a number of countries, and, as suggested earlier, were at least partly attributable to rising unemployment. In the United States, the phenomenon became a matter of protracted political controversy, as we shall see.

In fact, the proportion of workers receiving social security disability benefits in this country in the 1970s was much smaller than in four of the countries

Table 6.3. *Number of disability pensions in force as a percentage of number insured (A), or of labor force (B), selected countries, 1966 to 1977 or to 1981*

Country	1966	1970	1975	1977	1981
Australia	2.19% (B)	2.41%	2.73%	3.16%	3.26%
Belgium	3.42 (A)	3.73	4.37	4.70	
Finland	2.04 (A)	3.49	8.52	9.89	
France	1.94 (A)	2.07	2.06	2.35	
Germany (Fed. Rep.)		7.26 (A)	8.10	8.82	7.77 (B)
Netherlands		6.28 (A)	9.29	10.80	12.70 (B)
Switzerland		0.80 (B)	0.59	0.62	0.62
United Kingdom			1.75	1.88	
United States	1.28 (A)	1.58	2.42	2.61	2.51 (B)

Note: Where no (A) or (B) appears, the definition is the same as in the earliest year for which data are included.
Sources: Copeland (1981); *SSB: Annual Statistical Supplement, 1982;* country yearbooks or other official sources.

for which data have been assembled in Table 6.3, and was only slightly higher than in France and Britain. Switzerland alone stood out as having markedly lower disability rates than the United States. Moreover, the increase in percentage points was much more pronounced in Finland and the Netherlands than in this country.

Before considering the reasons for growth, where it occurred on a substantial scale, it is important to note that the differences in percentages of insured persons receiving benefits from country to country shown in Table 6.3 were strongly related to differences in the degree of disability required for eligibility for a full or partial disability pension, discussed above.

Highly significant, also, is the fact that in Finland, the Netherlands, and West Germany, determination of the degree of disability was broadened in practice, to take account of labor market conditions in the late 1960s and in the 1970s. In West Germany, rulings of the Federal Social Court in 1969 and in 1976 required pension institutions to place more emphasis on whether a suitable job existed in the economy before reaching an unfavorable decision. In Finland, legislation enacted in 1973 provided for easing the statutory disability definition so that the person's overall social situation could be taken into account. In the Netherlands, beginning in 1973, the degree of work incapacity was to be determined only after taking into account the chances that the disabled worker could actually be placed in suitable employment. As a result, many awards were granted for total disability even in cases of partial incapacity if no suitable work was available. In all three of these countries, in fact, the relative role of partial disability determinations declined (Copeland, 1981).[1]

Another factor that helped to explain the sharp increase in some European countries was a more pronounced rise in the proportion of older persons in the population than in the United States, reflecting the greater loss of life in the two world wars.

An interesting analysis of the situation in the Netherlands pointed out that persons who were threatened with unemployment were tempted to claim that they were ill and unfit for work, partly because unemployment benefits were lower than disability benefits and partly because they were limited in duration, though not for persons aged 58 and older (as we shall see in Chapter 11). The author of this study concluded that greater emphasis should be placed on such measures as early detection of the onset of disabling conditions, improved safety requirements in workplaces, retraining, and the like. He also recommended restructuring benefits to make retirement pensions more attractive than disability benefits, while at the same time making reduced early retirement benefits available from age 60 (Emanuel, 1980). In fact, the provisions were amended in 1986, so that disability ratings were to be based solely on loss of functional capacity, and partially disabled people could be treated as partially unemployed (*S&LB*, 1987 [3], 506–7).

A study in Finland showed, among other things, that disability pension applicants were more likely to be unemployed than persons in a study control group, and that nearly 70 percent of recipients of partial disability pensions in provinces with low unemployment rates were employed, compared with only 40 percent in provinces with high unemployment rates (Gould, 1981).

In the eyes of social security critics, the rise in the number of disability insurance beneficiaries in the United States in the 1970s, which seemed more spectacular in numbers than in percentages of insured – from 1.5 million in 1970 to 2.9 million in 1978 – was regarded as excessive. Charges were made that many beneficiaries were actually able to work and that administration was lax. A study conducted for the Social Security Administration concluded that the chief reasons for the increase were (1) the ratchet effect of rising unemployment (mentioned earlier), (2) increases in benefit levels, and (3) an increase in the proportion of workers aged 45 and over. Increasing awareness

---

[1] In West Germany, the number of persons receiving occupational (partial) invalidity pensions declined fairly steadily from 21.5 percent of all disability pensioners in 1973 to 8.0 percent in 1981, whereas in the Netherlands, the number receiving partial disability pensions declined from 18.2 percent of the total in 1970 to 15.4 percent in 1982. Most of the Dutch decline was among those with disability ratings of 45 to 80 percent (data from national statistical yearbooks).

of the program was also a factor, but one that was difficult to measure (Lando, Coate, and Kraus, 1979).

Another type of complaint was that significant proportions of beneficiaries were receiving benefits from several public and/or private pension programs simultaneously, sometimes resulting in total benefits that exceeded previous after-tax earnings, thus impairing incentives to work. This is a problem that is more likely to arise in the United States than in countries with more centralized governments, especially because industrial injuries programs are the responsibility of the states, which may make benefit decisions without regard to whether a recipient may be receiving federal social security benefits, although, as we shall see, federal provisions do call for certain offsets.[2]

Congress reacted to the various complaints in June 1980 by enacting amendments that were designed, among other things, to limit total family benefits, to increase incentives to return to work, and to improve the administration of the program.[3]

Even before these changes were adopted, however, the number of beneficiaries had begun to decline, and the decline has continued, partly because of tighter administration, and partly because the number of persons aged 55 to 64 was declining, reflecting the lower birth rates of the late 1920s and 1930s. Even so, the Reagan administration tightened procedures in March 1981, dropping beneficiaries from the rolls in large numbers. As a result, protests mounted over hardship cases, lawsuits were brought and won, and state agencies administering initial eligibility decisions refused to cooperate (in some cases with strong support of state governors, concerned about the increased welfare burden of the states).

Under amendments adopted in 1984, Congress provided for the use of more carefully defined standards in dropping people from the rolls (Collins and Erfle, 1985), and, early in 1985, the Reagan administration announced that the rules were to be relaxed somewhat.

A movement that has been significant in the United States, and also in some other countries, but which will not be discussed in detail, is the adoption of legislation to prevent employment discrimination against the disabled, and to ensure access to buildings and to public transportation. This has been associated with widespread voluntary movements to assist the disabled. In my own

---

[2] A special factor in the American context was the 1972 amendment that extended Medicare (the health insurance program for the aged) to disability beneficiaries who had been entitled to benefits for at least 24 consecutive months.

[3] Total monthly payments to a disabled worker with dependents were to be limited to the lower of 85 percent of the worker's average earnings before becoming disabled or 150 percent of the worker's primary insurance amount (PIA), but not less than 100 percent of the PIA. Reductions were to be made for workers' compensation or public employee benefits that would bring total benefits above these amounts.

city of Berkeley, California, there is a well-organized "Center for Independent Living" which is administered by a man who has lost his legs and lives in a wheelchair. Among other developments, there are ramps to assist those in wheelchairs at street crossings throughout the city.

Future problems

Much that has been said at the ends of Chapters 4 and 5 is relevant to future problems in providing for disability. Whether or not there is an increase in the proportion of elderly in the population, most industrial countries are experiencing a relative increase in the proportion of persons of advanced age within the elderly population. Sooner or later, many of these persons will need attendance. Especially in countries with high female labor force participation rates, adult daughters will not be available to provide the care. The large proportion of Britain's attendance allowances going to women aged 80 or more is indicative of a need that is likely to increase.

Given recent trends, it appears likely that attendance allowances and home helps will be expanded in an attempt to avoid the high costs of institutional care. And yet, there may be situations in which it is preferable, and less costly, to encourage the development of group living arrangements for elderly persons who do not need full nursing care but do need more limited services. The Scandinavian countries have led in the development of such institutions under public auspices, although current policy, at least in Sweden, favors caring for people in their homes whenever possible.[4] In the United States, retirement communities are proliferating, but usually under private auspices and available only for those with adequate incomes.

There are wide differences in the financing, coverage, and delivery of long-term care services among OECD countries (see OECD 1987a, 91–2). In Canada and the United States, persons needing long-term care are likely to be in medically oriented residential facilities, whereas in Europe relatively more of those needing long-term care are in nonmedically oriented facilities. On the other hand, proportions of persons receiving publicly funded home care services are highest in the United Kingdom and Sweden and lowest in Switzerland, Canada, and West Germany.

Long-term care is predominantly public financed and delivered in the Scandinavian countries, the United Kingdom, and the Netherlands, but in the United States, West Germany, and Switzerland there is considerably more private sector involvement in both financing and delivery.

In general, however, how to improve the provision of long-term care is a

---

[4] Interview with Ms. Monica Wikman, Assistant Under-Secretary, Ministry of Health and Social Affairs, Sweden, September 1986.

problem of increasing concern in country after country as the proportion of persons of advanced age within the aged population increases and the prospect of a huge increase in the number of elderly persons in the population in the early part of the twenty-first century has to be faced. In West Germany, the question of providing social insurance for long-term care has been debated, and in the United States, where the majority of those in nursing homes are financed through Medicaid (in many cases after exhausting their own resources during the early months or years after admission), bills were introduced in Congress early in 1988 providing for comprehensive long-term home health and nursing home insurance. Moreover, some large employers have adopted plans under which their employees may voluntarily purchase long-term health care insurance (Gajda, 1988). The issues are complex and promise to be among the most difficult of the problems that lie ahead in social security (see also ISSA, 1984a).

CHAPTER 7

Industrial injuries programs

We come now to industrial injuries programs, which in most countries represent the oldest form of social security. In the United States, following the British practice, they were usually referred to as workmen's compensation programs until the purging of sexist language led to use of the term workers' compensation, whereas in Europe they are usually called industrial injuries or employment injuries programs.

Before the adoption of industrial injuries legislation, the worker who was injured in the course of his or her employment could secure redress only by suing the employer.[1] Under the *codes civiles* on the continent of Europe, the defenses available to employers were more limited than under British common law, but the differences were not great. In the vast majority of cases employers were able to defend themselves against the allegation of fault, and very few cases were won by injured workers or their survivors.

Certain groups of workers, however, received compensation under special laws or provisions that date as far back as the eighteenth century, or in some cases even earlier, relating to disabled miners, seamen, and domestic workers. A Prussian law of 1838 made the railroad companies responsible for injuries to passengers and employees, except where the accident was attributable to the negligence of the injured person or an "act of God."

Prewar legislation

The German law of 1884

One of the earliest acts of the German Imperial Government, adopted in 1871, was an employers' liability law, which applied to factories, mines, and railroads. However, dissatisfaction with the experience under this law was expressed on the floor of Parliament repeatedly during the following decade. A report prepared in 1882 proposed a system of public accident insurance that would provide compensation for all accidents in industrial establishments without

---

[1] This chapter is based in considerable part on my two chapters on the development of industrial injuries insurance in Cheit and Gordon, eds. (1963).

regard to whether they were attributable to the negligence of the employer or of the injured worker, or to risks inherent in the business. Insurance with nonprofit government institutions was to be made compulsory for covered industries.

The original German law of 1884 covered only workers engaged in manufacturing and mining, but it was rapidly extended to certain other industries. Moreover, separate schemes were established for government employees (1886), persons employed in agriculture and forestry (1886), and seamen (1887). The laws were modified from time to time in other respects and were incorporated in the Social Insurance Code of 1911. Substantial amendments were also adopted in 1925, following the stabilization of the mark after the disastrous inflation of the early 1920s.

The German law provided from the beginning for joint liability of employers engaged in a similar industry in a given district, through accident associations (*Berufsgenossenschaften*). Covered employers were required to belong to these associations and to make insurance payments to them. The associations were quasi-public bodies with legal personality, conducted on a nonprofit basis and responsible for ensuring that workers employed in any of the affiliated undertakings received the compensation to which they were entitled. Failure of individual employers to make their insurance payments did not prevent their employees from receiving benefits.

Unlike the provisions of Germany's other early social insurance laws, employees were not required to contribute, nor were they subject to a duration of employment provision. This was consistent with the view that the employer was liable, on a no-fault basis, and characterizes the financing of industrial injuries insurance in most countries.

The law of 1884 applied to accidents occurring during the course of employment, unless the victim had caused the accident intentionally. Not until 1925 were specified occupational diseases brought within the scope of the law, although the victims of these diseases previously received some degree of protection under the sickness and nonoccupational invalidity schemes.

The accident had to be causally connected with the worker's employment. In general, this meant accidents occurring on the employer's premises and during customary working hours, but there were other circumstances that were considered to be "in the course of" employment. In Germany, as elsewhere, the tendency was to liberalize the scope of the law in this respect as a result of decisions in disputed cases. Accidents occurring in the course of work performed off the employer's premises but under the employer's direction were included. So were accidents occurring (1) while the worker was changing his or her clothes after arrival or before departure; (2) while he or she was resting, eating lunch, etc., on the premises; (3) while he or she was in living quarters provided by the employer; and (4) while he or she was traveling to and from work where special transportation was provided by the employer. In 1925, the law was amended to provide compensation for all accidents suffered on the worker's way to and from work.

Originally the law provided for two types of benefits: (1) medical benefits and (2) cash benefits designed to provide compensation for wage loss. Rehabilitation benefits were added in 1925. The victim was entitled to receive cash benefits amounting to 50 percent of his or her wage loss during the first four weeks after the accident and 66⅔ percent thereafter during a period of temporary disability. The benefits were provided by the sickness funds during the early weeks of disability.

For victims of permanent disability, the German law provided for a pension throughout "the continuance of disablement." In cases of total disability, the pension amounted to two-thirds of the worker's annual earnings in the year preceding the accident, whereas the partially disabled worker received a fraction of the full pension corresponding to the degree of his or her incapacity. A totally disabled worker who was so helpless as to require constant attendance was entitled to special assistance, in the form of nursing attendance in the home, institutional care, or a supplementary allowance.

The 1925 amendments added benefits for dependent children of permanently disabled workers whose earning capacity had been reduced by at least 50 percent. The amount provided for each child was 10 percent of the pension, subject to a family maximum of 100 percent of the basic wage.

In fatal cases, the German system provided for a modest lump-sum funeral benefit and for pensions for widows and children. It also provided pensions for certain surviving relatives if they had been dependent on the deceased, but total pensions provided to survivors could not exceed 80 percent of the basic wage.

The right to free medical treatment – to be furnished in the early stages by the sickness funds – was a feature of the German accident insurance system from the beginning. As time went on, and the Germans accumulated experience, more and more emphasis came to be placed on restoring the working capacity of disabled workers, as in the invalidity insurance program. Thus increasing attention was paid to supervising the quality of medical care, particularly in the more severe cases, and to the establishment of specialized institutions for the treatment of victims of industrial accidents. It was not until after World War I, however, that very much attention was paid to vocational rehabilitation, and, as in a number of countries, the needs of injured veterans provided the impetus for the development of rehabilitation measures.

To finance the accident insurance scheme, all covered employers had to make insurance payments based on the earnings of their workers and their risk class. Thus, the system incorporated the principles of rate determination which had developed in connection with the sale of private industrial accident insurance. We shall find that this method of financing, which placed a relatively heavy burden on employers in hazardous industries, continues to be commonly used today, although there are some exceptions, particularly in countries in which the financing of industrial injuries programs is merged with that of other social insurance programs.

Another important feature of the German law was the authorization of the accident associations to issue safety regulations and to impose penalties on workers and employers for failure to comply. Furthermore, an establishment could be shifted to a higher risk class or be required to pay supplementary charges for violation of the regulations. All expenditures for enforcement were met by the accident associations, which maintained their own corps of inspectors. However, the system did not completely replace the government factory-inspection system which had existed long before the adoption of the accident insurance law.

The German law eliminated suits against the employer in industries covered by the law, except where the employer was accused of intentionally causing the accident. It did not, however, eliminate litigation over such matters as the degree of incapacity, which became the basis of appeals to the insurance courts. The fact that the worker did not have to bear the expenses of litigation, which were met by the government, evidently played a role in encouraging appeals to the courts.[2]

The British act of 1897

Among the early industrial injuries insurance laws, the one that departed most widely from the German model was the British Workmen's Compensation Act of 1897, which subsequently exerted a strong influence on the laws adopted in most other parts of the British Empire and on the laws adopted by the states in the United States. On the continent of Europe, although many of the laws followed the German pattern with only minor modifications, others incorporated features that were clearly influenced by the British legislation. Thus the British law of 1897 played almost as important a role in the history of workmen's compensation legislation as the original German act.

The English law declared employers liable for industrial injuries to their employees but did not require them to carry insurance. Insurance was made compulsory in the coal-mining industry in 1934 but remained voluntary in other industries. In practice, most of the larger firms did take out insurance with ordinary commercial insurance companies or with mutual indemnity as-

---

[2] In this discussion of the early German legislation, I have not repeated all of the references included in my chapters in Cheit and Gordon. The most important references used were U.S. Commission of Labor (1911); Boyd (1913); Armstrong (1932); Sulzbach (1947); and Lauterbach (1960). A useful more recent source is Kohler and Zacher (1982).

sociations, but the Holman Gregory Committee estimated in 1919 that there were about 250,000 uninsured employers in Great Britain. The majority of claims for compensation were settled by agreement between the workers or their representatives and the employers or their insurance companies. Where an agreement was not reached, the case was carried to arbitration, usually before a county-court judge. There were also provisions for appeals to higher courts. However, there was no public administering agency and very little state control of the system (*Social Insurance and Allied Services*, 1942, appendix B; Chambers, 1948).

The British act did not rule out the alternative remedies of a suit at common law or under the Employers' Liability Act of 1880. Partly as a result of the gradual erosion of the defense of common employment through judicial decisions, the number of common-law cases tended to increase. There was also a good deal of litigation surrounding workmen's compensation proceedings. Although it had been hoped that the 1897 act would reduce the amount of litigation, the only sense in which this occurred was in the virtual disappearance of actions under the Employers' Liability Act.

Originally, the British act applied only to employment in certain hazardous industries, but gradually its scope was extended, and by 1933 all employees were covered except nonmanual workers with annual earnings above £350 and certain casual and family workers.

The 1897 act declared an employer liable for "personal injury by accident arising out of and in the course of employment." Problems growing out of the interpretation of this now-famous phrase gave rise to a vast amount of litigation, and the standard textbook on the act eventually included over 150 pages of close print devoted to the interpretation of this section (Frank, 1953). In 1906, the scope of the legislation was extended to certain specified occupational diseases, and provision was made for adding diseases to the scheduled list by administrative order.

The injured worker was entitled to receive cash benefits amounting to only 50 percent of his or her base weekly wage and subject, originally, to a maximum of 1£ a week, later to 30s. a week. Not only was the British benefit formula less generous than the German, but the benefit ceiling was considerably more restrictive in relation to average earnings. The act made no legal distinction between temporary and permanent disability benefits. It provided that if the worker had received weekly payments for not less than six months and was still incapacitated, the employer and worker had a right in all cases to settle a claim by payment of a lump sum.

In his vigorous critique of the 1897 act, Beveridge pointed out that this right – "which finds no counterpart in systems of most other countries" – "is extensively exercised, particularly in cases of permanent or prolonged disability." He went on to say:

Divergent views have been expressed as to the advantages or otherwise of this practice, but from the point of view of social security it is impossible to justify. It is certain that in many cases, whether because the sum agreed proves insufficient for the purpose or because it is injudiciously expended by the workman or used by him to meet pressing, but temporary, needs, the lump sum fails to provide any permanent source of income. It should be added that, in the process of bargaining about a lump sum the injured workman is discouraged from recovery or from taking any kind of work lest he should prejudice his bargain.

(*Social Insurance and Allied Services*, 1942, 36–7)

If a worker who was permanently and totally disabled received weekly payments, the amount was the same as for temporary disability. Partially disabled workers received reduced benefits which varied in accordance with the loss of earning capacity. From 1923 on, however, compensation in permanent disability cases could be adjusted to take account of changes in prevailing wages.

In fatal cases, the survivors did not receive a pension, but only a lump-sum payment, which was liberalized slightly under the 1923 amendments.

Insurance companies writing workers' compensation coverage in Great Britain varied their rates by risk classes, but relatively little use was made of merit rating of individual firms.

Other early laws

The country that modeled its system most closely after Germany's was the Austro-Hungarian Empire, whose law became the basis of legislation adopted after World War I by Austria, Czechoslovakia, and Hungary. The German influence was also strong in Poland.

The British law, as already suggested, strongly influenced legislation subsequently adopted in the United States, Australia, and New Zealand, although most of the Australian and American states called for compulsory insurance. The British act also applied originally in Ireland and influenced the subsequent legislation of the Irish Free State.

Certain European countries – France, Belgium, and Spain – adopted legislation characterized by voluntary provisions but with the protection of a special government security fund, maintained by contributions from employers, to guarantee the payment of compensation in cases in which employers did not carry out their responsibilities. Still another group of countries – the Netherlands, Denmark, Finland, Sweden, and most of the Australian states – had compulsory insurance provisions but permitted employers to choose their own insurers. In the Netherlands, however, employers were required to insure with the State Insurance Bank unless granted permission to self-insure or to carry their insurance with a private company.

More centralized than any of the systems discussed thus far were those of the countries that required insurance in an exclusive government fund or government-administered insurance system. This group included seven European countries, the Canadian provinces, and one Australian state (Queensland). The background of the decisions of the Canadian provinces to require insurance with a state fund was particularly interesting.

Five of the provinces enacted legislation between 1902 and 1911 that was modeled after the British law, whereas Quebec adopted a law in 1909 that was somewhat more liberal but was likewise based on the principle of voluntary insurance. Ontario, the largest and most industrialized province, was slow to act, but in 1910, Sir William Meredith, an eminent jurist, was appointed as commissioner to investigate the whole question. In his report, Meredith recommended collective liability under a state insurance system, stating his reasons as follows:

> It is in my opinion essential that as far as is practicable there should be certainty that the injured workman and his dependents shall receive the compensation to which they are entitled and it is also important that the small employer should not be ruined by having to pay compensation, it might be, for the death or permanent disability of his workman caused by no fault of his. It is, I think a serious objection to the British Act that there is no security afforded to the workman and his dependents that the deferred payments of the compensation will be met, and that objection would be still more serious in a comparatively new country such as this, where many of the industries are small and conditions are much less stable than they are in the British Isles.
>
> (quoted in Mackintosh, 1939, 1–31)

The 1914 Ontario act closely followed the Meredith recommendations and exerted a strong influence on subsequent legislation in the other Canadian provinces. Another important and unusual feature of the Ontario act was the provision that adjudication and administration were to be placed entirely in the hands of a board appointed by the lieutenant-governor in council, and there was to be no right of appeal from the decisions of the board. This principle was followed in most of the other Canadian acts. Decisions are frequently reviewed by the board, and some of the boards have organized internal review procedures, but the absence of the right of appeal has meant that there is no litigation in the courts over workers' compensation cases in most Canadian provinces. In the opinion of many observers, this principle has contributed to the development of the highly responsible and outstanding administration for which the Canadian boards, and particularly that of Ontario, are noted. Especially noteworthy is the careful supervision of medical care provided for victims of industrial accidents and the success of rehabilitation programs, to be discussed in Chapter 12.

We come, finally, to the laws enacted in the American states, where, as already suggested, the influence of the British act was predominant. Not until the federal government enacted legislation for its employees in 1908 was there an effective workers' compensation law in the United States. From 1911 on, however, legislation was enacted in state after state.

According to Armstrong (1932, 252), it was feared that compulsory legislation of the European type might not be constitutional. In consequence, an elective type of compensation law was devised, giving to both employer and employee the choice of either the new compensation system or the old damage suit procedure.

However, the compulsory type of compensation law received approval of the United States Supreme Court in 1917 as a proper expression of the police power. Even so, the elective type of law lingered on in many states for a considerable period, and a few such laws continue at the present time.

Most of the early acts applied only to hazardous industries, but the list tended to be expanded, and, by the 1930s, most states covered all types of employment with certain exclusions. As in foreign legislation, agricultural and domestic workers were the groups most frequently excluded. Another common type of exclusion applied to very small firms. Only a few of the early laws covered specified occupational diseases, but there was a tendency to add occupational disease provisions in the 1930s, when victims of such diseases were frequently unemployed and without any source of income.

In the usual manner, the cost of compensation was financed through employer contributions which varied by risk class. A few states provided for employee contributions, which were usually allocated to medical care. Moreover, some of the states placed neither a time nor a money limit on the medical benefits guaranteed (Armstrong, 1932, 256).

Benefits in most cases in the 1930s amounted to at least 60 percent of weekly wages, and in a few cases more, but the maximum amounts tended to be very restrictive. Moreover, in the majority of states compensation for permanent total disability was limited to a period ranging from five to ten years or to an amount varying from $3,000 to $15,000.

Except in Alabama, insurance was compulsory, through a state fund or a private insurance company or through self insurance. In seven states, employers were required to carry their insurance with the state fund, whereas in ten states and in Puerto Rico, they could carry their insurance either with the state fund or with a private insurer. This left the majority of states with only the private insurance option.

Workers' compensation laws in the United States have been improved in many ways since the 1930s, but there are still substantial variations from state to state, and excessive litigation and lump-sum settlements continue to be a problem in a number of states.

Postwar developments

Since the end of World War II, industrial injuries programs have been less affected by basic changes than have other social security programs, probably because they were older and more firmly established. Nevertheless, laws embodying extensive changes have been adopted in a number of countries.

The British act of 1946

One of the more important pieces of postwar legislation was the British Act of 1946, which largely followed the recommendations of the Beveridge Report. Beveridge's caustic criticism of lump-sum settlements has already been quoted, but he also expressed numerous other objections to the 1897 act, including (1) the fact that the system rested in the last resort on the threat and practice of litigation; (2) the absence of any machinery for assisting employees in presenting their claims, except where they could rely on help from their trade unions; (3) the problems resulting from failure of employers to insure; (4) disputes over the occupational origin of the injury in a setting in which workmen's compensation was completely divorced from other social insurance programs; (5) the high administrative costs of private insurance companies compared with those of mutual funds; (6) the difficulty of determining which employer should be held liable in the case of occupational diseases, which often developed over a considerable period of time during which the victim might have worked for a number of employers; and (7) the failure of the system to achieve what should have been its most important purpose – the restoration of the injured worker to employment (*Social Insurance and Allied Services*, 1942, 36–9).

In formulating his proposals, Beveridge considered whether, given the desirability of closer integration between workmen's compensation and other social insurance systems, there was a continuing need for distinguishing between occupational and nonoccupational disability. He argued that there was, primarily on three grounds: First, many industries vital to the community were also especially dangerous, and, because it was essential that workers should enter such industries, these persons should be assured of special provision against their risks. Second, victims of occupational disability were disabled while working under orders, which was not generally true of other types of disability. Third, only if special provision were made for the results of industrial accidents and disease, irrespective of negligence, would it be equitable to limit employers' liability at common law to those cases in which they could be found negligent.

The National Insurance (Industrial Injuries) Act of 1946 incorporated most of Beveridge's recommendations, with certain modifications recommended in the White Paper of 1944. The act provided that all persons in covered employment would be compulsorily insured against industrial injuries and specified occupational diseases. The system was to be financed by flat weekly employer and employee contributions and by a Treasury contribution, rejecting a recommendation that Beveridge had made for a premium for hazardous industries.

The former system of court review was eliminated. Claims were to be initially processed at local offices of the Ministry of Pensions and National Insurance, with the right of appeal to a local tribunal and then to the Industrial Injuries Commissioner, whose ruling was to be final.

Unlike the situation in Canada, the right to sue the employer was not abolished for those covered by the industrial injuries scheme. Under the Law Reform (Personal Injuries) Act of 1948, the right to sue became an additional rather than alternative remedy. This proved to be an important development, as we shall see at a later point.

The 1946 act also liberalized the rules applicable to injuries sustained on the way to or from work but did not go as far as the German law in covering such accidents.

A flat-rate benefit which exceeded the ordinary sickness benefit was formerly payable for a maximum period of 26 weeks from the date of the injury, but this was abolished in 1982. Injured workers thereafter received statutory sick pay (from the employer) for the first eight weeks, as did other ill workers, and then ordinary sickness benefits (*S&LB*, 1982 [4]: 546–7).

A permanent disability pension was payable if the injured worker was still disabled after 15 weeks or if, after the individual was able to return to work, he or she had a permanent impairment of 20 percent or more. The amounts of these flat-rate benefits have been increased frequently, but they are not indexed. In 1985, the weekly benefit ranged from £11.68 a week for a disability of 20 percent to £58.40 a week (or about 40 percent of average wages) for permanent total disability. The total disability benefit was considerably higher than in a case of nonoccupational disability.

The permanent disability rating was based, not on loss of earning capacity, but on a rating of the degree of physical disability resulting from the injury, as compared with the condition of a normal healthy person of the same age and sex. Ratings were at first provisional in most cases, but once a final rating was made, the worker with a disability of 20 percent or more was entitled to a pension for life even if his or her earning capacity was restored. Adoption of this principle, recommended by the 1944 White Paper, would, it was believed, maximize the incentive to undergo rehabilitation treatment, by removing the worker's fears that his or her compensation would be reduced if his or her earning capacity were improved or restored.

The injured worker receives medical care free of charge under the provisions of the National Health Service.

It has been estimated that about 16 percent of persons receiving industrial injury benefits have also received damages under the 1948 legislation permitting suits as an additional remedy. To win such a suit, the employee, or a survivor, had to prove that the employer was negligent. A survey by the Trades Union Congress (TUC) in 1971–2 indicated that these cases involved the more serious injuries and illnesses and were usually settled with the employers-insurers rather than with the courts, on a lump-sum basis (Barth, with Hunt, 1980, 198).

As in other programs, the flat-rate employer and employee contributions were subject to criticism, and in 1975 were replaced by a single earnings-related contribution from employers and employees that covers all social insurance programs.

Other postwar legislation

Insurance requirements and administration: During the postwar period, voluntary insurance schemes have largely disappeared in industrial countries, except in a few American states,[3] but there have continued to be excluded groups, such as agricultural employees, in a number of countries. The role of private insurance companies has also become less significant, as more and more countries have required insurance through a national insurance system or a public fund. There remained, however, in 1985, a few countries – Denmark and Finland – in which insurance was entirely through private insurers, and another group of countries – including some of the Australian states and Belgium – in which employers had the option of insuring with a public or a private carrier. This was also true in a number of American states, but in the majority of states insurance was entirely with private companies.

Another highly significant postwar development was closer integration of industrial injuries schemes with other social insurance and income maintenance programs, although only in the Netherlands has this resulted in complete integration of occupational and nonoccupational disability insurance through the repeal of the legislation on occupational injuries in 1967. Such a solution has, however, been proposed by committees of experts in Australia and Norway and has been reported to be under consideration in New Zealand (Voirin, 1980). In addition, both Switzerland and New Zealand have gone part of the way by covering non–work-related and work-related accidents in the same scheme. This has been the case in Switzerland since 1911, with

---

[3] Most of my discussion of current provisions of American laws is based on U.S. Employment Standards Administration (1984).

employers liable for contributions for work-related accidents and employees for nonoccupational accidents. The scheme was, however, limited to workers in industry, crafts, and agriculture until 1981, when it was made compulsory for all employees; self-employed persons were covered on a voluntary basis (Charles, 1984).

In New Zealand, the Accident Compensation Act of 1972 provided protection against income loss for work injuries and other injuries suffered by a regularly employed earner, along with no-fault compensation for motor vehicle accidents, applicable to earners and nonearners alike. It did not, however, go as far as a special committee had recommended, in that it did not cover housewives for accidents other than motor vehicle accidents. The scheme was financed by employer contributions varying by risk class, except for motor vehicle accident compensation, which was financed by a tax on motor vehicle owners (M. Anderson, 1973). It should also be noted that this was the only social security program in New Zealand that provided earnings-related rather than flat benefits.

The French Employment Injuries Insurance Act of 1946 replaced the former system of individual employer liability by a system of collective liability. The scheme was to be compulsory, private insurance was no longer permitted, and employer contributions varying with risk class were to be made to the social security funds. In addition, each employer was to be individually liable for a payment designed to cover an increase in the disability rating if the accident was found to be attributable to the inexcusable fault of employers or their subordinates (Rouast and Durand, 1960, 335).

In Eastern Europe, employment injuries insurance largely disappeared as a separate branch of social insurance for a time, although victims of industrial injuries were, as elsewhere, entitled to receive benefits without meeting the qualifying period requirements imposed for other social insurance benefits. They also received somewhat higher benefits than victims of nonoccupational disability under many of these systems, particularly in the case of the permanently disabled.

During the 1950s, however, there were indications of a reversal of the trend toward integration of employment injuries insurance with other social insurance programs, evidently in the interests of accident prevention. In both Czechoslovakia and the Soviet Union, the costs of medical services and certain long-term pension expenses were ordinarily met from general government revenues, whereas short-term cash benefits were generally financed through payroll taxes on establishments. However, under legislation enacted in Czechoslovakia in 1956 and 1961, and regulations adopted in the Soviet Union in 1957, the establishments were made liable for a greater portion of compensation costs in industrial injury cases under certain circumstances.

Types of workers covered: Expansion of coverage has continued under employment injuries insurance legislation, so that most countries included in this study now cover virtually all employees with very minor exceptions. Even coverage of the self-employed, which was very rare before World War II, has come to be required in most countries, although in 1985 the self-employed were not covered in Greece, the United Kingdom, the United States, or most of the Australian states, and were covered only on a voluntary basis in Norway and Switzerland. They were covered only partially in Hungary, Poland, Denmark, and West Germany.

Another significant excluded group consisted of agricultural employees, although they were much more likely to be covered than before the war. Jurisdictions that continued to exclude them were Greece, Italy, Japan (if they were employed in small enterprises), some of the Canadian provinces, and many of the American states. Domestic workers were also excluded in a number of systems.

Types of risks covered: There has been a pronounced tendency during the postwar period to broaden the coverage of occupational diseases. The typical practice continues to be limitation of protection to a specified list of diseases – often a two-column list, limiting coverage not only to specified diseases but to the industries in which each disease typically occurs – but there has been a tendency to grant a certain amount of administrative discretion in adding to the list. The number of occupational diseases recognized by experts has been increasing, partly as a result of a dramatic increase in the number of chemicals produced and used in industrial processes, partly reflecting increased exposure to radiation, and partly because of the growth of knowledge about the specific industrial origins of certain diseases – for example, certain forms of cancer.

However, the fact that the number of known occupational diseases has been growing does not necessarily mean that their incidence has been growing. The decline in employment in mining, for example, will in the long run result in a substantial decrease in the number of cases originating in mining, which has accounted for a very large proportion of compensated cases of occupational disease in countries where mining is important – exemplified by such diseases as silicosis, pneumoconiosis, carbon dioxide poisoning, and many others. The effect of the decline in employment on claims will be delayed, however, because many of these diseases develop slowly over a long period of time.

More recently, in Western Europe and in industrial countries in other parts of the world, there has been a decline in employment in manufacturing – accompanied in some countries by a decline in the relative proportion of production versus nonproduction workers in manufacturing – a trend that could

be expected to result in a drop in the incidence of occupational diseases because many of them are associated with factory blue-collar employment.
However, in the United States, there have been recent indications of a growth
of claims for work-related ''mental stress'' in white-collar employment, some
of them receiving court approval. A recent report for the workers' compensation insurance industry concluded that 11 percent of all occupational disease
claims in 13 states in 1980–2 were for mental disorders (Dworkin, 1985).

In his useful comparative analysis of policies relating to occupational diseases in the United States, seven European countries, and the province of
Ontario, Barth (1980) concluded that ''the most common and significant thread
running through each of these disease systems'' was that administrators depended to an important extent on a schedule of diseases. Even when the list
was not exclusive, it tended to define the range of compensable diseases. The
worker could be reasonably certain of compensation if his or her condition
was on the list, but could seek benefits from other sources of assistance if it
was not. The American situation differed appreciably because the lists tended
to be much more restricted and because disputed cases tended to wind up in
court, whereas in the other systems that Barth studied, the responsibility for
making decisions in disputed cases tended to be assumed by the administrators of workers' compensation in a nonadversarial atmosphere and relied heavily
on expert medical opinion. Moreover, the fact that workers were much less
likely to have access to other sources of support in the United States increased
their incentive to use attorneys' services to press their claims. Not only were
European workers much more likely to have access to comprehensive medical
benefits and short-term sickness benefits under nonoccupational programs than
their counterparts in the United States, but they might also be eligible for
permanent partial nonoccupational disability benefits, which were not available in the United States.

In spite of the heavy reliance on the schedule or list, administrators of
industrial injuries programs in Western Europe and in Ontario usually had
considerable latitude in approving compensation for an unlisted condition if
the evidence was clear that it originated out of and in the course of employment. Denmark has gone so far as to provide under 1976 legislation that
coverage was no longer to be limited to the diseases appearing on its schedule.
In West Germany, where Barth found the list to be limited to 55 occupational
diseases, the accident associations could compensate unlisted diseases, although this provision was rarely used. The situation in Switzerland was similar. In Ontario, also, although there was heavy reliance on a list of diseases,
it was not an exclusive list, and the Workers' Compensation Board could
approve a claim that was not routine, in large part on the advice of its medical
staff and specialized consultants.

It must be recognized, however, that the problems confronting decision-makers in occupational disease cases are frequently much more complex than in industrial injuries cases, where the injury clearly results from a single, identifiable event. An occupational disease can develop over a long period of time, can be attributable to more than one cause, and can affect a worker who has worked for more than one employer during the period when he or she was contracting the disease.

Heart cases present particular difficulties, owing to the fact that the cause of a heart problem in a given case is generally unknown. Largely because of this uncertainty, and because heart problems are responsible for a very large proportion of permanent disabilities and deaths, they were not covered in many industrial injuries laws in Western Europe, but the heart victim could seek nonoccupational disability benefits. Ontario did cover them, but they accounted for a small number of cases. Some American states permitted approval of claims for heart attacks, but only if the attack occurred immediately following an identifiable or in some cases an "unexpected" accident or injury in the course of employment.

The problem of cancer is somewhat different. Although the etiology of most cancer cases is unknown, there is a growing body of knowledge about the specific industrial origin of certain forms of cancer and thus a case for including these specific types of cases on lists of covered diseases.

In spite of the concern about occupational diseases, they tend to represent a very small proportion of permanent occupational disability cases – not more than 1 to 2 percent in most countries. Among the countries studied by Barth (1980), West Germany had the highest proportion of such cases – 8.9 percent of initially compensated claims in 1975.

Although there has been some tendency to include coverage of accidents to and from work in the postwar period, some countries have resisted such coverage or adopted legislation specifically excluding it.

Temporary disability benefits: Before considering amounts of benefits, it is important to note that the great majority of injured workers achieve recovery and return to work after a relatively short period. Some of them receive only medical benefits, and do not need to stop working, whereas others receive both medical and temporary disability benefits but never reach the stage of applying for permanent benefits. American data showed that the average number of work days lost by victims of occupational disability in 1982 was only 16.9 days.

Nevertheless, because permanent disability benefits and survivors' benefits are received over long periods, they account for a sizable proportion of total occupational disability expenditures in industrial countries.

Temporary disability benefits in industrial injuries programs in 1985 tended to be higher than in nonoccupational, or sickness, programs, although this was not always the case. Whereas in many countries, weekly sickness benefits amounted to around 60 to 70 percent of earnings, in industrial injuries cases they amounted to 100 percent of earnings in 11 countries and most Australian states. In three of these countries – Austria, Belgium, and West Germany – they were somewhat lower after an initial period of a month to six weeks, whereas in a number of the Australian states the benefits were lower or were converted to a flat-rate amount after 26 weeks. In Sweden, on the other hand, they amounted to 90 percent of earnings during the first 90 days and to 100 percent thereafter. Also noteworthy was the fact that benefits amounted to 100 percent of earnings in a number of the socialist countries, including East Germany, Hungary, Poland, the Soviet Union, and Yugoslavia.

In Czechoslovakia (for long-service workers) and in Denmark the benefits were 90 percent of earnings, and in other countries the benefits tended to range from 60 to 85 percent of earnings. Benefit amounts in nearly all American states were 66⅔ percent of earnings, but in a number of states, especially in the South, weekly maxima were very restrictive.

Maximum duration of benefits also tended to be longer in industrial injuries cases than in sickness programs. In 16 countries, and in most of the Canadian provinces, Australian states, and a large number of American states, temporary disability benefits could be paid until recovery or award of a permanent disability pension, or else no maximum period was specified. Norway essentially belonged in this category as well, because although temporary disability benefits were limited to 52 weeks, a rehabilitation allowance or a pension could be paid after that. Maximum duration was a year in Finland and the Netherlands, approximately half a year in Greece, Israel, and Poland, and 18 months in Spain. In the United Kingdom, where maximum duration was 28 weeks (following the initial period of employer sick leave), a permanent disability pension could be awarded at the end of 15 weeks, as we noted earlier.

One reason why countries are prepared to provide generous weekly benefits over a substantial period in industrial injuries cases is that abuse is much less likely than in the case of ordinary sickness benefits. The fact of the injury is known, reports are received on its severity, and in many countries medical care is subjected to scrutiny by the administrators of the program.

Dependents' benefits were relatively uncommon in provisions for temporary occupational disability in 1985. This was attributable partly to the concept of "compensation" for injury, partly to the fact that benefits amounted to 100 percent of the earnings, or not much less, in a good many countries, and partly to the availability of family allowances. Nevertheless, dependents' benefits were provided under temporary occupational disability programs in six of our countries – Australia, Austria, Greece, Ireland, New Zealand, and the United Kingdom. In the United States, dependents' benefits were provided in about one-fifth of the states.

Permanent disability benefits: Partial disability benefits played a relatively more important role in industrial injuries programs than in nonoccupational disability programs, particularly in compensating for very small degrees of disability. The minimum percentage of total disablement that could be compensated tended to be considerably smaller than in nonoccupational cases, and lump-sum settlements were in some cases provided for a disability that was rated below that minimum. The explanation, again, was the heritage of the concept of compensation for damages, even in cases in which the injury had no effect on actual earning capacity.

Nevertheless, estimated loss of earning capacity was an important factor in the determination of disability ratings in most countries. In his study of occupational disease policies, Barth (1980) found that the United Kingdom was the only country among the seven included in his study that rated disabilities on physical grounds only. An eighth jurisdiction, the province of Ontario, considered both socioeconomic conditions and physicians' evaluations of physical impairment in arriving at ratings. Similar findings in a study of EEC countries (Bouquet, 1979) were discussed in Chapter 6.

Although permanent total disability benefits amounting to more than 66⅔ percent of earnings were rare before World War II, there were 18 countries in which they amounted to more than 66⅔ percent in 1985, and in six of these they amounted to 100 percent. In several Eastern European countries they were less than 66⅔ percent, except for long-service workers who benefited from increments for added years of employment.

Moreover, unlike the situation before World War II, recipients of industrial injuries benefits were protected by indexing provisions in a number of countries by 1985, although such provisions were less common in industrial injuries programs than in other pension programs.

In the majority of countries, permanent partial disability benefits were related to the degree of disability, but in Eastern Europe they were more likely to take the form of a specific percentage of earnings or of the total disability pension, with a flat-rate minimum specified.

We have earlier noted that provision for constant attendance allowances in industrial injuries programs originated earlier than in nonoccupational disability programs, but by 1985 the number of countries providing them in industrial injuries programs was slightly less (18) than in nonoccupational disability programs (21). In most cases, they were provided in both types of programs, but in a few countries they were provided in only one. Several countries, however, that provided no constant attendance allowance in industrial injuries cases did provide considerably higher benefit amounts in such cases than in nonoccupational cases. Moreover, a few countries provided special benefits for lasting injury. In Denmark, for example, there was no constant attendance allowance in industrial injury cases, but there was a flat-rate supplement up to 25,500 kr. a year as compensation for lasting injury. Switzerland provided for lump-sum awards for lasting injury (according to a schedule of specified amounts for each type of injury) and a constant attendance allowance where needed.

Not unlike these lasting injury supplements was Britain's unemployability supplement, granted when total disability was expected to be permanent. As we saw in Chapter 6, in fact, Britain's combination of flat-rate allowances provided benefits that compared favorably in relation to earnings with those provided in other EEC countries, although Britain's relative position was less favorable in nonoccupational disability cases.

Financing: Employer contributory taxes, varying by risk class, continued to be the most common method of financing industrial injuries insurance in 1985, but the exceptions were numerous. In Austria, Ireland, and Sweden, costs were met by the employer but on the basis of a uniform percentage, whereas in Belgium, which had a separate fund for occupational diseases, employer contributions to that fund were uniform. Under the merged system of disability insurance in the Netherlands, financing was through a uniform employer contribution.

In addition, there were nine countries, primarily in Eastern Europe, in which contributions for work injuries insurance were merged with contributions for other social insurance programs. The employer contribution did not vary by risk class in four of these countries, involved a premium for arduous or unhealthy industries in Greece, and varied by industry or risk class in East Germany, Romania, and the USSR.

In Chapter 2, we noted that the cost of industrial injuries insurance tended to be a very small proportion of total social security expenditures, amounting to less than 1 percent of GDP, and often as little as 0.3 or 0.4 percent. Thus, where the employer contribution was a uniform percentage of payroll, it tended to be very small, varying from 0.4 percent in Ireland to 1.5 percent in Austria in 1985. The average employer contribution in countries where it varied by risk class also tended to be relatively small, amounting, in countries for which I have data, to 1 percent in Israel, 1.5 percent in West Germany, and about 1.8 percent in American states. France's average was unusually high, amounting to 3.7 percent of payroll in 1985. We shall find, when we consider data on industrial injury rates, that the number of work days lost as a result of industrial injuries per employed worker in manufacturing is relatively large in France.

The chief rationale for employer contributions that vary by risk class, apart from forcing employers in hazardous industries to bear a large share of the costs, is to provide employers with high contribution rates an incentive to give strong emphasis to safety and health measures that will reduce their injury rates and hence their contribution rates. Yet the evidence is unclear as to whether varying rates of employer contributions are a decisive factor in lowering injury and occupational disease rates.

Occupational health and safety

Such data as are available indicate that there has been a long-run downward trend in work injury rates in most industrial countries, not only because of declining relative employment in some of the most hazardous industries, especially mining, but also within most industry groups, suggesting that occupational health and safety measures have had some effect. Even so, of special interest are American data going back to 1926, indicating that the decline in the injury rate in manufacturing was very irregular and sensitive to what was happening to employment. The rate fell substantially in the depressed 1930s, rose sharply during World War II, declined under the looser labor market conditions of the 1950s, and rose again during the Vietnam War period of the late 1960s.

I have not found much evidence of a comparable rise in injury rates in other industrial countries during the full employment years of the 1960s, but, for whatever reasons, the 1970s and the first half of the 1980s were characterized by the enactment of legislation aimed at improvement of industrial health and safety conditions in country after country. Many of the new laws provided for increased employee participation in relation to safety conditions within their enterprises and were clearly associated with the movement toward increased worker participation in industry, especially in Western Europe. Other influences were increased awareness of the hazards associated with various chemicals, asbestos, radiation, noise, and certain technological developments, as well as the burden on employers of sharply rising medical costs.

One of the most significant of the laws – representing, as it did, a departure from the past practice of leaving such matters largely to the states – was the Occupational Safety and Health Act of 1970 in the United States. Enacted after three years of controversy and embodying features that had been supported by organized labor and opposed by employers, the law has continued to be a focus of controversy.

The legislation was clearly influenced by rising injury rates, and especially by a mining disaster, and had been preceded by the enactment of the Coal Mine Health and Safety Act of 1969, which provided for benefits for coal miners who were totally disabled as a result of pneumoconiosis (black lung disease) and for their dependents and survivors in death cases. The 1970 act provided for establishment of the Occupational Safety and Health Administration (OSHA) within the Department of Labor, charged with responsibility for carrying out a vigorous program of enforcing safety and health standards in all types of employment. The legislation also empowered workers to trigger inspections through written complaints and gave them the right to accompany compliance officers in their examination of workplaces and to point out alleged hazards (Collier, 1973). There were also provisions for phasing out the federal role in states that adopted laws at least as strict as the federal law and administered them successfully under the watchful eye of the federal government over a period of years.

OSHA developed a network of regional offices and a sizable program of inspections and enforcement. Under the Reagan administration, however, enforcement activities were relaxed in a number of ways, through examining employers' logs of on-the-job injuries rather than inspection of workplaces where injuries fell below the national average, and through a conciliatory approach to settling citations, preferring to give employers light fines in return for promises to remove hazards.

Meanwhile, a movement in Canada toward legislation giving workers rights in relation to the monitoring of safety and health measures was probably influenced by the American legislation. Workers' compensation boards in Canada had taken an active part in enforcement of industrial safety but had tended to work with management and to regard workplace safety as a management responsibility. However, labor organizations sought to become involved in health and safety matters, and in 1972 the province of Saskatchewan enacted an occupational safety and health act which specifically provided for worker participation in the identification and control of hazards, calling for joint health and safety committees with effective mandates to be established in all workplaces where ten or more persons were employed. Similar legislation has since been adopted in some of the other provinces (Clarke, 1982).

In addition to increased worker participation, other notable features of the laws enacted in this recent period have, among other things, included (1) a requirement that employers appoint plant physicians and safety engineers in their firms, in numbers varying by size of firm and type of industry (West Germany, 1973); (2) a requirement that employers be responsible for safety training of workers (France, 1976); (3) increased centralization of responsibility, where previously it had been diffused, through the creation of two national bodies for formulating policy and carrying out enforcement activities (United Kingdom, 1974); (4) a program for advanced training of specialists in occupational safety and health services (USSR, 1976); (5) the establishment of several national commissions concerned with occupational safety and health matters, which had previously been left largely to the states (Australia, 1983); (6) new regulations relating to shorter hours of work for workers in arduous and hazardous occupations (Poland, 1983); and (7) adoption of various EEC directives relating to occupational health and safety problems, including provisions for the protection of workers exposed to asbestos (1983).

In spite of the wealth of new legislation, actual implementation has often fallen short of the objectives, as several studies have indicated. A Dutch specialist conducted a review of the situation in EEC countries and found that the scope of codetermination rights was often ambiguous and that the success of worker representatives in exercising the rights bestowed on them was sometimes questionable (Gevers, 1983).

Recently the ILO has begun to publish more extensive data on industrial injuries (ILO, Annual, 1985), whereas formerly only data on fatalities had been made available. Great caution must be observed in interpreting these data because differences in industry "mix," not only overall, but within such sectors as manufacturing and mining, affect the comparisons. However, they show very substantial differences among countries. The number of injuries per employed worker in manufacturing, for example, was relatively high in Switzerland, the United States, and West Germany, but quite low in Czechoslovakia, the Netherlands, and Norway. On the other hand, the number of work days lost per employed worker showed a different pattern of variations (for a group of countries, that was not identical with the group for which number of injuries was available), and on this basis, the rate in the United States was relatively low, though not as low as in Czechoslovakia and Hungary. Countries with relatively large numbers of work days lost per worker in manufacturing included Spain and France, followed at some distance by Switzerland and Poland.

There is little question that occupational health and safety issues will continue to be a matter of concern in industrial countries, and the Bhopal disaster in India in 1984 has served to call attention to the issue of the responsibilities of multinational enterprises toward health and safety in their branch plants in less developed countries. Although the rise in the proportion of white-collar workers in the economy, along with the increasing proportion of nonproduction workers in manufacturing, clearly tends to reduce the proportion of workers exposed to industrial accidents, there is evidence, as we have seen, of job-associated stress among nonmanual workers. Moreover, the number of recognized occupational diseases is increasing, although decreased employment in mining is an important factor in reducing the number of workers exposed to occupational disease.

Finally, a dramatic example of possible future problems is the recent move of the Japanese Ministry of Labor to promulgate regulations for ensuring safety of robot work premises and technical installations. On the one hand, the ministry has taken the position that replacement of workers in harmful and dangerous jobs by robots should be encouraged, but, on the other, has stressed the need for occupational safety in robot work (*S&LB*, 1983, [3]:426–7).

The trend toward increased emphasis on national programs of occupational health and safety, with participation of labor and management at the plant level, tends to cast some doubt on the effectiveness of variable employer contribution rates as a tool for reducing the incidence of industrial injuries and occupational diseases.[4]

The problem of litigation

The problem of extensive litigation and lump-sum settlements, which Beveridge identified as a major weakness of prewar British workers' compensation, is no longer as pervasive a problem in Britain, but it continues to be a major problem in the United States, though once again varying considerably from state to state. A quarter of a century ago, when I was first involved in a study of industrial injuries programs, the problem of excessive litigation was recognized as a major weakness of workers' compensation in the United States by a number of those participating in the research project (Cheit and Gordon, eds., 1963). It is not clear that the problem of excessive litigation has become less serious since that time, although in other respects, such as coverage and benefit levels, there has been substantial liberalization in recent years under the impetus of the recommendations of the National Commission on State Workers' Compensation Laws of 1972.

The use of schedules setting forth maximum total benefit payments and the number of weeks for which benefits can be paid for specified types of injuries – a practice dating from the New Jersey law of 1911 – continued to be prevalent in 1985 and meant that many seriously disabled workers did not receive benefits on a permanent basis. The use of such schedules also encouraged lump-sum settlements. However, a California study showed that older workers with severe disabilities were able to qualify for social security disability benefits in many cases after their workers' compensation benefits were exhausted (Vroman, 1976).

A separate system?

In recent years, certain experts, as well as study commissions in several countries, have questioned whether there continues to be a case for maintaining the separation between industrial injuries systems and nonoccupational invalidity systems – a case that was made so convincingly by Beveridge in his 1942 report. As we have noted in several contexts, the Netherlands has abandoned the separation. The fact that in most industrial countries, coverage has

[4] Various studies had shown that the American record in industrial safety and health varied greatly among the states (e.g., Steele, 1963, 262). However, some of the insurance companies had an excellent record in accident prevention work, and a comprehensive study of workers' compensation in the early 1950s indicated that many employers had discovered that industrial health and safety programs paid for themselves, quite apart from their effect on insurance premiums (Somers and Somers, 1954, 278–9).

been extended to all types of employment removes some of the force from the argument that workers' compensation systems are needed to protect workers in hazardous industries from their special risks. Moreover, the adoption of mandatory no-fault compensation is no longer confined to industrial accidents. Nevertheless, a careful analyst of these trends concluded that the road to unification was likely to be "rocky" and was unlikely to "enlist the enthusiastic support of the managers, executives, or representatives of employers' and workers' organizations on the management bodies of the occupational accidents scheme in countries where it enjoys administrative autonomy" (Voirin, 1980, 39–40).

Probably the chief advantage of merging the two types of programs would be the elimination of the need to determine whether or not the injury or disease was work-related, particularly in the case of occupational diseases. However, Barth's (1980) study indicated that this was unlikely to be a serious problem in the countries in which the determination is made by a strong administrative agency relying on expert medical opinion.

In conclusion, after a century of industrial injuries programs, the benefits they provide appear to be relatively adequate in most countries, but problems remain. In some jurisdictions there is inadequate attention to rehabilitation, as we shall find in Chapter 12; in the United States the problem of excessive litigation is serious; and in many industrial countries, there is a need for evaluation of health and safety measures.

CHAPTER 8

The role of employer pension plans

Just as national pension programs have been expanded and liberalized during the postwar period, so also have employer pension plans been extended to more and more workers. Whereas before the war, employer plans were usually found only in a relatively small number of large companies, in some industrial countries today, one-half or more of workers in the private sector are covered by employer pension plans. Moreover, tax exemption of contributions to employer pension plans is a common practice and has played an important role in stimulating adoption of these plans.

The proportion of retired workers who actually receive benefits from employer pensions, however, tends in most countries to be considerably smaller than the proportion of employed workers who are covered, not only because workers in relatively new plans may not have had enough years of service to qualify for a pension, but also because workers who change jobs often lose all or part of their pension rights. In fact, as the coverage of employer pension plans has increased, there has been increasing awareness of many weaknesses in the protection they offer workers, and a growing movement for governments to enact regulatory legislation designed to overcome at least some of these weaknesses.

Before discussing the major issues relating to pension plans, a word about nomenclature is in order. In the United States, we usually refer to employer-sponsored plans as "employer" plans or "private" plans, whereas in Western Europe they are often called "occupational" plans. I propose to refer to them usually as employer plans because I believe that this will make my meaning clear to all readers. Even so, there is ambiguity in some cases.

Coverage

Among the major policy issues in employer pensions is the unevenness of coverage in most industrial countries. Employers are particularly prone to provide pension coverage for managerial employees, to encourage them to remain with the firm, move up through the ranks, and eventually retire at a normal or conventional retirement age with a reasonably adequate pension. Employers are also often more likely to provide pensions for white-collar workers than for blue-collar workers, since white-collar workers who are highly knowledgeable about the firm's activities are less easily replaced than blue-collar workers, whose skills are less likely to be specific to the individual firm. However, there has been a tendency in most countries for unions to press successfully for inclusion of blue-collar workers in employer pension plans during the postwar period, although there continue to be some countries, such as Austria and Belgium, in which employer pensions are largely confined to salaried workers.

In general, outside of France and Sweden, with their nationwide collectively bargained plans, and Finland and Switzerland, with their legally mandated schemes, there is a persistent pattern of more widespread coverage of highly paid workers, and sometimes of union workers, than of nonunion and lower-paid workers. Moreover, large firms are much more likely to have pension plans than small firms, and industries in which large firms predominate, such as manufacturing and utilities, are more likely to have pension plans than trade and service industries. In addition, workers aged 25 or more, male workers, full-time workers, and long-service workers are more likely to be covered than part-time, casual, female, and youthful workers.

Precise data on coverage of workers in private employment by employer pension plans are not readily available for all of our market-oriented industrial countries, but Table 8.1 brings together data from a number of sources that are not precisely comparable but do give a rough impression of differences in coverage of workers by employer pension plans. Among the countries included, coverage is most nearly complete in Finland and Switzerland, and in France and Sweden.

The development of comprehensive coverage of employees in the private sector occurred particularly early in France, where the national pension program, though expanded in coverage under 1945 legislation, was based on a 1930 law, under which full pensions at age 65 after 30 years of service would not be available until 1960, were not indexed, and would amount to only 40 percent of covered earnings in the last ten years before retirement. Also, higher-paid salaried employees had been excluded from the national scheme before the war, and in some cases were covered by employer plans, whereas the 1945 act brought them within the national scheme, but with a relatively low ceiling on covered earnings. Thus, *Cadres* (i.e., managerial, technical, and other highly paid white-collar workers) felt the need for pensions that would, when added to the national pension, provide a more adequate replacement rate. This led to the negotiation of an agreement in 1947 between the *Conseil National du Patronat Français* (CNPF) and several organizations representing the *Cadres*, which established a "complementary fund" and provided that when the "most representative employer and union organizations agreed to contracts, they would become binding on all employers and employees in the

Table 8.1. *Estimated percentages of private sector workers covered by
employer pension plans, selected industrial countries, years around 1980*

Country	Coverage
Australia	50% of male workers and 26% of female workers
Austria	Chiefly higher-paid salaried workers
Belgium	Chiefly salaried and white-collar workers
Canada	About 49% of men and 30% of women in the private sector
Finland	Mandatory, except for workers employed less than one month
France	About 80% of employees covered by the national social security system
Germany	About 65% to 70% of private nonagricultural wage and salaried workers in firms with more than ten employees
Italy	Less than 20%
Japan	About 43% of employees covered by the national Employee's Pension Insurance program
Netherlands	About 80% of labor force in private sector
New Zealand	About 20% of employees in private sector
Sweden	About 90% of employees in private sector (mandatory under nationwide collective bargaining agreements)
Switzerland	Mandatory for workers with earnings from 1,380 fr. to 4,140 fr. a month; optional for self-employed
United Kingdom	About 52% of men and 17% of women in the private sector
United States	About 49% of private wage and salaried workers

Sources: Wilson, ed. (1974); *Employment Gazette* (UK) (1977 [May]: 474–5); Horlick and Skol-
nick (1979); Horlick (1980); U.S. President's Commission on Pension Policy (1980); Munnell
(1982); Aaron (1984); *Statistical Abstract of the United States, 1985* (p. 318); other sources.

industry.'' Under a 1959 ordinance, mandatory adherence to these agreements was legalized for all branches of industry represented in the CNPF
(Rouast and Durand, 1960, 325–9; Beattie, 1974, 259). This pattern of development in postwar France, from collective bargaining agreement to legal
compulsion, has already been encountered in connection with prepension plans
and will appear in Chapter 11 when we discuss unemployment insurance in
France.

   Not long afterward, unions representing lower-paid white-collar workers
and also representing manual workers began to press for similar complementary plans for their members, who faced highly inadequate social security
benefits. During the decade following 1947, a series of employer–union
agreements was negotiated providing for complementary funds for lower-paid
salaried and manual workers. Eventually there developed two major systems,
Association Générale des Institutions de Retraites des Cadres (AGIRC), and
Association des Régimes de Retraites Complémentaires (ARRCO), a major

component of which was the *Union National des Institutions de Retraite des Salariés* (UNIRS). Together these organizations, which actually were umbrella organizations for a large number of employer or multiemployer plans, came to include about 80 percent of employees covered by the general social security system.[1]

Also under nationwide collective bargaining agreements are employer pensions in Sweden, and there, too, it was the highly paid salaried workers who first pressed for supplements to the national social security benefits. When Sweden adopted its supplementary earnings-related national system under 1959 legislation, the band of earnings included under the scheme involved a maximum that was high enough to cover total earnings of nearly all blue-collar workers and most white-collar workers, but not of higher-paid salaried employees. This led to negotiations that resulted in an agreement in 1962 between salaried employees and the Swedish Employers Confederation (SAF) for the creation of an employer pension plan for salaried workers (ITP). At first it was left to employers and employees to make voluntary agreements to adopt a plan, but in 1969 these agreements were changed into collective contracts and became compulsory for employers belonging to SAF.

It was not until 1971 that employers and unions agreed on two private plans for blue-collar workers, one to provide retirement pensions and the other to provide supplementary cash sickness benefits. The retirement plan is known as STP and, by the end of 1974, included about 55,000 employers, with about 90 percent of all blue-collar workers.

Finland's mandatory private pension program, adopted in 1962, resembles the supplementary earnings-related social security pensions in Norway and Sweden, except for the fact that employers are not obliged to make contributions to a government fund, but instead make mandatory payments to a separate fund, a private insurance company fund, or a pension foundation. All employees must be covered, except for those employed less than one month. Since 1970, additional employment-related pension programs have been enacted for temporary employees, self-employed persons, and farmers (U.S. President's Commission on Pension Policy, 1980).

Switzerland's mandatory plan was debated for a long time before it was finally adopted under 1982 legislation, a decade after voters had approved a constitutional amendment instituting the three-pillar concept of providing for old age. The first pillar or tier consisted of the national social security program; the second tier, of occupational pensions; and the third tier, of personal saving. Mandatory coverage was limited, however, to a band of earnings

---

[1] We have earlier noted the special schemes in France for such groups as civil servants, seamen, miners, etc. – all of them public schemes that in some cases provided relatively generous benefits. They have not been supplemented by employer schemes, except in the case of the miners (Lynes, 1967; Beattie, 1974; Horlick, 1980).

which in 1984 amounted to a minimum of 1,380 fr. per month to a maximum of 4,140 fr., to be adjusted for future changes in wages (Charles, 1984). This meant that significant numbers of low earners would not be included.[2] Moreover, the maximum of 4,140 fr. a month was only about 1.5 times the monthly average male earnings in manufacturing. Employers are, however, free to cover earnings above the maximum voluntarily (*ISSR*, 1983, *36* [1]: 95–7).

Mandatory coverage by employer pensions has long been debated in the Netherlands, and fairly detailed agreement has been reached about the provisions that would be involved, but actual enactment of legislation has been held back under the difficult economic circumstances of recent years. As Table 8.1 shows, the great majority of workers are included under employer pension plans in the Netherlands. The plans are of two general types: compulsory multiemployer plans, covering about 1.3 million workers, and voluntary company plans, covering about one million employees in 1979. The company plans are found chiefly in large firms (Horlick and Skolnik, 1979).

In Britain, the United States, and Canada, coverage ranges from considerably less than half of private employees in Canada and Britain to slightly less than half in the United States (these percentages would be larger if based on all employees meeting age and service requirements for participation). The absence of nationwide collective bargaining is an important reason for the contrast between these countries and some of the Western European countries. There are multiemployer plans with broad coverage, but all three countries display the uneven patterns of participation discussed earlier.

However, the uneven patterns of participation result from the absence of employer plans in small companies and certain industries (such as the trade and service industries) and not necessarily from the exclusion of workers from a given plan. Requirements in the United States have denied qualified tax status since 1942 to plans covering only officers, executives, or other very highly paid employees. These requirements were stiffened by the Employee Retirement Income Security Act of 1974 (ERISA), which provided that a company plan must permit all employees to participate who were aged 25 or more and had worked for the company at least one year. However, a plan could be limited to salaried employees or nonunion employees if the company also had a collectively bargained plan covering union employees (Bureau of National Affairs, 1974, 244). In addition, there were provisions for maximum contributions and benefits.

In 1984, largely as a result of complaints that plans often discriminated against women, amendments were adopted that were designed to make it easier for women who took time out for childrearing to meet participation and

---

[2] Interview with Roland Sigg, Research Officer, International Social Security Association, Geneva, June 1985.

vesting requirements. The minimum age of mandatory participation was lowered to 21, and vesting requirements (to be discussed later) were modified somewhat (*SSB, 1985, 48* [May]: 38–44).

Requirements in the United Kingdom are less strict, and large employers frequently have plans that include only certain types of employment, but membership must be open to men and women on an equal basis (Horlick and Skolnik, 1979).

As we saw in Chapter 3, under both the law enacted in 1959 and that adopted in 1975, employers with pension plans could contract out of the national supplementary earnings-related scheme, if the benefits they provided were at least equal to those provided by the national scheme. The contracting-out provisions essentially represented a compromise between the Tories, who would have preferred strictly private supplementary pensions, and the Labor Party, which, at least in 1959, preferred something more closely resembling the Swedish national supplementary earnings-related scheme. Both under the 1959 law and under that of 1975 (effective in 1978), a large proportion of employers did opt to contract out.

Then, in June 1985, the government presented to Parliament a Green Paper, intended to provide a basis for discussion of several proposals for revamping social security. The most important of these would be the phasing out of the State Earnings-Related Pension Scheme (SERPS), in favor of mandatory employer pensions with defined contributions instead of defined benefits. The proposal proved to be controversial, but under 1986 amendments, mentioned in Chapter 3, benefits under SERPS were made more restrictive, individual employees were permitted to contract out if they opted for a defined-contribution personal pension, and, significantly, employers would be allowed to contract out if they set up defined-contribution schemes. Such schemes, like the individual employee option, would qualify for the state subsidy of 2 percent of earnings. Contributions would have to be at least equal to the national insurance rebate for contracted-out schemes. The results remain to be seen, but the principle that employer pensions must provide benefits equivalent to SERPS has to some extent been abandoned.

Japan is another example of a country in which employers may contract out of the earnings-related portion of the Employees Pension Insurance program. Under legislation adopted in 1966, an Employees Pension Fund (EPF) could be established by individual employers or groups of employers, provided 1,000 or more employees were involved, and the labor union had consented. The establishment of the fund required the approval of the Ministry of Health and Welfare. Another provision permitted the establishment of so-called tax-qualified plans by contract between an individual employer and a life insurance company or trust company, under the joint supervision of the National Tax Bureau and the Labor Standard Supervising Office. Only employers with 20 or more employees were eligible for tax-qualified plans. In 1979, about 23 percent of employees within the Employees Pension Insurance Program participated in EPFs, whereas about 20 percent were in tax-qualified plans.

Among other countries not yet mentioned in this discussion, West Germany has had a relatively large percentage of workers included in employer pension plans – a percentage that increased somewhat following the enactment of regulatory legislation in 1974. The other countries included in Table 8.1 have tended to have considerably fewer than half of the workers in private employment covered by pension plans.

Is there an inverse relationship between employers' contributions to social security and their contributions to private pension plans? One might expect that there was, because employers required to contribute a large percentage of payroll to social security might be inclined to resist sizable contributions to private pensions, and vice versa. A recent OECD publication shed some light on this question (Saunders and Klau, 1985, 176), and incidentally indicated that the only countries for which the authors were able to gather the relevant data were the countries that I have been discussing in this chapter. Information on employer pensions in other countries is sparse.

The data did not reveal a consistent relationship between contributions to social security and to private pensions. To be sure, the United States, with relatively low employer contributions to social security, ranked well ahead of other countries in contributions to employer pension plans, but that still left total employer contributions considerably below those of countries like France, Sweden, and Italy. On the whole, the rank order of countries on the basis of contributions to social security was not changed very much when employer contributions to private pension plans were added, although the United States moved up significantly.

Benefits

Benefits under employer pension plans have tended to flow in large measure to higher-paid employees. There have been a number of reasons for this. In the first place, except in the countries with nearly universal coverage, employers with higher salaries and at higher occupational levels have been more likely to be covered, as we have seen, than those with low earnings and at low occupational levels. Second, in several countries, employer pensions for salaried workers have been based only or largely on earnings above the ceiling for contributions to social security. In the third place, the provisions of employer pension plans have included other features benefiting higher earners, such as, for example, the provision of flat-rate benefits for blue-collar workers that tended to be lower than the earnings-related benefits received by many white-collar workers.

Benefit formulas in employer pension plans have tended to resemble the benefit formula in the West German social security pension system, which, it will be recalled, provides for 1.5 percent of revalued earnings per year of insurance. In the early years of employer pensions, pensions were based on average annual earnings – not revalued – but more recently there has been a pronounced tendency, under the impact of rising wages and prices, to base pensions on some type of final earnings formula, such as average earnings in the last three or last five years before retirement.

Whereas benefits for white-collar workers have in most cases been related to final earnings, this has been considerably less true for blue-collar workers, whose pension rights have tended to accrue in the form of a flat-rate benefit per year of coverage and have usually provided the retired worker with a lower benefit than was received by most white-collar workers. Although there has been a trend away from these flat-rate benefits, they have continued to be found in many of the multiemployer collectively bargained plans in the United States and also in Canada, West Germany, Japan, and the United Kingdom. They have likewise been prevalent in industrywide plans in the Netherlands, where they have provided an addition to the social security flat-rate benefits.

In Sweden, employer pensions are fully integrated with social security pensions and are designed to provide a modest addition to those benefits. Employer pension benefits in the case of salaried workers are based largely on earnings above the social security ceiling and those of blue-collar workers on earnings up to the ceiling.

In the United States, apart from multiemployer collectively bargained plans, most pension plans have been integrated with social security, influenced by a provision adopted under the Revenue Act of 1942, which provided that public and private retirement benefits would be considered together in determining whether a plan discriminated against low earners. Integration has been achieved by two methods. The most common of these is the so-called offset method, under which the private pension is reduced by a portion of the social security benefit, most frequently by 50 percent. This method results in a proportionately greater reduction for the low earner, who may in some cases receive almost no employer benefits. In West Germany, use of the offset method was prohibited, under the law regulating private pensions adopted in 1974, because the private pensions, which were generally not indexed, tended to decrease as the indexed social security benefits increased (*SSB*, 1975, *38* [July]: 38–9). In some other countries, use of the offset method has been restricted.

The second method of integrating public and private pensions has been the "excess" or "step rate" method, resembling the provisions for salaried workers in France and Sweden, under which the private pension provided a larger percentage of earnings for those earnings that exceeded the social security ceiling than for earnings below the ceiling, thereby raising the replacement rate for higher-paid workers. However, there has usually been an upper limit on the earnings that could be covered by the higher rate, and, in the United States, there has been a legal limit on benefits as a percentage of these higher earnings.

In the United Kingdom, the better schemes have tended to provide at least $1/60$ of final earnings (or 1.67 percent) per year of service (Hemming and Harvey, 1983). Such schemes have covered nearly 60 percent of pension members. The remaining members have been about equally divided between plans providing less than $1/60$ and other arrangements (chiefly flat-rate amounts per year of service). How the benefits will be affected by the new provision permitting employers to opt out on the basis of defined-contribution plans remains to be seen. Moreover, unlike the situation in a number of other countries, nearly three-fourths of members of employer schemes in the private sector have been able to commute part of their pensions to a lump-sum payment at the time of retirement, according to a 1977 report (*Employment Gazette* [May]: 474–5). Also, tax provisions permitted pensioners to draw up to one-third of their pensions as a tax-free lump sum when they retired (*The Economist*, November 17, 1984).

The situation in Australia has been somewhat unusual. Percentages of men and women covered by employer pensions have been somewhat similar to those in Canada, although the Australian data include public as well as private employees. However, a very large percentage of members of Australian private sector plans have received only lump-sum payments at the time of retirement, and many workers have tended to prefer this, apparently because the lump-sum settlements have been, until very recently, almost entirely free of the income tax, whereas pension income was fully taxable (although, as we saw in Chapter 4, with a sizable personal exemption). In view of the prevalence of these lump-sum payments and in view of the fact that the income-tested old-age pension is not available for men until age 65, the sharp drop in the labor force participation rate of men aged 60 to 64 between 1970 and 1985 is difficult to explain. One wonders about the sources of income of the men who have left the labor force. However, according to Lansbury (1980), retirement policies and employer pension plans have encouraged early retirement, especially in the larger firms and in public employment. Moreover, as Aaron (1984) points out, there has been no limit to the duration of unemployment benefits in Australia. In fact, an older man has been able to leave his job voluntarily and qualify for unemployment benefits after six weeks of unemployment.

In at least six countries, there has been an official national goal relating to the overall replacement rate from social security and employer pensions combined. In most of these countries, the goal has been stated in terms of the percentage of preretirement income received by single men with average earnings in manufacturing and ranged from 50 percent in the United Kingdom to 80 percent in Italy in 1975.

Disability and survivors' benefits

Long-term disability benefits are often provided in employer pension plans, and the provisions, especially relating to the degree of disability required for eligibility, are usually tied in closely with those of the national invalidity program. In general, disability provisions in employer pension plans tend to provide a modest supplement to disability benefits in national programs, but there are very significant differences from country to country in their amounts, depending to a considerable extent on age and years of service requirements.

In Switzerland, employees have been covered for invalidity and death benefits from age 17 on under employer pension plans, but coverage for retirement benefits does not begin until age 24. The amount of the pension actually received, however, has depended on amounts paid into the pension fund and thus has been smaller for youthful disabled workers and for older workers in new plans (as has also been the case in the national program). In the Swedish ITP plan, employees have been covered for disability from age 18 on, and not until 28 for retirement benefits, but the disabled have tended to fare better than in Switzerland because benefits under the national program have been considerably more liberal. The STP plan (for blue-collar workers) has provided sickness benefits that, in combination with social security, allowed the worker 90 percent of his or her after-tax income until the degree of permanent incapacity was determined and he or she became eligible for national invalidity benefits (Horlick and Skolnik, 1979).

A study of employer pensions in medium and large firms in the United States in 1983 indicated that 91 percent of pension plan participants were covered by disability retirement provisions. Most of the plans provided for disability benefits only after ten or more years of service, but there were no age or years-of-service provisions in some of the plans. If the disability satisfied the plan's definition of total disability, pension benefits often began immediately. Production workers were considerably more likely to be in plans with immediate benefits than were white-collar workers. The provisions, however, like those in the social security program, appeared to be designed for workers with permanent total disability and made no provision for partial disability (see U.S. Bureau of Labor Statistics, 1984).

In West Germany, most employer plans have provided for disability benefits, and, in some cases, as in the national scheme, have treated disabled workers as though they had worked to age 55 in determining years of service.

Where there was no such provision, a disabled worker might well receive only a small employer pension (Horlick and Skolnik, 1979).

In the Netherlands, on the other hand, employer pensions have not usually provided for disability benefits, and this appears to be related to the relatively liberal disability provisions in the social security program.

There have been provisions for widows' benefits in most employer pension schemes, and, again, as in the case of disability benefits, there has been a tendency for the age and eligibility conditions to be closely related to those in the social security scheme, although this has not invariably been the case.

Financing

Major issues in the financing of employer pension plans include not only the role and tax treatment of employer and employee contributions, but also whether or not advance funding is prevalent or legally required, and what provisions exist to ensure that the benefit rights of employees will be protected in the event of termination of a plan, inadequate funding, or bankruptcy of the employer.

In most industrial countries, employer pensions have been financed by employer and employee contributions, with the employer contributions typically exceeding those of employees. Moreover, in many countries, both employer and employee contributions (as well as earnings from pension fund investments) have been wholly exempt from taxation. In fact, as we have seen, the favorable tax treatment of contributions to employer pension plans has played an important role in stimulating the development of such plans, and there has been a tendency to impose certain standards on plans under tax legislation as a condition for tax exemption, even when there has been no special legislation regulating employer pensions. However, as noted earlier, there has been a pronounced trend toward adoption of special regulatory legislation for employer pensions, usually involving prudent financing and investment requirements, prohibitions against plans that are limited to or unduly favor highly paid employees, minimum vesting requirements, and (less frequently) portability provisions.

There are a few countries in which employer pension plans have been financed entirely from employer contributions, contrary to the prevailing pattern. These include Finland, Sweden, and the United States, for different reasons. In Finland, the law of 1962 mandating employer pensions provided for employer contributions but did not require employee contributions. In Sweden, the reliance entirely on employer contributions resulted from the provisions of nationwide collective bargaining agreements. And, in the United States, the fact that employee contributions have not been tax exempt has clearly been a major factor in the adoption of plans solely financed by employers. However, another influence was the tendency of unions in the post-war period to press for fringe benefits that were entirely financed by employers – a tendency that showed up in private health insurance as well as in pensions.

In most industrial countries, the rates of contribution to employer pension plans have varied substantially, depending on the outcome of collective bargaining or simply on the factors influencing the employer, including the importance to the firm of a stable work force, on the one hand, and the advantage of tax concessions, on the other. However, rates have been more likely to be uniform, or to conform to a particular pattern, in countries with nationwide mandated or collectively bargained schemes.

In France, there was an obligatory minimum contribution of 6 percent for the employer and 2 percent for the employee at the beginning of the 1980s under the *Cadres* scheme, but voluntary supplementation was possible up to a total contribution of 10 percent for the employer and 6 percent for the employee.[3] Contributions were significantly lower under ARRCO, with a minimum of 2.64 percent for the employer and 1.76 percent for the worker, and voluntary supplementation up to an additional 4 percent for each party. But an unusual feature of the French schemes has been *repartition,* or redistribution, involving coordination, stabilization, and mutual support among the various plans. The objective has been to ensure that changes in the ratio of working to retired persons in particular industries would not result in fund deficiencies, heavy requirements for contributions, or lower benefit levels compared with other industries (Greenough and King, 1976).

A rather different example of pooling the risks has prevailed in the Swedish blue-collar plan, where the total cost of pensions has been calculated for the entire blue-collar sector in relation to payroll and the resulting rate has been applied to all employers equally. In 1981, the contribution amounted to 3.15 percent of covered earnings. Under the ITP agreement for salaried workers, however, the costs have varied considerably from company to company on the basis of such factors as age, sex, and salary distribution within the company, averaging about 9.7 percent of covered earnings in 1975.

Still another version of uniform rates from company to company is found under the Swiss 1982 legislation for mandated employer pensions. Contributions that vary with age were required, with combined rates for employer and employee ranging from 7 percent for men aged 25 to 34 to 18 percent for those aged 55 to 65, and for women from 7 percent for those aged 25 to 31

---

[3] More recent data, reported by Tamburi (1985), indicated that contributions under AGIRC were no longer limited to earnings above the social security ceiling, but ranged from 4.6 to 8.0 percent of earnings below the ceiling and from 9.0 to 16.0 percent for earnings between the ceiling and four times the ceiling (employer and employee contributions combined).

to 18 percent for the 52 to 62 group (the differing age breaks for women reflecting the earlier retirement age of 62). Employer contributions had to amount to at least half of total contributions. Although the contribution rates were designed to yield a pension (for those with 40 years of coverage) that, together with social security benefits, would amount to 60 percent of final earnings, pensions actually received were to be based on the accumulated pension funds. There was, however, also a requirement for minimum benefits.

In addition, Switzerland has had its own version of pooling in the form of a national guarantee fund that not only guarantees benefit rights in the event of insolvency of the employer but also subsidizes plans with a particularly unfavorable age distribution of the participants (see *ISSR*, 1983, *36* [1]: 95–7; Charles, 1984; Tamburi, 1985).

Funding, pension guarantees, and indexing

Issues of funding, pension guarantees, and indexing of pension benefits are closely interrelated and cannot be discussed separately. Before considering these issues, however, it is important to recognize that indexing of employer pensions has two aspects, just as does the indexing of social security pension benefits: (1) how to adjust earnings on which pensions are based to rising wage levels, and (2) how to adjust pension benefits received by retirees to rising wage or price levels. To a large extent the first aspect has been met in most countries by basing the pension awarded at the time of retirement on a final earnings formula (such as average earnings in the last three years) or on revalued earnings over the worker's years of service (as in the German social security model). It is, however, the second aspect, the indexing of pension benefits after retirement, that presents serious difficulties in funded employer pension plans because a provision for automatic indexing would greatly complicate actuarial estimates of future costs and would also very substantially increase the current cost of pension contributions in many cases.

For these reasons, indexing of retirement benefits under employer pension plans has rarely been required, although we shall find that there are a few exceptions. Occasional increases on an ad hoc basis have, however, frequently been granted, but the degree of protection provided by such increases has varied greatly. In some countries, they have been granted only occasionally by individual plans when the status of pension funds permitted it, whereas in countries like France and Sweden they have been granted regularly, and in West Germany they are required on a limited basis.

Although there are important exceptions, employer pensions have tended to be fully funded or partially subject to advance funding in most countries, either under legal requirements or as a matter of prudent practice. However, there are numerous questions that have to be answered in determining what should be considered prudent financing.

Shall past service liabilities (benefits for workers employed before the plan was adopted) be funded? Shall future benefits of all those currently covered by the plan be funded, or only vested benefits (benefits to which the employee has earned a right under age and years of service requirements even if he or she leaves the firm to take another job)? What assumptions shall be made about future employment in the firm? And then, of course, there are all the other variables that must enter into actuarial estimates, including life expectancy, wage rates, interest rates, and other factors. The sharp rise in interest rates that began in the 1970s and reached unprecedented heights in the early 1980s not only resulted in the accumulation of excess funds, as these higher rates produced their compounded effects over the years, but also greatly complicated actuarial estimates because of uncertainty about the future course of interest rates.

Full funding is a more critical need in relation to single-employer plans than in multiemployer plans, where the risks are spread over a large number of companies, or in nationwide plans, such as those in France and Sweden. At one end of the spectrum are countries like the United States and Canada, where full funding has been required, and at the other end is France, where employer pensions have been financed on something approaching a pay-as-you-go basis.

Let us begin with the United States. Before the enactment of the Employee Retirement Income Security Act of 1974 (ERISA), which was debated in Congress over a seven-year period, pension plans had been subject to certain standards required for tax-exempt status and to disclosure requirements under 1958 legislation, but there were many instances of inadequate funding and vesting, with the result that many workers did not receive benefits when they retired.

The new law included requirements relating to vesting, participation and coverage, funding, guarantee of benefits, joint and survivors' options, reporting requirements, rights of participants and beneficiaries to intervene in disputes over the legality of plans or the rights of beneficiaries, and it also covered certain other matters.

Other provisions relating to funding included the use of reasonable actuarial assumptions, a realistic method of valuing the assets of the funds, periodical actuarial reports, and standards of fiduciary behavior.

Of major importance, also, were the provisions relating to the guarantee of benefits. The law created the Pension Benefit Guarantee Corporation (PBGC) in the Department of Labor and required that all plans must purchase insurance from PBGC, which guarantees the payment of vested benefit rights.

In the first half of the 1980s, employers found their pension plans accumulating excess funds (beyond those required for adequate advance funding), as a result of high interest rates and rising stock market values. The excess funds proved to be very tempting. Companies began to attempt to capture these excess funds to finance take-overs, ward off take-overs, invest the funds in capital expansion, or serve other corporate purposes. ERISA does not permit the shifting of funds out of pension plans, but a company can accomplish this by terminating its pension plan, paying off vested benefit rights and retirement benefits in force (usually by purchasing annuities for the affected employees and retirees), and then using the remaining excess funds for the desired purposes.[4]

The growth of excess funds has also facilitated a movement to reduce contributions to pension funds. This movement has involved about three out of five major industrial companies, including such giants as American Telephone and Telegraph Company and International Business Machines Corporation (Smith, 1984).

Some of the companies that have terminated their pension plans are shifting to deferred profit-sharing or savings plans, in which contributions are defined and their amounts can be kept to a predetermined percentage of payroll.

On the other hand, some funds have been terminated in recent years to help financially troubled companies avoid bankruptcy. Some of these cases have concerned large companies with very substantial underfunding and a resulting strain on the resources of PBGC. Bills have been introduced in Congress to raise the agency's insurance premiums, and at least one of these bills provides that a company cannot terminate a pension plan unless it is in financial distress (Greenhouse, 1985).

The phenomenon of excess pension funds has also appeared in Britain in recent years. The response of the tax authorities has been to refuse permission to shift these funds back to the company, although this has been allowed in a few instances. However, employers have been permitted to discontinue contributions to pension funds for several years, and there have also been some instances of termination of plans, though evidently not on the scale experienced in the United States (*The Economist*, 1985, September 28).

British funding requirements, however, have differed substantially from those in this country. Employer plans that have contracted out of the national supplementary earnings-related scheme have not been required to be fully funded, except to cover the so-called guaranteed minimum benefit (GMB) and the rights of existing pensioners (Hemming and Harvey, 1983).

---

[4] A well-publicized case was that of Occidental Petroleum Company, which acquired Cities Service Company in 1982, terminated both its own pension plan and that of Cities Service, with combined funds of $700 million, replaced the two plans by a new one, and then applied about $400 million of its pension funds to meet part of the financing of the $4 billion acquisition. According to Porter (1985), more than 500 companies moved to terminate their pension plans between 1980 and 1985.

Another difference is that British provisions have called for indexing not only under the national scheme but also under contracted-out plans, at least so far as the GMB is concerned. Pension recipients have received annual increases based on either the rise in prices or in average wages, depending on which was more favorable to pensioners. In addition, as we saw in Chapter 4, the band of earnings on which supplementary pensions have been based has been adjusted upward each year in line with earnings. In contracted-out schemes, also, earnings have been revalued each year in line with the national scheme.

In West Germany, as in the United States, legislation regulating pensions was adopted in 1974, but funding requirements have been quite different from those in this country. For one thing, book reserve financing has been widely used in West Germany. This is a practice under which the firm establishes a book reserve to record amounts of contributions to pensions, but may actually use the funds for corporate investment. The practice started after World War II as a means of accumulating badly needed capital for rebuilding. The employer has had to provide a legal guarantee to employees for defined pension benefits. Moreover, pension liabilities have had to be reinsured through an insurance contract.

According to Heubeck (1984), advance full funding has been the practice followed in West Germany (even though funds have actually been maintained in the form of book reserves in many cases), and a large capital reserve has been built up.

Before the enactment of the 1974 legislation, most employees who left their jobs before retirement age lost their benefits. In other words, the legal guarantee to provide benefits applied only to those who stayed with the firm until retirement age (Menzies, 1974a). Under the 1974 law, employers have been required to preserve a terminating employee's pension benefit, even though he or she left before retirement age, so long as the employee had met the vesting requirements. The law has also provided that pensions be guaranteed against loss in the event that the company went bankrupt.

The German law has had a provision relating to indexing of outstanding pensions, but it has left a good deal to the discretion of the employer. It has provided that "at three-year intervals, an employer shall examine the possibility of adjusting regular benefits . . . and shall reach his decision on the basis of equity; the decision shall more particularly take account of pensioners' interests and the employer's economic situation" (ILO, 1974 – Ger. Fed. Rep. 9).

In view of the ambiguity of this provision, it is not surprising that it led to controversy and court cases. Implementation was delayed until 1978, by which time court guidelines called for increases of 50 percent of the increase in the consumer price index (U.S. President's Commission . . . , 1980).

However, one of the effects of the 1974 legislation was to lead to an increase in the number of employer plans. Unions, which had previously placed greater emphasis on increases in social security benefits, began to seek expansion of employer pensions, now that workers' pension rights had been made more secure.

In Switzerland, funding was made compulsory under the law of 1982, in connection with the financing of retirement pensions. However, there was a requirement that survivors' benefits and invalidity benefits that had been received for more than three years would be compulsorily adjusted to increases in the cost of living, and that these adjustments would be financed on a pay-as-you-go basis. Any cost-of-living adjustments in retirement pensions, on the other hand, would be on an ad hoc basis.

Other features

Vesting and portability

One of the most serious deficiencies of employer pension schemes has been the absence of adequate vesting provisions – that is, the right of the employee to retain prospective pension benefits from accumulated employer contributions even if he or she leaves the firm before retirement age. Contributions of employees themselves are not usually an issue because they are generally refundable, if an employee leaves the firm, either in the form of a lump sum or of a deferred annuity.

However, most of the countries that we have been considering now have vesting requirements, under special pension legislation, under mandatory pension systems, or under nationwide collectively bargained schemes. In some cases, vesting is immediate when an employee takes a job, whereas more commonly vesting is required after an employee has reached a certain age and/or has been a member of the pension plan for a specified number of years.

The American vesting requirements have provided for several options, one of which called for 100 percent vesting after ten years of service, and the other two called for gradual vesting leading to 100 percent vesting after 15 years of service. Under revised legislation adopted in 1984, all service performed after age 18 had to be counted when calculating the vested portion of a worker's benefit, and employees aged 21 or more, with one year of service, instead of those aged 25 or more, had to be included in the pension plan. Vested pension rights of job changers could be transferred if both employers agreed, but because plans differed substantially, agreement to permit transfer has been uncommon. However, workers covered by multiemployer plans have been able to transfer their rights freely from one employer to another.

British provisions for vesting and portability have been relatively complex.

Membership in an employer pension plan has been required after a waiting period (usually from one to five years) has been served. Pension rights have been vested for workers who have had five years of employment under the pension plan and were over age 26. Once an employee had met these requirements, refunds of an employee's own contributions were not permitted. If an employee who had met the vesting requirements left a job, the employer had four options, ranging from transferring the pension rights to another contracted-out scheme (with the employee's consent) to retaining responsibility for the GMB under several provisions relating to indexing.

Critics have complained that although this set of provisions indexed the GMB of a worker who changed jobs, it did not protect the remainder of a more generous pension from the impact of inflation, especially if a substantial number of years intervened between leaving a job and retirement.[5]

Closely related to the issue of vesting is that of portability – that is, the right of the employee who changes jobs to have his or her accumulated vested pension funds transferred to the new employer. In general, portability has been less likely to be legally required than vesting, although it has tended to be a feature of multiemployer plans, has been required under mandatory pension systems, and has been available with some limitations in the French and Swedish schemes.

Under the mandatory system in Finland, in which, as we have seen, all employees have had to be included in the required employer pension schemes, except for those employed less than one month, pension rights have been fully vested from entry into the scheme and complete portability is required by law.

In France, employees have not been eligible for employer pension coverage until age 21, but from that point on, pension rights have been fully vested. Transferability has also been provided in the case of an employee moving from one plan to another within the plans affiliated with ARRCO or with AGIRC, but there has been no coordination between the two schemes.

The Swedish situation has been similar, providing for portability within the scheme for salaried workers and that for blue-collar workers, but not between the two schemes.

In both West Germany and the United States, vesting requirements were included in the laws enacted in 1974 and were fairly similar in the two countries, but portability rights were not granted in West Germany and were very limited in the United States. In West Germany, accumulated pension assets have been vested for an employee who is aged 35 or more and has been a member of a plan for a specified period. In practice, however, there is very little labor mobility after age 35.

---

[5] This problem was emphasized by several British officials whom I interviewed in London in October 1983.

Early retirement provisions

The critical question to ask about the role of employer pensions in relation to early retirement is whether they have led in the movement for early retirement or have tended to follow changes in social security provisions. The answer is that they have led in some countries and followed in others, depending in large part on labor market developments and on the response of social security policies to those developments.

Countries in which employer pensions have led, or facilitated early retirement when social security policies did not, include Australia, the Netherlands, Sweden (for a time), and the United States (also for a time). We have earlier discussed the situation in Australia. In the Netherlands, also, the normal retirement age of 65 for men has long prevailed and has not been lowered under the labor market pressures of the 1970s. And yet, sizable proportions of men have retired before age 65, in many cases under the early retirement provisions of employer pension plans. Early retirement benefit schemes (known as VUT) were established under collective agreements in the early 1970s, for hourly and salaried employees. A worker could retire voluntarily, usually from the age of 62, and would receive a special early retirement benefit that would be paid until age 65 (*S&LB*, 1983 [1]: 117–18).[6] Clearly, also, the liberal Dutch social security invalidity benefit program has been a significant factor in inducing early retirement, as we saw in Chapter 6.

Special early retirement benefit provisions under collectively bargained employer pension plans were also adopted in the United States, but considerably earlier than in the Netherlands, and to some extent before the adoption of the provisions for early retirement at ages 62 to 64 under social security in the spring of 1961. They were a response of some of the large unions – particularly the Autoworkers and the Steelworkers – to the unemployment problem that developed in the 1957–8 recession and continued on into the early 1960s. There was no parallel rise in unemployment in Western Europe at the time, and the American situation involved a decided lag in blue-collar employment – a phenomenon that was not to appear in Western Europe until the 1970s.

Employer pension plans in both the United States and Western Europe frequently have had provisions for early retirement, but formerly called for actuarially reduced benefits. A major change in this respect occurred in the United States, not only in the late 1950s, but even more decisively as the economy moved into the less favorable conditions of the 1970s. A study by the Bankers Trust Company in 1975 showed not only a pronounced trend toward more liberal early retirement provisions (in 271 plans covering ap-

---

[6] It was reported in 1983 that about half of the workers in the construction industry and in the metal industries who were eligible for VUT benefits had elected to receive them.

proximately 8.4 million employees), as compared with an earlier 1970 study, but also a trend toward substantially higher early retirement benefits. Only 10 percent of the plans provided merely the actuarial equivalent – a sharp decline from 49 percent in the prior study. The majority of plans in 1975 paid a benefit greater than the actuarial equivalent but less than the full accrued pension (on the basis of years of service). However, there were also many plans that paid early retirees the full accrued pension with a 30-years-of-service requirement (Kleiler, 1978, 57–8). A 1983 study of employer benefits in medium and large firms showed that these trends had continued. Moreover, a conspicuous phenomenon of the recession of the early 1980s was a move by a number of large firms facing layoffs to "buy out" older workers through exceedingly generous early retirement provisions.

It will be recalled that the normal retirement age under social security in Sweden was 67, until it was lowered to 65, under 1975 legislation. Before that, the normal retirement age under the two large employer pension plans was 65, and a full retirement pension was paid under these plans for two years until social security benefits became available at 67, when the employer pensions were reduced. Once the normal retirement age of 65 became effective under the national scheme, however, the employer plans were revised accordingly. There has been a provision for early retirement with a reduced pension from age 55 on under the ITP plan, covering salaried workers, but there has been no provision for early retirement in the STP plan, covering blue-collar workers (U.S. President's Commission . . . , 1980).

In France, the normal retirement age under employer pensions was 65 until 1983, when all the complementary schemes based on collective agreements lowered the normal retirement age to 60 to bring them into line with the national provisions approved in 1982, which introduced full-career pensions at age 60 for all workers with 37.5 years of insurance (*S&LB*, 1983 [2]: 267–8).

In West Germany, the normal retirement age has been 65 in most pension plans, as in the social security program, although in some cases it has been 60 for executives and for persons in special trades, but when the provisions for more flexible early retirement under social security were adopted in 1973, there was a tendency for employer pensions to be revised to permit early retirement on a reduced benefit if they had not had such provisions previously (Horlick and Skolnik, 1979). Moreover, in West Germany, as in the Netherlands, the relatively liberal policies in awarding invalidity benefits have facilitated early retirement in a good many cases (Menzies, 1974a).

In Switzerland and the United Kingdom, the normal retirement age in employer pension plans has tended to be the same as under social security (differing for men and women). Provisions for early retirement have not been very common and have tended to call for reduced pensions where they did exist. The situation in Canada was similar until recently, but early retirement has become possible under redundancy provisions in certain industries, and federal provisions for both early and delayed retirement were adopted in 1986, as we noted in Chapter 5.

Equal treatment

We have encountered the issue of equal treatment of women in our discussion of eligibility for pension plans, noting that some countries have laws requiring women to be included in pension plans under the same conditions as men. However, another type of alleged discrimination against women has been a controversial issue in the United States. This was a tendency under some pension plans to provide for smaller pensions for female workers than for male workers, on the ground that the average life expectancy of women was longer and therefore pensions would be paid over a longer period. The controversy finally reached the United States Supreme Court, which declared, in a five to four decision on July 6, 1983, that employers who offer retirement annuity plans that pay smaller monthly benefits to women than to similarly situated men violate the ban against sex discrimination in employment in Title VII of the Civil Rights Act of 1964 (American Council on Life Insurance, 1984).

More recently, on May 13, 1986, a directive of the European Communities called for elimination of all discrimination based on sex in occupational pension schemes, with certain exceptions, by January 1, 1993 (S&LB, 1987 [1]: 165–6).

Conclusions

In many respects, employer pension plans work best in countries with nearly universal coverage, either under mandatory provisions or under nationwide collective-bargaining agreements. And yet, for other countries, the case for adopting legislation that would make employer pensions mandatory is not entirely clear. Such a requirement would be a burden on small firms and could well have an adverse effect on employment opportunities of women, minority groups, and low-paid workers generally. Special provisions calling for some means of pooling the risks, as in France and Switzerland, would be desirable.

Another serious problem that has arisen in the United States, Britain, and possibly in some other countries, is the attempt of employers to capture excess pension funds by terminating pension plans. Clearly legislation in the United States needs to be tightened – not so clearly in Britain – to impose restrictions on the right to terminate plans. Provisions that would require representation of both employers and employees on bodies administering plans would serve as something of a safeguard, because companies would usually not be free to move toward terminating their plans without encountering serious opposition from employee representatives. In Britain, one of the requirements for contracting out of the State Earnings-Related Pension Scheme (SERPS) is that both employers and employees must agree to the move. In the United States, employer and employee representation exists in multiemployer plans and in some other collectively bargained plans, but the situation contrasts sharply with that in many Western European countries, such as Belgium, France, the Netherlands, and the Scandinavian countries, in which agreement of the so-called social partners is invariably sought before legislation affecting their interests is considered.

Some critics (e.g., Munnell, 1982) question the tax exemption of contributions to pension plans, in view of the tendency for pension plan coverage to vary positively with employees' earnings. The practice of tax exemption is, however, so widely accepted that it is difficult to imagine its termination. Moves toward mandatory coverage, or at least toward broader coverage, seem more likely, especially in a country like the Netherlands, where plans for mandatory coverage have long since been developed.

The issue of discrimination against women is likely to be at least as prominent in the future as it has been in the recent past because issues of equal treatment go far beyond eligibility to be included in pension plans and touch on such matters as the rights of a divorced woman and equality of treatment for the many women in part-time jobs.

We can expect somewhat slower growth of membership in pension plans in most countries in the coming years, however, because of the shift of employment to the trade and service industries, where coverage is less common. But this very trend may lead to increased controversy over the unevenness of coverage.

CHAPTER 9

The economic impacts of pension programs

The income status of the aged

There is little question that the incidence of poverty among the aged has declined in most industrial countries during the postwar period, at least if poverty is defined as insufficient income for a subsistence level of living – sometimes referred to as "absolute poverty." There is also some evidence of a decline in relative poverty – for example, the relative proportion of the aged with incomes below, say, 50 percent of average earnings.

The primary reason for the decline in poverty among the aged has been the expansion and liberalization of income maintenance programs for the elderly, discussed in earlier chapters. Also of substantial importance has been the provision of free or heavily subsidized medical care and, in some countries, housing subsidies. On the other hand, the sharp decline in the labor force participation of elderly men has acted as a countervailing force because, on the average, income from employment tends to exceed retirement income. Thus we may view the changing income status of the aged as the net result of two conflicting forces: improved retirement income versus reduced employment income. We must also keep in mind the fact that improved retirement income has enabled many older people to live independently, whereas in former times substantial numbers of aged people, particularly women, lived with relatives in a state of dependency. The increase in the proportion living independently has tended to retard the increase in measured income.

United States

Once again, we begin with U.S. data, because they are more extensive than those of most other countries. In 1959, 35 percent of all persons aged 65 and older, compared with 22 percent of the population as a whole, had incomes below the official poverty threshold, as defined by the U.S. Social Security Administration.[1] Between 1959 and about 1970, the percentage of the U.S.

[1] In 1965, the U.S. Social Security Administration developed two criteria of poverty that became the officially approved measures used by federal government agencies in estimating the extent of poverty. The lower of the two measures, adopted as the poverty line or poverty threshold,

population in poverty declined substantially, but then it leveled off and, under conditions of rising unemployment, increased from 1979 to 1983. The percentage of the aged population behaved similarly, but was not especially affected by the rising unemployment after 1979 and actually fell slightly below the percentage in poverty of the population as a whole for the first time in 1983 (14.1 percent vs. 15.2 percent). A special study analyzing changes in income from 1980 to 1984 (using econometric techniques to project changes from 1983 to 1984) showed that elderly Americans fared better during this period than others because lower rates of inflation and income tax reductions more than offset the negative effects of greater unemployment and cuts in federal programs. Moreover, two of the most important sources of income to the elderly, social security and asset incomes, rose at a faster pace than other sources (Moon, 1986). And, as Moynihan (1986) has emphasized, the growth in the proportion of female-headed families, in which the percentage in poverty is high, was a factor contributing to increased inequality of income in the general population – a problem that will be discussed extensively in Chapter 13.

Within the aged population, however, there are wide variations in the incidence of poverty. Families headed by a person aged 65 or older (chiefly elderly couples) have been less likely to be poor than unrelated elderly individuals, and elderly unrelated women tend to be more seriously affected by poverty than either couples or unrelated men.

These variations are found not only in the United States but also in almost all other countries for which I have found relevant data. Elderly married men are more likely to be employed than elderly unmarried men, partly because they tend to be somewhat younger. Because of the longer life expectancy of women, there are relatively more of the very old than among unrelated men, and the very old women include many whose husbands died before becoming fully eligible for social security benefits or with access to benefits based on the much lower earnings that prevailed several decades ago.

Not surprisingly, elderly blacks and those of Spanish origin in the United States were considerably more likely to be poor than elderly whites. In 1983, 36 percent of black persons aged 65 and older were in poverty, whereas among elderly Hispanics, 23 percent were poor. Among aged whites, the proportion who were poor had fallen to 12 percent by 1983.

was based on a Department of Agriculture economy food plan for emergency use or when funds were low (Orshansky, 1966). On the basis of data indicating that low-income families spent about one-third of their incomes on food, the poverty line was set at three times the cost of the emergency food budget. The "nearpoor" level was based on a food plan that cost about one-third more than the emergency budget. In 1984, the poverty line (which is indexed to the consumer price index) for a two-person family with head aged 65 and over was $6,282 a year, whereas for a four-person family it was $10,609 a year (SBB: Annual Statistical Supplement, 1984–85, 70).

Another indication of the decline in poverty among the aged was a very substantial reduction over the years in the percentage receiving public assistance. In 1940, when social security payments had barely begun, 22 percent of the population aged 65 and older received public assistance, and this percentage changed very little between 1940 and 1950. From that point on, the proportion receiving assistance payments tended, on the whole, to decline, and by 1982 was only 7.5 percent (Reno and Grad, 1985, table 12).

Thus far, we have been considering absolute poverty, but what about the relative income status of the aged? In 1982, the median income of aged couples was 62 percent of that of nonaged families, compared with 54 percent in 1950; however, as a number of recent studies have indicated, when adjustments are made for the smaller average size of aged families and, in some of these studies, for the lower taxes paid by the aged, the median income of the aged was not much below that of the nonaged or, in some studies, was actually higher.[2] On the other hand, the median income of aged unrelated individuals was still far below that of nonaged individuals (Grad, 1984).

As Table 9.1 indicates, only 23 percent of all aged income units (couples with at least one member aged 65 or more and nonmarried persons aged 65 or more) had any income from earnings in 1980, but the likelihood of having earnings was directly related to income level; thus those with high incomes were much more likely to have earnings. Moreover, the proportions with income from a number of other sources varied directly with income level. The data on the share of income received from various sources indicate that social security was of critical importance for the two lowest income groups, and these two groups accounted for 66 percent of all aged income units. Only in the lowest income group was the share received from public assistance significant.

It is important to note, however, that these data relate to the entire population aged 65 and older. Surveys of new beneficiaries indicate that they are considerably more likely to have income from employer pensions than the aged population as a whole.

How important is asset income as a source of income of new beneficiaries? When I first began to study the income status of the elderly in the late 1950s, amounts of savings and other liquid assets tended to be very small in most

---

[2] As a number of recent studies have indicated, these comparisons are somewhat misleading, especially for elderly couples, whose average income is being compared with that of nonaged families, with their somewhat larger average family size. On the other hand, as Aaron (1982) has pointed out, because of economies of scale in the operation of houses, a two-person family needs more income per capita than a larger family for a given level of living. The roles of income in kind and home ownership also need to be considered. A study by Danziger et al. (1982) concluded that income comparisons between the aged and nonaged were very sensitive to the choice of income unit, and per capita household income of the aged after taxes was 92 percent of that of the nonaged.

Table 9.1. *Importance of income sources for aged income units, by total money income, United States, 1980*

	All	Less than $5,000	$5,000–$9,999	$10,000–$19,999	$20,000 or more
Percentage with income from:					
Earnings	23%	6%	19%	36%	58%
Retirement					
Pensions[a]	93	88	98	96	91
Social security	90	87	94	92	84
Government-employee	12	3	10	20	28
Private	22	4	24	39	36
Asset income	66	38	72	89	97
Public assistance	10	24	5	1	0
Share of aggregate income from:					
Earnings	19	2	8	17	33
Retirement					
Pensions	55	81	75	59	32
Social security	40	79	63	39	16
Government-employee	7	1	4	9	9
Private	7	1	6	10	6
Asset income	22	4	14	21	34
Public assistance	1	10	1	0	0

[a] Amounts of social security and railroad retirement are excluded from the separate items listed below for persons receiving both sources. Similarly, amounts of government-employee pensions and private pensions are excluded from items listed below for persons receiving both sources. All pension income is included in the retirement pensions category.
Source: Upp (1983, table 1).

cases, although a large proportion of the elderly, particularly among the married couples, owned their homes free and clear. Moreover, assets were highly correlated with income. By 1982, the proportion of new beneficiaries with some financial assets was high, but assets continued to be highly correlated with income, and median amounts of assets, although considerably higher than they would have been several decades ago, were not large enough to be a major source of income or a source of substantial dissaving (Sherman, 1985).

International comparisons

International comparisons of the income status of the aged or of the population as a whole tend to be tricky. If we are concerned with the incidence of poverty among the aged, we confront the fact that official measures of poverty thresholds vary from country to country and do not exist in many countries (especially where public assistance benefits are still to some extent a local matter). Moreover, comparisons of money income fail to reveal the differing significance of income in kind from country to country, particularly in the form of free or subsidized medical care and housing (or of food stamps in the United States).

Nevertheless, there have been a number of useful studies of comparative poverty, including comparative poverty among the aged, and I shall emphasize particularly those that have attempted to base estimates of the incidence of poverty on reasonably uniform standards (such as the percentage of income units with incomes below a certain percentage of average earnings in manufacturing).

Before reporting the results of these studies, however, it is useful to point out that social security payments are only one among many factors affecting differences from country to country in the income status of the aged. The age and sex structure of the elderly population, the percentage of farmers and of self-employed nonagricultural workers, and the relative inequality of income in the population as a whole have all been found to play a role in explaining differences in the extent of poverty among the aged.

Studies of income inequality in the 1970s have shown that inequality was less marked in Denmark, Sweden, Ireland, and the United Kingdom than elsewhere, and it was not quite as unequal in West Germany as in France, Spain, and the United States (ILO, 1984c, table A–2). It has also been found that transfer payments tend to play a more important role than taxes in reducing income inequality, because transfer payments account for a large proportion of the income of the poor, whereas the progressive impact of income taxes tends to be offset by the regressive impact of sales taxes, value added taxes, and social security taxes (see, e.g., Saunders and Klau, 1985, chapter 7).

The factors that tend to perpetuate inequality of income are much the same as those that tend to perpetuate poverty, mentioned in Chapter 1, such as the growth in the relative proportion of the aged in the population, instability of employment among the unskilled and poorly educated, immigration from low-income countries, and the growth of single-parent families. On the other hand, the rapid growth of employment in professional and managerial occupations has been a factor tending to maintain the proportion of income flowing to upper-middle and, to some extent, top quintiles.

An interesting point brought out by Sinfield (1980) in his discussion of income inequality in France is that the percentage of workers who are self-employed is relatively large and there is very substantial inequality of income among them. The United Kingdom Royal Commission on the Distribution of

Income and Wealth (1977) also showed that the proportion of entrepreneurial income was relatively high in France. However, in France, as elsewhere, the percentage of self-employed farmers in the labor force has been falling quite rapidly, whereas the percentage of nonagricultural self-employed has declined much more slowly, despite the increased competition from supermarkets and other large-scale retail outlets.

Cross-national studies: One of the earliest and most comprehensive cross-national studies of the aged was that of Shanas et al. (1968) conducted by social scientists in England, Denmark, and the United States. Reflecting the sociological interests of some of these scholars, the study was concerned not only with income but also with health, living arrangements, contacts with adult children, and attitudes toward work and retirement. Our discussion will be concerned only with the income data.

As Table 9.2 shows, the incidence of poverty among the aged in 1962 was highest in the United States and lowest in Denmark, with the United Kingdom occupying an intermediate position. At the time, old-age pensions were higher in relation to average earnings in Denmark than in either the United States or the United Kingdom. More of the aged couples in Denmark and the United States received employment income than in Britain, partly because relatively more of the husbands were self-employed, and the self-employed are more likely to go on working after retirement age. On the other hand, relatively more of the British husbands were receiving employer pensions. In general, however, the patterns of distribution by sources of income were similar in the three countries.

One unusual aspect of the Danish data was the very small percentage of elderly women who were in poverty, in contrast with the situation in the United States and Britain, and also with that in other countries. Single women were eligible at the time for an income-tested old-age pension from age 62 that equaled the pension for a man from age 67, whereas widows without children in their care were eligible for such a pension from age 55, and both types of pensions were indexed for price changes.

Another highly useful study of poverty by Beckerman and colleagues (1979) developed uniform standards for the poverty threshold in each of four countries and estimated the extent of poverty in the population as a whole as well as among those receiving old-age pensions (Table 9.3). The results showed that the percentages of pension recipients who would have been poor without benefits were very high in all four countries, and the differences among them were not very pronounced. After benefits, the percentages in poverty continued to be very high in Australia but were very substantially reduced in the other countries. The high incidence of poverty after benefits in Australia was explained in large part by the relatively low level of benefits in relation to

Table 9.2. *Percentage of old people in poverty in three industrial societies, 1962 (aged 65 and older)*

	Men	Women	Couples
United States	47%	60%	30%
United Kingdom	29	50	23
Denmark	12	12	20

Note: National standards for United States and United Kingdom; British standards for Denmark.
Source: Shanas et al. (1968).

GNP per capita, as well as the large proportion of the elderly who were receiving these low benefits (as noted in Chapter 3).

Also highly illuminating were the results of the third study, shown in Table 9.4, which compares poverty in the cities of Bristol in England, Rheims in France, and Saarbrucken in West Germany. The three cities were selected because they were somewhat similar in their social and economic aspects, even though the characteristics of their populations could not precisely mirror those of the nations in which they were located as a whole. The authors determined the average income of households in which the head was under retirement age and had a full-time job, and then defined as very poor households with less than 40 percent of that income and as poor households with less than 60 percent of that income.

Among those households in which the head had retired, the percentage who were either very poor or poor was lowest in Saarbrucken and highest in Rheims, with Bristol falling in between. However, only 1 percent of these households were very poor in Bristol, compared with 5 percent in Saarbrucken and 17 percent in Rheims. The data were gathered in 1979, so that the results are the most recent of any of those yet considered, but it should be kept in mind that the French old-age pension system was very substantially liberalized under 1982 legislation, as we noted in Chapter 4, whereas no major changes were made after 1979 in either Britain or West Germany.

Some of the households – about a fifth in each city – included someone who held a paid job, and these households were less frequently in poverty. The remaining households, which consisted predominantly of retired people living alone and retired couples, depended almost entirely on retirement benefits (including employer pensions).

In Bristol, more than 90 percent of the retired persons were receiving a state retirement pension under the national insurance program. About half of the households with retired persons were also receiving employer pensions,

Table 9.3. *Percentage of old people in poverty in four developed countries, 1973 (pension recipients, before and after benefits)*

	Single	Couples	Total
Before benefits			
Australia	86.7%	72.3%	81.7%
Belgium	72.4	80.6	72.4
Great Britain	89.6	85.5	88.2
Norway	88.3	80.0	85.2
After benefits			
Australia	73.7	54.6	67.1
Belgium	22.8	35.9	27.9
Great Britain	34.8	36.3	35.3
Norway	37.1	26.0	33.0

Note: Uniform standard (poverty threshold for a couple with no children is set equal to average disposable income per capita).
Source: Beckerman (1979).

but the amounts were very small (four-fifths were less than £70 a month, or about what the average working man in the survey was earning in a week). Reliance on supplementary benefits (public assistance) was extensive, with about two-fifths of the households that included a retired person receiving them and about the same proportion receiving housing subsidies. However, the virtual absence of households that were "very poor" reflected the general availability of supplemental benefits for those in need.

In Rheims, almost all of the households with a retired person and no income from earnings were receiving social security retirement benefits, plus complementary benefits (employer pensions) in many cases. Pensions were related to earnings, and there was wide variation in the amounts received. If the households in which someone was employed are excluded, 47 percent of the households with retired persons were poor and 20 percent were very poor.

There were two schemes for retired people with little or no benefit from social insurance. The first, specifically for the retired, was a special pension – *Retraite du Fonds National de Solidarité* (FNS) – and the second was the public assistance scheme for people in need – *Aide-Sociale*. However, very few were receiving these benefits, and the amounts were very small.

The inadequacies of public assistance in France will be discussed more fully in Chapter 14, but in 1979 there were also weaknesses in the French old-age pension schemes which helped to explain the high incidence of pov-

Table 9.4. *Percentage of households with retired persons in poverty, in Bristol, Rheims, and Saarbrucken, 1979*

	Bristol	Rheims	Saarbrucken
Very poor	1%	17%	5%
Poor	26	25	11

Note: Very poor households had less than 40 percent, and poor households less than 60 percent of the average income of households in which the head was under retirement age and had a full-time job.
Source: Mitton, Willmott, and Willmott (1983).

erty in households with retired persons in Rheims and which were at least partially overcome by 1980 legislation relating to widows and by the comprehensive amendments of 1982 discussed in Chapter 4.

The low incidence of poverty in households with retired persons in Saarbrucken was largely attributable to the fact that pensions under the German social insurance scheme tended to be considerably higher than those in France or Britain. The minority with little or no social insurance pension could apply for public assistance *(Sozialhilfe)*, but very few did so. Reluctance to apply apparently played a role in explaining this residual poverty.

In a discussion of the reasons for poverty in Bristol, the authors emphasized the low level of flat-rate benefits, not only for the retired, but also for the unemployed and the disabled. Whereas national assistance had been intended as a safety net to protect the few not adequately supported by national insurance, it had become a major form of support for large numbers of people.[3]

Other studies: In addition to these cross-national studies, there have been a number of studies of poverty in individual countries, with results generally consistent with those already discussed in some cases, if allowances are made for differences in definitions of poverty and differences in populations covered. Worthy of mention are the chapters on Belgium, Italy, and West Germany in a volume on poverty in the Common Market, edited by George and Lawson (1980), some of the findings of which have already been discussed.[4]

[3] Mention should also be made of a comparative study of aged isolated women in France, Italy, and West Germany, which showed that the percentage of these women in financial difficulty was higher in France than in either Italy or West Germany (Collot and Le Bris, 1981).
[4] Other important studies that should be mentioned are those of the Australian Government Commission on Inquiry into Poverty (1975), Townsend (1979), and the United Kingdom Royal Commission on the Distribution of Income and Wealth (1977, 1978).

Belgium's move to introduce a guaranteed minimum income for the elderly, mentioned in Chapter 3, was followed in 1974 by an act establishing the "right to a subsistence minimum" for every Belgian citizen. Thus, Belgium became one of the first countries to adopt a specific provision for a guaranteed minimum income, although elsewhere, as in Britain, the public assistance system operated in effect to provide such a guarantee. However, the minimum income provided in Belgium was low: The original guarantee for the elderly, which was also used in the later more general guarantee, amounted to only 20 percent of average wages of male industrial workers for couples and 13.5 percent for single people, although this was somewhat modified by exemption of a specified amount from the means test. A study conducted in 1976 by the Center for Social Policy at the University of Antwerp showed that 38 percent of single pensioners and 36 percent of retired couples were in poverty (Berghman, 1980).

Of particular interest is the chapter on Italy, where poverty in the general population and also in the aged population continues to be severe, in spite of Italy's rapid economic growth during the 1960s and parts of the 1970s. Its earnings-related old-age pension system has provided for a relatively high replacement rate (see Table 4.1), but many Italian workers reach the age of retirement with broken earnings records and become dependent on the "social" minimum pension. As Moss and Rogers (1980, 167), authors of the chapter on Italy, point out, "neither the steady increase in GNP nor the growth in per capita income appears to have made serious inroads into the overall range of economic inequalities in Italian society." Moreover, Italy's public assistance program is very weak, as we shall find in Chapter 14.

The chapter on West Germany (Lawson, 1980) shows that the percentage of those with incomes below the meager social assistance level was greatest among the elderly and households headed by women. The latter included elderly widows, as well as single, separated, and divorced women over age 65.

Policy implications: An OECD (1976, p. 71) study of public expenditure on income maintenance programs concluded that, in general, "the relative level and changes in income maintenance expenditures do not bear much relationship to the extent or change in relative poverty." There is perhaps a bit more evidence that relative expenditures on pensions bear some relationship to the extent of poverty among the aged, although comparable data are not available for enough countries to draw firm conclusions. West Germany, for example, spent a larger proportion of GDP on pensions in 1979–80 than did either Britain or France and had relatively less poverty among the aged. Sweden was also a relatively heavy spender on pensions and had little poverty among the aged. A study conducted in 1977 indicated that pensioners formed only 4 percent of public assistance recipients (*S&LB,* 1978 [4]: 329–30).

A more interesting question is whether there is a relationship between the *structure* of old-age pensions and poverty among the aged. West Germany and Italy both have had relatively liberal earnings-related pension systems, but Italy has had much more poverty among the aged than West Germany.

One might expect that the countries that combine universal old-age pensions with earnings-related supplements would have the least poverty among the aged, and there are indications that this may be true of the Scandinavian countries.

One thing that does emerge clearly from our review of data on poverty in old age is that an effective public assistance system is usually essential to protect those who, for one reason or another, fall through the net of the regular pension system.

The savings controversy

The Feldstein finding

In 1974, an article by Martin Feldstein reported on his finding that social security reduces saving in the United States by some 30 to 50 percent (Feldstein, 1974). The article received a great deal of attention and not only generated a controversy that continues to this day, but also stimulated a great deal of research on the issues involved in the United States and in a number of other countries.

Feldstein's approach to the issue was based on the life-cycle model of saving, initially developed by Harrod (1948) and later elaborated by Ando and Modigliani (1963). According to the life-cycle hypothesis (sometimes referred to as LCH), individuals save in their working years for consumption during retirement. In other words, positive saving may be expected during working years and negative saving (or dissaving) during retirement. According to Feldstein, the model implies that social security, by providing income during retirement, reduces the amount of saving during the working years. In other words, as individuals acquire social security wealth (the present value of expected social security benefits), they will perceive less need for personal saving. In fact, if social security taxes and benefits have no net income effect, ''savings will be reduced by just enough to leave consumption during retirement unchanged.''

Feldstein's study was based (like that of Ando and Modigliani) on a time series analysis in which consumption was specified as a function of permanent income and of the stock of household wealth at the end of year t. The theory that saving was related to permanent income (or expected income based on average experience in the relatively recent past) had been developed by Friedman (1957) and was widely accepted by economists. Feldstein's innovation was to add a variable for gross social security wealth, or the present value in year t of the retirement benefits that could eventually be claimed by all those in the labor force or already retired in year t. His finding that social security substantially reduced saving implied a serious loss of saving for the economy because the social security system was on a pay-as-you-go basis and thus generated no significant saving.

Feldstein also argued that social security has a dual effect on saving. It induces retirement because of the "earnings test," which sharply limits the amount that can be earned while one is receiving social security benefits. On the other hand, individuals who plan to retire early will be inclined to save more during their working years in order to provide adequately for their needs over a longer period of retirement. These two countervailing effects make "the net impact of social security ambiguous" (Feldstein, 1974, 908).

There followed a number of studies that variously supported or contradicted Feldstein's conclusions. Then the debate entered a new phase when Leimer and Lesnoy (1980) published results indicating that Feldstein's estimates of social security wealth were incorrect. Later, in an extensive review of the results of a large number of studies, Lesnoy and Leimer (1985) reached the conclusion that if all the available empirical evidence – whether based on time series analysis, the results of household surveys, or international comparisons – is considered, the evidence is inconclusive. Similarly, a thorough review of the literature on the impact of transfer payments on the economy reached the conclusion that the estimates of the impact of social security on savings were small and often statistically insignificant (Danziger, Haveman, and Plotnick, 1981).[5]

It is not my purpose to review all of the literature on this issue, although I shall discuss briefly some of the research based on international comparisons, as well as my own search for the factors responsible for wide differences in savings rates among industrial countries. Before reaching that point, however, let us consider the empirical data on changes in income and expenditures over the life cycle, because they suggest that typically families save very little until the later stages of working life (approximately ages 45 to 64) and that at all stages of the life cycle the rate of saving varies directly with income, tending to be negative for those with very low incomes and to rise with advancing income.

The most recent consumer expenditure survey conducted by the U.S. Bu-

---

[5] Reviews of various studies of the impact of social security on saving by Juster (1981) and Munnell (1982) also reached the conclusion that the findings were inconclusive.

reau of Labor Statistics (1986) based on 1980–1 data, indicates, as have earlier surveys, the manner in which disposable income (income after direct taxes) and consumption expenditures vary over the life cycle. Disposable income rises to a peak among income units headed by a person aged 45 to 54, and then declines. Saving is negative for the youngest age group and is very modest for those aged 25 to 44; it is significant only for those in the 45 to 64 age group. Moreover, the data indicate that at all stages of the life cycle, savings tend to be negative for low-income groups and substantial only for those with incomes in the $30,000 and over range.

Typically, young couples go into debt to purchase a house and consumer durable goods, and the proportion of income units in debt rises to a peak in the 35 to 44 age bracket, after which it declines. This pattern is indicated clearly in the 1983 survey of consumer finances conducted by the Board of Governors of the Federal Reserve (*Federal Reserve Bulletin,* 1984, *70* [December]: 857–68).

The data suggest a very modest median amount of dissaving among families headed by someone aged 65 or more. However, as we have seen, assets are highly correlated with income in the population aged 65 or more, reflecting the correlation of savings with income throughout the life cycle (see Table 9.1). Those with significant amounts of assets do not need to dissave to meet living expenses, whereas those with low incomes hold very small amounts of assets and thus cannot dissave on any substantial scale.

In an extensive review of the studies of the impact of social security on saving, Cartwright (1984) goes so far as to question the validity of the life-cycle model if used as an explanation of aggregate savings. He stresses the importance of the fact that the percentage of income saved varies with income level, and that the accumulation of social security wealth could be expected to have far more effect at low income levels than at higher levels, both because the formula is tilted toward the lower earner and because higher earners will not regard social security retirement benefits as adequate. These higher earners will be inclined to seek supplementation of social security benefits through both employer pension plans and private saving.

International comparisons

Among studies involving international comparisons of saving, that of Modigliani and Sterling (1983), based on data for 21 industrial countries, is of particular interest. The authors concluded that their results provided strong support for the life-cycle hypothesis. Estimates of the impact on the savings rate of income growth, demographic factors, and the length of retirement were quite close to those suggested by the life-cycle hypothesis. On the other hand, the direct income replacement effect of social security was "harder to pin down,'' whereas the indirect effect of social security in inducing earlier retirement – that is, lengthening the span of retirement – was quite large. In fact, the weak direct and strong indirect effects tended to offset each other, with the result that the impact of social security was close to zero. Interestingly, the authors found that the low savings rate in the United States was accounted for by a below-average rate of growth of income and a relatively high dependency ratio (the proportion of children in the population). On the other hand, the very high rate of saving in Japan was explained largely by its high rate of economic growth.

This study, like a number of others based on comparative international data, was designed to test the life-cycle hypothesis and the impact of social security on saving. Another way of going about the problem would be to seek to determine what factors are associated with differences in savings rates among industrial countries, without basing the analysis on any particular theory. In such an attempt, I found a significant inverse relationship between direct taxes as a percentage of income and savings rates. This is scarcely surprising. In the three Scandinavian countries for which I could obtain data, for example, savings rates (averaged over the 1971 to 1980 period) were relatively low, while direct taxes represented a comparatively high percentage of income. Moreover, income taxes in the Scandinavian countries tend to be quite progressive, thus extracting large amounts from the income groups that are most likely to save.

I also found a positive relationship between the percentage of the labor force who were self-employed and the savings rate – a result that could be expected in view of the fact that savings rates of the self-employed tend to be comparatively high, reflecting the uncertainty of their incomes and probably, also, in some cases, a desire to accumulate capital to invest in their enterprises. The long-run decline in the percentage of self-employed in the labor force could be one of the factors responsible for the much-studied failure of the savings rate to rise with the increase in real income in many industrial countries.

My results confirmed those of others who have found a significant relationship between social security and early retirement, using social security expenditures as a percentage of GDP as the measure of the impact of social security and the percentage of men aged 55 or more who were out of the labor force as the measure of early retirement. As we found in Chapter 5, the liberalization of both social security benefits and provisions for early retirement has been accompanied by a sharp drop in the labor force participation of older men. And yet, I am skeptical of treating this as a simple income-conditioned choice between work and leisure, as explained in Chapter 2.

As we have seen also, however, there is a growing group of men (and women) who welcome early retirement, not because they have become involuntarily unemployed or encountered reduced earning capacity but because they can look forward to an adequate retirement income consisting of an employer pension on top of social security. Moreover, it is only among this latter group that it seems reasonable to assume that plans for early retirement may induce higher saving during working life (and especially during the later years of working life when most saving occurs). Thus, I am skeptical of the general hypothesis, stressed by Feldstein and others, that we can expect higher savings rates as the age of retirement declines. Moreover, I have not found a positive relationship between the proportion of men aged 55 or more who are out of the labor force and the rate of saving.

Differences in the age structure of the population from country to country might be expected to affect savings rates. For example, a large proportion of persons aged 65 and older in the population might be expected to be associated with lower savings rates, and this association may be a factor in the low savings rate of a country like Sweden, although I have not found a significant negative relationship across countries between the percentage of elderly persons in the population and savings rates. Moreover, a study of savings in Sweden (Bentzel and Berg, 1983) showed not only a positive relationship between wealth and age up to the retirement age, but also relatively large holdings of net wealth among pensioners. As in the United States, savings rates were negative in the youthful population (in this case, among those under age 31) and tended to become positive and to increase with advancing age. The authors characterized as particularly interesting their finding that pensioners tended to accumulate substantial savings. A possible explanation, they noted, was the growth of both public and private pension plans in Sweden and the significant redistribution of income in favor of pensioners since 1975.

Even though there may be no significant relationship across countries between the age structure of the population and the savings rate, this does not mean that changes in the age structure may not have a significant influence on savings rates in some instances. There is little question, for example, that the pronounced increase in the proportion of income units headed by persons aged 25 to 40 in the United States in recent years has had a negative effect on overall personal savings, as these members of the baby boom generation went into debt to acquire homes and consumer durables (see *Federal Reserve Bulletin*, 1980, *66* [August]: 613–26).

The relatively small proportion of elderly persons in Japan's population probably plays a role in explaining Japan's exceptionally high rate of savings, but clearly a number of other factors, particularly the high rate of economic growth, are important. A recent study by Shinohara (1983) identified a number of others, including (1) the comparatively high proportion of self-employed workers in Japan, (2) the low rate of spending on social security benefits, (3) the relatively high percentage of income received in the form of bonuses in Japan, along with a tendency for bonus amounts to increase with advancing age, (4) the fact that installment credit has only recently become widely available, and (5) the influence of Confucianism, particularly in rural areas.

Employer pensions and saving

The issue of the impact of employer pensions on savings rates is less controversial than the question of the impact of social security because pension plans are generally funded, although not always fully, and thus generate substantial savings. Even if individuals covered by employer pension plans were to reduce their personal saving by the full amount of pension plan contributions, this would not necessarily reduce total saving greatly. In fact, the savings generated by employer pensions are sometimes emphasized as an argument for shifting some of the responsibility for providing retirement income from social security to employer pensions. Moreover, in France, where employer pensions are virtually on a pay-as-you-go basis, the argument is sometimes advanced that they should be funded in order to provide savings.

In a most useful summary of the data relating to the impact of private pensions and social security on saving, Munnell (1982) pointed out that, according to the life-cycle model, in an ideal world pension plans would have no effect on saving because individuals would reduce their saving by precisely the amount of pension plan contributions. However, in the real world, this result may not be observed because of the impact of favorable tax treatment of pensions, uncertainty about the amount of an individual's future pension benefits, induced retirement, and other complications. She concluded that from a theoretical point of view the net effect of private pensions on aggregate saving was indeterminate.

Contradicting the results of several early studies by Cagan (1965) and Katona (1964) indicating that persons covered by private pensions tended to save more than those who were not covered, Munnell's review of several more recent empirical studies suggests that workers reduce their own saving by about 65 percent of every dollar of saving through pension plans, resulting in a net increase in aggregate saving of about 35 cents. However, a British study by Hemming and Harvey (1983) concluded that nonpension retirement saving was unaffected by pension expectations, although there were tentative indications of some reduction of life insurance contributions. These authors stressed the point that pension contributions provided a poor guide to pensions ultimately payable, even though they influenced the expectations of many individuals.

Bonus or tax exemption plans for savings

In a move to stimulate savings, a number of countries have adopted bonus or tax exemption plans for savings. One of the earliest of these was inaugurated in West Germany not long after the war, but it differed markedly from those of several other countries in that it applied only to lower- and lower-middle income groups and provided in considerable part for bonuses rather than for tax exemptions.

The plan in West Germany was originally designed to promote the reconstruction of the economy, with particular reference to private housing. Later the emphasis shifted to encouragement of private savings as an end in itself. Under a three-pillar theory, much like that in Switzerland, personal savings of workers would supplement social security and employer pensions. However, it was found that low-income families did not save, and government policy shifted to stimulating the savings of those who otherwise would be dependent solely on social security in old age.

There has been a plan both for the general public and for savings through employers. In the plan for the general public, individuals have opened their own savings accounts, and the federal government has paid them an annual bonus on savings held for seven years. However, there has been a maximum deposit eligible for a bonus, and those with annual taxable income above a certain level were not eligible for the plan. In the corresponding plan under which employers could make nontaxable deposits on behalf of employees, there was also a limitation to workers with incomes below a certain level. The number of participants in these plans rose from 50,000 in 1961 to 16 million in 1975, the peak year. There was also a plan providing tax incentives for higher income savers (*SSB*, 1981, *44* [October]: 39–40).

The provision for individual retirement accounts (IRAs) in the United States permits tax deferral on limited amounts of savings and on the income from those savings. Originally adopted in 1974, the program was greatly liberalized under the Reagan administration's tax reduction program in 1981, which provided for increases in tax deferral amounts and for eligibility of workers already covered by employer pension plans, whereas originally only those not so covered were eligible.[6]

The result of the 1981 amendments was a large increase in the number of persons establishing IRAs – to 12 million out of 95 million federal taxpayers on 1982 income – and in total amounts of IRA payments – to $28.4 billion, compared with $4.7 billion on 1981 income tax returns. The extremely high

---

[6] Mention should also be made of the Keogh tax exempt savings provisions for the self-employed, which have been liberalized several times and attract substantial savings.

interest rates prevailing at the time made IRA accounts particularly attractive, but expansion has continued in subsequent years. However, the percentage of taxpayers having IRA accounts has varied directly with income. More recently, the Tax Reform Act of 1986 removed those who were covered by employer pension plans from eligibility.

The experience has been somewhat similar in Canada, where a plan providing for tax deferral of limited amounts of savings has been in effect since 1962.

Clearly, the German approach has been much more effective in creating an incentive for saving by low earners. Under a progressive income tax system, low earners are liable for very limited income taxes, and thus very little can be gained through tax deferral, whereas a bonus for saving could be expected to have a more positive effect. The limitation of eligibility to relatively low earners is also clearly designed to encourage saving by those whose savings tend to be very small. The approach in the United States and Canada, on the other hand, provides tax advantages to those who would probably save substantially in any case.

Whether special measures are needed to induce saving is a matter of debate among economists. The Keynesian view, born of the Great Depression, was that underconsumption, not undersaving, was the problem. Economic policy should be directed toward measures that would stimulate consumption, which would stimulate investment and more rapid economic growth, which in turn would encourage saving. This view has been disputed in the past several decades, but not all economists agree that there is a deficiency of saving, even in the United States, where the personal saving rate is relatively low. As Eisner (1981) has argued, business investment as a proportion of GNP has remained quite high, except in recessions, and, moreover, the national income and product accounts do not reflect all of the capital accumulation that occurs outside of the private business sector.

It must also be kept in mind that income transfers from higher to lower income groups through social security programs will tend to increase aggregate consumption because lower income groups are likely to spend a large fraction of increments of income. Furthermore, the initial effect on consumption may be augmented by a secondary effect if there is a further increase through the multiplier (cf. M. S. Gordon, 1963a). However, these effects are much more welcome when the economic position is unfavorable than when the economy is at full employment, and additional consumption is likely to stimulate inflation.

CHAPTER 10

Health benefits

Unlike most of the items in the cost of living, the costs of illness vary greatly from family to family and from person to person. In any given month or year, serious and extremely costly illnesses strike only a relatively small proportion of the population, but their costs can be catastrophic, especially in this era of astronomical hospital charges. Even the less severe illnesses that result in a few days' loss of work are unevenly distributed. Hence the pooling of risks through insurance is particularly appropriate in meeting the costs of illness, and, as we have noted in Chapter 3, the mutual aid funds and friendly societies that were formed in the nineteenth century were especially concerned with meeting the costs of short-term sickness. They tended to provide modest cash benefits for loss of work and a portion of medical expenses.

Not only does the incidence of illness vary among persons generally, but also certain groups in the population are particularly prone to experience illness, as the data in Table 10.1 show. Women are more likely to have restricted-activity days than men (partly due to pregnancy and childbirth), blacks than whites (partly, at least, because they are more likely to be employed in heavy labor), and persons aged 65 and older than those under age 65 by a very large margin. Particularly striking, also, is the pronounced inverse relationship to income. The high average days of illness in the two lower income groups reflect to some extent the interdependence of ill health and low earnings, and also the large proportion of elderly people in the low-income population. Average days of work lost tend to be considerably lower than restricted-activity days, averaging 4.6 for men and 5.3 for women in 1981.

As we turn to health benefits, we need to recognize that they involve complexities not found in other social security programs, because they provide both cash benefits and services. Relations with those who provide the services – doctors, dentists, nurses, hospitals, and increasingly the numerous technicians and assistants who perform tests and handle x-rays – bring a type of controversy that does not exist in the provision of cash benefits.

Table 10.1. *Average number of restricted-activity days per year per person, by sex, race, age, and family income, 1981*

Sex, race, and age					
Male	Female	White	Black and other	Under age 65	Age 65 and over
17.3	20.7	18.8	21.7	16.5	39.9

Family income			
Under $5,000	$5,000–9,999	$10,000–14,999	$15,000 and over
35.9	28.2	18.4	14.1

Source: Statistical Abstract of the United States, 1984 (p. 121).

Early legislation

The German act of 1883

The pioneering law in the health insurance field was enacted in Germany in 1883. Its major features were strongly influenced by the miners' relief funds, mentioned in Chapter 7, and by the many existing local and voluntary institutions that had been providing sickness and accident protection for workers.

The original sickness insurance law, as it was called, covered only specified occupations: workers employed in the extractive industries, transportation, construction, manufacturing, mechanical trades, and establishments using power machinery. Coverage was later extended to other groups of workers, but generally white-collar workers were covered on a compulsory basis only if their earnings were less than 2,000 marks a year (about $500). This exclusion of higher-income workers was followed in other countries, at least in part because physicians wanted to continue to serve higher-income families on a regular private practice basis. To qualify for benefits, an individual must have been insured for three months out of the last six.

The German program was highly decentralized. The principal insurance organizations were the "local sickness funds," which were established for members of occupations or groups of occupations in local areas. Workers and their employers made contributions, in the ratio of two to one, to these local funds, which were administered by directors, two-thirds of whom were elected by the workers and one-third by the employers. Certain administrative costs were met by the imperial government. Provision was made for the continuance of mutual aid societies, to accommodate workers who wished to continue in these organizations, but the employer was not obliged to contribute to their costs.

The contributions of workers and their employers varied somewhat from fund to fund, but generally amounted to about 3 to 4½ percent of wages, of which, as we have seen, the worker paid two-thirds. The law specified minimum benefits, and it was anticipated that some of the funds would provide more than the law required. The benefits were payable during sickness, at the time of childbirth, and at the death of the insured (funeral benefits). Sickness benefits consisted of a cash benefit of at least 50 percent of the worker's wage, plus medical attendance, drugs, and therapeutical supplies. The cash benefit was payable from the third day of disability for a maximum of 13 weeks. In 1903, the maximum duration was raised to 26 weeks.

One of the largest of the funds was in Leipzig, with about 150,000 members in 1887, as a result of the consolidation of 18 local funds for various occupations in the city. The consolidation of the funds helped to facilitate a move to provide free choice of physician in many cases. By 1900, the fund had 297 physicians under contract, of whom 97 were specialists. The doctors were paid a lump sum annually on the basis of the membership of the fund – that is, so much per worker – a method of payment that came to be known as a "capitation fee."

The doctors were opposed to the capitation fee method of payment, the closed panels of physicians, and the fact that the procedures and methods of pay were not negotiated with the doctors' representatives but were often announced unilaterally by the funds. In 1904, the Leipzig physicians went on strike. A settlement was eventually reached, but the medical association prepared to "accumulate a heavy war chest" in preparation for the next battle (Marshall, 1967, 55). Gradually the physicians became more effectively organized, and payment by fee-for-service became more common. Dissatisfaction continued, however, because fees were low, especially during the Great Depression of the 1930s (Glaser, 1970).

According to Armstrong (1932), the most serious weakness of the prewar German system was the limited access of workers to hospital care. The funds were permitted to grant hospital care, but the family suffered a 50 percent reduction in the cash sickness benefit while the worker was in the hospital. Even though about half of the funds paid more than the usual cash benefit that the law required, this reduction left the family with too little income and often deterred the worker from applying for admission to the hospital. On the other hand, a great strength of the German system was its emphasis on prevention and cure of illness.

Other early legislation

The countries that followed Germany in enacting sickness insurance legislation at an early date were Austria (1888), Hungary (1891), Sweden (1891), Denmark (1892), and Belgium (1894). Then, in the years from 1909 to 1912, a second group of countries adopted legislation, including Italy, Norway, Great Britain, Romania, Switzerland, Russia, and the Kingdom of the Serbs, Croats, and Slovenes. Following considerably later were Poland (1920), Japan (1922), France (1928), and Spain (1929).

The most important distinction among these laws was that some of them were compulsory, as in Germany, whereas others simply provided for a modest government subsidy to voluntary mutual funds. In the latter group were Belgium, Denmark, Sweden, Switzerland, and the Australian state of New South Wales. In most of these cases, the subsidies were small, but in the Danish case, the subsidies were significant, and the voluntary system that developed was in some respects superior to some of the compulsory systems. The Danish, French, and British systems were studied by Armstrong (1939), with particular reference to the role of the doctors and the hospitals, revealing differences that are of interest because in some respects they persist nearly five decades later.

Under the Danish act of 1892, the mutual aid societies were offered several types of government subsidies, on condition that they registered with the government, met certain requirements in their membership policies, and offered benefits of specified minimum standards. The subsidies were available, however, only on behalf of "unpropertied" members – those with incomes and property below certain amounts. Benefits included cash payments, as well as medical care and hospital treatment for members and their children for a maximum period of 13 weeks. This period could be extended for needy persons at the expense of the commune, and dues for unemployed persons were paid by the communes. Additional benefits, such as the cost of drugs, might be provided by some of the funds, and members paid varying premiums according to the benefits desired. Wives had to join and pay premiums in order to be covered.

Provision for medical and hospital care not only for members but also for their children would have been very costly for the funds, except for the fact that the hospitals were largely publicly owned and financed from local taxes. Hospital care included the services of the medical and surgical staff.

By 1913, almost two-fifths of Denmark's population was receiving both medical and hospital care through the health insurance scheme, while the societies in Copenhagen were also providing specialists' services. In the late 1930s, direct government subsidies amounted to more than 40 percent of membership dues, while at least 90 percent of the costs of hospitalization of insured persons was financed by public taxes. Doctors were paid chiefly on a capitation basis, although this had not always been the case. The terms of insurance practice were settled by collective agreements between district medical associations and district federations of health insurance societies.

Armstrong (1939) found that Danish doctors were generally enthusiastic about the system, not only because it greatly improved access to medical care but also because it stabilized doctors' incomes, relieving them of the necessity of seeking to collect payments from low-income patients and maintaining the dues of persons who were unemployed.

The French scheme differed from that of Denmark in very significant ways. Coverage was compulsory for workers in industry, commerce, and agriculture, but, as in the old-age pension program, there were separate schemes for such groups as miners, seamen, and public employees. Nonmanual workers were included only if their earnings did not exceed certain limits.

Mandatory contributions were equal for employers and workers, and there was a government subsidy that varied in amount with the reduction in poor relief expenditures. Both medical and cash benefits were provided, but the medical benefit consisted only of partial reimbursement of the member's payment to the doctor. The French medical profession had opposed the provision of medical services and favored, instead, a system that provided for free choice of physician and direct payment to the doctor by the patient on a fee-for-service basis.

The British act of 1911

The British act of 1911 is of special interest because both its strengths and weaknesses helped to prepare the ground for the adoption of the British National Health Service and generalized sickness insurance after World War II. Its strengths included the fact that physicians were satisfied with its operation, including the capitation fee system of payment, which they had initially opposed, and which was continued for general practitioners after the war. Its weaknesses included the pattern of membership in the friendly societies, the failure to provide for hospital or specialist services, the failure to provide any benefits for dependents, and other limitations.

The leading role in framing and supporting the legislation was played by Lloyd George, then Chancellor of the Exchequer, who made a trip to Germany to observe the operation of health insurance there. One of the problems he faced was the insistence of the friendly societies on a role in the proposed scheme. Although he provided for their participation in the cash sickness benefits scheme, he decided that they could not be made responsible for medical care because the doctors were opposed to any system in which sickness funds negotiated with physicians.

The British act covered on a compulsory basis all manual workers and all nonmanual workers earning less than £160 a year, with certain exceptions, such as government employees for whom there were sick leave provisions. In addition, voluntary insurance was permitted for persons whose earned income was less than £160 a year.

The law provided for flat-rate contributions and benefits, unlike the German law with its earnings-related contributions and benefits, and there were no benefits for dependents. The benefit was payable from the fourth day of illness and, as in many of the continental European laws, for a maximum period of 26 weeks. However, there was no disability insurance program to "take over" when the sickness benefit expired, but a disablement or invalidity payment of 5s. a week was payable under the sickness program. As we saw in Chapter 6, Britain did not adopt invalidity insurance until 1971.

The medical benefit included the services of a general practitioner (GP), as well as necessary drugs and medical and surgical appliances. Obstetrical care and operations not ordinarily performed by a GP were not guaranteed, and neither hospital care nor nursing services were provided except where necessary in cases of tuberculosis. The law did provide for a maternity benefit for both female workers and wives of insured workers.

The act did not specify the method of payment, but the capitation method was adopted by most funds, except in Manchester, where a fee-for-service system was tried initially but was found to encourage abuse on the part of a small number of doctors and was therefore abandoned in favor of capitation in 1928.

Although the British medical profession had bitterly opposed the legislation when it was being discussed in 1909–10, the attitudes of the doctors gradually changed to enthusiastic approval, according to Armstrong (1939). A major reason for this, as in Denmark, was the improvement and stabilization of physicians' incomes. Even in depressed areas where unemployment was severe in the 1920s and 1930s, the health insurance rights of the unemployed were protected by governmental appropriations.

The omission of hospital benefits was largely explained by the prevalence of "voluntary hospitals," as well as public municipal hospitals in large cities. The voluntary hospitals started as private institutions, and before World War I most of them made no charge whatever for the care of patients, deriving their funds from contributions coming in large amounts from the wealthy and in small amounts from others. They were open to any sick person, but those with high incomes generally entered nursing homes that were run for profit by physicians and surgeons. Only members of the voluntary hospital staff could attend patients, and these often included prominent physicians and surgeons who provided their services free of charge.

The most significant departure of the British system from that of other countries was in the structure and functions of the friendly societies. The sickness funds in Germany and elsewhere were composed of all workers in the same occupation or group of occupations in an area. Thus, the workers tended for the most part to be normally distributed according to age. In Britain, however, workers could apply for membership in societies that were not necessarily limited to an occupation and that could reject applicants, though not on the ground of age. The result was substantial variation in the average cost experience of the societies. On this and other grounds, Beveridge argued strongly against continuing the approved societies in his 1942 report (*Social Insurance and Allied Services . . .* , 1942, 29–30).

Postwar trends

Whereas most prewar health benefit systems were modeled after the German law and operated through sickness funds, developments in the health benefits field in the postwar period have led to a situation in which health services are provided under three major types of systems and several hybrid or mixed systems. In 1985, as Table 10.2 indicates, five countries in Western Europe – Austria, Belgium, France, West Germany, and the Netherlands – continued what I call "traditional sickness insurance," under which coverage is basically employment-related and the system operates through sickness funds. Yugoslavia also had such a system.[1]

The schemes that are classified as "national health insurance" systems tend to be of more recent origin, to cover all residents in most cases, and to be operated on a national basis (or, as in Canada, on a federal–provincial basis).

The third major type of system is a national health service. Britain led the way in adopting this type of system in 1946, although New Zealand came close to adopting a national health service in its 1938 legislation, and the Soviet Union had had a national health service since about 1926. A national health service covers all residents and basically provides medical and hospital services free of charge, although there are some exceptions, most frequently in the form of a portion of the cost of prescribed drugs. Dental care is usually covered, but sometimes on a limited basis. Most of the countries of Eastern Europe have followed the Soviet example in providing for a national health service; likewise Italy in the late 1970s and Greece, more recently under the Papandreou Government, have adopted national health services. I have classified Denmark and New Zealand as having national health services, although in Denmark an individual or family may opt out of the system and pay for medical care, and in New Zealand care outside of public hospitals is not free of charge.

[1] For a similar classification, see ILO (1985a).

Table 10.2. *Basic structure of health benefit systems, selected industrial countries, 1985*

Traditional sickness insurance	National health insurance	National health service	Mixed systems
Austria	Canada	Czechoslovakia	Australia
Belgium	Finland	Denmark	Ireland
France	Germany (Dem. Rep.)	Greece	Japan
Germany (Fed. Rep.)	Norway	Hungary	Switzerland
Netherlands	Spain	Italy	United States
Yugoslavia	Sweden	New Zealand	
		Poland	
		Romania	
		USSR	
		United Kingdom	

Source: USSSA (biennial, 1986).

The remaining countries – Australia, Ireland, Israel, Japan, Switzerland, and the United States – had programs that did not fall under any of the three major classifications in differing ways, as we shall see.

Another major difference from the prewar period is that, whereas in most countries before the war the provision of cash sickness benefits was a major function of the sickness funds, the provision of cash benefits is now frequently quite separate from the provision of medical benefits, except insofar as doctors may be required to certify a worker's illness and his or her capacity to return to work. In Britain, for example, cash sickness benefits have been provided through the national insurance system and have been financed through employer and employee contributions that also finance other cash benefit programs, although, since 1982, the first eight weeks have been provided by the employer. Medical care, on the other hand, has been provided largely free of charge and financed chiefly through general government revenues.

In Canada, which did not provide for cash sickness benefits until 1971, they have been administered through the unemployment insurance system, whereas health care has been administered by the provinces under a federal – provincial financing program.

Moreover, although cash sickness benefits typically accounted for most of the expenditures of the sickness funds under early legislation, they have become a diminishing proportion of expenditures during the postwar period, even though they have been expanded and liberalized. The reason is that expenditures on medical care have mounted rapidly, as people have become more accustomed to seeking medical care; furthermore, provision has been made for care of dependents, access to hospitals has been improved in most countries, the use of specialists has become more common, and technological progress has been accompanied by the use of costly equipment and highly specialized personnel. For these reasons, I shall devote my attention primarily to health care rather than to sickness benefits in the remainder of this chapter.

The years since 1945 can be divided into two periods: From the late 1940s – or in some cases the 1950s – expenditures on health benefits rose sharply in most industrial countries. Coverage of insurance programs was expanded, benefits were liberalized, access to hospital care was improved, new hospitals were built, modern equipment was installed, and specialists played an increasingly important role in the provision of medical care.

In the 1970s, however, there were signs of growing concern about inflation in health care costs, particularly after the oil crisis of the mid-1970s. The rate of increase in the costs of medical care extended to exceed the rise in the general consumer price index. Belt tightening measures were adopted, frequently involving increased patient charges and in many cases involving growing governmental control over drug prices, fees, and total health expenditures. Limitations were imposed on increases in hospital capacity, and measures were taken in some cases to control the supply of physicians through restrictions on access to medical schools, influenced by the research of Fuchs (1974) in the United States and similar findings elsewhere, that less emphasis should be placed on increasing the supply of physicians, especially specialists in some oversupplied fields, and more on increasing the supply of physician assistants.

The German system

Although coverage is broad in West Germany, salaried workers and some categories of self-employed persons were covered on a compulsory basis in 1985 only if their earnings were less than DM 48,000 a year (about $16,000). Although the ceiling has been raised several times and eventually was indexed, it has continued to be controversial, especially because a number of other countries have dropped such a provision. On the other hand, the German system has covered the unemployed and disabled, as well as the employed, while pensioners and students have been covered for medical benefits though not for cash benefits.

In 1985, the employer was required to provide benefits amounting to 100 percent of earnings during the first six weeks of an illness, whereas benefits in the early weeks were well under 100 percent in Britain. However, West Germany has been by no means alone among European countries in calling for employer payment of 100 percent of earnings during the early stages of illness, but in some cases the sickness funds have been required to reimburse the employer for all or part of the cost. After the first six weeks, the German provisions have called for sickness funds to pay 80 percent of covered earnings for up to 78 weeks in a three-year period. The lengthening of maximum duration of sickness benefits to 78 weeks (compared with the prewar provision of 26 weeks) reflects the trend mentioned in Chapter 6 to encourage rehabilitation.

Maternity benefits in West Germany and elsewhere are a much more important feature of the provisions than they were under the early laws, and there has been a pronounced tendency to improve these benefits. Although they are usually formally under sickness programs, they are of special interest in connection with family policies and will be discussed in Chapter 13.

Although an individual has been required to join one of the sickness funds, he or she could go to any doctor who had been admitted to insurance practice. The doctor submitted a bill to the local insurance doctors' association and could not charge an additional amount unless the patient requested a home or office visit which the doctor deemed unnecessary. The total amounts required to pay medical practitioners have been negotiated within each state *(Land)* by the medical association and the associations that represent the various types of sickness funds.

Despite concerns over rising health costs, the federal government, under the Social Democrats, adopted a number of significant liberalizing measures in 1974, the most important of which was a provision for entitlement to hospital treatment of unlimited duration. However, the situation changed dramatically in 1977, following an unusually sharp rise in health care costs in 1976. A cost containment act was adopted, providing for a conference at the federal level, consisting of all of the associations and organizations directly concerned with matters of health, including the federal ministries and the provincial governments. The purpose of the meeting was to arrive at recommendations relating to the total remuneration of doctors and dentists for the following year, as well as other expenses such as drugs. The recommendations had to be acceptable to the sickness funds and practitioners' representatives, and, if no decision could be reached, these representatives were to negotiate, and, if necessary, go to binding arbitration.

Among other provisions of the 1977 act, probably the most significant was a requirement increasing the share of pensioners' medical costs to be met by the sickness funds to 50 percent by 1980 (the most recent share had been 30 percent). This change was expected to force the sickness funds to increase their members' contributions.

In the early 1980s, and especially after the Christian Democrats gained control of the government in 1982, cost containment measures were intensified. For the first time, patients were required to pay a small daily charge for the first two weeks of hospital care and for each day of convalescent care.

Table 10.3. *Total and public expenditures on health as a percentage of GDP, OECD countries, 1960 to 1984*

	Total expenditures					Public expenditures				
	1960	1970	1975	1980	1984	1960	1970	1975	1980	1984
Australia	5.1%	5.7%	7.6%	7.4%	7.8%	2.4%	3.2%	5.6%	4.6%	6.6%
Austria	4.4	5.3	6.4	7.0	7.2	2.9	3.4	4.1	4.4	4.4
Belgium	3.4	4.1	5.5	6.1	6.2	2.1	3.5	4.5	5.3	5.7
Canada	5.5	7.2	7.4	7.3	8.4	2.4	5.1	5.7	5.4	6.2
Denmark	3.6	6.1	6.5	6.8	6.3	3.2	5.2	5.9	5.8	5.3
Finland	4.2	5.6	5.8	6.3	6.6	2.3	4.1	4.9	4.9	5.4
France	4.3	6.1	7.6	8.5	9.1	2.5	4.3	5.5	6.1	6.5
Germany	4.8	5.6	7.8	7.9	8.1	3.2	4.2	6.3	6.3	6.4
Greece	2.9	3.9	4.0	4.2	4.6	1.7	2.2	2.5	3.5	3.6
Ireland	4.0	5.6	7.7	8.5	8.0	3.0	4.3	6.3	7.9	6.9
Italy	3.9	5.5	6.7	6.8	7.2	3.2	4.8	5.8	6.0	6.1
Japan	3.0	4.6	5.7	6.4	6.6	1.8	3.0	4.0	4.5	4.8
Netherlands	3.9	6.0	7.7	8.2	8.6	1.3	5.1	5.9	6.4	6.8
New Zealand	4.4	4.5	5.2	5.7	5.6	3.3	3.5	4.3	4.8	4.4
Norway	3.3	5.0	6.7	6.8	6.3	2.6	4.6	6.4	6.7	5.6
Spain		4.1	5.1	5.9	5.8		2.3	3.6	4.3	4.2
Sweden	4.7	7.2	8.0	9.5	9.4	3.4	6.2	7.2	8.7	8.6
Switzerland	3.3	5.2	7.1	7.2	7.8[a]			4.7	4.7	
United Kingdom	3.9	4.5	5.6	5.6	5.9	3.4	3.9	5.1	5.1	5.3
United States	5.3	7.6	8.6	9.5	10.7	1.3	2.8	3.7	4.0	4.4

[a] 1982.

Source: OECD (1987a, 11 and 55).

The charge per prescription was increased, the building of new hospitals virtually ceased, and a list of nonessential drugs that could not be prescribed under health insurance was developed. Interest began to be expressed in shifting from a daily hospital charge to a scheme – resembling that adopted in 1983 under Medicare in the United States – of making an overall charge on the basis of diagnosis of the patient's ailment (Abel-Smith, 1984).

Compared with the experience of other industrial countries, the rise in health care expenditures as a percentage of GDP was particularly pronounced in West Germany from 1970 to 1975, but after that public expenditures as a percentage of GDP leveled off, and total expenditures rose only slightly (Table 10.3). The data also show that other countries with traditional sickness funds – Austria, Belgium, France, and the Netherlands – experienced continuing increases in both public and total expenditures. On the other hand, countries with national health services – Denmark, Italy, New Zealand, and the

United Kingdom – were relatively successful in holding down expenditures, although it must be recognized that the national health service in Italy dates only from 1978 and has only gradually been implemented.

The increase in costs was particularly large in the United States, for reasons that will be discussed later, while costs also rose to a comparatively high level in Sweden. Moreover, public expenditures accounted for a particularly large percentage of total expenditures on health in three of the Scandinavian countries – Denmark, Norway, and Sweden – but they were also relatively high in 1984 in Australia (which had recently changed its provisions), Belgium, Ireland, Italy, and the United Kingdom. On the other hand, private expenditures formed a large proportion of the total in the United States. Significantly, however, whereas the share of public expenditures in relation to total expenditures rose from 61 percent in 1960 to 79 percent in 1984, on the average in OECD countries, the increase slowed down after 1975 and the public share remained virtually unchanged after 1980. This has led to speculation as to whether this leveling off will be followed by a decline as countries continue to cope with financial stringency (OECD, 1987a, p. 54), and, in fact, there has been a slight decline in a few countries.

Other traditional systems

In the other four OECD countries with traditional sickness insurance, coverage provisions in 1985 did not differ greatly from those in West Germany, although France continued to have a number of special systems for various groups of workers. In the Netherlands, salaried employees were excluded from the compulsory system if their earnings exceeded a certain level.

Provisions for cash sickness benefits were, on the whole, somewhat less generous than those in West Germany, especially in France, where there was a qualifying period of employment before benefits could be paid, a three-day waiting period, and benefits that amounted only to 50 percent of earnings, although they were raised to two-thirds of earnings after the first 30 days for a worker with three or more children. The maximum duration of benefits was one year.

The provision of health care benefits in France has continued to be marked by controversy between the insurance funds and the medical profession. For a time after the war, the doctors managed to retain the payments system that had formerly prevailed, but after de Gaulle returned to power in 1958, the National Assembly gave him emergency powers to solve the Algerian crisis and adjourned. There followed a period of government by decree, in which, among other things, several long-debated reforms affecting medical care were carried out. In May 1960, a decree was issued, which provided that fee schedules were to be binding on nearly all doctors and would cover nearly all patients. A government commission could set ceilings on the negotiated fee schedules.

There followed an abortive strike by the medical profession, which failed because most doctors, except for the more militant physicians in Paris and Lyons, were content to accept the official fee schedules which, according to Glaser (1970), were among the world's highest.

In France, as in West Germany, the period since 1977 has been characterized by a series of cost containment measures along somewhat similar lines (Abel-Smith, 1984). There have also been some cost containment measures in the other countries with traditional systems.

National health insurance systems

Sweden: Among the countries with national health insurance systems, Sweden is of special interest because it has long ranked well on such measures as life expectancy and infant mortality, while it is also among the largest spenders on health benefits among industrial countries. Somewhat similar comments, however, apply to the other Scandinavian countries.

Sweden has been classified as having a national health insurance program because its coverage has been nearly universal, even though it has operated to some extent through sickness funds. Its hospital system, however, has resembled a national health service in that care has been available to all free of charge, although the system has been administered and financed in large part by counties and municipalities. Most hospitals have been owned and operated by the counties, or in some cases by municipal governments, and have served the community rather than only the poor. Their expenses, including the services of specialists, have been met almost entirely from local taxes, supplemented by a small subsidy from the central government.

Historically, voluntary sickness funds received modest government subsidies in Sweden, and compulsory sickness insurance was not enacted until 1947. Moreover, the legislation did not become effective until 1955, after a long period of consultation with the medical profession and other groups on how the program would be administered.

Cash sickness benefits have been comparatively generous and have been unique in providing for housewives and dependent husbands, as well as for employed persons. In 1985, they amounted to 90 percent of earnings up to a ceiling, with a maximum of 403 kr. a day and a minimum of 8 kr. for housewives and dependent men.

Under the provisions effective in 1955, physicians' outpatient services were to be paid for by newly constituted sickness funds distributed throughout the country. However, private practitioners outside of the hospitals did not have to enter into a contract with the sickness funds. Patients paid them directly for services and were reimbursed by the local sickness fund for three-fourths of the official fee in the case of GPs and less in the case of specialists. The official fee schedule was negotiated between the Swedish Medical Association and the Federation of County Councils and had to be observed by certain categories of doctors, but not by full-time practitioners, professors of medicine, and chiefs of hospital service in Stockholm, who were free to set their own charges, whether or not the patient sought reimbursement from the sickness fund.

Although increases in fees were not particularly pronounced in Sweden, according to Glaser (1970), costs did rise somewhat and major reform legislation was adopted in 1970, under which the patient was to pay any doctor practicing under the insurance system a fee of 7 kr. for an office visit and 15 kr. for a house visit.

By 1985, the charge to the patient for a visit to a private doctor was 55 kr. (about $6.40 at the prevailing exchange rate). The fee was somewhat less for a public doctor, who usually received his or her basic income from a hospital or institutional salary. The hospital charge after 365 days was 30 kr. a day. There were also charges for most drugs, for a portion of the cost of dental care, and for part of the patient's travel costs in connection with doctor or hospital visits.

Although the hospitals have been funded largely at the local level, the central government has had great influence through its responsibility for allocating medical staff throughout the country. The National Medical Board has determined staffing ratios and quality criteria, and the Swedish hospitals have been widely regarded as maintaining high-quality standards (Anderson, 1972).

The fact that public expenditures accounted for a very large percentage of total health expenditures in the early 1980s (Table 10.3) was partly explained by the fact that hospital care was largely free of charge. Moreover, although patients did go to private practitioners, the great majority of the practitioners were associated with hospitals or with public dispensaries, and their private fees supplemented their basic salaries from public sources. Only 5 percent of Swedish doctors had fully private incomes in 1985 (ILO, 1985a). As for Sweden's high rate of spending on health, a major explanation is the large proportion of aged in the population (16.2 percent aged 65 and older in 1980; see Table 4.5).

Canada: The health insurance system in Canada is of particular interest, especially in the United States, because conditions of medical practice have historically been similar in the two countries, and yet Canadian doctors have accepted a compulsory health insurance program without too much of a battle, whereas American physicians have successfully fought off any such program, except for the aged and some of the disabled.

In an interesting analysis of the development of the "welfare state" in the two countries, Kudrle and Marmor (1981) pointed out that despite many similarities the two countries differ in important respects. Canadian political attitudes have been much more supportive of state action for national and provincial development, and the Canadian parliamentary system has involved a high degree of party discipline, in contrast with the situation in the United States, in which members of Congress are intensively lobbied by interest groups seeking to block legislative proposals that they dislike.

In both countries, the hospitals were largely voluntary, and physicians were paid on a fee-for-service basis. Moreover, the training and outlook among physicians and nurses were similar. Yet, in contrast with the position taken by the American Medical Association, the Canadian Medical Association began issuing policy statements that were generally favorable to compulsory health insurance as early as 1934. Moreover, in the immediate postwar years, several provinces, led by left-leaning Saskatchewan, began to develop compulsory health insurance programs. Meanwhile, the development of private health insurance in Canada closely paralleled that in the United States.

In 1957, the federal government of Canada adopted a hospital insurance program, under which the federal government was to pay to participating provinces approximately 50 percent of the cost of comprehensive hospital insurance providing ward accommodation, with no limit on duration, and hospital outpatient diagnostic services. All of the provinces eventually participated and were required to adopt insurance programs that were available to all residents under uniform terms and conditions.

Nine years later, in 1966, the Medical Care program (called Medicare) was enacted, empowering the federal government to provide grants-in-aid for about one-half of the costs of provincial medical insurance plans meeting certain minimum criteria. All medically required services had to be covered without exclusions or financial barriers, and all Canadian residents were to be eligible. The plan had to be administered on a nonprofit basis by a public authority accountable to the provincial government. By 1971, all ten provinces and two territories were participating.

Sources of financing have varied from province to province. Gradually, however, provinces that had initially provided for premiums paid by the insured persons found that premium collection was difficult and costly, and there has been a tendency to shift to financing from general revenues (see Comanor, 1980, on the changes in Ontario). In 1985, flat-rate premiums still had to be paid by insured persons in several provinces, but these covered only a small portion of the costs, and low-income persons were usually exempt. In Quebec, the employer paid a 3 percent payroll tax.

Insured persons have had free choice of physician, and doctors have been free to choose where to practice. However, some provinces have offered financial incentives to doctors willing to locate in areas where there was a shortage of physicians. Payments to doctors have been on a fee-for-service basis, in conformity with a provincial schedule of fees, but physicians associated with government or institutional programs have sometimes been paid on a salaried basis. Physicians have been permitted to opt out of the system and bill patients directly rather than through the public authority. However, charges in such cases could exceed the scheduled fee, and patients were not fully reimbursed.

In 1984, the Canada Health Act, replacing the former hospital insurance and medical care laws, came into effect. The major purpose of the new legislation was to aim at eliminating the practice in some of the provinces of imposing charges on patients (*ISSR*, 1985, *38* [1]: 77–8). Thus, Canada was refusing to join the ranks of the countries resorting to such charges.[2]

Nevertheless, the Canadian situation is not without its problems. There are shortages of hospital beds in some areas, fears that appropriations will be inadequate, and complaints by physicians over the restrictions on fees. On the whole, however, the system of universal health insurance is immensely popular (Malloy, 1988).

The British National Health Service

Among postwar developments in health care, the British National Health Service (NHS) has probably attracted more attention than any other development and has been intensively studied by scholars both in Britain and in other countries.

As proposed in the Beveridge Report (*Social Insurance and Allied Services. . .*, 1942, 158–9):

A comprehensive national health service will ensure that for every citizen there is available whatever medical treatment he requires, in whatever form he requires it, domiciliary or institutional, general, specialist or consultant, and will ensure also the provision of dental, ophthalmic and surgical appliances, nursing and midwifery, and rehabilitation after accidents.

The plan put forward by the national government in a White Paper issued in 1944 called for a comprehensive national health service, but left the hospitals much as they were. However, the decisive architect of the plan that was

---

[2] The Canada Health Act did not go into effect without protest. After Ontario enacted conforming legislation in June 1986, the Ontario Medical Association struck, but public opinion was against them and the strike was not successful. The doctors now have to accept the controlled fee, and the patient pays nothing. This, I was told by several doctors in Ontario, has its good and bad aspects. There is some abuse, for example, in the form of unnecessary referrals to specialists.

finally adopted in 1946 was Aneurin Bevan, Minister of Health in the Labor government elected in 1945, who insisted on nationalizing the hospitals.

The British Medical Association was generally supportive of the legislation. Although the GPs objected to a proposal to put them under regional authorities, they were satisfied that free choice of doctor and capitation fees were to be retained. In the end, they were left much as they had been, receiving capitation fees in accordance with the number of patients on their panels, and, in the customary British manner, practicing almost entirely outside of hospitals and referring their patients to hospitals as needed.

The central government has determined the capital and current budgets of regional health authorities who in turn have distributed budgets to district health authorities. These budgets have financed the hospitals and community services, such as home nurses. The central government has also exercised broad control over the number of positions on hospital medical staffs and the costs of administration of health authorities (Abel-Smith, 1984). The payments to practitioners have been handled by local executive committees.

There is little question that the NHS is immensely popular with the British public, and in many ways deservedly so. More than 80 percent of respondents in various opinion polls express enthusiasm for it. They feel confident that they will receive care when they need it. Numerous commentators on NHS also refer to the high morale that generally prevails among its health workers, though there are complaints and exceptions.

All of this has meant that governments have been reluctant to adopt a restrictive attitude toward the system. Even the Thatcher government, with its drive toward "privatization," has been hesitant to make any serious changes in NHS, although recently some changes have been proposed.

On the whole, moreover, the evidence points to a substantial improvement in access to care, although lower-income groups do not tend to seek services more frequently than those with higher incomes, despite their greater incidence of health problems (Walters, 1980).

According to Anderson (1972), in his comparative study of health care in Britain, Sweden, and the United States, the hospital organizational structure has enormously improved the distribution of specialists. Although few hospitals have been built, they have been upgraded in quality. Other writers (e.g., Gill, 1980) maintain that there is still an acute problem of maldistribution of hospital facilities.

Probably the most damaging criticism of NHS, reiterated by many critics, is that it has benefited the middle- and upper-income groups more than those with low income. The higher-income groups tend to be more knowledgeable about how to seek the best service and are more likely to live in areas with an adequate supply of doctors and hospitals. A number of writers emphasize shortages of doctors in poverty areas, despite policies aimed at overcoming geographical maldistribution. Moreover, although patients needing emergency surgery are promptly admitted to the hospital, there are long waits for admission of those whose needs are less acute. Those with ample means can avoid this problem by seeking private care.

A basic underlying problem is that appropriations have never been adequate to provide the comprehensive free care that was contemplated when NHS was founded. Almost from the start, concern over rapidly rising costs resulted in budgets that were held to modest increases over those of previous years, especially in terms of a percentage of GDP. As Table 10.3 shows, British expenditures on health care, public and total, have risen very modestly and in 1984 were close to the bottom among industrial countries, with public expenditures amounting to 5.3 percent of GDP and total expenditures to 5.9 percent. In some ways, this is an impressive achievement, attributable to budgetary controls and probably also to the fact that doctors are paid basically by capitation fees, or, if on hospital staffs, by salaries. Compensation is negotiated from year to year but is not subject to the extremely inflationary pressures associated with "third party" payments on a fee-for-service basis in the United States.

Services have not been entirely free under NHS. As reported by Titmuss (1963), patients desiring privacy in hospitals could pay a weekly charge representing part of the cost. A charge of 1s. was made for each drug prescription outside of the hospital, and there were charges for surgical appliances and for hospital treatment following road accidents. Adults over the age of 21 (except expectant and nursing mothers) had to pay all or part of the cost of dental treatment, and roughly half of the cost of dentures. Patients also had to pay part of the cost of spectacles.

Cost containment measures adopted in recent years have resulted in a number of increases in charges. By 1985, the charge per prescription had increased to £2, although 70 percent of such items were exempted, chiefly for the elderly and children. There were also increases in dental and ophthalmic charges, and the age limit for free dental treatment for young people was lowered from 21 to 18 in 1981 (Abel-Smith, 1984).

The role of the GP in Britain has been a matter of controversy. The tradition of barring the GP from hospital practice has been criticized by some, but this is also the practice in Denmark, Sweden, and West Germany.[3] In Britain, moreover, as one expert put it, although general practice was supposed to be the cornerstone of the NHS, the expansion of medical staff took place in hospitals rather than in general practice. (Forsyth, 1973, 25). Yet the decline in the proportion of doctors who are GPs has been less pronounced in Britain

---

[3] Some of this discussion of GPs is based on an interview with Professor Brian Abel-Smith, London School of Economics, October 1983.

than in some other countries, especially the United States. The trend has been associated with the advance of scientific medicine, which has given rise to more specialties and to increasing demand for specialists' services.

British GPs are not barred from the hospital entirely. Under NHS, diagnostic services have been available to GPs on a direct-access basis. Moreover, some GPs have held hospital posts (Titmuss, 1963).

Although the basic compensation of GPs takes the form of the capitation fee, doctors receive additional payments for a number of services, including maternity services, treatment of temporary residents, the training of assistants, and others. They also receive a higher capitation fee for elderly patients. The great majority of GPs are now in group practice, and the number of community health centers has expanded rapidly (Forsyth, 1973). In the larger group practices and in health centers, there is a certain amount of specialization among the doctors, and experience has shown that larger numbers of patients can be accommodated on the doctors' panels.

Meanwhile, as a better understanding of the realtionship between family background and health status has developed, there has been a trend toward reemphasizing the family doctor. There has been a similar trend in the United States, where there is now a family practice specialty, requiring three years of residency training (Carnegie Council . . ., 1976).

In 1986, the Minister of Health and Social Services recommended, among other things, that doctors be paid more to work in underserved inner city areas and that there be a "good practice allowance"–paying more for excellence. He also proposed increasing the proportion of compensation–at present, less than one-half on the average–to be derived from capitation fees.

Meanwhile, there has been a significant growth of membership in private health insurance schemes in Britain. According to Walters (1980), there were over one million subscribers to private health insurance in 1976, mostly on an employer-sponsored basis. Other estimates are higher.

The Soviet system

Health care in the Soviet Union is more thoroughly "socialized" than in Britain. Health workers are all employed by the state on a salaried basis, and there is no such thing as private practice. Moreover, the development of health services has been part of the five-year plans since 1926.

In the early 1970s there were 36,600 polyclinics and some 25,000 hospitals (Venediktove, 1973). More recent data, for years around 1981 indicated that the population per hospital bed in the Soviet Union was 80, which compared quite favorably with comparable data for other industrial countries–for example, 127 in the United Kingdom and 171 in the United States (*Statistical Abstract. . .*, 1985, 844).

Expenditures on health care in the Soviet Union in 1979–80 amounted to 6.2 percent of GDP–less than in such countries as Sweden and Norway, but comparable with those in such countries as Belgium, Finland, Japan, and the United Kingdom. Interestingly, also, the percentages were very similar in other Eastern European countries, ranging from 5.6 percent in Hungary to 6.9 percent in East Germany (Appendix 1).

The Russian hospital network is formed on a "pyramidal" system with increasing specialization toward the apex, and with each superior hospital acting as an organizational and methodological center for the smaller hospitals at the next level down. The central hospitals provide consultative services and take patients requiring specialized treatment.

Most of the Soviet writers on health care emphasize the importance attached to preventive care. Sizable groups in the population are under systematic observation, and there are medical departments in many large enterprises where a worker may receive prompt attention in the event that he or she develops an ailment. There also has been great emphasis, as in some of the other Eastern European countries, on encouraging the development of sanitoria and health resorts for persons with early symptoms or who are recuperating from an accident or a serious illness.

Under the influence of *glasnost,* however, we are beginning to learn about serious weaknesses in the Soviet health care system. Hospitals are old and run down, lacking sanitation, and doctors in neighborhood clinics have been required to see eight patients an hour. Moreover, contrary to the experience of other industrial countries, life expectancy has declined and infant mortality has increased to a level far above that of most other developed countries. A plan for vast improvements, with emphasis on prevention, was announced in August 1987 (D'Anastasio, 1987).

Cash sickness benefit amounts per week have varied with years of service, and this has also been true in a number of other countries in Eastern Europe. Traditionally, in the Soviet Union, the trade unions have played a role in the administration of sickness benefits and also in the improvement of working conditions.

The American system

We come now to the situation in the United States, which has been described as "chaotic." In spite of efforts to achieve the adoption of a national health insurance system, especially during the Truman administration, we continue to be the only industrial country lacking such a system. Moreover, our record is not impressive on the basis of measures used to compare health status across nations. It was reported early in 1988 that we ranked 17th among industrialized nations in infant mortality, with a rate of 10.6 per 1,000 live births, compared with less than 5 per 1,000 in top-ranking Japan (Perlman, 1988).

During the early 1960s and especially as the "war on poverty" got under way, those who had supported national health insurance legislation came to regard that cause as hopeless and turned their attention to the plight of the aged, who faced heavy premium costs or very limited protection in attempts to purchase private health insurance. Attention was also given to the needs of the poor, who were most unlikely to have private health insurance.

The result of this shift in emphasis was the enactment of two important pieces of legislation in 1965: Medicare, which provided insurance benefits for the aged; and Medicaid, which provided grants to the states for part of the cost of medical assistance for the poor. This was an important accomplishment, facilitated by the landslide election of President Lyndon Johnson and of a large Democratic majority in Congress in 1964. It had, however, one unfortunate consequence. It singled out for federally sponsored programs two groups–the aged and the poor–with very heavy average health costs. The great majority of people continued to be in private health insurance schemes. This meant that the benefits of "averaging," or offsetting the high costs of the aged and the poor with the lower costs of the average employed worker, that countries with national health insurance plans enjoyed, were not available to the government. The cost per person protected in the Medicare program is exceedingly high, compared with costs for the average person; in the Medicaid program, costs are also high, but costs and benefits vary a good deal from state to state. Exacerbating the problem of Medicare, many of the technical advances requiring costly services and equipment have related to the diseases of old age.

From slow beginnings in the 1930s, private health insurance developed rapidly, spurred on both by wage control policies in World War II that permitted employers to adopt fringe benefits in lieu of wage increases and by legal decisions after the war that required employers to bargain over fringe benefits.

By 1983, 81 percent of private consumer hospital expenditures and about 62 percent of physicians' charges were met by private insurance. In terms of proportion of the population covered, 83 percent were covered for hospital expenses, 76 percent for surgical expenses, 75 percent for physicians' expenses, 45 percent for major medical expenses, and 46 percent for dental expenses. Dental expenses had been infrequently covered until the 1970s, when it became the popular new fringe benefit (*Statistical Abstract. . .* , 1986, 90 ff). Some of the insurance was carried on a group basis with private insurance companies and a substantial proportion with nonprofit Blue Cross plans (for hospital insurance) and Blue Shield plans (for medical expenses).

A serious problem is that the people omitted from coverage tend to be those least able to meet the cost of individual insurance, which is more costly than group insurance because of the problem of adverse selection of risks (persons in poor health are more likely to seek insurance than those in good health). This problem is avoided in the typical employment group. Those not covered include many part-time workers, employees of small firms, and many of the working poor (Davis, 1975, 35). A serious deficiency has been the lack of coverage for the unemployed, in contrast with the situation in most other industrial countries, in which some type of provision for coverage of the unemployed is common. Belatedly, this problem is being partially rectified. Effective July 1, 1986, employers with 20 workers or more have been required to continue health insurance for up to 18 months for employees they dismiss and for up to 36 months for widows, but initially the beneficiaries have had to pay the full cost of the insurance, plus an additional 2 percent for administrative costs.[4]

The absence of a national health insurance program does not mean that there is no sickness insurance. Five states – California, Hawaii, New Jersey, New York, and Rhode Island – and Puerto Rico have compulsory temporary disability insurance, as we saw in Chapter 6, and Hawaii has compulsory health insurance, adopted in 1975. Moreover, most firms provide sick leave.

One of the features that has distinguished private health insurance in the United States from health insurance in other countries is that in a large proportion of cases employers have paid the entire premium cost as a fringe benefit. Employees have not been required to contribute and have had no voice in managing the program. In contrast, under the compulsory sickness funds that developed in Western Europe, employees paid part of the cost (typically one-half) and were represented on the governing bodies that administered the funds. Both employers and employees were interested in holding down costs, and we have seen how the German doctors rebelled against this effort in the period before World War II. Recently, however, under the impact of sharply rising health benefit costs, U.S. employers have succeeded in seeking employee contributions, which were imposed on 41 percent of the workers in firms with 100 or more employees in 1986 (James, 1987).

When the federal government adopted Medicare in 1965, it did not become directly involved in the control of costs. The Johnson administration entered into agreements with state agencies and private organizations to secure their assistance in administering the program. Hospitals nominate an intermediary, such as a Blue Cross plan or a commercial insurance company, to process

---

[4] Bills have also been introduced recently that would require an employer to continue contributions to health insurance for a certain period of time for terminated workers.

claims, whereas medical insurance claims are processed by Blue Shield plans and insurance companies.

Thus we have developed a system in which "third-party" agencies handle most claims for payments, and typically there is no particular incentive for the third party to hold down hospital and medical costs. In fact, it has become widely recognized that this lack of incentive to control costs, in a setting in which the demand for hospital and medical services has been increasing rapidly, has been largely responsible for the extremely high rates of inflation of costs in the American health scene. Also a major factor is the fact that physicians make the decisions that determine whether a patient enters a hospital and what types of services he or she receives, although doctors have no control over hospital charges and often are not fully informed about the costs of services they recommend. The result has been an exceedingly sharp increase in medical care prices. On a base of 1967 = 100, the medical care price index had reached 379.5 in 1984, compared with 311.1 for the overall consumer price index. Physicians' costs had increased about as much as the medical care price index, but it was hospital costs that had risen astonishingly, to 670.9 in 1984 (*Statistical Abstract. . ., 1986*, 90 ff).

In a presentation of the reasons for these mounting costs, Enthoven (1980) made a strong case for adoption of a federal policy that would significantly alter the pattern of financing of health care and support the expansion of Health Maintenance Organizations (HMOs). In this type of organization, of which one of the earliest and best known is the Kaiser-Permanente Medical Foundation, centered in Oakland, California, the insured member pays a fixed individual or family monthly premium, in return for which he or she receives care free of charge, with certain minor exceptions, such as a modest charge for a home visit. The insured does not have free choice of physician but must instead choose one of the physicians on the HMO staff. However, in the larger HMOs the member has substantial choice. Doctors are paid on a capitation fee basis or on a salaried basis, and there is no incentive to hospitalize a patient unless it is necessary. The result is that costs in traditional HMOs tend to be considerably lower than those in private insurance company plans or Blue Cross/Blue Shield plans.[5] Moreover, insurance company plans are more likely to include deductibles and special charges that are not found in HMO plans, and there is no guarantee that the physician will not charge the patient more than the amount the plan is prepared to cover.

Writing in the late 1970s, Enthoven commented on the slow growth of

---

[5] In 1986, for example, the University of California (Berkeley Campus) paid monthly premiums ranging, for a single person, from $74.50 for an employee joining the Kaiser Foundation plan to $114.00 for one joining the "high option" Prudential Insurance Company plan; in the latter case, the employee also had to pay $27.52, resulting in a total premium of $141.52. The range was similar for family coverage.

HMO plans and the need to stimulate more rapid growth. Since then the situation has changed dramatically. Whereas there were only about six million persons in HMOs in 1976, HMOs enrolled about 28 million persons, or nearly 12 percent of the population by 1987 (Rundle, 1987).

There have been several important reasons for this development. The cost to employers of employee health benefits had, by the 1980s, risen so sharply that firms began a determined effort to reverse this trend, negotiating to shift some of the costs to employees, providing employees a choice of plans that would enable them to join an HMO, and resisting annual increases in health benefit costs. Meanwhile, the increase in the supply of physicians had caught up with the demand and in some areas had overtaken it, although there continued to be shortages in low-income and in rural areas. The number of physicians per 100,000 population had risen from 151 in 1960 to 228 in 1983, while newly licensed doctors (some of them graduates of foreign medical schools) had increased over the same period from 8,000 to 20,600 a year. Clearly some of the newly licensed physicians were finding the prospect of successfully entering private practice unpromising and welcomed the opportunity–formerly scorned by many–to join the staff of an HMO.

Not only had membership in HMOs increased rapidly, but the number of HMOs had risen substantially, to 650 in 1987. Some of the newer HMOs were operated for profit, and HMOs came in all shapes and sizes, with some operating on a nationwide basis. In addition, increasing numbers of physicians are in preferred provider organizations (PPO), which are similar to HMOs except that the patient chooses from a range of doctors and hospitals which offer their services at a discount to their members. The fact that some of the HMOs advertised their services vigorously indicated that competition was keen. Another sign of the changing environment was a decline in the rate of increase of physicians' incomes, a trend that was also appearing in a number of other industrial countries (ILO, 1985a).[6]

Meanwhile the sharply rising costs of Medicare constituted a problem of major concern. Medicare provides for compulsory hospital insurance for virtually all persons aged 65 and older, financed by a contributory tax of 1.45 percent on employers and an equivalent tax on employees (a tax rate that has risen over the years). The program also provides for voluntary supplementary medical insurance (SMI) in which nearly all persons aged 65 and older enroll. SMI receives about 75 percent (originally one half) of its revenue from general federal revenues and the rest from a monthly premium ($24.80 a month in 1988), which is deducted from the monthly benefits of those receiving cash social security benefits. Persons who go on working beyond age 65 pay the premium on a quarterly basis.

---

[6] Recent reports, however, do not suggest a declining rate in the United States.

In 1972, Medicare was extended to include persons under age 65 who had been receiving federal disability insurance benefits for at least 24 months, as well as to childhood disability beneficiaries and persons suffering from terminal kidney disease.

Benefit provisions are rather technical and will be discussed only briefly. In 1986, benefits included up to 90 days in a hospital in a benefit period,[7] but the patient had to pay a deductible which was adjusted each year and in 1986 amounted to $492 for the first day of hospitalization. There was also a co-insurance payment equal to 25 percent of the deductible for the 61st through the 90th day. After the 90 days were exhausted, each beneficiary had a lifetime reserve of 60 days of hospital care but at a cost of 50 percent of the deductible per day. A semiprivate room and all the customary hospital services were included.

Nursing home services have been covered on a very limited basis, following hospitalization of at least three days, for a maximum period of 100 days, but after the first 20 days patients have had to pay an amount equal to 12 1/2 percent of the hospital deductible per day for each of the remaining days. Thus, nursing home care has been provided only in connection with the type of acute illness that would require hospitalization, and there has been no provision for the person who needs to enter a nursing home on a long-term basis. There has been a provision, however, for payment of the reasonable cost of home health services.

There is no question that access to health care for the elderly has improved greatly as a result of both Medicare and Medicaid, and yet in the mid-1980s, less than half of the expenditures of the elderly for medical care were met by Medicare, whereas only about 14 percent were met by Medicaid (Davis and Rowland, 1986, 33). As Medicare costs have risen, there has been a tendency to increase deductibles and coinsurance payments, as well as monthly premiums. In response, many of the elderly, especially those in middle- and upper-income brackets, have purchased private insurance to supplement Medicare.

In 1983, the Reagan administration inaugurated a new approach to containing hospital costs by shifting away from reimbursement of charges per day to lump-sum payments for treating specific illnesses under so-called diagnosis related groups (DRGs) in the Medicare program. Although this appears to have resulted in some slowing down of the increase in hospital costs of the elderly, hospitals have responded in many cases by discharging patients sooner, to the detriment of some patients who have needed longer hospital care.

Cries of alarm about the impending insolvency of Medicare are a frequent occurrence, chiefly because hospital costs have been rising at a much more

[7] A benefit year begins when the individual enters a hospital and ends when the person has not received inpatient hospital or skilled-nursing facilities services for 60 days (*SSB*, 1986, *49* [January]: 19).

rapid rate than the revenue from the contributory taxes that finance the hospital insurance portion of the program, and this trend is expected to continue. The catastrophic illness bill of 1988 provided for free hospital care after payment of the deductible, limited an individual's liability for doctor bills, and partially met drug costs – to be financed by an increase in the monthly premium and an income tax surcharge on upper-income elderly persons.

In the long run, what is needed is a shift to universal health insurance to overcome the serious inequities in the present situation and to reduce per capita costs of public insurance by bringing the high-cost elderly and the lower-cost members of the under-65 population into a single insurance scheme.

The political climate in recent years has been extremely unfavorable for such a move, given the concern about the federal deficit and the conservative bent of the Reagan administration. In the longer run, however, the prospect may be more favorable, partly because the younger generation of physicians, many of them working in HMOs and similar settings, are likely to be more receptive to a universal health insurance plan than their older colleagues. Many of them are not joining the AMA, which now enrolls less than half of all physicians (Hume, 1986). Moreover, opinion polls have shown that the great majority of persons favor adoption of a national health insurance system.

Other mixed systems

Apart from the United States, there are a number of other countries whose health benefit systems do not fall neatly into any of our classifications, but they will be discussed rather briefly.

In Australia, most of the population has been covered by voluntary health insurance, but attempts to make coverage mandatory have seesawed with changes in government (see Aaron, 1984, for a good summary of the changes). However, pensioners and low-income persons have generally benefited from special provisions and have been entitled to free care in public hospitals. In fact, most of the hospitals are public – owned by the states and receiving lump-sum appropriations from state governments, which in turn receive grants from the Commonwealth.

Japan has had two main schemes, much as in old-age insurance: a mandatory scheme for employees in firms with five or more employees (with a contracting-out provision) and a national health insurance scheme for other residents who were not covered by any health insurance program. There have also been special schemes for persons aged 70 or more, farmers, public employees, and other industry groups. Japan received "high marks" in a survey of health care in five countries conducted for *The Economist* (April 28, 1984) for its low expenditures per capita while achieving low infant mortality and high life expectancy. Much of its success was attributed to emphasis on preventive medicine and extensive use of physician extenders and assistants.

Ireland has had a history of emphasis on public hospitals that have provided care free of charge, except that patients with income above a certain level have had to pay for consultants' services. Israel has not had a national health insurance scheme but has had an extensive private scheme which has developed over a long period, largely through the initiative of Histadrut, the general labor federation.

Switzerland is another country with its own unique pattern, which has left the main responsibility for health insurance to the cantons, but has imposed certain federal standards. Membership has been compulsory in some of the cantons, and in certain cities in other cantons, but the compulsory feature has usually applied to residents with incomes below a certain level.

Per capita expenditures

Before concluding the present chapter, it is of interest to consider comparative data on per capita expenditures on health recently developed by OECD (OECD, 1987a, 21).

In terms of dollars at current exchange rates in 1980, per capita expenditures were highest in the United States, but West Germany was a close second (Table 10.4). Also high were per capita expenditures in the Netherlands, Norway, and Denmark. They were considerably lower in Canada than in the United States, probably reflecting at least to some extent the more effective controls on hospital charges and physicians' fees in Canada. Also of interest were the low per capita expenditures in the United Kingdom. Not surprisingly, Greece and Spain were at the bottom of the list.

However, when per capita expenditures were adjusted for differences in health prices, the rank order of countries was appreciably altered. The adjustment consisted of computing the ratio of health prices in each country to the average in all countries and dividing per capita expenditures in each country by these ratios. The results provide a measure of volume that reflects the valuation of each country's health services relative to the average international prices of those services. On this basis, Norway ranks at the top, followed by France, the Netherlands, Finland, Japan, Austria, and West Germany, with the United States ranking seventh. Greece and Spain were again at the bottom of the list. As the OECD reports point out, there are many factors (including, for example, the age structure of the population), that help to explain differences in per capita expenditures. Of special interest, however, is the fact that the report showed that both hospital charges and physician fees for various specific types of services were far higher in the United States than elsewhere.

Table 10.4. *Per capita health expenditures in OECD countries in U.S. dollars, 1980, converted on the basis of current exchange rates and after adjustment for purchasing power parities*

Country	Current exchange rates	Adjusted for purchasing power parities
United States	$1,087	$ 809
Germany (Fed. Rep.)	1,065	825
France	1,036	941
Netherlands	983	865
Norway	963	1,071
Denmark	879	665
Canada	787	663
Belgium	747	675
Austria	718	828
Finland	677	853
Japan	569	832
United Kingdom	530	653
Ireland	480	509
Italy	479	636
Spain	334	405
Greece	175	289

Source: OECD (1987a, 21).

Conclusions

Although there was a pronounced trend in the first several decades after World War II toward providing health care free of charge either under broad compulsory insurance programs or through the provision of free services, this trend has been reversed in a number of countries in the 1970s and the 1980s under the impact of inflation, through the imposition of new or increased charges on patients and through nationwide programs to control the increases in health expenditures. To a large extent, however, the patient charges do not apply to low-income persons and to pensioners. The imposition of charges on patients, provided they are moderate, may not be undesirable, but a good deal depends on whose financial burden is being relieved by these charges. There is also a case for exempting from the charges those with low incomes.

Meanwhile, the postwar experience has indicated that greatly increased expenditures on health care have not led to commensurate improvements in health. To quote from Abel-Smith (1983b, 166), the author of several comparative studies of health care:

The rapid increase in spending in real terms has not led to a commensurate improvement in standardised mortality rates; this is the case although nearly all the pharmaceuticals prescribed today were invented over the past 40 years and advanced medical technology has been introduced over the last 20 years;

There are no clear correlations between standardised mortality rates and the proportion of GNP spent on health care, physicians per 1,000 population or hospital beds per 1,000 population . . . ;

In countries which have data, there has not been a narrowing of relative differences in mortality rates between different social classes.

There may be some exceptions to this rather gloomy assessment. Life expectancy has increased in a number of countries, if not at a rate commensurate with increased spending. Fuchs (1986, 276–7) has pointed out that in the United States the relation between income and life expectancy has tended to disappear, but that there is one factor – education – that consistently appears as a correlate of good health. There is evidence in a number of countries that higher-income and better-educated persons are more likely to seek high-quality care and to live in areas where high-quality care is available. In addition, as we shall find in Chapter 14, funds are often inadequate to meet the needs of those who must resort to public assistance to finance their care.

Thus, despite impressive progress in access to health care, there is much progress yet to be made. As the ILO experts put it: "We are in no doubt that the development of services for prevention and rehabilitation should receive the highest priority in social security policy for the period up to the year 2000 and beyond" (ILO, 1984b, 108).

CHAPTER 11

Unemployment compensation

Unemployment was the last of the risks confronting the worker in modern industrial societies to be protected by a compulsory social insurance system. Benefits for the aged and the ill were, on the whole, less controversial, whereas deeply embedded in poor relief policies was the notion that the "able-bodied poor" were responsible for their own idleness and therefore must be harshly treated. In England, toward the end of the nineteenth century, this meant that, in general, they were to be denied "outdoor relief" and were to be sent to the workhouse. Policies in some of the continental European countries were less harsh, but were nevertheless punitive (see, e.g., de Schweinitz, 1943, and Heclo, 1974).

Moreover, prevailing economic thought weighed against intervention on behalf of the unemployed. Say's "law of markets," first proclaimed by the French economist in 1803, held in its simplified version that supply creates its own demand and that therefore the economy will adjust to its potential without need of government intervention. It was not until the latter part of the nineteenth century that economists like Knut Wicksell in Sweden undertook studies of business cycles and confirmed the existence of recurring involuntary unemployment. Even then, adjustments at the micro level, such as wage reductions, were the preferred response. It was not until after the publication of Keynes's *General Theory* (1936) that the principle that governments should be responsible for maintaining full employment began to take hold. Keynesian policies were dominant in the first few decades after World War II, but in the 1970s some economists began to question the notion that most unemployment was involuntary. In the United States, although "mainstream" economists continued to regard most unemployment as involuntary, proponents of the "search theory" or "turnover theory" of unemployment questioned this, and some economists held that unemployment insurance prolonged unemployment. We shall come back to this controversy later.

Prewar developments

Ghent system

The response of trade unions in various parts of Europe to recurring unemployment was to develop voluntary insurance funds, to which workers contributed, and which provided partial compensation for wage loss to members who became unemployed. In Britain, by the first decade of the twentieth century, about 80 of the largest unions, with about three-quarters of a million members, maintained such funds (Gilbert, 1966). But it was on the continent that a movement developed for municipal subsidization of union unemployment funds. Known as the ''Ghent system'' because an early move toward subsidization of voluntary funds was made in that Belgian city in 1901, the scheme was subsequently adopted by many town governments in Belgium and by cities in the Netherlands, Denmark, France, Germany, and Italy (Gilbert, 1966). Legislation establishing the subsidies on a national basis was enacted by France, Norway, Denmark, and Belgium in the years from 1905 to 1908.

According to Armstrong (1932), the limitations of the Ghent system lay in the fact that the labor unions involved were composed of skilled workers and engaged actively in placing their members in employment. Subsidized municipal voluntary unemployment insurance funds, which had been tried in a few German cities and Swiss communes in the 1890s, were unsuccessful because they attracted only those who were especially likely to experience unemployment, and the subsidies required were far greater than the contributions.

The British act of 1911

By the first decade of the twentieth century, the need for reform of the outmoded poor relief policies toward the able-bodied poor had come to be widely recognized in Britain, and the 1909 report of the Poor Law Commission included a thoroughgoing indictment of the current poor relief policies, although the Majority and Minority reports differed in the policies that they recommended (Sidney and Beatrice Webb, 1910).

If Lloyd George was the father of health insurance, it was Winston Churchill, as president of the Board of Trade, who became convinced that unemployment insurance was essential and who was instrumental in achieving enactment of the Labor Exchanges Act of 1909, which empowered the Board of Trade to establish labor exchanges in places that needed them and to develop regulations for their management.

There followed a period of intensive debate over the framing of the unemployment insurance act, with the result that the carefully planned British legislation of 1911 incorporated a number of principles that subsequently became embodied in unemployment insurance in other countries. Many of its provisions were influenced by the experience of the voluntary funds. Initially, the act was to apply only to trades in which cyclical unemployment was prevalent, because it was felt that there was too little information about unemployment in other sectors of the economy to justify broader inclusion. The scheme was to be financed by employer and employee contributions of 5d. a week for each worker, half of which was to be deducted from the employee's wages. The state was to be obligated to pay one-third of the combined contributions. The benefit was to be 7s. a week, payable after a one-week waiting period, for a maximum of 15 weeks within a 12-month period. Not more than one week of benefit could be given for each five weeks of contributions.

Provisions for disqualification under certain circumstances were strongly influenced by the experience of the voluntary funds. No benefit could be paid when the individual's unemployment was attributable to a strike within the establishment in which he or she was employed. If a worker quit a job without good cause or was fired for misconduct, he or she was to be denied benefit for a period of six weeks. There was, however, a right of appeal, and according to Gilbert (1966), the regulations rarely denied benefits to a worker who was eligible on the basis of weeks of contributions. No attempt was made to use the denial of benefits to punish an alcoholic or otherwise improve working-class habits of life.

The act came into effect under favorable circumstances. There was relatively little unemployment in the years preceding World War I, in contrast with the situation that was to develop after the war.

The first important revision of the act in 1920 extended coverage to practically all manual workers and most nonmanual workers. The groups excluded, as in many other countries, were the self-employed, domestic workers, and agricultural workers. However, the legislation was not destined to provide benefits in the form contemplated. After a brief postwar recovery, the basic competitive weaknesses of Britain's main export industries – coal, cotton and textiles, shipbuilding, and engineering – began to be apparent. Hampered by old equipment and old work practices, their plight was made worse by the return to the gold standard in 1925, which resulted in an overvalued pound sterling. The unemployment rate rose to 17 percent in 1921 and was followed by rates ranging from 10.3 percent to 14.3 percent during the remainder of the 1920s. Rates were even higher in the worst years of the Great Depression of the 1930s (Johnson, 1985, 164).

To meet this crisis, contribution rates were increased several times, and the Exchequer loaned money to the unemployment fund, which became heavily indebted. The duration of benefits was also extended. The act of 1927 was designed to provide a permanent model, with a requirement for 30 contributions in the previous two years to establish eligibility for benefits. Eligibility, once established, was to continue for the duration of unemployment. Transitional arrangements required fewer weeks of contributions.

With the onset of the Great Depression, additional drastic changes were made necessary. During 1930, unemployment rose to include one-fifth of all insured persons. Between December 1929 and December 1931, the debt of the unemployment insurance fund more than tripled to £110 million (Heclo, 1974, 119). The controversy over what should be done about unemployment insurance was involved, along with broader issues of economic policy, in bringing down the MacDonald Labor government in 1931, and replacing it with a national coalition government. On October 7, transitional unemployment benefits were replaced by means-tested "transitional payments" administered by local public assistance committees with funds from the Exchequer. Although there were additional changes during the course of the 1930s, assistance payments, which came to be known as the "dole," were the primary source of unemployment relief throughout the decade. This was also true in a number of other countries.

Other early legislation

Apart from the British law, the enactment of compulsory unemployment insurance legislation awaited the end of World War I. By 1931, among the countries included in this study, there were seven with voluntary subsidized systems, and seven with compulsory systems. In addition, the Australian state of Queensland had a compulsory system, whereas Switzerland had a hybrid system (as in sickness insurance), in which the federal government provided subsidies to unemployment funds, which were also subsidized by the cantons, including some cantons with compulsory systems and others with voluntary systems.

Interestingly, the USSR adopted a compulsory system in 1922, but it was suspended in 1930 in one of a series of moves aimed at adjusting the supply of labor to the objectives of the five-year plan. A number of measures were taken that greatly limited the freedom of workers to choose their places of employment, or to refuse a job or retraining (Rimlinger, 1971, 271). Since then there has been no unemployment insurance system, although in recent years there have been occasional reports of special payments to workers, including managerial workers, who have been affected by layoffs. We shall find that a few of the other countries of Eastern Europe now have unemployment assistance systems, despite the prevailing doctrine, at least until recently, that there is no unemployment in socialist countries.

In 1931, the jurisdictions with voluntary systems included Belgium, Czechoslovakia, Denmark, Finland, France, the Netherlands, Norway, and 14 Swiss cantons, whereas those with compulsory systems included Austria, Germany, Great Britain, the Irish Free State, Italy, Poland, nine Swiss cantons, and Queensland.

Most of the provisions governing the subsidization of voluntary systems called for contributions by workers but not by employers, and they did not provide for a standard benefit, although they did provide for a maximum benefit, usually amounting to one-half to two-thirds of the prevailing wage.

In other respects, however, there were many resemblances between the two types of systems. They usually included a qualifying period of required contributions, a waiting period before benefits could be paid, and a provision for maximum duration of benefits. Under both types of laws a worker who quit his or her job without good cause or was terminated for misconduct could be disqualified for a certain period (although in some of the voluntary systems he or she was denied benefits for an indefinite period).

In many of the laws, also, there were provisions relating to "suitable work." A worker was permitted to refuse a job if it provided less than the prevailing wage and in some cases if the job required a change in the worker's usual occupation. Generally, however, workers who had been receiving unemployment benefits for a certain number of weeks without finding a suitable job could be required to lower their aspirations.

The German decision to enact a compulsory unemployment insurance law in 1927 is of interest, because it was so long delayed after the initial move to social insurance in the 1880s. For one thing, unemployment tended to be somewhat less severe in the years before World War I in Germany than in Britain, according to trade union data, which were the only data available (Armstrong, 1932, 470). For another, the Germans were evidently somewhat uncertain that unemployment could be precisely enough defined to determine eligibility for insurance benefits.

Under the German law, the provisions for public employment offices and unemployment insurance were closely linked, and both were administered by the Imperial Institute for Labor Exchanges and Unemployment Insurance, a public body under the supervision of the federal minister of labor.

A large proportion of the working population was covered by the German law, although salaried workers with earnings above a certain level (as in sickness and old-age insurance) were excluded, along with self-employed farmers, tenant farmers, and casual workers.

Contributions and unemployment benefits were earnings-related, and the benefit formula was tilted toward low earners, with benefits ranging from 75 percent of wages for the lowest wage group to 35 percent for the highest group. There were modest dependents' benefits and a maximum duration of benefits of 26 weeks. Those who exhausted their right to benefits could receive means-tested benefits for a limited period.

The law was enacted at a time of low unemployment, but unemployment rose rapidly from 1928 to 1932. The result was a series of crises, including various types of restrictive measures and increases in contribution rates. Meanwhile the number on poor relief mounted and resulted in a heavy drain on local governments, some of which were on the verge of bankruptcy.

Thus, the German experience, like the British, indicated that unemployment insurance, financed in the usual way and with benefits provided as a matter of right, tended to break down in a period of severe unemployment. The main difference between this experience and that of recent years of high unemployment in Western Europe results from the fact that most Western European countries during the course of the postwar period developed national unemployment assistance systems, or public assistance for which the unemployed could qualify, with relatively little stigma, when they had exhausted their rights to insurance benefits. This has made it possible to maintain such features as limitations on the duration of unemployment insurance benefits, although, as we shall see, these have been stretched somewhat, especially for older workers. Another highly significant difference has been the much more substantial emphasis on labor market policies providing for retraining, public service employment, relocation allowances, and other measures aimed at reducing unemployment.

In Sweden, although there was much interest in unemployment insurance from around the turn of the century, the political situation did not favor enactment of legislation until after 1932, when the Social Democrats acquired a majority in Parliament.[1] Moreover, by that time, and foreshadowing the policies that were to be developed by the Social Democrats in the period following World War II, the party leaders had become convinced that countercyclical public expenditure was the primary need in combating unemployment and that unemployment insurance was secondary. In this they were strongly influenced by British proposals stressed by Keynes and the British Liberal Party as early as 1928, eight years before the publication of the *General Theory*.

Early in 1933, the new government adopted a plan for an unprecedented 200 million kr. to fight unemployment, at a time when the conventional wisdom in most countries continued to support wage reductions and retrenchment of government expenditures as the primary tools for overcoming unemployment. There followed a move to adopt an unemployment insurance program that took the form of subsidization of voluntary union funds.

In the United States, there was strong interest in unemployment insurance

---

[1] They had also held a majority in the 1920s, but it was narrow and short-lived.

within a limited circle of intellectuals throughout the early decades of the present century, and bills were introduced in a number of state legislatures, but it was not until 1932 that a measure was enacted in Wisconsin. One of the obstacles to enactment of legislation was that it was not until 1932 that the American Federation of Labor supported unemployment insurance. Another obstacle, at the state level, was the fear of employers that the imposition of a payroll tax would weaken their ability to compete with employers in other states.

When President Roosevelt, a longtime proponent of social insurance, moved to establish the Committee on Economic Security to frame social insurance legislation in 1934, one of the most difficult issues before the committee was whether unemployment insurance should be wholly federal or a mixed federal–state arrangement.[2] After a lengthy controversy, the committee chose to support a federal–state system under which employers in all the states would be subject to a federal payroll tax, most of which would be excused if they were contributing to a state unemployment insurance system that embodied certain features set forth in the federal act. The device proved to be extremely effective. Within two years after adoption of the Social Security Act, all the states had enacted unemployment insurance legislation.

As originally enacted, the law called for a federal payroll tax of 3 percent, with employers liable for only 10 percent of that amount if they were contributing to a state system. The proceeds of the federal tax have been used for grants to the states to meet administrative costs, and for advances to states with insufficient reserves. States are subject to a number of requirements, including (1) making benefit payments through a public employment office; (2) depositing their unemployment insurance funds in a special account maintained by the federal treasury, in order to ensure centralized management of the investment of the funds; (3) providing unemployed workers with the right of appeal to impartial tribunals in disputes over benefit claims; and (4) permitting unemployed workers to refuse jobs that do not meet prescribed standards without having their benefits withheld.

In addition, the federal law influences the state laws in other ways. Certain types of employment that are exempt from the federal unemployment insurance tax are also likely to be exempt from state laws, although there are exceptions, as we shall see. However, the states are free to frame their own provisions on such vital features as amount and duration of benefits, eligibility provisions, and, to a large extent, their tax schedules.

One of the exceptional features of unemployment insurance in the United States, found almost nowhere else, is the system of taxation that prevails

[2] For an account of this controversy, see Bernstein (1960). See also National Conference on Social Welfare (1985).

under the state laws. For one thing, in the great majority of states, the system is financed by an employer payroll tax. Only a few states provide for an employee contribution. Second, the employer tax is subject to "experience rating" – that is, employers who experience little unemployment in their firms pay a very low tax (at times, zero in some of the states), whereas employers with relatively high unemployment, as in the construction industry, pay a much higher tax. The notion underlying this approach, which was stressed in Wisconsin under the leadership of Professor John R. Commons of the University of Wisconsin, was that employers would be induced to stabilize their employment if they could therefore be subject to lower payroll taxes.

We shall have more to say about how this has worked out in connection with postwar developments, but at this point it should be noted that it was vigorously opposed by such experts as Eveline M. Burns and Paul H. Douglas at the time of its adoption and has been opposed by many experts since then (e.g., Lester, 1962).

Postwar developments

The behavior of unemployment

In connection with unemployment and unemployment insurance, the years since World War II fall into three periods. The 1950s and 1960s were years of rapid economic growth and very low unemployment, especially in Western Europe, but also in such countries as Japan and Australia. Thus, unemployment insurance revenue tended to exceed needs, and in West Germany, for example, unemployment insurance funds were used to finance retraining and other labor market programs. Beginning around 1973–5, the picture changed dramatically. High and rising unemployment rates created a strain on unemployment insurance funds. Although at first the reaction was to raise contributory rates and increase government allocations, as well as to extend the maximum duration of benefits in some cases, in the early 1980s there was something of a reversal toward restrictiveness.

Despite the predominantly upward trend in unemployment rates from the mid-1970s on, as we saw in Chapter 1, there were differences from country to country, and a few countries managed to escape increases. Although a detailed analysis of the differences is beyond the scope of this study, a brief discussion is in order, if only because in right-wing circles in some countries there is a tendency to attribute prolonged unemployment to overly generous income maintenance for the unemployed.

Why were unemployment rates in the 1950s and 1960s in the United States and Canada considerably higher than in Western Europe? This question was investigated by the U. S. President's Committee to Appraise Employment and

Unemployment Statistics (1962), which arranged for a special study to develop comparable unemployment data for a number of Western industrial countries and to analyze the reasons for the differences in rates.[3]

The results of the committee's study indicated that, after all adjustments were made, the unemployment rate was still considerably higher in the United States and Canada than in the six other countries included – France, West Germany, Great Britain, Italy, Japan, and Sweden. The analysis indicated that differences in methods of measuring unemployment played only a minor role in explaining the differences. Much more important were the exceedingly rapid rates of growth achieved by the other countries during the period, along with pronounced productivity gains in Germany, Japan, Italy, and France. Other factors were also mentioned, including the prevalence of policies in other countries, and especially in Japan, that tended to deter employers from laying off workers who had been with the company for a considerable period of time.

In very recent years, the relative position of countries has been strikingly different. The unemployment rate fell in the United States and to some extent in Canada from 1982 to 1986, whereas in Western Europe it tended to remain "stuck" at high levels, although there were signs of some improvement during the course of 1986 in some countries.

There has been a tendency to attribute the relative persistence of high unemployment rates in Western Europe to the rigidity of real wages. Lindbeck (1985) among others has argued that one of the most important prerequisites for a return to low levels of unemployment in Western Europe is more flexibility of real and relative wages. He goes on to identify differences between the United States and Western Europe as follows:

The problem is not that real and relative wages are 'fixed' in Western Europe, but rather that they sometimes change in the 'wrong' directions . . . while at other times they adjust too slowly in the 'right' direction. It would seem that, in this respect, the economic system functions much better in the United States than in Western Europe. In particular, it is striking to note that since 1973 more than 20 million jobs have been created in the United States, while there has been a virtual stagnation in Western Europe. It is also interesting to note that the average period of unemployment is much longer in Western Europe than in the United States, where unemployment 'rotates' among a somewhat larger fraction of the labour force than in Western Europe. The better performance of the American economy . . . is reflected in this ability not only to absorb an increasing labour force but also to recover from recessions and to shift resources – labour as well as capital – to expanding industries.

(Lindbeck, 1985, 158)

---

[3] The committee was appointed by President Kennedy following the appearance of several articles in popular magazines charging that the official unemployment statistics overstated the amount of unemployment. The committee concluded that this was not the case, but did recommend certain improvements, which were largely adopted.

Unlike some other economists who have emphasized wage rigidity, however, Lindbeck contends that restrictive fiscal policies during the first half of the 1980s have been a major reason for the drastic increase in unemployment.

The view that real-wage rigidity has been the key problem has been challenged by R. J. Gordon (1986) on the basis of an analysis that distinguished between manufacturing and nonmanufacturing industries in 14 countries. Another recent study of the situation in ten countries of Western Europe (Soskice, 1987) concluded that the low unemployment countries – Austria, Norway, and Sweden[4] – have benefited from an interlinked "package" that included (1) company and industry level adjustment; (2) macro-real-wage moderation with work-force consensus; and (3) a political bargain, in exchange for using aggregate demand management as far as possible and maintaining employment security.[5]

Most economists would probably agree that a substantial portion of unemployment in Western Europe in recent years has been "structural" – that is, calling for shifts from declining industries or occupations to others that may be difficult to achieve because unemployed workers do not have the skills required in the expanding occupations or industries.

The evidence that much unemployment in Western Europe is structural is found primarily in what has been happening to employment in manufacturing, compared with what has happened in the United States and Japan. In the United States, there was very little change in total manufacturing employment between 1970 and 1985. Declines in some industries hard hit by foreign competition, such as textiles and steel, were offset by gains in the electronics and related industries. In Japan, there was a modest increase in total manufacturing employment, reflecting a preponderance of gains over losses. In contrast, many of the countries of Western Europe experienced sharp losses in manufacturing employment, and the resulting effects on overall employment were very pronounced because factory employment had represented a relatively large proportion of total employment at the beginning of the period.

This is not to say that there have not been difficult adjustments in employment in the United States and Japan. Not only has there been the problem of absolute declines in some manufacturing industries, but there has also been an increase in the proportion of nonproduction workers in manufacturing, especially in "high tech" industries. This change was already far advanced in California in the mid-1960s, with its high proportion of employment in the

---

[4] Soskice explained, in delivering his paper (at a session which I attended), that he had not included Switzerland in this group because its success in holding down unemployment had been due largely to "sending" foreign workers back home.
[5] In another recent study, McCallum (1986) concluded that cross-country differences in unemployment performance since 1979 had been due largely to fiscal and monetary policy, with the real-wage variable playing a minor role.

aerospace industries. It has contributed to the problem of a "mismatch" between the qualifications of the unemployed and the requirements of available jobs. In fact, many displaced factory workers in the United States have had to take lower-paying jobs in trade and service industries.

Exacerbating the problem of opening up job opportunities for displaced manufacturing workers was the fact that they were frequently concentrated in particular regions or areas, as in the familiar case of the concentration of heavy industry in the Midlands and the north of England. In West Germany, unemployment has been particularly pronounced in the area of Bremen, with its shipbuilding industry, and much less pronounced in Baden-Württemberg in the south, with its electronics and aerospace industries.

Characteristics of the unemployed

In the 1950s and 1960s, unemployment tended to be more severe among young workers newly entering the labor force and among older workers than among middle-aged workers. This pattern continues to prevail, but unemployment of youth is now a much more severe problem in most countries, while the situation of older workers varies. In countries that have taken decided steps to increase incentives for early retirement, the unemployment rate of older workers is in some cases no higher, or even lower, than that of middle-aged workers (Table 11.1).

The problem of unemployment among older workers is not that they become unemployed more often than middle-aged workers. In fact, many of them enjoy a relatively high degree of job security. However, when an older worker does become unemployed, he or she often has great difficulty in achieving reemployment and tends to fall into the category of the long-term unemployed. And, it is scarcely necessary to add that in a period of prolonged high unemployment the proportion of long-term unemployed, especially among older workers, rises substantially.

Unemployment rates for youth rose sharply between the late 1960s and the early 1980s, to a point that in some countries was alarming (Table 11.2). At the same time, there were pronounced differences from country to country that largely reflected differences in patterns of transition from school to work. In Japan, the teenage unemployment rate was relatively low in both 1968 and 1984, reflecting both the low overall unemployment rate and the very high school-retention rate (Kato, 1978; Umetani and Reubens, 1983).

On the other hand, in West Germany, where the overall unemployment rate was much higher than in Japan, the teenage unemployment rate was surprisingly low in both 1968 and 1984, explained in large part by the fact that a very large proportion of "school leavers" who do not go on to higher education are hired as apprentices and are employed continuously throughout the apprenticeship period of several years.

Table 11.1. *Unemployment rates by age and sex, selected countries, 1984*

Country	United States		Canada		Japan		Austria		Germany (Fed. Rep.)		Italy	
	Male	Female	Male	Female	Male	Female	Male	Female	Male	Female	Male	Female
All ages	7.4%	7.6%	11.2%	12.2%	2.7%	2.6%	0.9%	1.7%	6.6%	8.8%	6.7%	6.9%
15–19[a]	19.6	18.0	20.5	18.1	8.5	5.1	0.5	1.1	6.6	9.2	35.9	52.7
20–24	11.9	10.9	9.5	14.4	3.8	4.9	1.0	1.9	9.5	12.0	22.9	34.4
25–44	6.3	6.6	10.4	12.2	1.9	2.9	0.9	2.0	6.3	8.9	3.8	11.8
45–54	4.6	5.2	7.1	9.0	1.7	1.9	0.8	1.7	4.7	6.2	1.9	5.5
55–59	4.9	4.6	7.0[b]	6.3[b]	4.0	2.2	1.0	1.4	9.4	10.0	2.1	2.1
60 and over	4.4	3.8			4.3	1.4	0.7	1.0	6.0	3.7	0.5	1.5

[a] 16–19 in the United States.
[b] Rate for age 55 and over.
Source: Computed from data in ILO, *Yearbook of Labor Statistics, 1985.*

Table 11.2. *Unemployment rates of teenagers and persons aged 20 to 24, selected countries, 1968 and 1984*

Country	Teenagers		Aged 20 to 24	
	1968	1984	1968	1984
United States	12.7%	18.9%	5.8%	11.5%
Canada	11.3	20.0	6.3	16.8
Australia	4.2	22.3	1.9	12.9
Japan	2.3	6.9	1.8	4.6
France	7.3	30.7[a]	3.5	18.8[a]
Germany (Fed. Rep.)	3.8	6.9[b]	1.4	8.0[b]
United Kingdom	7.0[c]	22.8	4.8[c]	18.8
Italy	12.4[d]	26.6[a]	9.3[d]	15.6[a]
Sweden	5.6	5.0	3.0	6.7

[a] 1983.
[b] 1982.
[c] 1971.
[d] Data not adjusted to U.S. concepts.
Sources: U.S. Bureau of Labor Statistics (1978, 35–6); Moy (1985, 18).

Even in periods of low overall unemployment, the unemployment rate for teenagers is often somewhat higher than that for adults, because young unemployed persons include a substantial proportion of new entrants to the labor force, who tend to go through a "floundering" period with a number of job changes before they obtain a stable job. Numerous studies have shown that this occurs not so much because they are "choosy" as because the jobs they get are often temporary or seasonal. The difficulty became more serious in a number of countries in the 1960s or in some cases later because of the high birth rates that prevailed for a time after the war, which led to a sharp increase in the number of young people entering the labor force 15 or 16 years later.

However, there are widespread predictions that the youth unemployment problem will not "go away" even if full employment is restored in many industrial countries in the coming years. The reasons for this stem from developments on both the demand and supply sides of the labor market and therefore can be more appropriately discussed when we come to consider labor market programs for youth in the next chapter.

Unemployment among blue-collar workers and especially among the unskilled continues to be more severe than among white-collar workers; however, in an era when many firms have been closed or "bought out," unemployment among white-collar workers has tended to become somewhat more important in the overall unemployment mix than was formerly the case. Interestingly, also, some of the unemployed have gone into self-employment. Contrary to earlier trends, nonagricultural self-employment increased 50 percent in the United States and 47 percent in Britain between 1970 and 1985. There were also sizable increases in Canada and Australia, but not in most continental Western European countries (OECD, 1987b), where in some cases high marginal tax rates may discourage investment in small business. Interestingly, also, it was reported in the fall of 1986 that the Soviet Union was adopting new policies aimed at encouraging self-employment. The move was consistent with the Gorbachev policy of greater reliance on market forces. Another significant development in the United States has been an increase in the number of persons employed in relatively small firms, as large firms have been affected by take-overs and mergers that have resulted in displacement of workers at all levels.

Postwar unemployment insurance

During or soon after World War II, a number of countries that had not had unemployment insurance systems before the war enacted unemployment insurance or assistance laws. Canada adopted a compulsory insurance law in 1940 that was greatly strengthened in 1971. Australia, conforming to its usual pattern of favoring assistance schemes, enacted legislation in 1944 providing for a means-tested unemployment assistance system like that adopted in New Zealand some years earlier. Greece adopted compulsory unemployment insurance in 1945, Japan in 1947, and Israel in 1970.

Postwar developments in France were somewhat exceptional. The country emerged from the war with a weak unemployment assistance system, and the first move toward unemployment insurance was the negotiation of a collective bargaining agreement between the major labor federations and the federation of employers providing for unemployment insurance in the firms included in the agreement (i.e., most firms in industry and commerce) in 1958. Financed originally entirely by employer contributions, and later also by an employee contribution, the scheme was made compulsory in 1967 legislation for all firms in industry and commerce.

Departing from the usual pattern in Eastern Europe, Hungary adopted an unemployment assistance system in 1957, as did Yugoslavia some years later. On the other hand, East Germany, which had continued its unemployment insurance system after the war, formally dismantled the system in 1977, when it adopted a constitutional provision guaranteeing the right to employment.

In 1985, the great majority of unemployment compensation systems took the form of compulsory insurance. There were, however, a number of exceptions, including the unemployment assistance schemes in Australia, New Zealand, Hungary, and Yugoslavia. Switzerland gradually moved from its combination of compulsory and voluntary insurance to a nationwide compulsory system under legislation adopted in 1976 and 1982. Although the cantons were given a role in implementing the federal law, minimum standards for benefit levels and duration of benefits were governed by the federal law, unlike the situation in the United States. Denmark, Finland, and Sweden continued their voluntary union funds, but both Finland and Sweden had adopted legislation in the 1970s providing for a nationwide unemployment assistance system.

In general, the trend has been toward liberalization of coverage, benefits, and maximum duration (cf. Alber, 1982), but in recent years there have been some restrictions in response to severe financing difficulties.

Coverage: Unlike some of the early laws, which covered only workers in industries particularly likely to experience unemployment, by 1985 coverage in most unemployment insurance systems was broad, and the trend had been toward limiting exclusions.

Probably the most common exclusion was of self-employed workers, largely because it was not easy to determine whether unemployment was involuntary in their cases. However, they were covered in Denmark, along with employees belonging to voluntary funds, which were found in all types of industries, and in which membership was compulsory for union members in those industries. The self-employed also tended to be eligible for assistance in countries with general unemployment assistance schemes (discussed in Chapter 14).

There were upper and lower age limits in the systems of most countries. The lower age limit generally coincided with the school-leaving age, whereas workers above the normal retirement age were usually excluded either on the basis of age or by the exclusion of old-age pensioners.

Many of the laws also excluded casual workers or workers with very low earnings, as well as family workers. Exclusion of agricultural employees, which used to be quite common, was infrequent. In Japan, however, coverage was voluntary for employees in agriculture, forestry, and fishing in enterprises with fewer than five employees. Agricultural employees had long been excluded in the United States, but this was no longer true; although the federal law covered only workers on relatively large farms, some of the states had brought in those on smaller farms.

Qualifying requirements: In order to qualify for unemployment insurance, a person must have worked in covered employment for a certain period of time. Moreover, in order to test recent attachment to the labor force, the work experience must have been in a recent period, generally referred to as the "base period." Probably the most common base period in 1985 was a year, and a particularly frequent requirement was that the individual must have been employed in covered employment for at least six months, or 26 weeks, during the year preceding his or her claim for benefits. However, a number of countries required a record of employment over a longer period. In West Germany, for example, a claimant must have had 360 days of insured employment in the last four years (raised from three years in 1984).

In some countries, such as Belgium and France, the requirements were relatively complex, providing for a minimum and a maximum period of coverage. In Belgium, for example, the claimant must have had from 75 days of insured employment in the last ten months to 600 days in the last 36 months, with the required period of employment rising with the age of the claimant. This was clearly related to the fact that until recently there has been no limit on duration of benefits in Belgium, and older workers, family breadwinners, and certain other groups have continued to be eligible for benefits indefinitely.

State laws in the United States usually define the base period as the first four quarters of the last five completed calendar quarters preceding the claim. During these quarters a claimant must have earned a certain minimum amount.

Danish requirements appeared to be relatively lenient, calling for 26 weeks of employment in the last three years, but to qualify for the maximum duration of benefits, the 26 weeks must have immediately preceded the period of unemployment. There was no longer a limit on duration, as we shall see, but benefits were reduced after a period of time.

In a few countries, including Austria and Japan, the base period could be extended to include periods of sickness, employment in noncovered firms, and certain other contingencies.

Young persons entering the labor force with no work experience were usually not eligible for unemployment benefits, but there were some important exceptions in 1985. In Belgium, benefits were payable to claimants under age 25 who had completed their education or training if they had been registered as seeking employment for a specified period of time. The benefits were payable for up to one year, but could be extended for time spent in military service or under other special circumstances. In the United Kingdom, school leavers could qualify for supplementary benefits (public assistance) without regard to parental income, but had to wait from July until September to receive them. In France, young persons aged 16 to 25 registering for the first time at an employment agency, or young persons supporting a family, were entitled to allowances that were not means-tested.

Denmark had an unusual provision under which youth allowances were provided for young persons aged 16 and 17 under the family allowance system even though they were not continuing in school, as long as the family income did not exceed a certain (relatively high) maximum amount. Those who had participated in training programs were immediately eligible for special compensation for loss of income if they could not find work. Sweden also had a provision under which young people without work experience could receive unemployment assistance from age 16 on, provided they had been actively seeking work for at least three months (ILO, *Legislative Series* 1973 – Swe. 3; Blaustein and Craig, 1977, 91–2). Also, in West Germany, a young person had to have completed ten weeks of remunerated employment (much less than the standard requirement) to receive unemployment benefits, but the completion of vocational education or a college education could be considered the equivalent (*SSB*, 1984, *37* [March]: 41–5).

In general, however, young persons receiving these income maintenance payments had to meet the usual requirements of being registered for work, available for suitable work, etc. Moreover, these and other countries had provisions for allowances for youth in training programs.

If there were substantial differences in minimum periods of qualifying employment from country to country, there were strong similarities in other eligibility conditions. Universally, claimants had to be involuntarily unemployed, actively seeking work, and available for work. They could be disqualified for a certain number of weeks if they had quit their jobs voluntarily without good cause or if they had been discharged for misconduct. Also, they were not eligible if involved directly in a strike.

To be considered available for work, a claimant had to be willing, able, and ready to accept "suitable" employment. This is the broad principle that underlies decisions as to availability, but it leaves unanswered many of the questions that arise in particular cases. Much of the difficulty arises over what is considered suitable work. As Blaustein and Craig have put it, in their useful comparative study of unemployment insurance systems:

The definition of the term *suitable* work varies among the countries. Many of the criteria . . . relate to concern for the protection of labor standards or codes established through law or collective bargaining or custom. They generally reflect the view that temporary involuntary unemployment should not be the occasion for damage to the status achieved by the worker in his line of work. The main factors taken into account are (1) the rate of pay and terms of employment; (2) the location of the new job in relation to the worker's home and to transportation facilities; and (3) the relationship of the new job offered to the worker's previous occupation, skills, experience, and physical capabilities.

(Blaustein and Craig, 1977, 47)

Policies in most countries, however, tend to lower standards of suitable work for those who have been unemployed for a considerable period of time.

Also nearly universal are requirements that an unemployed worker register at the public employment office and report regularly to learn of any possible job opportunities.[6]

---

[6] An exception is Britain, where registration for employment ceased to be a condition of entitlement to unemployment benefits in October 1982, except for young people under age 18. The

Waiting periods: The practice of imposing a waiting period from the onset of unemployment until the worker is entitled to benefits was common, but not universal, in 1985. The exceptions were Belgium, Denmark, France, West Germany, the Netherlands, Spain, and nine American states. In addition, no waiting period was stipulated under the unemployment assistance schemes in Hungary and Yugoslavia. Elsewhere, the waiting period varied from three days to a week in most cases, but in Canada it was two weeks, whereas in Switzerland it was only one day.

A waiting period can be justified on the ground that most workers are in a position to experience a very short period of unemployment without great hardship. From an administrative point of view, it has the great advantage of not involving processing of applications from the large numbers of workers who experience short temporary layoffs or who have patterns of irregular employment.

Benefit provisions: Comparison of statutory provisions for unemployment benefits does not yield an accurate measure of the relative proportions of earnings replaced, for several reasons. In nearly all countries except the United States, for example, children's allowances continue to be paid to families of the unemployed, sometimes in addition to dependents' benefits, whereas in the United States, but not elsewhere, many of the unemployed are eligible for food stamps, which subsidize their food costs. Housing subsidies are also received by families of the unemployed in some countries.

Moreover, statutory provisions that provide for earnings-related benefits, as most do, often specify a certain percentage of gross earnings, whereas, in fact, the percentage of take-home pay received by an unemployed worker in the form of insurance benefits may be considerably higher than the percentage of gross earnings because the worker's take-home pay has been reduced by contributory social security taxes and by the withholding of income taxes. The unemployment benefits he or she receives, however, are not subject to contributory taxes, and, though subject to the income tax in a number of countries, it is chiefly those with a working spouse, or comparatively high earnings, and therefore high benefits, who are likely to be liable for a significant income tax.

Other complications arise from ceilings on contributory taxes, provisions for maximum benefits, differences in waiting periods before unemployment benefits can be received, and provisions in a few countries (e.g., Britain and,

change was recommended by a special committee as a way of increasing administrative efficiency and making public employment offices more attractive to employers and job-changers. The unemployed, however, still had to report regularly to unemployment benefit offices (*ISSR*, 1983, *36* [2]: 271–2). The policy is not without its critics, who argue that it has encouraged malingering (e.g., *The Economist*, December 7, 1985).

until recently, France) in which unemployment insurance benefits may be supplemented by assistance payments. Finally, of course, differences in maximum duration of benefits have an important effect on income replacement, especially for the long-term unemployed.

Unemployment insurance benefits were earnings-related in most countries in 1985, but they were on a flat-rate basis in Italy (except for special allowances), and they have been entirely on a flat-rate basis in the United Kingdom since 1982, when the former earnings-related supplement was discontinued.

In 1985, Finland, France, and Ireland had two-tier systems in which an earnings-related benefit supplemented a basic flat-rate benefit. Elsewhere the benefits were entirely earnings-related, but formulas varied in a number of respects. In the United States, a uniform percentage of base-period earnings – 50 percent in most states – was usually specified, but relatively restrictive maxima tended to result in lower percentages for a large proportion of workers. In Spain, and in Belgium for single workers, the percentage of earnings specified declined, at stipulated intervals, as the period of unemployment lengthened.

Even in countries that lacked such complications, insurance benefits varied greatly as a percentage of earnings. A relatively high percentage was provided in Denmark (90 percent), and, as we shall see, there is no limit on the duration of benefits, but under 1985 amendments an unemployed person who ceased to meet the qualifying conditions would receive only 70 percent of previous earnings for the first 12 months and subsequently 50 percent for an unlimited period (*S&LB*, 1987 [1]: 156–7). In Switzerland, benefits were 80 percent of previous earnings for a married person and 70 percent for a single person. Elsewhere, percentages ranged from 40 percent in Greece to 60 percent in Canada and 70 percent in the Netherlands (down from 80 percent in 1983). In Sweden, benefits varied slightly among the funds.

Moreover, a number of countries had restrictive maxima, like those in American states, that resulted in earnings replacement rates that were well below the statutory percentage for many workers.

Some countries provided both dependents' supplements for children and family allowances (plus a spouse's allowance in some cases), whereas other countries provided only family allowances. In the United States, among the larger states, Illinois, Massachusetts, and Pennsylvania provided for dependents' benefits, but California and New York, along with the majority of states, did not.

Although data on replacement rates based on net income or take-home pay are not as readily available as those based on gross earnings, the number of studies concerned with this type of measure is increasing. Particularly useful are the data presented by Burtless (1986), based in part on a study of five countries by the Centre d'Étude des Revenues et des Coûts (CERC, 1982) in the French government. They will be discussed only briefly here.

In Britain, after the removal of supplementary earnings-related benefits in 1982, the replacement rate for a worker with average earnings ranged from 28 percent for a single worker to 54 percent for a married worker whose wife earned less than a modest amount and with two children. Moreover, supplements for children were discontinued in 1985. French replacement rates in 1982 were considerably higher, especially for workers dismissed for economic reasons, ranging for a worker with average earnings from 76 percent for a single worker to 78 percent for a married worker with two children. In West Germany, the replacement rate for a worker with average earnings and children was 68 percent of net earnings in 1986, whereas that for a single worker was 63 percent (Bundesregierung, 1986c).[7]

In Sweden, insurance benefits varied somewhat from fund to fund, and ranged for a worker with average earnings from 63 percent for a single worker to 69 percent for a married worker with two children in 1982. In the United States, the situation was much more complex, with benefits varying substantially among the states, and with much shorter duration (generally 26 weeks or less) than in most countries of Western Europe. Burtless cites OECD estimates for 1984 showing replacement rates for average production workers ranging from 35 to 41 percent, depending on a worker's family situation. Food stamps augmented the income of some, but not all, of the unemployed (for a discussion of the food stamp program, see Levitan, 1985). As an indication of their amount, they would have increased the weekly income of an unemployed worker with average earnings in California by about 12 to 13 percent.

Most countries have provisions relating to the partially unemployed designed to meet situations in which the employer finds it necessary to shorten hours of work for a temporary period. The provisions do not apply to workers who are regularly employed on a part-time basis. They vary a good deal and will not be considered at length. Sometimes the workers concerned accept reduced earnings, which are supplemented by a compensatory allowance paid by the employer or under a statutory unemployment insurance program or through a special partial unemployment insurance fund. In the United States and Canada, workers employed temporarily on a part-time basis have received benefits based on total unemployment from which any earnings they were receiving were deducted. Usually, however, only earnings exceeding a certain minimum amount were deducted (Blaustein and Craig, 1977, 70–2).

---

[7] See, also, measures developed by Burtless (1986), showing variations in replacement rates in West Germany over time, as the composition of the unemployed at various earnings levels changed.

Duration of benefits: Among the most significant differences from country to country are those relating to maximum duration of benefits, because they have a very important bearing on replacement rates for the long-term unemployed. Moreover, under conditions that have prevailed since the mid-1970s, there has been some tendency for maximum duration to be increased and also for provisions to become more complex. We have considered at length in Chapter 5 the special provisions aimed at inducing early retirement, some of which have been financed through the unemployment insurance system. Provisions that relate the maximum duration to the age of the worker have been adopted in several countries, whereas provisions relating maximum duration to length of employment in the base period have long been common.

In two countries with unemployment compensation systems, there was no limit on the duration of benefits in 1985. These were Australia and Denmark. Belgium had long had no limit on duration, but benefits were reduced with lengthening unemployment, and in 1986 procedures were introduced that would make possible exclusion of some claimants from receiving benefits indefinitely (*S&LB*, 1987 [1]: 102–3). In Denmark also, under relatively recent amendments, there was a provision for reduction of benefits with lengthening unemployment, gradually reducing them from 90 percent of earnings to 50 percent, as we have seen.

In three other countries, there was a single maximum duration provision. These were Hungary (six months), New Zealand (26 weeks), and the United Kingdom (52 weeks).

Provisions were more complicated in many other countries. In the Netherlands, with one of the lengthiest periods of potential benefits, the provisions were substantially revised in 1986. Unemployment insurance benefits were to amount to 70 percent of earnings, below an upper ceiling and subject to a national minimum. The maximum duration of benefits was to be six months for those meeting the minimum employment requirement, but could be extended up to five years depending on the age and previous duration of employment. When the earnings-related benefit was exhausted, an additional year's benefit of 70 percent of the minimum wage was to be granted to applicants under age 57 1/2 on becoming unemployed, and, for other applicants, until they reached age 65.

Unemployment assistance was to be provided for those aged 50 or more on becoming unemployed, on an income-tested basis after exhaustion of insurance benefits, and amounting to 70 percent of the minimum wage for a single worker, 90 percent for single-parent families, and 100 percent for couples. Partially disabled persons were to be treated as partially unemployed (*S&LB*, 1987 [3]: 86–7). It will be recalled that provisions relating to the disabled were made more restrictive, as we noted in Chapter 6.

Italy has been another country with a uniform maximum duration of benefits – 180 days – in its basic program, but the situation has been complicated by the fact that in all industrial sectors, provided unemployment was attributable to a specific event such as a plant shutdown, there was a provision for special unemployment benefits for up to 12 months. Moreover, the special benefits amounted to 80 percent of earnings, in contrast with the meager flat-rate benefits provided by the basic scheme (Ricci, 1981).

Many of the remaining countries have had provisions under which maximum duration varied with length of insured employment. In West Germany, for example, in 1985, maximum duration varied from 17 to 52 weeks, according to the length of employment in the base period. Japan's provisions were more complicated, with maximum duration varying with both length of employment and with age, ranging from 90 to 300 days. There was also a provision for extension of benefits when the unemployment rate reached a certain level.

Two countries that varied maximum duration with age were Norway and Switzerland. In Norway, benefits were payable for up to 80 weeks during any two consecutive calendar years for those under age 64, and for 52 weeks in each calendar year if older, whereas in Switzerland the more liberal period applied to persons aged 55 or more.

Provisions in France are of special interest because they have evolved over a long period under a series of collective bargaining agreements, and some of the provisions for prepensions discussed in Chapter 5 have been dropped since retirement benefits available from age 60 on were liberalized under provisions adopted in 1976 and 1982. The unemployment insurance system was changed quite substantially under the provisions of collective bargaining agreements adopted and ratified by the government in 1984 and 1985. The changes resulted in a clearer distinction between two schemes: unemployment insurance proper, financed by employer and employee contributions; and a "solidarity" scheme providing benefits for young persons and others not entitled to insurance benefits, that is financed entirely by the government.

Insurance benefits under these provisions were of two types: a basic allowance and an end-of-entitlement allowance. The maximum duration of the basic allowance varied from three months to 45 months according to length of qualifying employment, but could be as long as 60 months for persons over age 55. After a period varying with length of membership and age, the basic allowance was replaced by a flat-rate end-of-entitlement allowance, which was doubled after a year for persons with 20 years of insurance, and was subject to a maximum duration that varied with age but could be as long as 15 months for workers over age 55.

Under the solidarity scheme, a so-called integration allowance could be paid to jobseekers who had not previously received more than three months of unemployment benefits at any one time and were in one of the following groups: young persons aged 16 to 25 registering for the first time at an employment agency, young persons supporting a family, freed prisoners, and single women who were family heads and had been seeking work for at least five years. These benefits were not means-tested, but there is also an unemployment assistance scheme under the solidarity program (*ISSR*, 1984, *37* [3]: 316–17; 1986, *39* [1]: 72).

Thus, the French provisions are particularly sensitive to the needs of unemployed youth and unemployed older workers.

In the United States, the maximum duration of benefits was 26 weeks in a benefit year in most states in 1985, but in only eight states was the maximum uniform for all claimants. In other states, the maximum varied with the amount of base-period earnings or employment. In addition, four states and Puerto Rico provided for extended benefits when unemployment reached a certain level.

In 1970, the federal law was amended to provide for extended benefits, financed equally by the federal employer tax and by the states, when unemployment in a state reached a certain level. In addition, during several periods of high unemployment at various times since 1958, the federal law has provided for extra periods of benefits, most recently from 1982 to 1985.

Financing: In most Western industrial countries, unemployment insurance is financed on a tripartite basis, with contributory taxes paid by employers and employees, and a government contribution determined in a variety of ways, but in a number of cases designed to meet "any deficit." The chief departures from this pattern in 1985 were in Italy, where there was no employee contribution, and in the United States, where the entire system was financed by employer contributory taxes, except in three states – Alabama, Alaska, and New Jersey – which imposed a very small tax on employees.

As would be expected in a period of rising unemployment, contributory tax rates have increased considerably since the end of the 1960s. The increases have been particularly pronounced in countries that have experienced a sharp rise in the unemployment rate and have tended to affect the employer contribution more than the employee contribution. In 1985, the employer contributory rate was relatively high in France (4.08 percent), Canada (3.29 percent), and Spain (5.2 percent). In the United States, the basic state employer rate was 5.4 percent, but under experience rating the average was about 3.1 percent.

In varying degrees, general government contributions have also tended to rise over this period, not only because of increased unemployment insurance costs but also because of rising public assistance costs and, in some cases, expenses associated with special early retirement provisions.

Unemployment insurance systems have been subject to stresses and strains, particularly in those countries in which employer taxes play an important role in financing. French employers have balked on occasion at increases in employer taxes and have succeeded in reaching compromises with the government.

Employers have resisted higher tax rates in the United States, with the result that a severe crisis in the financing of unemployment insurance has developed, involving, among other things, heavy borrowing from the federal government's unemployment insurance fund by the states (Vroman, 1986). Moreover, experts who had opposed experience rating initially had argued that it would not be effective in inducing employers to stabilize their employment because most unemployment, particularly of the cyclical type, was attributable to forces beyond the control of the employer. What they did not fully foresee was that experience rating would result in controversies over how the burden of increased costs would be distributed among employers. One of the striking effects has been success on the part of employers experiencing little unemployment in holding down the ceiling on the taxable earnings base, thereby shifting a large percentage of the costs to employers with seasonal or intermittent employment and low average annual wages.

The recommendations of the U.S. National Commission on Unemployment Compensation (1980) would, among other things, have mandated substantial increases in the federal taxable earnings base, but, issued toward the end of the Carter administration, its recommendations were largely ignored.

Does UI prolong unemployment?

In a number of countries, there is a school of thought among conservative and right-wing circles to the effect that overly generous unemployment benefits prolong unemployment, even if they do not actually create it. In the last few decades, largely originating in the United States but also influential to some extent in Britain, there has also developed a school of thought, mostly among younger economists, that adopts something closely resembling the classical theory mentioned at the beginning of this chapter, but adds a new "wrinkle" to the effect that the tendency of workers to prolong their job search in order not to be forced to accept a job at unsatisfactorily low wages has the effect of prolonging unemployment. Some of these economists, in fact, go so far as to maintain that all unemployment (in excess of frictional unemployment) originates on the supply side of the labor market because it is caused by utility-maximizing job searchers (cf. Lucas and Rapping, 1969). And because unemployment insurance facilitates job search by restoring at least part of the lost wages of the unemployed worker, it can have the effect of prolonging unemployment.

To an economist who came to adulthood in the Great Depression, the notion that unemployment originates on the supply side of the labor market is utterly unconvincing. Moreover, eminent economists have convincingly argued that much unemployment is involuntary – for example, Solow (1980, 1985) and Hahn (1987). To me, the evidence seems clear that a rise in unemployment can nearly always be traced to developments on the demand side of the labor market. Moreover, the fact that there is very little long-term unemployment in prosperous periods, and that long-term unemployment becomes important only as a recession deepens, has always seemed to me to indicate that most unemployed workers are not inclined to prolong their unemployment when job opportunities become favorable.

On the part of those who hold that unemployment insurance prolongs unemployment, a mamber of empirical studies have been conducted – based either on time series or on cross-sectional data – to test their hypothesis (e.g., Feldstein, 1976). Yet, in a careful review of this literature, Hughes and Perlman (1984) found that, although UI benefits did have a significant effect in raising the level of unemployment, the effect was very small. More recently, Layard (1986) has argued convincingly that the rise in unemployment in Britain could not be attributed to an increase in unemployment benefit replacement rates (discussed more fully in Chapter 14). Burtless (1986) also concluded from his study of five countries that there was little evidence that differences in jobless pay provisions explained the differential trends in unemployment in Western Europe and the United States.

This is not to deny that there may be some situations in which liberal unemployment provisions have tended to prolong unemployment. Economists at the University of Bonn called my attention in 1986 to the fact that provisions for prolonged severance pay in the event of plant closures in West Germany (under the codetermination provisions calling for labor–management agreements over the terms of job terminations in such situations) could have such an effect. Similar complaints have been made about redundancy provisions in other countries.

In Canada, the Forget Commission recently conducted an extensive review of the unemployment insurance provisions and, I was told in Ottawa in October 1986, was expected to recommend tightening of some of the provisions. Workers who had exhausted their right to benefits after one spell of unemployment could requalify for benefits after ten weeks of employment if they lived in areas where the unemployment rate was over 11.5 percent (Canada, Health and Welfare, 1986). The report of a commission in Newfoundland, where the unemployment rate was 21 percent, issued in October 1986, made the charge that this encouraged neighbors to "rotate jobs," each working for ten weeks, and then quitting to live on unemployment insurance while a neighbor took over the job. Even so, the commission recognized that Newfoundland was suffering from a problem of declining employment in primary industries, with little expansion of industrial employment, and that tightening the UI provisions would have to be accompanied by other moves to combat poverty (*Globe and Mail* [Toronto], October 7, 1986).

A basic problem with much of the neoclassical literature is that it is focused on the income of a worker when employed in relation to the family income when he or she is unemployed, losing sight of the fact that a worker may have concerns other than merely that of lost income. The leisure that accompanies unemployment may not be viewed as a very desirable state in many cases. There is the stigma involved in unemployment, the boredom, and the lost sense of functioning as the family provider. Furthermore, there have been many empirical studies, especially in the United States, that have shown the seriously adverse effect of unemployment on family living standards, and the mounting difficulties, as the length of unemployment increases, in meeting consumer debt and mortgage payments.

To be sure, in this era of two-earner families, the impact is less severe if one member of the couple is employed, and this may help to explain why the high unemployment rates in many countries in recent years have not given rise to more vigorous insistence on government action. Even so, as Layard has shown with reference to Great Britain, such families do suffer serious loss of income, particularly if the higher earner (usually the husband) is unemployed.

Critics of unemployment insurance also tend to ignore the important role it plays as an automatic stabilizer, providing benefits that almost immediately help to maintain purchasing power in a business downturn. And, finally, the debate over unemployment is necessarily inconclusive until we have considered the role of labor market policies, to which we turn in the next chapter.

CHAPTER 12

Labor market policies

Introduction

As World War II drew to a close, and industrial countries began to consider the economic problems that would face them in the postwar period, memories of the disastrous unemployment of the 1930s were uppermost in the minds of statesmen and the general public.[1] Everywhere it was taken for granted that sooner or later – perhaps after the most urgent postwar reconstruction needs had been met – nations would once more be faced with relatively serious unemployment problems, at least in cyclical recessions. At the same time, in varying degrees, there was determination – influenced by Keynesian doctrines – to pursue national economic policies that would ensure the maintenance of full employment.

As it turned out, as we have seen, most of the countries of Western Europe largely escaped serious unemployment in the 25 years following the war, except for an initial adjustment period, especially in those countries, like West Germany, that had suffered severe war damage. This achievement, however, was attributable not only to policies emphasizing the pursuit of full employment on the demand side of the labor market, but also, at least to some degree, to training, retraining, and other labor market adjustment policies on the supply side.

Early postwar labor market legislation was designed in large part to serve three purposes: (1) to increase the employability of the unemployed; (2) to facilitate the return to civilian employment of veterans, war workers, former prisoners of war, and similar groups; and (3) to help relieve the shortages of labor anticipated in certain occupations, particularly the building trades, where the ranks had been depleted by long years of reduced construction activity during the depressed 1930s and the war, and whose workers would be needed in greatly increased numbers for postwar reconstruction.

Nevertheless, even in this early stage in the formulation of postwar economic policies, training and retraining programs were regarded in several countries as a permanent instrument of labor market adjustment policy, rather

---

[1] The first part of this chapter is based to a considerable extent on M. S. Gordon (1965b).

than as merely a means of facilitating the transition to a peacetime economy. The British White Paper of 1944 on *Employment Policy*, which set forth the guidelines for a postwar full employment policy, was particularly explicit on this point (United Kingdom, Office of the Minister of Reconstruction, 1944).

The economic environment in which labor market policies were pursued in the full employment years was very different from that which developed in the 1970s. Under conditions of full employment, training and retraining could be emphasized with reasonable confidence that those completing training would be placed in suitable jobs. Similarly, moving allowances could assist workers to move from relatively depressed regions – for example, coal mining areas – to areas of expanding job opportunities. As unemployment rates increased in country after country from about 1973 on, policies changed. One of the first reactions in a number of countries, as we saw in Chapter 5, was to ease older workers out of the labor force through more liberal early retirement provisions, with a view to opening up job opportunities for young people. However, these measures failed to overcome the problem of youth unemployment, and there was a strong movement in many countries from the mid-1970s on to provide increased training and job opportunities for youth. At the same time, the impact of plant closings or heavy layoffs was mitigated by redundancy policies that required advance notice of such developments and special severance payments for workers being displaced. In some countries, but by no means all, expenditures on job creation or work relief increased substantially.

However, the "mix" of labor market policies varied greatly from country to country, as did amounts expended on such policies. Comparable data on labor market expenditures are much less readily available than they are for social security expenditures in general. Moreover, a thorough discussion of the evolution of labor market policies in a substantial number of countries would require not a chapter, but a book. For these reasons, my approach in this chapter will differ considerably from that in most other chapters. I shall consider first the labor market policies of the two countries that have pursued such policies particularly vigorously and consistently, Sweden and West Germany, and then discuss very briefly how policies in a number of other countries differed. Programs relating particularly to youth and the disabled will be discussed in the latter part of the chapter.

The Swedish model

Sweden was one of the first countries to emphasize countercyclical policies of a Keynesian type, as we saw in the last chapter. However, it was not until the late 1950s, under the influence of two economists associated with the Swedish labor federation (LO), Gösta Rehn and Rudolph Meidner, that Sweden developed a comprehensive set of policies relating to both the demand and supply sides of the labor market. A particularly comprehensive discussion of what he calls the Rehn version of these policies has been provided by Lundberg (1985, 17):

This version is based on the recognition that in the real world, the various regions and sectors of the economy would differ markedly in their distance from full use of capacity and full employment. . . . Therefore, a different approach should be pursued. Overall fiscal and monetary policy should be kept sufficiently restrictive in order to prevent the appearance of excess demand and profit inflation in the most exposed sectors and regions. The lowering of demand pressure would mean that there would appear 'islands of unemployment' in the weaker sectors and regions of the economy. These unemployment problems should not be solved by inflating the economy but by *selective measures,* designed to create jobs on the spot as well as to support the movement of manpower after vocational training to expanding sectors and firms.

Lundberg went on to point out that an important element of the Rehn policy scheme was its demand for "solidaristic wage policy," which meant a narrowing of wage differentials and the same pay for the same type of work regardless of profitability and productivity in the various branches and firms. A necessary condition of the success with which this policy was pursued was the centralization and growing strength of the trade union movement. Moreover, the central organizations of employers and workers had met in Saltsjöbaden in 1938 and entered into a general agreement on the aims and means of peaceful collective wage settlements. The "Saltsjöbaden spirit" became an important element of the Swedish model.

Expenditures on labor market policies rose from about 1 percent of GNP in the beginning of the 1960s to 6.1 percent in 1982–3, when the unemployment rate peaked at 3.3 percent. They fell to 4.8 percent with a slight drop in unemployment in the following year (Sweden, Delegation for Labor. . . , 1984, 11). However, the unemployment problem is somewhat more serious than the official data suggest. In recent years, around 4 to 5 percent of the labor force has been involved in training programs, public works, sheltered workshops, and schemes to support inventory buildup. Sweden's practice in counting such persons as employed is no different from that of other countries. The difference is that no other country has as large a percentage of the labor force engaged in such activities.[2]

Central responsibility for labor market policies is in the hands of the National Labor Market Board (*Arbetsmarknadsstyrelsen,* or AMS). Funded by the government, the AMS has a tripartite governing body, with labor, business, and government representation. It also functions through regional of-

---

[2] Moreover, as Rehn has pointed out, in Rehn and Petersen (1980), Sweden has its share of discouraged workers who have dropped out of the labor force.

fices and supervises the county labor market boards and the public employment service (Ginsberg, 1983).

The first director of AMS to adminster the new policy of greatly increased emphasis on labor market policies was Bertil Olsson, who, among other things, emphasized the central importance of a strong employment service (Olsson, 1967). The public employment service has much broader powers than in many other countries (cf. Lester, 1966), and private employment agencies are not permitted.

Initially, emphasis was placed on retraining for the unemployed, chiefly in the metal trades. As time went on, however, course offerings were greatly diversified and training opportunities for women were given increased emphasis. Data for 1983–4 showed that women accounted for 37 percent of the trainees and that there continued to be marked contrasts between the sexes in the types of training for which they were enrolled (Sweden, National Labor Market Board, 1985, table 3).

Labor market training is intended primarily for the unemployed or for persons at risk of becoming unemployed. In addition, a limited number of persons who are employed are admitted to labor market training. Participants receive a training grant payable for five days a week and taxable as income. Training is also intended for persons aged 20 or more, although under certain conditions persons aged 18 to 19 are admitted. Those under age 18, if not enrolled in academic programs, are encouraged to enroll in the highly developed program of vocational education in the regular school system. Moreover, some of those in labor market training are referred to training in the vocational schools. However, with its continuing problem of youth unemployment in recent years, Sweden has developed a program of "youth teams," to which we shall refer later.

Sweden's experience demonstrates the fact that training programs tend to be more successful in years of full employment, when those completing training can readily be placed in jobs, than in periods of substantial unemployment. The number enrolled in training programs (other than in-plant training) rose to a peak in 1979 and then fell off somewhat. On the other hand, those on work relief jobs peaked in 1979 and 1983, the latter a year of relatively high unemployment. Meanwhile, there was a persistent increase in the number in sheltered and semisheltered employment, reflecting increased resources for those programs, as well as the difficulty in placing handicapped persons in normal employment. Persons in in-plant training increased considerably in 1977, when there was special emphasis on subsidized training for workers threatened with redundancy, but have been less important in the 1980s.

Although policies to assist workers to meet the cost of moving to areas with favorable job opportunities have been an integral part of labor market programs, expenditures on geographical mobility have represented a relatively small percentage of labor market expenditures. Moreover, although they were an important part of the Rehn–Meidner model, they became somewhat controversial. Especially in the depressed areas in the north, there has been strong support for regional economic development assistance, which would increase job opportunities there rather than encourage out-migration (cf. Ginsburg, 1983).

Of particular interest is the rise in the percentage of AMS expenditures on unemployment benefits, from about 10 percent in the early 1970s to 28 percent in 1983–4. Thus Sweden, despite its emphasis on labor market policies and its comparatively low unemployment rate, has not succeeded in avoiding a sizable increase in expenditures on unemployment benefits.

Along with a number of other countries in Western Europe, moreover, Sweden reacted to rising unemployment by enacting "redundancy" legislation. The Security of Employment Act, in effect since 1974, requires reasonable cause for dismissal and calls for advance warning to the employee and the union. Age, illness, or reduced working capacity are not sufficient reasons for layoffs of individuals. Only if the employee cannot perform any work at all is dismissal permitted, but in that case a disability pension is recommended instead. The Law for Promotion of Employment, enacted in the same year, permits a county labor market board to obtain information from a firm about its work force. Seniority is the main principle operating when a firm must reduce its work force, but old or disabled workers and workers in semi-sheltered employment as a rule may not be dismissed (Wadensjö, 1984a). Under the Codetermination Act, which became effective in 1977, layoffs cannot occur without negotiations with the union, and the number of jobs to be eliminated is subject to such negotiations. In addition, the county labor market board must be notified in advance of any projected layoffs, and that board or the local employment service must work actively to minimize the impact of the layoffs, locate other jobs for those laid off, and see that handicapped and older workers receive special protection, as required by law. Although providing valuable protection to workers, these provisions are resisted by employers and regarded as an obstacle to necessary labor market adjustments.

The Swedish model has worked somewhat less well in recent years, largely because adverse economic conditions, and especially the problem of Sweden's competitive position in international trade, have created a much more difficult environment for policy decisions. The decision of the Social Democrats, when they returned to power in 1982, to undertake a sharp devaluation of the currency was a major factor in bringing about a restoration of economic growth. However, disagreements over how to meet changing economic circumstances have created a less favorable climate for labor–management relations, and opposition of the "bourgeois" parties to the proposal of LO and the Social Democrats for the creation of "collective wage earners" funds – adopted in a modest version in 1983 – has been intense.

Opponents are particularly critical of the wage determination process based on centralized collective bargaining, which they charge generates "excessively high nominal wage increases" (Meyerson, 1985, 184). Also of concern is the heavy concentration of employment in the public sector, which is, of course, associated with the pronounced growth of public expenditures as a percentage of GDP – from 30 percent in 1965 to 60 percent in 1984 (the highest of any Western industrial country).[3]

Nevertheless, a comprehensive study of the Swedish economy by the Brookings Institution found little evidence that Sweden's welfare state and high taxes had caused serious market rigidities. Summarizing some key results, Rivlin (1987, 19) stated:

While the American team sees difficult economic and political choices to be made, it finds no evidence that Sweden cannot sustain domestic growth and international competitiveness if the economy is managed well. Despite the heavy commitments to wage equalization and high employment, the economy has proved responsive to the need for structural change.

Although policy changes of one sort or another are under discussion, I have not encountered, in my conversations with Swedish experts, any expectation of a dismantling of the "welfare state." As Lundberg concluded:

The fundamental targets contained in the conception of the Swedish Welfare State are being preserved together with the main structure of the social insurance system built up since the 1930s. An underlying egalitarian spirit, a 'passion for equality,' lies behind the successful policies leading to the abolition of poverty and to reduced tensions among social classes.

(Lundberg, 1985, 34)

West Germany

In its consistent emphasis on labor market policies, especially further training and retraining, West German policies resemble those of Sweden, but there are significant differences, and West German expenditures have been considerably lower, as a percentage of GDP, than those of Sweden.

Very similar to the role of the AMS in Sweden is that of the Federal Institute for Employment (or *Bundesanstalt für Arbeit)*, which I shall refer to as the *Bundesanstalt*. Not only does it have broad responsibilities relating to labor market policies and unemployment benefits, but, as in Sweden, there

---

[3] These percentages are from OECD (1987d, table R-7). Both Lundberg (1985) and Meyerson (1985) mention a figure of 70 percent.

has been great emphasis also on maintaining an effective public employment service, which is well informed about labor market developments. Private employment agencies are banned, as in Sweden.

Training programs in West Germany may be sponsored by the public employment offices or by technical colleges, vocational schools, or centers sponsored by industrial associations or trade unions. In general, I was told in 1963, selection tests were seldom used in admitting persons to training, and upper age limits were not rigid (in contrast with the situation, say, in France).

Labor market policies were strengthened by the Employment Promotion Act of 1969, which broadened the functions of the *Bundesanstalt* and set forth a policy of prevention of unemployment and underemployment as the major goal. Training allowances for persons enrolled in approved further training or retraining programs were to amount to 120 percent of the unemployment insurance benefits for which the individual would qualify, in order to strengthen incentives to enroll in training programs. The act also provided for liberalizing the subsidies payable to employers to encourage the hiring of unemployed workers, so that they amounted to a maximum of 60 percent of standard local wage rates for comparable jobs and were payable for a maximum of two years. In addition, provisions relating to training allowances for women were liberalized. The *Bundesanstalt* was also to administer the program of unemployment assistance for persons who could not qualify for unemployment insurance.

As employment conditions worsened in the mid-1970s, the *Bundesanstalt* began to emphasize such policies as (1) encouraging a reduction in hours of work, (2) increased emphasis on job creation measures, and (3) increased promotion of vocational training activities (Leve, 1981). Provisions for early retirement were also liberalized, as we saw in Chapter 5. Moreover, legislation was enacted to combat redundancy. Under the law of the Constitution of the Firm of 1972, and the Codetermination Act of 1976, firms were obliged, in case of impending changes that would adversely affect employment, to agree with the works council on a social plan that would mitigate the economic impact on employees. Chiefly involved were payments to employees who lost their jobs when a firm closed down or moved, or when there were technological or organizational changes that led to layoffs of certain workers (Hax, 1982).

Total expenditures relating to employment, which had been extraordinarily low during the prolonged period of full employment, rose from 0.5 percent of GDP in 1965 to 2.9 percent in both 1982 and 1983, after which they fell somewhat. In 1965, about 28 percent of these expenditures were for training, about 31 percent for mobility measures, and about 42 percent for unemployment benefits. In 1984, when the unemployment rate had risen to 8.5 percent, expenditures for unemployment benefits (including unemployment assistance) had increased to two-thirds of the total, whereas expenditures for training mounted to a little more than one-fifth, and for mobility to slightly more than one-tenth (Bundesregierung, 1986d). A more detailed breakdown indicates that work creation accounted for a considerably smaller percentage of total expenditures than in Sweden. Also significant was the fact that the direct expenditures of the federal government rose from 1.2 billion DM in 1980 to 8.7 billion in 1984, largely reflecting payments for unemployment assistance (*Statistisches Jahrbuch. . .* , 1985, 409).

In recent years German women have shown an increased tendency to enter the labor force. In 1984 and 1985, 80 percent of the growth in employment was attributable to increased employment of women. The government has responded by stressing the need to improve training opportunities for women and by specific measures that will, among other things, permit a mother (or father) to remain out of the labor force as long as five years following the birth of each child without losing eligibility for training allowances or for placement in a work creation program (Bundesregierung, 1986b).

Although the Kohl government may make some minor changes in labor market policies, it is most unlikely that there will be a major shift away from emphasis on them. Results of opinion surveys conducted in the years from 1982 to 1986 indicated that the most important goal of public policy must be the reduction of unemployment. In West Germany, as in Sweden, a very high value is placed on the opportunity to work rather than live on transfer payments.

Other countries

Among other industrial countries, Britain's experience with labor market policies has been more complicated and controversial than that of most countries of Western Europe. An early move by the government to expand training in government training centers was thwarted after an unusually severe winter in 1946–7 when there was substantial unemployment among building trades workers. Widespread complaints arose among workers over a government policy of adding to their ranks in the midst of unemployment, and under pressure from union representatives on the national advisory committee, the government agreed to limit training in the building trades to the disabled. The problem of union restrictionism was not confined to the building trades. It prevailed, also, to a certain extent in the engineering trades and other occupations. The result was that the numbers enrolled in government training centers remained very small in the 1950s and early 1960s (M. S. Gordon, 1965b, 64). There was, however, considerable emphasis on regional development measures.

The problem of union restrictionism in Britain was not paralleled in most other Western European countries, where the various labor federations tended to provide vigorous support for government training programs. The narrow craft organization of the British union movement has generally been regarded as responsible for this restrictionist attitude.

Meanwhile, apprenticeship remained the main instrument of industrial training, but the numbers involved represented a much smaller percentage of entrants to employment than in West Germany, and apprenticeships for young women were largely confined to hairdressing. However, in 1964, an important step was taken to stimulate employer-sponsored training with enactment of the Industrial Training Act, which provided for industrial training boards for each of about 30 industries. The boards would be responsible for the overseeing of training policies in their industries and had authority to raise levies from all employers in their branch, with the proceeds to be used to provide grants to firms undertaking training. For a time, the effect was to stimulate training activities, especially in the engineering and construction industries.

Another significant move was the enactment of the Employment and Training Act of 1973, which created the Manpower Services Commission (MSC) to be responsible for employment and training programs. Six of its members were drawn in equal numbers from employers and trade unions, with minority representation from local government and education. MSC received strong backing from the government for a number of years, supported as it was by the trade union movement and the governing Labor Party (Maclure, 1979). In the mid-1970s, MSC developed a number of courses below full skill level in response partly to growing levels of unemployment.

The industrial training boards, meanwhile, encountered opposition by some employers on the ground that they were too ''bureaucratic,'' and openings for trainees declined as employment stagnated. In 1982, the Thatcher government announced that steps were being taken to abolish 16 of the industrial training boards and reduce the scope of three of the remaining seven (*Employment Gazette*, 1982 [June]). As youth unemployment became a serious problem in the late 1970s, the emphasis of Britain's labor market policies tended to shift to an unusually comprehensive program to stimulate training and employment opportunities for youth, as we shall see.

The postwar history of labor market policies in the United States bears some resemblance to that in Britain, with numerous changes in policy associated with changes in the political party in power in the federal government. The changes have affected the relative responsibilities of the federal government and the states, the relative degree of emphasis on programs targeted to the disadvantaged, and the magnitude of expenditures.

The United States did not move as quickly as countries in Western Europe in developing labor market policies after the war. There was a long-standing, but small, vocational rehabilitation program, but it was not until 1962 during the Kennedy administration that the Manpower Development and Training Act (MDTA) was enacted to provide training for the unemployed. It had been preceded by the Area Redevelopment Act of 1961. Congress also adopted the Trade Expansion Act in 1962, providing for special retraining and income maintenance for workers displaced by increased import competition. Although this program has tended to be relatively modest, its expansion is under consideration.[4]

The initial emphasis under MDTA was on institutional training for the unemployed and underemployed, but the training allowances were low (equaling unemployment benefits), and limitations on the duration of courses were restrictive. As time went on, and especially after the initiation of the "war on poverty" in 1964, there was a tendency to shift emphasis to the disadvantaged, with particular attention to minority youth. The programs were expanded to include basic education, while training allowances were liberalized and skills centers were developed in communities throughout the country. MDTA also included provisions for subsidized employer training, but institutional training predominated.

In 1973, during the Nixon administration, a move was made to give states and local communities greater responsibility for the implementation of the program, under the Comprehensive Employment and Training Act (CETA). Moreover, under CETA job creation in the public sector – or public service employment, as it came to be called – received increased emphasis and reached a peak of 750,000 enrollees in 1978 (Levitan, 1985). During the Carter administration, also, there was increased emphasis on expanding the number of occupations in which apprenticeships were available and on innovative programs for youth.

However, major changes occurred after the Reagan administration came into power in 1981. The public service employment program was eliminated, and the emphasis shifted away from institutional training to employer-sponsored training under the Job Training Partnership Act (JTPA), which replaced CETA in 1983. JTPA gives greater emphasis to placement in the private sector and low training costs. Training allowances are no longer available. Thus, the main thrust of the changes, along with greatly reducing the role of the federal government, was to shift emphasis away from the disadvantaged, as employers tend to emphasize qualifications in selecting trainees.

French labor market policies in the period immediately following the war were distinctive in that they were much more selective and oriented toward the furnishing of needed skills than were programs elsewhere, partly because

---

[4] For an interesting recent account of the reasons for limited activity under this program, see Wilensky and Turner (1987, 22–3).

there was very little unemployment in France after the war and partly because manpower planning became an integral part of national economic planning. Government training centers were developed throughout the country, and many of them were on a large scale, providing residential facilities.

Originally intended for the unemployed, the centers from 1946 on were no longer confined to the unemployed but were to recruit their trainees among candidates presented by the manpower service. Standards of admission were relatively rigorous. Every applicant had to undergo a medical examination and a psychotechnical examination, and upper age limits were very restrictive. Although formally the upper age limit was 35, I was informed by a training official in 1964 that in practice the limit was 28 or 29.

As time went on, the French centers increased their emphasis on training for high-technology occupations, with liberalized provisions for training allowances and for the duration of courses. There was also increased emphasis on subsidized on-the-job training. However, with the development of a serious unemployment problem, the expansion of training was almost halted after 1975, and more varied types of labor market policies were developed. One of the earliest steps was the encouragement of early retirement, discussed in Chapter 5. Another, which received consideration in other countries, and was emulated in some, was a program under which employed workers could apply for leave for partial pay for purposes of further education and retraining, under stipulated conditions, but neither in France nor elsewhere was this program utilized to any significant extent (von Moltke and Schneevoigt, 1977).

During the early postwar period, Italy's unemployment problems centered to a relatively great extent on youth. Courses for the unemployed tended to cater to workers under age 40. Moreover, Italy's policies differed from those of most other countries in that there was substantial emphasis on courses for unemployed juveniles. This was explained not only by youth unemployment but also by the fact that traditional vocational education facilities, in the form of either technical schools or apprenticeships, were decidedly underdeveloped in Italy. Decisive steps were taken to improve this situation through an apprenticeship act and later through a vocational training act of 1978 (Ricci, 1981), but Italy continues to be plagued by disastrously high youth unemployment rates.

Canada has had a substantial program of institutional training since the late 1960s and of subsidized on-the-job training since the early 1970s. However, in 1985, concerned over the persistent problem of unemployment, the government announced the development of a much more comprehensive labor market program, on which $4 billion would be expended over the next two years (Canada, Health and Welfare, 1985b). The program would consist of six parts: (1) a job entry program that would help young people and women entering the labor market, through a combination of training and work experience; (2)

a job development program providing assistance for the long-term unemployed; (3) a skills shortages program that would be oriented toward the overcoming of critical skills shortages; (4) a community futures program that would provide assistance for workers in communities facing chronic high unemployment, plant closures, or mass layoffs; (5) an innovations program to stimulate a search for innovative solutions to labor market problems; (6) and a skill investment program aimed at upgrading the skills of employed workers through part-time or full-time leave, somewhat like that in France. Australia has also moved toward a more comprehensive and varied set of labor market programs, as have a number of other countries, including Austria and Denmark. Almost everywhere, also, there has been increased emphasis on programs for youth, to which we now turn.

Programs for youth

In spite of problems of fiscal stringency and budget deficits, expenditures on training and job opportunities for youth have been intensified in most Western industrial countries in recent years. There is little question that concern over the social problems associated with heavy youth unemployment has been one of the factors responsible for this emphasis, along with recognition of the need for providing work experience and skills.

In the United States and Canada, an increase in the supply of young people played a role, though not necessarily the dominant one, in increasing youth unemployment in the 1960s before the problem became serious in Western Europe, where the impact of an increase in the teenage population on the numbers of young people seeking employment was offset by a sharp rise in secondary school enrollment rates. Moreover, it was not customary for students to hold part-time jobs in Western Europe, as it has been in the United States and Canada. During the course of the 1970s, however, as job markets for graduates became less favorable, the increase in enrollment rates in both secondary schools and higher education slowed down or reversed, whereas in some countries – West Germany, for example – the teenage population was continuing to increase because the peak in the birth rate had come somewhat later than in other countries. Moreover, the influx of married women into the labor force created competition for youth, especially in the trade and service industries, although American data showed that women and youth tended to be affected similarly by changes in demand in various occupations and that it was largely in jobs involving driving that women were getting hired in preference to youth (Gordon, with Trow, 1979). However, many of the changes occurring on the demand side of the labor market in a number of countries were impairing job opportunities for youth. As I put it:

The situation that seems to be common to nearly all industrial countries is the set of forces on the demand side of the labor market that impair job opportunities for youth. These forces will remain for a long time, and they require vigorous policy measures if the youth unemployment problem is to be held within reasonable bounds. In fact, the long-run forces that have been decreasing the relative demand for young people in the labor market may well be intensified rather than reversed.

(Gordon, with Trow, 1979, 29)

What are these forces on the demand side of the labor market? Some are reflective of long-run trends and others of more recent developments. They may be summarized as follows:

1. *The decline in the relative importance of unskilled jobs in manufacturing, construction, and utilities.*
2. *Growing rigidities in the labor market.* Young people are barred from a number of different kinds of jobs (e.g., those involving working near moving machinery) by protective labor legislation.
3. *The costs of employing young people.* Because of the inexperience and frequently the lack of skills of young people, employers cannot afford to hire them at wages comparable to those paid to adult employees. In many European countries, collective bargaining agreements – and sometimes legislation – establish wage rates that are low for young people but that gradually rise until the age of 20 or 21. However, wages of young people relative to those of adults have risen in the United Kingdom and Sweden, while everywhere increases in payroll taxes and employer-sponsored fringe benefits have added to the costs of hiring young people. In the United States, proposals to provide a reduced minimum wage for youth have been supported by employer organizations and strongly opposed by organized labor.

Perhaps the most important point, however, is that, although a decline in the size of the youthful population has been occurring in some countries, and will soon occur in others, reflecting the fall in the birth rate from the mid-1960s on, the fall is likely to be less pronounced among minority groups who are disproportionately represented among the unemployed. This is clearly the case in the United States and presents something of a problem in Britain, France, and West Germany, among others.

Frequently overlooked in discussions of youth unemployment in the United States is the fact that although the unemployment rate of white teenagers has recently been higher than in most earlier years, there has been no long-run upward trend in the ratio of the white teenage unemployment rate to the overall unemployment rate. On the other hand, the ratio of the black teenage unemployment rate to the overall rate has been considerably higher since the mid-1960s than in earlier years. A major reason for these differing trends was the migration of the black population from rural to urban areas (Killingsworth, 1966; Gordon, with Trow, 1979). Whereas unemployment tends to be low in rural areas (or at least hidden in the form of underemployment), unemployment rates were much higher in the urban ghetto areas into which blacks were moving. Moreover, unemployed blacks in ghetto areas tended to include a large proportion of school dropouts. The problem was serious, also, among Hispanics. This is not to suggest, however, that discrimination in the job market did not play a role.

Although I have not been able to obtain similarly detailed time series on unemployment rates of minority youth in other countries, the pattern of higher unemployment rates in recent years among young Jamaicans in England, young Algerians in France, and the children of *Gastarbeiter* (guest workers) in West Germany is clear, as is the tendency for the unemployment rate to be higher among white and minority youth who have dropped out of secondary schools. As the eminent Swedish education expert, Torsten Husén put it, ''A new under-class is emerging in Europe composed of those who are neglected in one way or another and have given up'' (Husén, 1977).

As the Carnegie Council (1979) report on youth emphasized, the problem is as much a challenge for the schools as for labor market policies, and too often the problems of the secondary schools and the labor market problems of youth are analyzed quite separately. Influenced by the proposals of Janne (1979) and others, as well as my own contacts with professionals engaged in cooperative education, I have long been convinced that problems of dropping out and absenteeism in American high schools need to be attacked by providing youngsters with a combination of education and work experience. Enrichment of classroom vocational education is not very likely to increase the holding power of the schools. As Reubens (1974) showed, dropout rates were higher for vocational students than for students in other programs, even when the data were controlled for ability and socioeconomic status.

In view of the fact that programs affecting youth have proliferated in recent years, it will be necessary to be selective and to emphasize approaches in several countries that might bear emulation in other countries.[5]

United Kingdom

The British program to stimulate training and job opportunities for youth is of interest because it is relatively comprehensive, in a country that has been

---

[5] The Carnegie Council on Policy Studies in Higher Education sponsored studies of youth education and employment in a number of countries, to some of which I refer in this section. Although the council no longer exists, some of the studies are available free of charge from the Institute of Industrial Relations, University of California, Berkeley CA 94720.

deficient in its training programs in the past. Moreover, the Thatcher government, despite its thrust toward privatization and cutbacks in spending for social purposes, has expanded and strengthened the youth program that it inherited from the previous Labor government. There seems to be little question that concern over the social problems associated with youth unemployment, especially after the inner city riots of the summer of 1981, has probably played a role, though not necessarily the dominant one, in stimulating this effort. There has also been growing recognition of the importance of adequate training of youth as Britain seeks to overcome its lagging performance in adaptation to technological change.

Beginning in the early 1970s, a number of different types of programs to provide improved training and job opportunities for youth were initiated. However, the proliferation of separate programs was increasingly criticized, and in the autumn of 1976, the Manpower Services Commission set up a special working party, under the leadership of Geoffrey Holland, to examine the feasibility of a universal guarantee of employment or training for unemployed youth (Maclure, 1979). The result was the government's decision to adopt a program for unemployed young people aged 16 to 18 under which they would be guaranteed uniform compensation of £18 a week for participating in a variety of work experience or training programs. A number of existing programs, including community programs, would be merged in the new scheme. It would begin by serving about half of unemployed youth aged 16 to 18.

A uniform compensation rate of £18 a week was intended to eliminate any element of financial advantage of one program over another that might affect the young person's choice. Yet it posed a serious dilemma, which Maclure expressed as follows:

> Most obviously, the work-experience program is likely to affect teenage economics: each boy or girl accepted into a work-experience scheme will qualify at once for £18 a week – considerably more than the educational maintenance allowances offered by the education authorities to children from poor families who remain in school or college beyond the age of 16. Concern has been expressed by the Manpower Services Commission and by the education authorities about the difficulties this may cause when children who take advantage of a work-experience opportunity later recognize the need to return to full-time education.
>
> (Maclure, 1979, 12–13)

Maclure here highlights a problem found in a number of countries in connection with programs for youth. Payment of much less than £18 a week would have been opposed by the trade unions as a move that would have created "unfair" competition and downward pressure on wages for the employed. Similarly, in the United States, a serious controversy arose in 1977 over a provision in a program for expanded training and work opportunities for youth that would require payment of at least the minimum wage.

In the early years of the Youth Opportunities Program (YOP), as it came to be called, jobs held by youth were often provided by community programs and other work creation measures. However, the Thatcher government favored greater emphasis on training, and in a series of moves both expanded the program and stressed employer-sponsored training. The first of these, announced in August 1981, was adoption of a new scheme under which employers would be offered a weekly payment of £15 for all young employers under the age of 18, provided they were in their first year of work and that their earnings were below £40 a week (*Employment Gazette*, 1981 [August], 339). This came to be known as the Youth Work Scheme (YWS).

In yet another and more decisive step in the same direction, the MSC in May 1982 proposed a guarantee of an early offer of training for all 16-year-old school leavers, numbering 460,000 in 1983–4. Training would last a year, be approved by the MSC, and be provided by employers, voluntary organizations, and other groups on a subsidized basis (*Employment Gazette*, 1982 [May], 187).

The new scheme was to replace YOP and was to be called the Youth Training Scheme (YTS). Scheduled to begin in September 1983, the scheme received a favorable response from employers, but there was skepticism on the part of some government officials as to whether there would be enough jobs available for young people completing the program. By 1985, three-fourths of entrants into the program were in employer-based training places (*Employment Gazette*, 1986 [January], 36). However, the government had concluded that one year of training was inadequate in many cases and in February 1986 announced the conversion of YTS into a two-year program.

Evaluations of the results of the one-year program have yielded mixed findings. MSC has estimated that only 6 percent of 16-year-old school leavers did not participate in the program, but about 15 percent of those who did participate in YTS left early without completing the training. Both the nonparticipants and the early leavers tended to have a record of truancy in school, and many of them were from families receiving supplementary benefits (*Employment Gazette*, 1986 [July], 271–3).

Employers were reported to appreciate the opportunity to screen young people in training before offering them permanent employment. Large firms were particularly likely to participate, and about a third of first-year apprentices had been brought into the scheme (Sako and Dore, 1986). However, an evaluation of YWS, which had been started in 1982, indicated that although a large proportion of those who completed their training stayed on their jobs, many of these jobs were not additions to, but substitutes for, those already available (Bushell, 1986, 145–52).

Thus, Britain's experience, though partially successful, indicates some of the problems involved in conducting a large-scale program for youth in a country in which employment has not been growing. On the other hand, the shift from emphasis on job creation to training may have more desirable long-run effects on the quality of the work force than would greater reliance on job creation.

West Germany

We turn now to West Germany, which contrasts with Britain in maintaining a large apprenticeship program, which is regarded as an important factor in explaining its low teenage unemployment rate.

The German apprenticeship system, under which a young person (or the parents) enter into a contract with a training firm, has been traditional since the 1920s (and to some extent even earlier) and was continued after World War II. It is based on detailed analyses of the skills required of the worker in different occupations and industries and the steps involved in achieving skills. Moreover, unlike the apprenticeship systems in some other countries, the standards distinguish between skilled and semiskilled occupations and the length of the period required to achieve them. The specifications are subject to continuous revision as production methods change (Williams, 1963).

The countries that appear to be closest to West Germany in maintaining large-scale apprenticeship programs are Austria and Switzerland, both of which have had comparatively low youth unemployment rates.

In West Germany, about three-fourths of young people who have left school with or without a certificate from compulsory school and about two-thirds of those with an intermediate school certificate enter an apprenticeship. The proportion who leave school without a certificate is relatively high among the children of foreign workers. As a share of the entire cohort of those aged 15 to 19, apprentices represent about 45 percent. They receive an allowance from the firm, which increases in amount each year, and the training period usually lasts three years. Trainees are obliged to attend public vocational school for 6 to 12 hours a week, depending on their state of residence.

One criticism that is frequently made about the German system, however, is that children are divided at ages 10 to 11 among different types of schools (Schober, 1983), and those who enter the main upper primary school *(Hauptschule)* have virtually no opportunity to go on to advanced technical or to university education. Only those who enter the *Gymnasium* and receive the certificate *(Abitur)* are qualified to enter universities. A movement to develop comprehensive secondary schools, open to all along the lines of those in Britain, has met with strong opposition from parents who want to retain the *Gymnasium*.[6]

---

[6] I was told when I was in Bonn in 1986 that a group of parents had sued the state *(Land)* government to stop the development of comprehensive schools.

Although the supply of apprenticeships was generally adequate during the 1950s and 1960s, there was criticism of the quality of some of the training. This criticism led to enactment of the Vocational Training Act of 1969, which raised the legal standards for the quality of vocational training, strengthened the rights of apprentices, and at the same time made training more difficult and more expensive. Moreover, scientific developments were making it necessary for an increasing part of education to be transferred to the theoretical level, a factor that reduced the usefulness of apprentices.

According to von Dohnanyi (1978, 53), the inevitable consequence of these changes was a decline in the number of training positions, just at a time (in the early 1970s) when the number of school leavers was beginning to rise. The Edding Commission, appointed by the federal government, concluded that a relatively small number of firms financed all of the industrial training. A significant number of trainees, particularly in crafts, trained in small firms and then went to work for large industrial firms. The commission therefore recommended a general levy on all firms to provide funds to finance training positions in those firms that were prepared to conduct training. The proposal was resisted by employers on the ground that it would raise the costs of training, and a modified law, which would have imposed levies only on large firms, was not implemented, in 1977, when firms engaged in training agreed voluntarily to add 100,000 training positions.

The expansion of training institutes outside of firms has also been encouraged by the federal government. They were designed to meet the problem posed for middle-sized and small firms that found it difficult to provide training of adequate quality in response to technological changes.

The number of new apprenticeship contracts rose from 558,000 in 1977 to 706,000 in 1984, but there were both some unfilled places and some unplaced applicants; in the early 1980s, with growing unemployment and, in the first few years of the decade, a rising number of school leavers, the number of unplaced applicants rose – from 17,000 in 1980 to 58,000 in 1984 (Roberts, 1986, 110). Moreover, with substantial unemployment among young adults (see Table 11.2), university graduates were in some cases competing with teenagers for apprenticeship positions.

Although the number of apprenticeship places available continued to increase in the mid-1980s, there was a substantial problem of unemployment after completion of the apprenticeship. The highest rates of unemployment were among those who had been trained in artisan occupations such as baker, pastry cook, and hairdresser, in which the ratio of apprentices to employees had risen sharply in the last decade, as employers substituted apprentices for higher-paid adult workers.

The Christian Democratic government of Helmut Kohl which came into power in 1982 resisted any move to introduce government controls over the apprenticeship system, but adopted a number of other measures to meet the youth unemployment problem, especially among youth from low-income families. These measures took the form of an increased job creation program, and assistance to young people from low-income families to meet the costs of participation in training programs sponsored by the *Bundesanstalt*. Included are courses to overcome educational deficiencies of those who did not complete the *Hauptschule* (Bundesregierung, 1986b). Experts tend to predict, however, that intervention by the government will sooner or later be essential to overcome problems of maladjustment between types of training offered and types of training needed in a changing economy.[7]

United States

Labor market programs for youth in the United States, along with labor market policies generally, have undergone numerous changes associated with changes in the party in power in the federal government, and this is one of the few Western countries that has curtailed expenditures for youth programs in the 1980s.

Historically, there have been vocational education programs in the schools, and apprenticeship programs that were largely confined to the building and metal trades, with restrictions on entry imposed by unions. During the Carter administration, Secretary of Labor Ray Marshall sought with some success to expand apprenticeship into new fields, and this effort has continued to some extent in the 1980s.

Greatly increased emphasis on programs for youth, however, dates from adoption of the Economic Opportunity Act of 1964, which included provisions for two youth labor market programs, the Neighborhood Youth Corps (NYC) and the Job Corps (JC), both of which, as Bullock (1985) has pointed out in his useful history of youth programs, resembled programs that had been developed during the 1930s and later discontinued.

The NYC provided part-time jobs, usually at the minimum wage, to students from low-income families and young people who were not in school, with substantial emphasis on summer employment, especially after the inner-city riots of the 1965–7 period. The JC was a much smaller program providing residential training for a limited period to hard-core unemployed youth who not only needed training but who also might benefit from removal from an undesirable inner-city environment.

The NYC program was designed to keep low-income young people in school, get them back to school, or increase their chances of becoming employable if

---

[7] According to Dr. Michael Bolle, who visited Berkeley in 1987, a research program on changing needs for vocational training in Western Europe is being conducted at the Forschungsstelle Sozialökonomik der Arbeit, Freie Universität, Berlin.

they were school dropouts. Apart from the summer program, in which 567,000 young people were involved in 1971, NYC was quite small.

Evaluations of the program yielded somewhat mixed results. There was little clear evidence that it prevented dropping out or improved the employability of the young people involved. However, one study showed favorable results in relation to the extent of involvement in crime and delinquency, and it was generally shown that the income maintenance involved helped the young people and their families (Carnegie Council. . . , 1979, 111).

JC centers have been operated both by government agencies and by private industry. Until 1977, the program enrolled about 40,000 youths at some point every year, or about 20,000 at any given time. Its limited size was at least partly explained by the fact that costs per trainee were far higher than in other training programs, largely because of its residential character, and also because some of its enrollees needed special medical or other services. Early in the Carter administration, a decision was made to double the size of the JC. The newer centers were to be both residential and nonresidential, and were to train for a wide variety of skills.

Although results of early evaluations of the JC were frequently somewhat negative, later studies revealed that although the dropout rate from the program was high, the placement rate for those who completed the program was very encouraging. Moreover, in terms of lasting tenure on jobs and gains in earnings for those who completed the program, the JC came out well.

In 1973, under CETA, NYC was dropped, and emphasis on youth was somewhat reduced. However, the Carter administration displayed serious concern about youth unemployment, and in 1977, the Youth Employment and Demonstration Projects Act was adopted, calling for four different types of youth programs. Although a full discussion of all of these is not feasible, a brief description of one of them, the Youth Incentive Entitlement Pilot Projects, seems appropriate, because it exemplified a promising way of combining education and work experience.

The pilot projects were carried out in 17 large and modest-sized communities over a period of 18 months. Economically disadvantaged young people were guaranteed work if they agreed to finish high school. The 17 communities were selected on the basis of proposals submitted in a competitive process. Employment during the school year could not exceed 20 hours a week, and summer employment was to be full-time or a combination of part-time work and training. All sponsors involved in the project received the funds needed to pay wages (at the minimum wage level) plus the costs of administration.

Evaluation of the project indicated that its impact in providing employment opportunities for the young people involved and inducing them to remain in school (as long as the program lasted) was very encouraging, but that relatively few of those who were dropouts when the program began ultimately completed school, although some of them later obtained a general education certificate.[8]

Interestingly, in spite of the cutbacks in expenditures for labor market programs in the 1980s, the JC has survived, having gained the support of some conservatives as well as liberals in Congress.

There are other American youth programs worthy of attention, including efforts of private and nonprofit community organizations, but I should like to call attention to the highly significant role of the community college (or public two-year college) system in providing opportunities for youth and adults to enroll in either academic or vocational education with few formalities and usually little expense. They have been called the ''open-door'' colleges (Carnegie Commission. . . , 1970), and in 1982 they enrolled 4.5 million students in 939 institutions (*Statistical Abstract. . . , 1985*, 152). In at least some of the states, they are open to all adults who can be expected to benefit from the instruction, whether or not they are high school graduates. However, their policies and methods of financing are determined at the state level, and there are differences from state to state. California, which has the largest community college system, has long emphasized a wide variety of vocational and academic programs, open admission, and until very recently no tuition (now there is a modest charge of $50 per semester). The point to be stressed is that these colleges provide an opportunity for young persons who have dropped out of high school to return to education, as well as educational opportunities for adults of any age.

There are examples of similar institutions in other countries, including colleges of further education or technical education, but usually they are open only to graduates of secondary schools.

Other countries

There are many other examples of innovative market and educational programs for youth that cannot be discussed here, but mention should at least be given to the occupational orientation centers for youth in Belgium (Janne, 1979); to the national system of centers organized to provide counseling and training opportunities for unemployed youth in France (*S&LB*, 1983 [1]: 145–7); to the residential centers for unemployed youth in Denmark, described by Petersen (Rehn and Petersen, 1980); to the ''youth teams'' (offering guaranteed temporary employment, usually part-time, in government agencies) in Sweden (Sweden, Delegation for Labor Market . . . , 1984); and to the

---

[8] Because one of the communities was Berkeley California, where I live, I was able to learn in some detail about the types of job opportunities developed there.

industry-sponsored residential programs in Japan, combining high school education and skills training for youth (Kato, 1978).[9]

In Eastern Europe, the transition from school to work is not without its problems, although it is unclear to what extent unemployment is involved (except in Yugoslavia, where youth unemployment has been substantial). According to Kurilin (1986), young people with high levels of education in the Soviet Union are frequently dissatisfied with their jobs. This results in a high rate of job mobility among young workers, a problem, he argued, that could be solved only by further mechanization of manual tasks, which government policy aims to achieve.

In Hungary, school leavers are said increasingly to possess qualifications that lead them to choose mainly office work or other nonmanual work, although there is an acute need for manual workers. Moreover, redundancy dismissals and changes in the structure of employment affect young people first, especially those who have only recently entered employment (*S&LB*, 1983 [2]: 239–40). This implies that there may be a problem of youth unemployment, and it will be recalled that, unlike most countries in the Soviet bloc, Hungary does provide for unemployment assistance.

Liberska's (1979) illuminating account of youth education and employment in Poland indicated that some students dropped out of secondary schools, that the dropouts were likely to come from families of low socioeconomic status, and that more than half of the students enrolled in higher education were from families belonging to the "intelligentsia." However, the government has tried to combat this elitism in higher education, as have other countries in the Soviet bloc, by providing that students who have graduated form either general or vocational secondary schools are eligible for admission to all types of institutions of higher education.

I shall defer comments on the future of programs for youth to the concluding chapter, where I shall be concerned with the importance of recognizing the relationship of educational policies and social security policies in general, as well as that between labor market programs and educational policies for youth.

Rehabilitation of the disabled

There are wide variations from country to country in the effectiveness of rehabilitation programs for the disabled, and they seem to be attributable as much to the manner in which programs for the disabled are organized as to the amounts spent on them. As Beveridge emphasized in his discussion of

---

[9] For a comprehensive and useful recent summary of social security provisions for youth, see Fisher (1986).

industrial injuries programs, the aim of the programs should be "to restore the injured worker to employment" (see Chapter 1). Clearly, this should also be a major aim of programs for the nonoccupationally disabled.

I first became aware of the wide differences in rehabilitation programs nearly three decades ago when I was involved in a study of occupational disability programs (Cheit and Gordon, eds., 1963). At the time, the Canadian provinces, and especially Ontario, were known to have particularly effective rehabilitation programs for injured workers. I visited the offices of the Workmen's Compensation Board in Toronto, as well as the Downsview Rehabilitation Center outside of Toronto, and learned that some of the elements responsible for the effectiveness of the board's rehabilitation program were the following:

1. Their insistence on ensuring access to high-quality medical care and early assessment of the need for vocational rehabilitation. This sometimes involved flying injured workers from remote areas, such as the northern lumbering areas, to the Downsview Center, where specialized medical care, as well as vocational counseling, were available.

2. Maintenance of a staff of medical experts in the central offices of the board, who received and examined x-rays of the injured limbs or body parts and, wherever indicated, telephoned the physician handling the case to discuss methods of treatment.

3. Provision of vocational rehabilitation services, as soon as possible, for those deemed to need them and capable of benefiting from them.

4. The policy of not permitting appeals to the courts from the board's decisions. As we saw in Chapter 7, this was in sharp contrast to the situation in the United States, where in many of the states cases are frequently appealed to the courts, usually with respect to the degree of the injury, creating a disincentive for recovery and return to employment.

5. The policy of maintaining contact with the injured workers' employers to seek their cooperation in reemploying the workers as soon as they were able to return to work.

The result of these policies was not only a record of effectiveness in restoring the injured worker to employment, but also relatively low costs in the insurance program, attributable largely to the fact that there were comparatively few cases of residual serious permanent disability.

In 1986, on a return visit to Toronto, I learned that the board was, if anything, placing even greater emphasis on early access to rehabilitation, but was not quite as satisfied with its success as I had found earlier. A major reason, I was told, was that with the growth of population and industrial employment that had been occurring in Ontario, the resources available to the board had not entirely kept pace. There was, for example, a shortage of physical therapists. And yet, the board's record in restoring the injured worker to employment continued to seem very impressive. Among 5,581 workers rehabilitated in 1985, 87 percent were employed and the board played an important role in placement activities not only for those who went back to their former jobs but also for those placed in other employment (Ontario, Workers' Compensation Board, 1985).

An important reason for the board's success, clearly, is the fact that one agency is involved in supervising the entire process, from start to finish. Although similar concentration of authority can be found in some other occupational disability programs, the situation is frequently more complicated in nonoccupational disability programs, where a number of government agencies, as well as private agencies, are often involved. This tends to interfere with achievement of prompt access to vocational rehabilitation for those in need of it. And yet, the importance of early initiation of vocational rehabilitation is generally recognized by experts.

In their comprehensive study of public policy toward the disabled, in eight countries, Haveman, Halberstadt, and Burkhauser (1984) identified Sweden, the Netherlands, and West Germany as having mature systems with relatively well-integrated transfer, rehabilitation, and work programs. Countries with less developed systems and relatively uncoordinated programs included Italy, France, Israel, the United Kingdom, and the United States.

Although the emphasis on rehabilitation of the disabled in West Germany reflects a tradition established in the early years of social insurance, rehabilitation policies were greatly strengthened by legislation that became effective in 1974. A comprehensive system of medical and vocational rehabilitation was to be available to all handicapped persons regardless of the cause of the disability. Medical and vocational rehabilitation services were to be coordinated, with rehabilitation to begin in the hospital and to continue until the handicapped person was fully reestablished in working life and society. Income maintenance of handicapped persons and their families was to be ensured during the entire period of rehabilitation by the payment of a sickness or transitional benefit amounting to 80 percent of the worker's previous earnings.

Not only were all cases to be referred to the *Bundesanstalt*, but also that agency was to be responsible whenever there was a dispute as to what institution was responsible for rehabilitation, until the dispute could be resolved. A disability pension could not be awarded until rehabilitation measures had been carried out, or when, in view of the severity of the handicap, they could not be expected to be successful (*ISSR*, 1975, *28* [1]: 59–70).

Although the number of persons in rehabilitation programs and expenditures on rehabilitation have increased very substantially since 1974, Pfaff and Huber (1984) concluded that coordination among the institutions involved in rehabilitation left something to be desired. The most important of these institutions were the old-age and invalidity pension program, the workers' accident program, health insurance, veterans' benefits, public employee programs, and public assistance. Each of these institutions was concerned about its own budget and might dispute its responsibility in particular cases. Thus the pronounced differentiation existing among the social security institutions had an adverse effect on the pursuit of rehabilitation measures. However, on the basis of examination of a number of cost–benefit studies, they concluded that "rehabilitation must be considered one of the most efficient investments in human capital" (Pfaff and Huber, 1984, 217).

In addition to vocational rehabilitation and training, there are three other types of programs for the disabled in West Germany: (1) sheltered workshops, (2) wage subsidies for employers hiring the handicapped, and (3) a quota system under which all public and private employers with at least 16 employees must reserve a minimum of 6 percent of their positions for disabled persons. These three types of programs are found in a number of other countries, but their relative importance varies greatly, and we shall consider them only briefly.

In Sweden, the central role of the National Labor Market Board (AMS) is an important factor in encouraging access to vocational rehabilitation, and yet several of the experts whom I interviewed in Stockholm in 1986 said that lack of coordination among the various institutions involved was an obstacle to achieving optimal access to rehabilitation services.[10] An important development was the introduction of employability assessment institutes in 1980. In 1981, there were 50 such institutes, and ten more were being setup. They are intended for job applicants who find it difficult to decide what kind of job they want, as well as for those with reduced working capacity. The internal organization of the institutes is based on working teams ranging from two to six persons. A team might consist of two work consultants, a psychologist, and an employment officer. They are assisted by specialists, including a welfare officer, a physiotherapist, a nurse, and a doctor. There are also more specialized assessment institutes for specific categories of handicapped people. The assessment proceeds in stages over a period of about three weeks, including introduction, investigation, guidance, and individual planning during the first two weeks. For those not placed in jobs, there follows more prolonged work assessment and finally referral to a training center or an on-the-job training position (Bratfisch, 1981).

Data provided by Wadensjö (1984b, 48) indicated that the number of persons in vocational rehabilitation programs rose from 1,275 in 1961 to 4,890

[10] Interviews with Oswald Bratfisch, National Labor Market Board, and with Professor Eskil Wadensjö, Director of the Institute for Social Research, University of Stockholm, September 1986.

in 1983. However, the number of disabled persons in archive work, semi-sheltered work, and sheltered work also rose sharply and greatly exceed the number in vocational rehabilitation, totaling about 61,000 in 1983. Wadensjö (1984a) has argued that the preferred alternative is to increase access to the workplace. To enlarge opportunities for the disabled to work, requirements have gradually been introduced relating to the design of buildings, access to transportation, and access to places of work. Moreover, a major effort has been made to improve the mobility of the disabled through transportation assistance, including grants or loans for the purchase of specially equipped automobiles.

Sweden took a major step toward restoring disabled workers to their former places of employment in a law that became effective at the beginning of 1986. Employers were to be required to provide jobs for employees who had become disabled, whether the disability was occupational or nonoccupational. If an employer could not place a worker in his or her former job or another job, the employer could seek advice from the employment office, but this was conditional on the physician's recommendation. Services were to be provided by the employment assessment institutes, with particular reference to re-arrangements at the place of work that would facilitate the capacity of the disabled worker to perform adequately.[11] The results of this new law will be of great interest.

An exceedingly thoughtful report by the Manpower Services Commission (MSC) in the United Kingdom (1981) pointed out that although public provision for rehabilitation was limited, a great deal of employment rehabilitation occurred within industry, as firms made efforts to readapt a disabled employee into the work force. Public provision for rehabilitation was provided chiefly through 27 Employment Rehabilitation Centers (ERCs) conducted by the MSC. However, most ERC clients, though classified as disabled, were not people who had left their jobs because of recent sickness or disability but persons who had incurred their disability some time ago and had experienced long periods out of work.

The average length of stay for adults at an ERC was six to eight weeks, and the maximum duration of a course was 26 weeks. The courses provided assessment and work experience in relatively simple jobs rather than skills training. Follow-up results for those completing courses from April to September 1979 showed that 37 percent of those responding were employed, whereas 12 percent were in training courses. The remaining 51 percent were not employed. The report noted that the success rate was much higher in the 1960s when the unemployment rate was low.

In their study of disability policy in the United Kingdom, McCrostie and

---

[11] My information about this new law is based on my interview with Oswald Bratfisch.

Peacock (1984) commented that the information available on disability was extremely sparse in comparison with that of other countries. This did not reflect a lack of concern, but rather the fact that the system developed out of the activities of a considerable number of voluntary bodies, and that when government became the main source of support for disabled persons, government departments concerned with health, education, and employment were going through periods of large-scale reorganization.

They concluded that there was a serious need for reform of the welfare system, which was complex, inequitable, and inefficient. They also noted that in sheltered employment the benefits outweighed the costs, whereas the success rate in reintegrating people into the work force had not been great and the reasons for failure were not clear.

It is important to note that in both Britain and the United States, disability benefits are provided only for those who are completely incapacitated for work, except for the cases of the occupationally disabled. In the United States, this is true of the social security disability insurance program and also of the supplementary security income (means-tested) program. And yet, those who are partially disabled are more likely to be successfully rehabilitated. Vocational rehabilitation is carried out by state agencies, but is funded chiefly by federal grants. A part of the funds comes from an allocation by the Social Security Administration of 1.5 percent of expenditures for disability benefits in the preceding year. Expenditures from federal funds have increased substantially over the years; they reached $1.4 billion in 1984, after which they were cut somewhat (U.S. Office of Management and Budget, 1985). According to Levitan (1985, 121), there were 954,000 cases in 1984, and 220,000 persons were rehabilitated.

Yet it seems clear that there is lack of coordination and that inadequacy of funds available to the state rehabilitation agencies limits the number of disabled persons who can be accepted. Moreover, income maintenance and access to health services in the early stages of disability are by no means as certain as in most countries of Western Europe. A disabled person is not eligible for federal disability insurance benefits until after a waiting period of five months, and the required number of years of insurance coverage is larger than in many other countries, as we found in Chapter 6. Workers living in the five states with temporary disability insurance programs and in Puerto Rico can receive temporary disability benefits, generally for up to six months. Elsewhere, the majority of workers are covered by employer sickness and health benefits, but these generally expire not long after the termination of employment, although there are now special provisions for the involuntarily unemployed. Moreover, the training allowances formerly available for disabled persons admitted to government training programs are now no longer available under the Job Training Partnership Act (JPTA). Medicare services are available for disability insurance beneficiaries, but not until two years after the first receipt of benefits. However, those who can qualify for SSI means-tested disability can receive the benefits, as well as Medicaid services, without a long waiting period. Limitation of available funds at the state level may, nevertheless, restrict access to adequate Medicaid benefits.

When it provided for the allocation of Social Security funds for vocational rehabilitation, Congress stipulated that savings (in the form of benefits that would not have to be paid to disabled workers who were rehabilitated and returned to work) must equal or exceed the trust fund expenditures for services. This provision led to a number of studies, both within and outside the SSA, to determine cost–benefit relationships in the use of these funds. Although there has been disagreement over the methods used in these studies, they have generally shown, as have studies in other countries, that the benefits exceed the costs by wide margins. However, as Reubens (1970) pointed out, such a narrow focus on efficiency would be considered unacceptable in a number of European countries; similarly, according to Haveman, Halberstadt, and Burkhauser (1984, 181), the "reluctance to employ rehabilitation efforts as more than a cost-reducing mechanism in the United States is in sharp contrast to many of the other countries studied. . . ."

Moreover, the United States has avoided quota systems for hiring the disabled, like that in West Germany – systems that have rarely been well enforced. Instead, this country has emphasized policies to guarantee the disabled "equal access" to education, employment, and mobility. There has also been a substantial growth of voluntary agencies to serve the needs of the disabled, including sheltered workshops that are privately run but subsidized by the government.

It is important to recognize that rehabilitation is given considerable emphasis in some of the countries of Eastern Europe and is closely associated with their policies of maximum utilization of manpower. The way in which disabled persons are classified in the Soviet Union was described in Chapter 6. Czechoslovakia's extensive program of rehabilitation has been described by Kubernátová (1986), showing, in contrast with the situation in some Western European countries, that the vast majority of those receiving disability benefits receive partial disability pensions and that the number of disabled persons who are employed has been increasing rapidly.

An interesting postwar development in Poland has been the growth of invalids' cooperatives, which provide a comprehensive program of rehabilitation, in addition to medical and social services. By the early 1960s, gainful employment was provided in 393 invalids' cooperatives for about 100,000 severely disabled persons, or about 12 percent of the total number of handicapped persons in Poland. They produced a wide variety of products, and state assistance, chiefly in the form of tax relief, helped these enterprises to compete with firms employing the able-bodied. According to Futro (1964), the development was unique in giving the disabled workers the opportunity not only to work but also to serve on the governing boards of the cooperatives.

To recapitulate, there is a need, met in only a few countries, and not entirely effectively even in those few, for integrated programs for the disabled and for access to vocational rehabilitation at an early stage. Although, in general, the aim should be to restore the disabled worker to normal employment, this is difficult to achieve in a period of high unemployment rates. Thus, sheltered workshops may logically be given an increased role in such periods, as is clearly the case in Sweden. In many countries, these enterprises are subsidized quite heavily by the government, even though they may be organized on a voluntary basis.

Conclusions

In an overly long chapter, I have not been able to do justice to the numerous evaluation studies, especially in the United States, where they have proliferated. However, in conclusion, let me refer to the findings of one of the few comparative evaluations which was very recently published in the form of a symposium (see Wilensky; Haveman and Saks; Casey and Bruche; Rehn, 1985).

Drawing on data from a number of countries in Western Europe and the United States, the authors conclude that, among the various types of labor market programs, training and placement programs are the most cost-effective. Even if training programs do not lead to immediately available jobs, they "may reduce long-term unemployment and increase adaptability and thereby be economically cost-effective" (Wilensky, 1985, 4). Moreover, participation in a training program may prevent, at least for a time, the loss of self-respect and social isolation often experienced by the unemployed.

A second need is for strong, stable funding and a tripartite administrative structure using well-trained professionals in placement, counseling, and training. This is similar to my finding (M. S. Gordon, 1965b) that training programs should be permanent; stop-and-go programs are likely to suffer from shortages of manpower and facilities when they need to start up again. Moreover, changing skill requirements occur continually.

The authors also commend the close link between secondary schools and apprenticeships exemplified by such countries as West Germany, Austria, and Switzerland, in contrast with the sharp separation between education and work in the United States. Moreover, in contrast with the situation in Sweden and West Germany, the United States has a weak, understaffed employment service, whose operations are only loosely related to school counseling.

There is little question that the need for vigorous labor market policies will continue, even though the unemployment problem may become less serious in the coming years. We shall have more to say about this in the concluding chapter.

CHAPTER 13

Family allowances and family policies

Family allowances

Introduction

Family allowance systems are frequently referred to as children's allowance schemes because in most countries the allowance provided to the family is so much per child. However, in a number of countries allowances are also paid for the wife or for a single parent. For this reason, I shall refer to the schemes as family allowances. I also prefer this term because of the growing trend to link family allowances with family policies, which will be discussed in the latter part of this chapter.

Among the countries in this study, the United States alone does not have a family allowance system, and it is unlikely to adopt one in the foreseeable future. All of the other countries do have family allowance systems, but there are vast differences among them – in amounts per child and in other features.

The first country to adopt a family allowance system was New Zealand, in 1926, but unlike most of those adopted later, the scheme involved an income test and was designed to assist low-income families. It was not until 1946 that New Zealand's scheme became universal. The Australian state of New South Wales followed with a similar scheme in 1927, a scheme that was replaced by a comprehensive Commonwealth scheme in 1941.

Rather different in their origins were family allowance schemes in France and Belgium. During World War I, under pressure for higher wages to meet rising living costs, more and more French employers turned to children's allowances as an alternative, thus avoiding a rise in general wages but assisting families with children. Until the end of the war, employers paid allowances directly to their own employees, but in a move toward consolidated administration of the benefits and broader distribution of the cost burden, local "equalization funds" were established and financed by employer groups in 1918, disbursing allowances among eligible employees. During the 1920s and 1930s, there was growing concern about lagging birth rates, and, in 1932, the family allowance system for wage earners in industry was made compulsory. Financed by an employer payroll tax, the system was designed not only to combat falling birth rates but also to achieve greater equality among wage earners (Haanes-Olson, 1972). The history of family allowances in Belgium was very similar.

Early debates over proposals for family allowances in the United Kingdom and Sweden were less concerned with demographic considerations than with the welfare of children. Prominent among the advocates in Britain was Eleanor Rathbone (1947), whereas in Sweden the seminal work by Alva Myrdal on family policy (1941) tended to favor free services for children rather than cash allowances.

By the beginning of World War II, seven countries – New Zealand, Belgium (1930), France (1932), Italy (1936), Spain and Hungary (1938), and the Netherlands (1939) – as well as New South Wales had adopted family allowance legislation. Australia, Canada, Finland, Ireland, Romania, some of the Swiss cantons, and the USSR adopted legislation during the war years, and in the immediate postwar period the movement continued.

By the early 1950s, all of the countries included in this study, except for Israel, Japan, and the United States had family allowance systems. Israel followed in 1959, and Japan, with a system limited to families with three or more children, in 1971.

Although there has been some support for adoption of a family allowance system in the United States, it has largely been limited to specialists in social welfare and a few other social scientists or government leaders with a special interest in the issue. A serious obstacle has been the high cost of a family allowance system that would provide a significant addition to the income of families with several children. There is little question, moreover, that a good many people would be prejudiced against such a proposal for fear of encouraging minority group families or individuals to have more children.[1]

Varying provisions

Relative expenditures: Probably the most significant difference among family allowance systems is in rates of expenditures as a percentage of GDP. Countries with large expenditures tend to have relatively generous allowances per child, broad coverage, and special features such as larger allowances for single-parent families. We referred briefly to expenditure differences in Chapter 2, as shown in Appendix 1, for 1959–60 and 1979–80.

In the earlier of these two years, France ranked highest in expenditures in

---

[1] In 1969, at a hearing held in New York City by the U.S. President's Commission on Income Maintenance Programs, of which I was a member, Professors Vera Shlakman and Alfred J. Kahn presented a proposal for a federal children's allowance program. They suggested an allowance of $50 a month per child, which they estimated would cost, net of reduced tax allowances and of income taxes on the children's allowances, about $28.5 billion a year and would reduce the number of children in families in poverty by about 77 percent. The reaction of most of the commissioners on the hearing panel was that such a cost would be prohibitive.

relation to GDP (2.9 percent), followed by Czechoslovakia, New Zealand, Belgium, Italy, and Poland. At the opposite end of the scale, with very low expenditures in relation to GDP, were Switzerland, West Germany, the USSR (with allowances only for very large families), Denmark, the Netherlands, and Norway.

There followed some rather substantial changes. By 1979–80, although France and Belgium continued to rank near the top, Hungary had crept to the top of the list, with 3.0 percent, followed by Czechoslovakia, with 2.8 percent. Also ranking high in 1979–80, with expenditures exceeding 2.0 percent of GDP, were Austria, the Netherlands, and Israel.

In the first 25 years or so after World War II, family allowances were typically allowed to erode in relation to price and wage changes, but in the 1970s there was something of a reversal of this trend, as countries became concerned over falling birth rates and the persistence of poverty among large families, as well as the rise in the proportion of single-parent families. Even so, there has continued to be erosion in a number of countries, reflecting the fact that only about one-fourth of our countries provide for indexing of allowances.

Coverage and financing: There have been two types of family allowance systems in terms of coverage and financing: (1) employment-based and financed by an employer payroll tax, and (2) residency-based and financed from general government revenues. In the late 1950s, there were 12 countries, all in continental Europe, in which the systems were based on employment (usually covering social insurance beneficiaries as well as employees). The British Commonwealth countries, Ireland, and the Scandinavian countries – probably influenced in most cases by the Beveridge Report – covered all residents (usually with a very modest requirement relating to length of residence, or in some cases requiring citizenship) and financed the system entirely or largely through general government revenues.

By 1985, the number of systems based on residency had increased, with Austria, France, East Germany, West Germany, and the Netherlands joining the ranks of countries covering residents with children. Israel and Japan, which had adopted systems in the interim, based coverage on residency. Overall, moreover, the number of countries that did not include the first child or the first two children had declined, although France continued to exclude the first child in its main system. Another significant change was a contribution from general government revenues in countries that had previously relied entirely on an employer payroll tax, sometimes accompanying a move toward special allowances for single-parent or low-income families.

Amounts of allowances: Differences in amounts of allowances in 1985 were wide – measured in relation to average wages in manufacturing – with the

Table 13.1. *Family allowances as a percentage of average wages in manufacturing, for families with two children or four children, selected countries, 1985 (basic system only)*

Country	Two children	Four children
Austria	10.1–10.6%	20.2–21.3%
Belgium	11.8 or more	33.8 or more
Canada	3.5 or more	6.9 or more
Czechoslovakia	22.6	59.7
Denmark	2.6 or more	5.2 or more
Finland	6.8 or more	16.9 or more
France	9.5	64.3
Germany (Fed. Rep.)	4.3 or more	14.2 or more
Greece	5.1	13.1
Hungary	16.8	39.5
Ireland	3.4	6.8
Japan	None	3.3
Netherlands	9.1 (1980)	21.5 (1980)
New Zealand	5.8	11.6
Norway	8.0	19.4
Sweden	9.4	25.9
Switzerland	6.2 or more	12.4 or more
United Kingdom	9.2	18.5

Sources: Computed from data in USSSA (biennial, 1986) and ILO (1986 [4]). The 1980 data for the Netherlands are from Bradshaw and Piachaud (1980, table 13.5). Data relate to the basic family allowance system and do not include special supplements; moreover, they are approximate only, because it was necessary to convert hourly wage data to monthly data or to make other conversions in many cases.

highest allowances being provided in countries that were high spenders on family allowances (Table 13.1). A glance at the data, moreover, reveals the fact that in many countries total allowances for a family with four children were considerably more than twice those for a family with two children. This trend reflects not only a tendency to increase the amount per child with each additional child, but also the omission of the first child, or the first two children, in a few instances.

Although a uniform payment for each child was common in the first few decades of family allowance systems, relatively few countries retain such provisions today. Even where the basic program provides for uniform allowances, there are often supplements under certain conditions.

The most common type of variation in the amounts of allowances in 1985 provided for a fairly steady increase for each additional child in a family, although frequently the increases stopped after a total of four or five children. A dozen or more countries varied allowances in this manner, including Australia, Belgium, Czechoslovakia, Finland, East Germany, West Germany, Greece, Israel, the Netherlands, Norway, Romania, and Sweden, whereas the USSR increased amounts for each additional child after four. In Yugoslavia, the rates varied with the number of children in a family but also among the Republics and Autonomous Regions.

In this type of system, the increases tended to be quite substantial, in recognition of the heavier costs associated with large families and of the fact that such families are often poor. In Australia, for example, the allowance was $22.80 a month for the first child, $32.55 for the second child, $39 each for the third and fourth, and $45.55 for the fifth and each subsequent child.

Of particular interest were the systems that provided for an increase in the allowance for each additional child up to a certain point and then a decrease. In Czechoslovakia, for example, the allowance increased quite substantially for each additional child through the fourth, and then dropped off for the fifth and each subsequent child. France and Greece had somewhat similar formulas. This seems to reflect at one and the same time a recognition of the needs of large families while discouraging parents from having more than a certain number of children.

Austria did not vary the allowance by number of children, but did provide a slightly larger allowance for older children, and, like many countries, provided a relatively large amount for a permanently disabled child. Belgium, France, and the Netherlands also provided larger amounts for older children as well as increases by number of children. In Canada, the federal system provided for a slightly larger allowance for a child aged 12 or more, whereas Alberta varied allowances by age of children for four age groups, and Quebec increased amounts by number of children up to the fourth (Canada, Government of, 1986).

Single-parent and low-income families: A particularly significant trend, especially since the early 1970s, has been the adoption of provisions for supplementary allowances for low-income families or single-parent families, or, alternatively, larger basic allowances for such families. If this trend continues, it will result in a fundamental change in family allowance systems – from evenhanded provision of allowances for all families with children to systems more closely resembling public assistance (or social assistance, as it is often called in Europe). The trend is explained by growing recognition of the persistence of poverty among families with children as well as the greater prevalence of poverty among large families and among single-parent families. The rising unemployment in the 1970s and 1980s has also, of course, tended to bring about a substantial increase in the proportion of families in poverty. Moreover, as in the case of universal old-age pensions, some governments have tended to favor the less costly procedure of raising allowances for low-income or single-parent families over the much more costly path of providing a general increase in allowances for all families.

Although the increased concern for low-income families and single-parent families is understandable, it may conceivably have one undesirable result – creating an incentive for separation of the parents, or "family-splitting," in order to permit one of the parents (usually the mother) to qualify for larger benefits. Universal family allowances, on the other hand, are neutral in their effect on marital status. Generally, they flow to the children regardless of the marital status of the parents. In my conversations with experts in various countries, I have not found serious concern about this, although here and there the problem has been mentioned.

On the other hand, frequently objections are raised to the provision of family allowances for middle- and upper-income families, who do not need them. In fact, there has been some tendency to exclude high-income families or to provide reduced allowances for them. Denmark adopted a provision in 1977 that called for a modest reduction in benefit amounts for families with incomes above a certain ceiling, but the proportion of families subject to the reduction is quite small. A few other countries have similar provisions, including Italy and several Eastern European countries. As Kamerman and Kahn (1982, 380) pointed out, "an important element in the shift away from social assistance . . . has been the development of income-tested benefits which are entitlements and are not stigmatized." They noted that several countries had been successful along these lines, as they developed income-tested programs that covered large portions of the population. "A combination of such programs with some taxation of universal benefits could well be the path towards universalism without inefficiency," (Kamerman and Kahn, 1982, 380).

There may, however, be a problem with a shift to income-tested allowances for other reasons. Both employer and union organizations in France – especially the trade unions – have been opposed to recent moves toward income testing, as exemplified in the supplementary allowances scheme (to be discussed below) on the ground that it is a shift away from a family policy toward assistance (Fragonard, 1983). Proposals for income testing have also been controversial in the Netherlands (Van Der Reijden, 1983). It is easy to see why union members might be opposed to a trend toward income testing, which could well result in exclusion from family allowances of workers with average or above-average incomes.

The proportion of single-parent families has been increasing in most industrial countries. Data collected by Kamerman and Kahn (1982, table 9) indicated the following percentages of single-parent families among all families with children: Australia, 12.7 percent; Canada, 12.3 percent; France, 13 percent; West Germany, 11 percent; Israel, 4.3 percent; Sweden, 27 percent; the United Kingdom, 12 percent; and the United States, 19.5 percent. Other relatively recent data showed comparatively high percentages in Belgium and Hungary and a relatively low percentage in Czechoslovakia (Mattyasovszky, 1985).

Illegitimacy rates have been reported to vary widely, ranging in 1969 from 2.2 percent of live births in the Netherlands to 16.3 percent in Sweden (United Kingdom, Government of, 1974). Later reports have indicated relatively high rates for Denmark and Sweden.

The problem of single-parent families assumes major dimensions in the United States. Although the increase in the proportion of women heading households was small between 1960 and 1970, it accelerated sharply after that. By 1985, 23 percent of children under 18 were in families headed by a single parent: Among blacks, 54 percent of the children were in single-parent families; among whites, 18 percent; and, among children of Spanish origin, 29 percent (U.S. Bureau of the Census, 1986, 8). The rise in the divorce rate, a high fertility rate among young unmarried women, and a dramatic lessening of the stigma against unwed mothers have been cited as reasons for these trends.

A particularly striking difference between the United States and some other industrial countries is in the prevalence of teenage pregnancies. The number of teenage pregnancies has been around one million a year in recent years, and the rate has been about 96 per thousand women aged 15 to 19 in the United States, compared with 14 per thousand in France, 14 per thousand in the Netherlands, 44 per thousand in Canada, 45 per thousand in England and Wales, and 35 per thousand in Sweden. According to a study by the Guttmacher Institute, the countries with the lowest teenage pregnancy rates were those that had the most open attitudes about sex, the most extensive school sex education programs, and the readiest access to contraception for young people (Jones et al., 1985). Thus the solution is more of an education problem than a social security problem. Although the majority of Americans are reported to favor sex education in the schools, a highly vocal minority that is opposed to sex education (and also to abortion) has tended to intimidate the schools. Recently, however, with growing concern over the spread of acquired immune deficiency syndrome (AIDS), the federal government has begun to advocate increased emphasis on sex education in the schools.

Study after study in various countries has shown that the proportion of children who are poor is relatively high in large families and in female-headed families (e.g., the Australian Government Commission on Inquiry into Poverty, 1975; Townsend, 1979, on poverty in Britain; Mitton, Willmott, and Willmott 1983, on poverty in Bristol, Rheims, and Saarbrucken; George and Lawson, eds., 1980, on poverty in Common Market countries; Borowczyk, 1986, on poverty in Poland; and annual reports by the U.S. Bureau of the Census). Nevertheless, it is important to recognize that although percentages of poor children are high in such families, children in small two-parent families form a large percentage of the poor.

All in all, at least 16 of our countries had some type of special provision for low-income families or for single-parent families, or in some cases for both, in 1985. There were special allowances or supplements for single-parent families in Denmark and Norway, for the first and second child of a single parent in Hungary, for children of unmarried mothers in the Soviet Union (not limited to those with more than three children as in the regular system), and for the first child of a single parent in Britain. These allowances or supplements were not income-tested, except for the income ceiling previously mentioned in Denmark. In Greece, widows and widowers with children received higher allowances than other families.

In Australia there were income-tested allowances for single parents, although regular family allowances were not income-tested. They included an allowance for the parent that was equal to the income-tested old-age pension for a single person, plus allowances for children, rental supplements, and a mother's guardian allowance. There was also a supplemental allowance for low-income families.

There were 12 other countries with special allowances for low-income families by the end of 1986. In Belgium this took the form of means-tested allowances for families that were not eligible for regular family allowances (i.e., families that did not include employed persons or social insurance beneficiaries or did not belong to the special systems for self-employed or public employees). In Japan, the allowance for each child beyond two in low-income families amounted to 7,000 yen a month, compared with 5,000 yen a month in other families. In the Soviet Union, there was an allowance of 12 rubles a month for each child under 12 in low-income families; in the United Kingdom, a law enacted in 1971 provided for a family income supplement for low-income families in which the head was employed on a full-time basis, whereas families with a full-time worker were not eligible for public assistance.[2]

The history of supplemental benefits in France is particularly interesting because it showed a trend toward greater use of income-tested benefits and, at least until 1985, away from rewarding mothers who stayed at home with their children toward a more neutral policy for working mothers. However, discussion of this trend will be deferred to a later section on family policy in France.

In Israel, needy families were eligible for income-tested support if the usual allowances did not meet their needs (Honig and Shamai, 1978), whereas in

[2] For a detailed discussion of the British family income supplement, see Brown (1983); and for a discussion of one-parent families in Britain, see Popay, Rimmer, and Rossiter (1983).

Poland allowances were inversely related to income, and there was an overall income ceiling.

Among recent additions to countries with supplements for low-income families are Italy (1983), Ireland (1986), and New Zealand (1986). Significantly, moreover, all three of these countries adopted provisions (perhaps influenced by that in Britain) under which the supplements were to be provided only to families in which at least one parent was working. Growing recognition of poverty in the families of low earners, as well as avoidance of disincentives to work, probably played a role (S&LB, 1983 [4]: 594–5; 1984 [2]: 321; 1986 [1]: 162; 1986 [1]: 163). Another country to adopt supplements for children in low-income families recently is West Germany (Bundesregierung, 1986a).

Although Sweden was not one of the countries with a special family allowance for a single-parent family, it nevertheless ranked at the top of nine countries studied by Kamerman and Kahn (1982, table 4) in the generosity of its income maintenance provisions for a single-parent family consisting of a mother who was not working, with two children. Major reasons were its advance maintenance payments (child support payments later to be collected from absent fathers) and its extensive program of income-tested housing allowances. Ranking after Sweden were France and West Germany, whereas the United States, Canada, Australia, the United Kingdom, and Israel continued to rely very heavily on public assistance in meeting the needs of families of this type, and income maintenance payments were much smaller in relation to average earnings.

Age ceilings and other features: In general, family allowances are payable for children up to the school-leaving age, although a number of countries provide them to considerably later ages for young people enrolled in education or training programs. Much depends on the relationship between the family allowance system and education grants or loans, especially for those enrolled in higher education. Where family allowances are not available beyond the school-leaving age, grants or loans for those enrolled in higher education tend to be available in many of our countries.

In some countries, families in certain circumstances may receive both family allowances and supplements for children under other social insurance provisions. However, as we have seen, supplements for children are considerably less common under sickness and unemployment insurance schemes than in old-age and invalidity insurance. Moreover, countries with relatively generous family allowance systems do not usually permit the payment of children's supplements under insurance schemes as well. This leaves a relatively small number of countries in which some families may receive both family allowances and children's supplements under other schemes, chiefly old-age and invalidity insurance. Sweden has a provision for subtracting family allowances received from children's supplements under other programs, and West Germany has a somewhat similar provision.

Finally, the number of countries with special provisions for allowances for handicapped or disabled children has been growing – a trend mentioned in Chapter 4. In many cases, these allowances are larger than for nondisabled children, and they are sometimes available to a later age. Many countries also have special provisions for orphans, under which allowances are frequently higher than for other children.

The birth rate

Although a desire to stimulate an increase in the birth rate has been one of the reasons for adopting family allowances in some countries, there is little evidence that they have been an important factor in inducing changes in the birth rate. For one thing, in most cases the allowances do not begin to be large enough to meet the costs of an additional child. For another, birth rates in industrial countries have tended to change in much the same manner, responding to broad social and economic changes, such as the prosperity that prevailed in most countries in the 1950s. Moreover, there is no evidence that the *relative* generosity or meagerness of family allowances has had any influence on differences in birth rates from country to country (see Burns, 1968; Fragonard, 1983; and many other sources).

Family policies

The Myrdals

The concept of a family policy owes much to the writings of Alva and Gunnar Myrdal on this problem in the early 1930s and the later, more comprehensive work by Alva Myrdal (1941). In an introduction to a later paperback version of Alva Myrdal's book (1968), Daniel P. Moynihan (now Senator Moynihan) wrote that "in the nature of modern industrial society no government, however firm might be its wish, can avoid having policies that profoundly affect family relationships. . . . The only option is whether these will be purposeful, intended policies or whether they will be residual, derivative, in a sense, concealed ones."

Noting that, as a result of a declining birth rate, a decline in total population was impending in Sweden, the Myrdals argued that the practical problem of averting that fate involved social reforms creating a foundation for the institution of the family. Furthermore, they pointed out that the reforms they proposed were consistent with the policies for social security and increased welfare then being launched by the Social Democrats. Later in her 1941 book (p. 128 ff), Alva Myrdal listed these reforms as follows:

Free delivery, and free prenatal and postnatal care for all mothers
Free medical and health care for all children, including dental care, mental hygiene, and medicines
Subvention of rent and other housing costs in relation to family size
Reduction of food costs for children through a free school meal and price discounts on certain foodstuffs in relation to family size
Free education all the way
Free nursery education
Somewhat reduced costs for clothing, eventually through free availability of the more expensive and necessary garments
Reduced costs and improved facilities for family recreation through cheap fare for families, vacation villages, etc., free summer vacation camps, afternoon clubs, etc., for children and adolescents, and free vacations for mothers in various forms
Increased security of employment for both fathers and mothers and coverage of costs for periods of lessened physical resistance
Social responsibility for the children in all incomplete and handicapped families

She then went on to discuss the pros and cons of family allowances, taking the position that, in general, it was preferable to provide benefits in kind or in the form of services rather than in cash, although she recognized the need for cash payments for children without a family supporter. Sweden did, however, adopt a family allowance system in 1947, undoubtedly influenced by the Beveridge Report, and by the recommendations of a special commission.

Although education policies are among the most important aspects of family policies, they are beyond the scope of this study, as are housing policies; health benefits have been discussed in Chapter 10 and will not be considered further. I shall consider primarily those aspects of family policy that are most closely related to family income and the problems of labor force participation for married women bearing and rearing children.

In the highly useful book edited by Kamerman and Kahn on family policies in 14 countries (1978), the editors concluded that the countries should be divided into three groups:

1.   Countries with an explicit and comprehensive family policy – Sweden, Norway, Hungary, Czechoslovakia, and France
2.   Countries in which family policy was a field of concern – Austria, West Germany, Poland, Finland, and Denmark

3. Countries in which family policy was implicit and reluctant – the United Kingdom, Canada, Israel, and the United States

We shall find, at a later point, that there have been indications of increased concern more recently in some of these countries, especially Canada and Israel.

Our discussion will first focus on several of the countries with explicit and comprehensive family policies and then will consider how various elements of family policy – for example, maternity benefits and provision for child care – are manifested in different countries.

Individual countries

France: The history of family policies in France is of special interest because it was one of the first countries to develop an explicit family policy and because there have been significant changes in French family policy over the course of the postwar period. We have earlier noted the enactment of the law requiring employers to provide children's allowances in 1932. This was followed by the adoption of the Family Code in 1939, shortly before the outbreak of World War II, at a time when the French public was deeply concerned over a longtime decline in the birth rate, in the face of a larger population in Germany. The code was also aimed at improving the well-being of families and encouraging the raising of large families (Rouast and Durand, 1960).

The former allowance for the first child was discontinued, and allowances for the third child and additional children were increased. There was also a single-earner allowance which, modified somewhat in later legislation, provided supplementary allowances to the family if the wife of an employed man with children did not work or worked only on a part-time basis. Also provided were premiums payable in respect of first births, loans to young married couples setting themselves up in agricultural occupations, assistance to needy families, and revision of the tax system so that the incidence of the tax burden would be inversely proportional to family responsibilities. Moreover, all family schemes were absorbed into a single system.

In 1946, the family allowance program was broadened to extend eligibility to persons whose employment had been interrupted or who could not be employed for one reason or another, including the unemployed, widows, single mothers, and disabled heads of households. Two new allowances, providing for prenatal and maternity benefits, replaced the premium for the first birth. Moreover, there was a requirement that, as a condition for maternity benefits, births should take place at specified intervals after a marriage.

In 1948, means-tested benefits were introduced to assist families to meet housing expenses. Later, in 1972, means-test limitations were extended to apply to certain existing allowances, such as the single-earner allowance, and the proportion of family allowances paid under a means test rose from 14 percent in 1970 to 35 percent in 1976. It was in 1972, also, that allowances were provided for certain specific groups, such as orphans and handicapped children.

Despite the use of means tests for certain benefits, family allowances were not considered to be public assistance, but rather payments to which eligible families had a right.

An important change was made under legislation effective in 1978, which replaced several existing allowances, including the single-earner allowance (except for those already receiving it), by a supplementary allowance for low-income families. The supplement was payable subject to two conditions:

1. The family must have at least one dependent child under age three or at least three dependent children.
2. The income of the family must not exceed a ceiling which depends on the number of dependent children.

The supplement was payable whether the mother worked or not (for data on the income ceilings in effect in 1980, see Bradshaw and Piachaud, 1980, 59). Notable was a shift away from policies encouraging families to have more than three children toward emphasis on the second and third child and, more recently, toward fewer special benefits in relation to the third child (Questiaux and Fournier, 1978; Fragonard, 1983).

Family allowances clearly are only one of many types of family benefits in France. All in all, according to Bradshaw and Piachaud (1980, 57), there were 14 types of family benefits at the end of the 1970s:

Prenatal allowances	Orphan's allowance
Postnatal allowances	Special education allowance
Family allowances	for handicapped children
Family supplement	Benefits for handicapped adults
School costs allowance	Removal expense grant
Housing allowances	Loans to young couples
One-parent allowances	Improvement loans for homes
Paternity leave	

These were the benefits administered through the family allowances funds *(Caisses des Allocations Familiales)*. They included some items that would have been administered by other agencies in most countries.

In 1985, the prenatal and postnatal allowances (as well as certain supplements) were replaced by an infant allowance and a parental infant care allowance. Payments were to begin after the third month of pregnancy and continue until the child was three months old. If the family income was below a certain ceiling (high enough to include 80 percent of families), however, payments could continue until the child's third birthday. Moreover, the new provisions were intended to compensate employees of either sex partially for the loss of income from stopping work or reducing hours of work to care for a child under age three. The purpose was to enable employees to take full advantage of the right to parental leave, which had been introduced in 1977 (*S&LB*, 1985 [3–4]: 556–7).

The new policy resembled Sweden's parental leave provisions along with Hungary's provision for an allowance to a mother who stayed at home until the child was age three. It was adopted in spite of the fact that earlier proposals for an extended period of paid leave for the mother had been opposed by unions and a large section of feminist opinion (Fragonard, 1983).

France has also followed the lead of the Scandinavian countries in providing alimony advances, financed by family allowance funds, and to be claimed later from the defaulting parent (*S&LB*, 1981 [2]: 210).

Although there are complaints in France as elsewhere about the shortage of places in child care centers, the free public kindergartens (*écoles maternelles*) were reported in 1978 to be open to 2½ million children aged two to five. In 1973–4, nearly 75 percent of children aged three were attending these schools, and nearly 95 percent of children aged four and about 100 percent at the age of five were enrolled. According to Questiaux and Fournier (1978), the methods in these schools were designed to suit each child's personality. They have been widely admired in other countries as well as in France. Moreover, by no means do all of these children have mothers at work. In 1976, 44 percent of mothers of children aged three to six were in the labor force (Kamerman and Kahn, 1981).

Among working mothers' children under age three, the majority were cared for at home or by private individuals away from home, including grandparents, but there were also others who were cared for in *crèches collectives* or *crèches familiales* (supervised family day care), or public nursery schools, and a particularly large number were in licensed or unlicensed family daycare centers (called *nourrices*). These facilities are partially financed from public funds, but parents pay a fee that is graduated according to income.

Until 1985, French policies could be seen as tending toward greater emphasis on allowances for low-income families and as moving toward more evenhanded support of mothers who worked. Now the trend is not quite so clear. The adoption of the infant care allowances represented a move toward encouraging the mother or the father to care for children, but presumably it would be the mother who would do so in most instances. Moreover, the extended infant allowance was not targeted toward low-income families but set an income ceiling that qualified 80 percent of families.

Hungary: The development of family policy in Hungary in the postwar period has been very similar to that in other Eastern European countries, especially in Czechoslovakia and in certain respects in the Soviet Union. It has been characterized by a shift away from Marxist attitudes toward the raising of children, as the socialist countries have confronted falling birth rates and unstable family relationships. It has also encouraged the labor force participation of women, while at the same time, at least in part for the purpose of encouraging population growth, providing special allowances to the mother of very young children who stays at home.

According to Ferge (1978) there was a period of active development of social policy in the three or four years following the end of the war, but a slowing down thereafter, attributable not only to the scarcity of resources but also to the officially held belief that socialist development would result in the "withering away" of social problems – from poverty to alcoholism to delinquency. Moreover, the radical view was that the family was the most important determinant of social positions and of the persistence of social inequalities. Communal education of children was therefore an integral part of radical ideologies.

Even so, it was recognized in Hungary in the 1940s and the 1950s that the development of high-quality communal education was not economically feasible and that the institution of the family had to be safeguarded. Madison (1968) has traced at length a similar development in the Soviet Union. Moreover, from the end of the 1950s it was becoming clear that economic and social progress were not resulting in the disappearance of social problems, but to some extent were aggravating them.

Family allowances in Hungary date from 1938 and were also subject to legislation enacted in 1946, which provided for a universal flat-rate benefit. However, the allowances remained very low until the end of the 1950s, after which they were raised on several occasions, with emphasis on adequate provision for large families and those that were members of cooperatives. No allowance is provided for the first child, but in 1985 the allowance for the second child was 980 forints a month (about $49), 660 ft. for the third and for the fourth child, 630 ft. for the fifth child, and 610 ft. for the sixth and each other child. A single parent received 710 ft. for the first child and 660 ft. for the second. There were also relatively high allowances provided for families with one or two disabled children.

A particularly significant step was the introduction of a child care grant in 1967, offering a mother who had been employed about a year or more prior to the child's birth the choice of staying at home after the expiration of her fully paid maternity leave or returning to work. The mother who chose to stay at home could receive a monthly grant until the child was age three. In 1985, the grant for the first child amounted to 910 ft. a month (after 16 weeks of maternity leave following the birth and 4 weeks before the birth). The grant for the second child was 1,010 ft., and that for the third child was 1,110 ft. There was also a birth grant amounting to 2,500 forints for each birth.

Initially, the introduction of these child care grants was followed by an increase in the birth rate, but this did not last, even though a large proportion of mothers (around 70 percent) chose to receive them. In 1980 the birth rate in Hungary was 13.9 per thousand population – higher than in most Western European countries, but considerably lower than in other countries of Eastern Europe. In fact, the number of mothers taking advantage of the option to stay at home decreased somewhat after 1977. In spite of its popularity, moreover, it was criticized by Western feminists as an interference with a woman's career development. Significantly, women employed in intellectual jobs tended to stay at home for only a year or a year-and-a-half, whereas mothers who had been employed in routine jobs tended to stay at home for the entire three-year period.

In Hungary, as elsewhere in Eastern Europe, child care institutions are emphasized in order to promote the cause of women's emancipation and the collectivist education of children. According to Nagy and Szabady (1983), 16 percent of children under age three were in infant's nurseries in 1980, whereas the rest were cared for by their mothers either on childbirth leave or on child care leave. The capacity of day nurseries had been expanded rapidly: About 87 percent of children aged three to five were in day nurseries, while about 38 percent of elementary school children were in child care centers part of the day.

The development of family policy continues to be taken very seriously in Hungary, and all parties participating in the development of five-year and longer-term plans are required to consider all the decisions having implications for family policy. There is also concern over the rise in the divorce rate, the prevalence of single-parent families (about 11 percent of families with children around 1980), and a tendency for children brought up in unstable families to experience disruption in their own family life.

Sweden: Sweden, like Hungary and France, has developed a comprehensive and purposeful set of family policies, but they do not appear to have been as pronatalist as were those of France at one time. Moreover, in the country with the highest female labor force participation rate among Western industrial democracies, there has been greater emphasis on training and retraining opportunities for women with children. Also, as we have seen, Sweden was the first country to provide opportunities for fathers, as well as mothers, to take paid leave in order to care for young children.

Sexuality among the young is accepted, as is access to contraceptives. The rate of illegitimacy has been high (Liljeström, 1978), but recent reports (Ljung,

1986) indicate a leveling off at about 20 percent in the proportion of all couples living together who were not married in the first half of the 1980s. Moreover, a very high proportion of single mothers with children work, and, according to a survey conducted in 1971, nearly two-thirds of mothers with illegitimate children cohabited with the child's father.

Sweden adopted universal and uniform family allowances in 1947, but the amounts were small. Gradually, however, the amounts have been increased, and, by 1985, Swedish family allowances amounted to 400 kr. a month (about $47) for the first child and increasing amounts for each child after two. Educational grants and loans were available through the education authorities and were quite extensive in Sweden, with considerable emphasis on loans for students enrolled in higher education.

Although there has been emphasis on the development of day nurseries and municipally run and supervised child-minding homes, only 26 percent of the children with working mothers had access to such care in 1974. I was told when I was in Stockholm in 1986 that despite a pronounced increase since then, there was still a shortage of places, and the government had promised to overcome the shortage by the early 1990s. In view of the insufficiency of places, priority is given to the children of single parents and to children from "socially disadvantaged" families, such as children of alcoholics.

In Sweden, I encountered some concern over the possible family-splitting effect of advantages given to single-parent families, but little definite information about it. Moreover, the prevalence of cohabitation with the fathers of illegitimate children meant that mothers of illegitimate children were less likely to be destitute than in some other countries. Also very important was the policy on maintenance advances in Sweden, and in Norway and Denmark as well. Amounts of maintenance are set by the state. They are designed to guarantee a monthly maintenance level to all children of unmarried, separated, or divorced mothers, when added to the family allowances. Payment of these advances is associated with procedures for investigating paternity, fixing the amount, and enforcing the payment of private maintenance by the father. It was reported in 1974 that in Norway and Sweden, if paternity was not established, the child was eligible for the publicly guaranteed maintenance payment until age 18 (United Kingdom, Government of, 1974).

All of these factors help to explain why mothers of illegitimate children are much less likely to become dependent on public assistance than in some other countries – the United States, for example.

Mothers in Sweden have long been entitled to maternity benefits under the sickness insurance scheme, but in 1974 a new law on parental insurance came into effect, providing that gainfully employed parents were entitled to apportion between them seven months of "child leave." During this period they would receive a daily amount equal to 90 percent of their earnings. The fathers also were to share the right to 60 days of leave a year in order to stay at home with a sick child. By 1985, the total period of shared leave amounted to 360 days, of which 270 days were at 90 percent of earnings and 90 days at 48 kr. a day until the child was age four. Although fathers have taken advantage of this right to some extent, it has been the mothers who have taken most of the leave. In 1983, about 85 percent of the cost of benefits under the sickness insurance scheme was met through an employer payroll tax of 9.5 percent, while the remaining 15 percent was met from general government revenues.

Although the important features of Swedish family policy are strongly supported by public opinion, there continue to be some matters of controversy – for example, over shorter hours of work for parents of small children. Moreover, the trade unions and feminist organizations have opposed extended maternal paid leave along the lines of the Hungarian and Czechoslovakian policies.

Tax policies and other provisions

Intimately related to family allowances are income tax policies as they relate to children. Most industrial countries have provided for tax deductions for family members, including children. However, as the interest in combatting poverty has grown, a substantial number of countries have abolished tax deductions on the ground that they benefit chiefly high-income families who are subject to high marginal tax rates. In a number of cases, this move has been accompanied by an increase in family allowances, thus providing greater relative assistance for low- and middle-income families. This type of change has occurred in at least ten countries, including Australia, Austria, Belgium, Denmark, West Germany, Israel, Italy, the Netherlands, New Zealand, and the United Kingdom. In Sweden, tax deductions for children were discontinued when family allowances were adopted in 1947.

In the United States, the Tax Reform Act of 1986 has substantially increased tax deductions for family members.[3] Although this will benefit high-income families, the marginal tax rates are being reduced at the same time, so that the impact of the deduction will be somewhat modified. Meanwhile, those low-income families who will be subject to no tax liability as a result of the larger deductions for family members will clearly benefit.

Initially, family allowances were usually not taxable, but by 1976 five countries – Canada, Italy, New Zealand, Switzerland, and the United Kingdom – were taxing them (Messere and Owens, 1979, table 1). The changes

---

[3] Previously the amounts of personal tax exemptions had lagged far behind changes in wage and price levels.

took account of the fact that middle- and higher-income families had less need for family allowances and could well afford to pay taxes on them, whereas low-income families were subject to little or no income taxes.

The move toward providing tax credits for children is relatively recent and has clearly been influenced by debates over the negative income tax. A "tax credit" is a deduction from taxes to be paid, rather than from income, and usually is the same for all families. Therefore, its effect relative to income is greater for low-income than for high-income families. Moreover, tax credit programs sometimes provide that families liable for no taxes will be paid the tax credit by the government and those liable for a tax that is less than the tax credit will receive the difference. This type of plan resembles the "social dividend" proposal made by Lady Rhys-Williams (1943) in Britain under which every man, woman, and child would receive a social dividend payment that would replace all other social security benefits and would be financed by a proportional income tax on all other income.

Canada's program, effective in 1979, provides a tax credit that is payable in full to all families with income below a certain maximum. It is designed to provide additional assistance in meeting the costs of raising children in low- to middle-income families. The benefit is in addition to the regular family allowance and in 1986 amounted to $384 for each eligible child if the family income in 1985 did not exceed $26,330. The benefit was reduced by $5 of every $100 of income above that ceiling (Canada, Health and Welfare, 1986, 20).

The tax credit compared with the family allowance of $379 a year in 1986 (both indexed to changing prices). Together they yielded $763 per child and provided, of course, a very substantial increase in total amounts payable to large families.

Thus, in a series of moves, Canada has tilted its federal payments for children toward low- and middle-income families, even though it retains a universal allowance in its basic federal family allowance system.

In the United States, several proposals for versions of a negative income tax failed of adoption, but, after considerable debate, Congress did adopt, in 1975, an earned income tax credit. In 1987, this was available for families with one or more children if they received earned income of less than $15,425. The credit could be claimed by a married couple filing a joint return, or by a single parent with the status of widow(er), head of household, divorced, or separated, if there were one or more dependent children. The credit rose from $2 for zero earnings to $851 for earnings between $6,075 and $6,925 and then declined steadily to zero with earnings of $15,425 or more. Both the maximum credit and the maximum earnings below which the credit would be available were considerably higher than they had been in 1986. According to Moynihan (1986, 157), by the 1980s between six and seven million families were receiving benefits, which amounted to $2 billion a year, about one-third of which took the form of reduced taxes and two-thirds of cash payments. There is also a tax credit for child and dependent care expenses.

Israel's tax reform act, enacted in 1975, brought about a comprehensive integration of the income-maintenance and tax systems. According to Roter and Shamai (1976), the effect was to develop a combined system of tax credits for children and children's allowances. The system was regarded as a first step toward a negative income tax, but the guaranteed income program adopted in 1980 took the form of a comprehensive and unified national assistance scheme rather than a negative income tax program (*S&LB*, 1981 [2]: 212).

According to Messere and Owens (1979), Austria, Belgium, Finland, and Italy also had tax credits for children in 1976. Moreover, in 1972, a comprehensive tax credit scheme was proposed by the Conservative government then in power in Britain (United Kingdom, Government of, 1972). Under the 1986 amendments, however, a modest scheme of family tax credits was adopted to replace the Family Income Supplement. It is designed to be paid to families in which the breadwinner is working at least 24 hours a week, at rates intended to ensure that most families are better off on a low wage than on income support.

Birth grants: Closely related to family allowances are birth grants, which were provided in most of our countries in 1985. In nine of these countries, they were provided from family allowance funds, whereas in ten they were provided, like maternity benefits, through the sickness insurance system. A few countries also gave a special allowance for a limited period to a mother nursing her child.

Birth grants, or maternity grants as they are sometimes called, vary quite widely in amount. In Austria and Belgium, they amounted to about 50 percent of average monthly wages, whereas in some of the Eastern European countries they were higher. On the other hand, amounts were considerably lower in Finland, West Germany, Ireland, and the United Kingdom. In Switzerland, birth grants were provided in some of the cantons.

In most countries the amount was the same for each birth, but in the Soviet Union the amount increased quite steadily with each birth up to the 11th. On the other hand, in Belgium the amount decreased from the first to the second, and from the second to the third, staying constant thereafter.

Although the provision of birth grants may appear to be pronatalist in some cases, as in the USSR, the purpose in many cases is to encourage the mother to have the appropriate number of medical examinations both before and after the birth. In fact, in some countries the birth grant is conditional on a specific number of examinations or is lower for the mother who does not have them.

Significantly, also, the provision of these grants is not income-tested, although in some countries where the grant is provided through sickness insurance, it may be dependent on a required number of weeks of insurance.

Parental leave: Prenatal and postnatal maternity leave is generally provided through sickness insurance programs for specified maximum periods before and after confinement, with compensation for loss of earnings usually amounting to a relatively large percentage of earnings and in some cases to 100 percent. Generally the mother must have been employed and insured for a specific period of time although in Austria she may qualify if her husband is insured, whereas in Israel she may qualify if she is the spouse of a deceased insured worker. The previous employment required of the mother is in most cases quite limited, amounting in some cases only to current employment or in others to a year, in order to insure that she has not become employed after the onset of pregnancy for the purpose of qualifying for benefits.

In Austria in 1985, maternity benefits amounted to 100 percent of earnings for eight weeks before and eight weeks after confinement, but there was also provision for extended leave up to one year and there were higher leave payments for single mothers. West Germany and the Netherlands also provided 100 percent of earnings, but only for six weeks before and eight weeks after the birth in West Germany and six weeks before and six weeks after in the Netherlands. In Eastern Europe, however, benefits were generally 100 percent of earnings for considerably longer periods, and we have earlier noted the special provisions for paid leave in Hungary and Czechoslovakia. Poland followed their example in 1981 with an allowance that was inversely related to income (like the regular family allowance in Poland) and that was payable for up to 24 months and until the child reached the age of four (Borowczyk, 1986, 176).

In three countries – Czechoslovakia, Denmark, and Sweden – benefits were 90 percent of earnings. Sweden's provisions have been discussed earlier, as have those of Czechoslovakia. Denmark's provisions have recently been liberalized, providing benefits for a total of 24 weeks (*S&LB,* 1986 [3–4]: 542).

In other countries, benefits ranged from 50 percent to 80 percent of earnings, and duration provisions were generally similar to those of Austria. In Britain, however, under the 1986 amendments, a woman who had worked six months for the same employer received a flat-rate payment for 18 weeks, but if she had worked for the employer two years, the benefit was 90 percent of earnings for the first six weeks. In Ireland, maternity benefits were a combination of flat-rate and earnings-related benefits.

Denmark, Finland, and Norway have followed Sweden's path in providing for leave for fathers, but the provisions tend to be somewhat less liberal than Sweden's.

In the United States, it is only in the five states (plus Puerto Rico) with temporary disability insurance (see Chapter 10) that pregnant women can qualify for legally provided benefits. Elsewhere, women may be eligible for disability benefits under employer plans, and the Pregnancy Discrimination Act of 1978 required that pregnant employees be treated the same as employees with any type of temporary disability. However, as Kamerman (1983) has pointed out, policies vary as to when a pregnant woman is considered sufficiently disabled to leave work and even more when she is considered able to return to work.

The situation is changing, however. Early in 1987, the United States Supreme Court upheld a California law that requires unpaid leave and reinstatement in the job for a pregnant woman, and bills have recently been introduced in Congress providing for parental leave.

Child care centers: Issues relating to child care have become increasingly important since the 1960s, as more and more mothers of very young children have entered the labor force, whereas the earlier postwar pattern was for mothers of very young children to stay out of the labor force. Policies relating to child care centers in France, Hungary, and Sweden have been discussed earlier in this chapter. I shall deal rather briefly with policies elsewhere, since a full discussion of the extensive available data would extend this chapter unduly.[4]

Although there is in general considerable agreement about the need for high-quality child care centers for children aged three to five or six, the question of the provision of nursery care for children under age three is a matter of controversy in some countries, and policies differ. As we have seen, the policies of Hungary, Czechoslovakia, Poland, France, and, to a less pronounced degree, the Soviet Union are designed to induce the mother of very young children to remain out of the labor force. On the other hand, East Germany has stressed the development of high-quality day care centers for children under age three, as well as an extensive kindergarten system for those aged three to six. In 1977, over 48 percent of children under age three were in day care centers – or 60 percent if we exclude children under 20 weeks of age, whose mothers received paid maternity leave and were not admitted to child care centers (Kamerman and Kahn, 1981).

The situation in West Germany has been quite different. Organized child care for children under three has not been encouraged. Even so, labor force participation of mothers of young children has been increasing, and the majority of the children under age three of working mothers in 1975 were cared for by grandmothers and other adult family members, while a minority were in group care outside of the family environment. On the other hand, enrollment of children aged three to six in kindergartens has been extensive. With

---

[4] The series of studies written or edited by Kamerman and Kahn (e.g., 1982) provide a wealth of information on child care and other aspects of family policy.

the recent acceleration of the flow of women into the labor force, there is likely to be increased pressure for expansion of child care facilities.

Kindergartens tend to be free of charge, providing for children from age three to five or six, but in many countries they are largely on a part-day basis and thus do not fully meet the needs of mothers who work full-time. On the other hand, programs providing day care, whether for children under three or those aged three and over, usually charge a fee on a sliding-scale basis in relation to income, with a government subsidy of varying relative importance from country to country.

Among the countries studied by Kamerman and Kahn (1978 and 1981), the proportion of children aged three or more in kindergartens and other types of preschool programs that provided all-day care was particularly high – in the range of 80 to 90 percent – in Eastern Europe. The percentage enrolled was also very high in France, but only 44 percent of mothers of children in this age group worked in 1976, whereas in Eastern Europe the percentages in the labor force were much higher.

According to Rimmer and Wicks (1983), the proportion of children under age five receiving some form of day care in Britain increased markedly during the 1970s. Among children aged two to four, the percentage attending nursery or primary school rose from 10 percent in 1971 to 21 percent in 1979; the proportion of those under age five attending play groups or day nurseries rose from 11 percent to 29 percent in the same period. Even so, surveys indicated that parents found the current level of provision far from adequate.

In the United States, apart from free public kindergartens, which are largely on a part-day basis, there has been only modest public funding of child care centers either at the federal or state levels. Nevertheless, the need has been there, and various types of child care facilities have been developed under private auspices – profit or nonprofit or sometimes religious – as well as substantial provision of family day care in private homes, licensed or unlicensed, depending on the degree of supervision in the various states. Public funding that was provided by the federal government and some of the state governments has been cut back in the 1980s, although recently a few of the states have increased funding for child care centers as part of programs aimed at stimulating employment and training of AFDC (Aid For Dependent Children) recipients. Early in 1988, several bills providing for increased federal funds for child care were introduced in Congress.

Although there continues to be a shortage of organized child care centers, the number of children of working mothers cared for in such centers has increased rapidly and accounted for 23 percent of children of working mothers under five years of age in 1984–5 (*San Francisco Chronicle*, May 9, 1987). One of the results of the dearth of publicly supported child care centers in the

United States has been the growth of pressure on employers to provide child care facilities in or near the firm, and some have responded.[5]

In an exceedingly interesting discussion of the trend toward "community care" (essentially more localized and privatized care), Bryson and Mowbray (1986) criticized the move of the conservative Fraser government toward family day-care in Australia. Federally subsidized and administered by local governments, this was a scheme in which women cared for children under age five in their own homes, receiving very low pay. Although this policy was to some extent reversed by the succeeding Labor government, in favor of child care centers, a severe shortage continues.

In Canada, a special task force on child care (the Cooke Task Force) issued a report in March 1986, charging that Canada's child care situation was in a "state of crisis, with the current supply of licensed child care spaces able to accommodate less than 9 percent of children requiring nonparental care on a full-day basis" (Canada, Government of, 1986). It recommended a gradual approach to improving the situation, beginning with short-term grants from the federal government to the provinces and territories, followed by a cost-sharing program in which the provisions and territories would cover a portion of the cost. In the long run, child care would be fully funded by the federal and provincial/territorial governments on a cost-shared basis (Canada, Government of, 1986).

Conclusions

The social developments of the postwar period have virtually forced governments to pay increasing attention to issues of family policy, whether or not they had a tradition of consciously pursuing a family policy. The increasing instability of families, the rising proportion of working mothers, and the persistence of poverty among families with children have created an entirely different environment for issues of family policy than in the early postwar years. And yet, there continues to be a wide gulf between countries with a comprehensive and purposeful family policy, such as France and Hungary, and countries that have responded to the new needs in a piecemeal manner, like the United States.

We now move on to public assistance, which is also an important element of family policy, whether purposefully or not.

---

[5] Interestingly, also, the City of San Francisco, with a predominantly liberal Board of Supervisors, recently became the first major city in the country to require office developers to make provision for child care services (*San Francisco Chronicle*, October 8, 1985).

CHAPTER 14

Public assistance and guaranteed income proposals

Introduction

Modern public assistance is usually the path of last resort for the needy who cannot qualify for benefits from other programs. It is more humane than old poor relief systems, less restrictive in applying the means test, and much less stigmatizing. Moreover, in many countries it is now subject to national standards and wholly or partly financed from national budgets, even though it tends to be administered locally. Nevertheless, it has not altogether lost its stigmatizing tendency, and this, along with ignorance of the provisions, helps to account for the fact that what the British call the "take-up" rate (the proportion of eligible persons who apply for and receive public assistance) tends to be far below 100 percent.

In the Middle Ages, poor relief was the province of the Church and was governed by Canon law. The Church distinguished between the holy voluntary poverty of a St. Francis of Assisi and idle parasitism. It also distinguished between the "able-bodied poor" and those who were poor because they were ailing or too young or too old to work – that is, between the deserving and undeserving poor. It was the duty of the wealthy to provide for the poor – this was the way to heaven. The role of the parish was central in the administration of poor relief, and this was the basis of the important role played by the parish after the Reformation. The medieval hospital also played an important role, as did the lord of the manor, who was expected to care for aging serfs, and the medieval guilds, which had mutual funds to care for ailing and aging members in some cases (Tierney, 1959).

The breakdown of medieval poor relief has frequently been attributed, at least in England, to the enclosure movement and later to the Reformation. This was only a part of the picture. A complex set of forces involving the breakup of the feudal system and the growth of a money economy led to the appearance of a class of landless rovers. The problem of relieving the poor became intertwined with the problem of suppressing vagrancy. After the Reformation, moreover, in countries that became predominantly Protestant, the "Protestant ethic" (the belief that all able-bodied persons should work) played an important role, whereas in Catholic countries the Church continued its

306

charitable activities, sometimes along with public and other private bodies, in aiding the poor.

In England, the poor laws began with the Ordinance of Laborers of 1349, which called for the suppression of begging. Then, gradually, the statutes from Henry VIII to Elizabeth I established the principle that each parish was responsible for the relief of its poor, with local financing and local adminis-tration for local residents (de Schweinitz, 1943). On the Continent, poor laws developed at about the same time in a number of European cities. On the whole, they were less punitive than in England.

The Law of Settlement, adopted in 1662, embodied an extreme form of localism, under which the justices of the peace were empowered to return to his former residence any person who came to occupy a property renting for less than £10 a year and who, in the opinion of the overseers, might at some future time become needy. The result was that such persons scarcely ever succeeded in gaining settlement in a new neighborhood, unless they acquired it through apprenticeship, employment, or the paying of taxes. Not until 1795 was the law amended to prevent a person from being removed unless he had actually applied for relief. The heritage of this policy was still being experi-enced in the United States during the Great Depression when occasionally one read of poor families being shipped from one state to another, or from one local community to another.

In the long history of amendments to the poor laws, the changes resulting from the recommendations of a special commission that issued its report in 1834 were particularly significant. The first of these proclaimed the doctrine of "less eligibility," under which the amount of relief granted had to be less than the earnings of the lowest paid laborer who was not receiving relief, lest it should be advantageous to avoid work. It had its successor in the "wage stop" that was in effect in Britain until 1976. Moreover, the workhouse was designated as the mechanism through which this doctrine was to be carried out. The poor were to live in an institution that was essentially penal. The commission's second recommendation, however, embodied a movement away from extreme localism. A central board was to be established to control the administration of the poor laws. It could combine parishes for the establish-ment and administration of workhouses and promote the provision of qualified and paid local personnel for relief administration.

British poor relief policies influenced the policies adopted by the states and local communities in the United States, as well as those adopted in the nine-teenth century in such countries as Australia, Canada, and New Zealand.

Poor relief developed rather differently on the Continent, although there was a good deal of communication between England and continental countries over poor relief issues. At first, poor relief tended to center around programs developed in local communities and only considerably later were national laws enacted requiring communities to provide poor relief. A model for other European communities was a program developed in the 1520s in the Belgian city of Ypres. There administration was placed in the hands of four leading citizens who were to see that the poor were fed and clothed, that young men were sent to school or trained in handicrafts, and that beggars who were able to work were to be compelled to work. Funds for the program were acquired on a house-to-house collection basis, as well as through boxes at churches.

Somewhat similar programs were developed in Hamburg and Munich, but they were financed by a combination of public and private funds. According to de Schweinitz (1943), by 1769 Hamburg had developed the most thorough and comprehensive program of its time, with estimates of relief needs developed from a survey of 3,500 families and a scheme of assistance that included employment, aid to dependent children, child placement, day nurseries, and provision for education. The principle of minimum relief was similar to the doctrine of "less eligibility" under the British recommendations of 1834, but the administration was less punitive.

Influenced especially by Malthus, and his doctrine that poor relief simply encouraged the poor to have more children and led to pauperism, a school of thought developed in the nineteenth century not only in Britain but also in some of the continental countries, and in the United States which was exceedingly hostile to poor relief. William Graham Sumner, a professor at Yale University, stressed the principle of natural selection, which enabled "those best adapted for survival to come out on top and left the unfit to succumb in the struggle" (Rimlinger, 1971, 49). The poor included not only those who were lazy and shiftless but also those who were intemperate.

It was not until the latter part of the nineteenth century that a movement developed to provide more humane assistance, especially through the development of separate programs of assistance for the aged, as in Denmark and Britain, and through the development of social insurance programs. Gradually, also, there were modifications in poor relief policies, especially during the Great Depression, when assistance to the unemployed was seen as imperative. It is not my purpose, however, to review these gradual changes, but rather to devote the remainder of this chapter to developments after World War II, when there was a widespread movement toward national standards and to some extent toward national financing, as well as humane administration. It should be kept in mind, however, that the New Zealand legislation of 1938, as we have noted earlier, was pathbreaking in providing for a comprehensive national social security program based for the most part on income-tested benefits. Moreover, Australia and New Zealand continue to rely to a large extent on income-tested benefits, thus continuing to differ from the prevailing pattern in which means-tested benefits are a residual part of social security programs.

Table 14.1. *Social assistance expenditures as a percentage of GDP, selected OECD countries, 1970–85*

Country	1970	1975	1980	1983	1985
Canada	4.4%	5.0%	4.6%	5.2%	5.2%
United States	2.5	3.6	3.3	3.2	2.8
Japan	1.3	1.3	2.2	2.1	1.9
Australia	5.4	8.6	8.8	9.9	9.7
Austria				5.9	5.7
Belgium	1.8	2.2	2.4	2.3	2.4
Finland	1.2	1.3	1.8	2.0	2.1
France	2.2	2.4	2.3	2.5	2.5
Germany (Fed. Rep.)	2.3	3.5	3.0	2.9	2.7
Ireland	5.7	7.7	7.2	9.1	
Netherlands	1.8	3.5	3.8	6.5	6.0
Sweden	2.9	3.2	2.9	3.1	3.2
Switzerland			2.3	2.5	2.6
United Kingdom	2.5	3.0	4.2	5.8	6.0

Source: OECD (1987c).

Expenditures on assistance

During the early years of the postwar period, there was a general expectation (clearly spelled out in the Beveridge Report) that, as social insurance expenditures became more comprehensive, the need for public assistance (or "social assistance," as it is generally called in Europe) would gradually diminish. This expectation proved to be inaccurate, partly because countries were confronted with the persistence of poverty among groups not fully eligible for social insurance or receiving only inadequate benefits, and, from the 1970s on, because of the rising burden of unemployment, which led to dependence on public assistance on the part of unemployed persons who had exhausted their benefit rights or were not eligible in the first place.

Table 14.1 shows that in 1970, social assistance expenditures were relatively high as a percentage of GDP in Canada, Australia, and Ireland. I have used the OECD data because they are available for the early 1980s (whereas ILO data are not), but also in recognition of the fact that they are more useful for comparing changes over time in each country than for comparisons between countries. The OECD definition of social assistance is very general,[1] and it appears that countries make their own determination as to just what

[1] The OECD defines social assistance grants as "grants to individuals and households by public authorities, private nonprofit corporations, and corporate and quasi-corporate enterprises, except social security benefits and unfunded employee benefits" (OECD, 1986b).

expenditures are included under public assistance. Australia's social security expenditures, for example, are classified entirely as social assistance expenditures, even though a few categories, such as industrial injuries insurance and basic family allowances, are not income-conditioned. On the other hand, no part of Denmark's expenditures is classified as social assistance, even though old-age pensions, for example, are partially income-conditioned. The ILO follows a different practice, classifying income-conditioned pensions as "pensions," and this and other differences mean that ILO data differ from those of OECD (see Appendix 1).

Between 1970 and 1983, when the unemployment rate reached its peak in most countries, the rate of spending on social assistance rose in nearly all of the countries included in Table 14.1, but the increase was particularly pronounced in Australia, Ireland, the Netherlands, and the United Kingdom. The slight increase in Belgium is something of a surprise in view of the sharp increase in its unemployment rate (see Figure 1.3), but, as we saw in Chapter 11, there has been until recently no limitation on the duration of unemployment insurance benefits. France also experienced only a slight increase in social assistance expenditures as a percentage of GDP from 1970 to 1983 because the special payments to older workers came from unemployment insurance funds, because certain other income-conditioned payments were charged against sources of funds other than *Aide Sociale*, and also because *Aide Sociale* tends to be very limited in amount and duration (Marmor and Rein, 1969; Mitton, Willmott, and Wilmott, 1983).

On the other hand, the United Kingdom is a clear case of a country in which the increase in expenditures on supplementary benefits (as assistance expenditures have been called in Britain) was largely explained by the rising burden of unemployment. Not only were unemployed persons who had exhausted their unemployment benefits eligible for supplementary benefits, but supplementary benefits were available to augment inadequate unemployment insurance benefits. The unemployed rose from 27.3 percent of recipients of supplementary benefits in 1966 to 53.2 percent in 1981 (United Kingdom, Department of Health and Social Security, 1982a, 186), and I was told when I was in London in the fall of 1983 that they had reached 60 percent of the total. Moreover, as long-term unemployment increased, and the number of unemployed who had exhausted their benefits rose, the percentage who were receiving supplementary benefits to augment their insurance benefits declined to a relatively small percentage of the total.

Ireland was another country with a sharp rise in expenditures on social assistance as a percentage of GDP, to a level exceeding that of any other country in the table except Australia, which is a special case. Ireland's unemployment rate has been exceptionally high, averaging about 14 percent of the civilian labor force in 1983 and 18 percent in 1985 (OECD, 1987b).

Another country with a pronounced increase in expenditures on social assistance has been the Netherlands, where the rise in the unemployment rate was sharp until 1986, where the maximum duration of unemployment insurance benefits was 26 weeks per benefit year, but where there was a non-means-tested unemployment assistance system that provided benefits for up to two years, or to seven years for those aged 58 or over. Unemployed persons under age 65 could qualify for means-tested benefits thereafter (Rikkert, 1981; but see also the recent legislation discussed in Chapter 11).

Although there was a slight drop in the rate of spending on social assistance in most countries from 1983 to 1985, as the unemployment rate fell, there were exceptions (see Table 14.1).

As the ILO data in Appendix 1 show, public assistance expenditures tend to be minimal or nonexistent in Eastern Europe. At a later point, we shall have more to say about the situation in the Soviet Union.

Unemployment assistance

One of the most significant developments of the 1970s and 1980s is that, faced with a growing problem of long-term unemployment, many countries moved to make unemployment assistance more readily available for those who had exhausted their unemployment insurance benefits or were not eligible in the first place. Ten of our countries had special provisions for unemployment assistance in 1985 (not including Australia and New Zealand, which rely entirely on unemployment assistance). Not all of these provisions originated after 1970, but a number of them did, and previous policies were frequently liberalized to meet the needs of the long-term unemployed.

With few exceptions, all of the programs involved a means test or an income test, but the test frequently applied only to income and did not force workers to use up savings before becoming eligible. In some cases, moreover, the unemployment assistance was provided by the same agency that handled unemployment insurance rather than through the public assistance administration, thus sparing the unemployed worker the stigma of seeking public assistance, and including those on unemployment assistance under the jurisdiction of the agency that was enforcing availability for work requirements for those receiving unemployment insurance.

In 1985, Denmark did not have special unemployment assistance programs but provided unemployment insurance benefits that were unlimited in duration, although they declined in amount with the passage of time. Belgium, as we have seen, has had no limits on duration of insurance benefits until recently, and limits did not apply to older workers or family breadwinners. Also unlimited in duration were assistance payments in six of the countries with special provisions. Elsewhere, as in Britain, there were a number of countries that had no special unemployment assistance programs but provided payments of unlimited duration under general social assistance programs.

Sweden's labor support program was adopted under 1973 legislation and provides assistance to persons who are not insured, have not yet fulfilled the eligibility conditions, or are ineligible for insurance for other reasons (ILO, 1973, *Legis. Series* – Swe. 3). The benefits have been flat-rate, amounting to 130 kr. a day in 1985, and with maximum duration varying from 150 days for persons under age 55, to 450 days for those aged 60 to 64.

France's solidarity scheme provided benefits without a means test to specified groups, such as youth, but required a means test for other groups.

Provision for unemployed workers who have exhausted their eligibility for unemployment insurance or were not eligible in the first place is somewhat uncertain in the United States. In 1961, Congress authorized federal participation in Aid to Dependent Children of Unemployed Parents (AFDC-UP), thus opening the federal assistance program to unemployed persons for the first time. The Aid to Families with Dependent Children (AFDC) program had provided assistance only if one parent was incapacitated or absent from the home. However, only 27 states have implemented the AFDC-UP program (most of the Southern states have not), and eligibility conditions and payment amounts vary widely. As an adjunct to AFDC, the program makes no provision for unemployed persons who are not parents and is administered by the "welfare" agencies in the various states. Moreover, the means test tends to be very restrictive. There is also the General Assistance program, financed by state and/or local funds in 36 states and certain territories, but eligibility conditions are very restrictive and would exclude the unemployed in some cases, and payment amounts are generally below those provided in the AFDC program, and sometimes vary within a state.

Finally, unemployment assistance payments in most countries are financed by general government revenues and have, of course, played an important role in straining budgetary resources in the countries that have had persistently high unemployment rates.

Public assistance in individual countries

We turn now to a discussion of public assistance in individual countries, in order to convey contrasting relationships between public assistance and other social security provisions. The discussion of each country will be brief and will concentrate on the major characteristics of its public assistance provisions. I have selected countries that differ substantially from one another in their provisions but also on which I have been able to assemble adequate information. Comprehensive comparative data are not as readily available on public assistance as on other aspects of social security.

United Kingdom

The Beveridge Report envisaged a social insurance system with benefits that would ensure at least a subsistence level of living. Public assistance, although important during a transition period, would in the long run become a residual program, meeting the needs of those who, for one reason or another, could not qualify for insurance benefits. However, the reality in postwar Britain has been the persistence of a major role for public assistance, for reasons that have already been mentioned. Moreover, the British system is highly centralized.

The National Assistance Act of 1948 repealed the old poor law and certain related laws and provided for a new scheme of national assistance administered by the National Assistance Board, with jurisdiction over the local agencies involved. Any needy person could apply for cash assistance under the new program, but assistance could not be provided for a person (or for that person's dependents) who was engaged in full-time work, or to a worker who was not working because of a strike at his or her place of employment (ILO, 1948, *Legis. Series* – U.K. 1). Independent local appeal tribunals were provided and were to include worker representatives. In general, the scales of payment adopted by Parliament were to be followed, but discretionary deviation was permitted in individual cases.

One of the most significant changes from old poor relief practices was the specific limitation of relatives' responsibility to the nuclear family. The National Assistance Board could proceed in court to recover the cost of assistance or services from persons liable for maintenance payments, such as deserting, separated, or divorced fathers. The board could also require that a person be registered for employment as a condition for assistance, or in appropriate cases be required to enter a training program.

Although amounts of payments were increased from time to time, the first major change in the law was the adoption of legislation in 1966 changing the name of the program to the ''supplementary benefits'' program (SB) and providing that benefits were to be a matter of right. Then, in 1980, legally defined rules of entitlements removed some of the discretion formerly exercised by the Supplementary Benefits Commission.

For many years the controversial principle of the ''wage stop'' was followed, providing that the family's total income could not exceed what it would be if the father were working full-time. According to Lynes (1968), this was effective mainly in cases in which the father was unemployed but available for work. It was discontinued in 1976.

Moreover, the exclusion of the family of a full-time worker from receiving supplementary benefits became somewhat less significant after the adoption of the Family Income Supplements program (FIS – mentioned in the previous chapter) in 1971. This provided a weekly allowance to families with children if the main breadwinner was in full-time employment and if the combined earnings of husband and wife fell below a certain level that varied according to the number of dependent children in the family. The scheme was somewhat effective in reducing poverty, even though the take-up rate was far from 100 percent, ranging from 50 to 75 percent, in spite of substantial government publicity (George, 1980). It has now been replaced, as we saw in the previous chapter, by a family tax credit scheme, which may be more effective in reaching eligible families.

Beginning in 1973, a distinction was made between the ordinary or short-term benefit, provided for families of the temporarily sick or unemployed, and the long-term higher rate, provided for the aged or permanently disabled. This was another example of concern over possible disincentives to return to work.

An unusual aspect of SB in Britain has been that benefits have tended to exceed flat-rate unemployment insurance or old-age insurance benefits. Moreover, SB recipients are entitled to housing costs, whereas recipients of social insurance may or may not be receiving housing subsidies. According to Layard (1986, 47), in January 1986 a married man with two children, with average male manual earnings, and the sole earner in his family, would have received an unemployment insurance benefit, including dependents' benefits, of £63.25 a week, or 45 percent of after-tax earnings, compared with SB benefits for such a family of £91 a week, or 65 percent of after-tax earnings. Even if account is taken of the large proportion of families of the unemployed in which one spouse was working, the data showed that most families experienced a substantial loss of income when the husband was unemployed.

After careful examination of the evidence, moreover, Layard concluded that only a very small percentage of the rise in unemployment, at most, could be attributed to a rise in replacement rates, especially because replacement rates had not risen since the late 1960s. Other studies have come to a similar conclusion. Layard did point out, however, that many of the long-term unemployed have ceased looking for work, not because of the generosity of benefits but because they have become "discouraged workers."

Experts on British social security have tended to be very critical of a situation in which a rising proportion of the population has become dependent on means-tested benefits, and yet there have been wide differences of opinion as to the changes that should be made (for a discussion of divergent views, see Hemming, 1984). Meanwhile, Britain's SB program has tended to provide a more effective "safety net" than policies in a number of other countries, and, as we found in Chapter 9, does tend to come close to eliminating extreme poverty.

However, the government acted, under the 1986 Social Security Law, to abolish the SB system and replace it, in April 1988, by a new system of income support. The new scheme provides a basic allowance plus premiums for particular groups, such as families, single parents, pensioners, and disabled people. The purpose has been reported to be to focus more aid on the "truly needy" and low-income working families. Housing benefits are to be provided on the same basis to people in the same financial circumstances, but this would involve ending housing benefits for about one million persons and has been partially modified in response to protests. Family income supplements, as we saw in the preceding chapter, will be replaced by a new family credit, and single people under age 25 will receive about £7 less than other claimants (*S&LB*, 1987 [1]:163–4).

West Germany

A comprehensive modern social assistance law was adopted in West Germany in 1961 and was officially consolidated and amended in May 1983 (ILO, 1983, *Legis. Series* – Ger. F. R. 1). Its provisions were in some ways more restrictive than those in Britain and in other ways less so. The purpose of the law was stated to enable the recipient to lead a life that is in keeping with "human dignity."

Relatives' responsibility was retained, however. A person could not receive assistance if that individual could help him- or herself or could receive the necessary assistance from other parties and, in particular "from members of his family or from the carriers of other social benefit schemes" (ILO, 1983, *Legis. Series* – Ger. F. R. 1, p. 2). This provision has been a deterrent to applying for social assistance, as we saw in Chapter 9, even though the requirement for relatives' responsibility is hardly ever enforced.

Social assistance is granted by local and interarea carriers, who are to ensure that the work of the social assistance scheme and the activities of voluntary welfare agencies effectively supplement each other, to the applicant's advantage. There is no specific exclusion of the family of a full-time worker, as in Britain. An applicant is expected to seek work and to accept an offer of suitable work. Moreover, the definition of suitable work is considerably broader than in the usual unemployment insurance provisions. A worker cannot refuse a job, for example, because it is not in his or her former occupation or because the working conditions are less favorable. Those who cannot find work are normally provided with employment opportunities in work relief and other similar programs.

Cash benefits are provided at standard rates, determined by federal agencies but subject to minor modification by the states to reflect local differences in the cost of living. The standard rates are to be fixed so that, taking into account average housing expenses, they are below the "net average working income of the lower income brackets" (ILO, 1983, *Legis. Series* – Ger. F. R. 1, p. 7). Indexing of the rates occurs at the same time and at the same rate as adjustments in old-age insurance benefits. Benefits are 20 percent above the standard rates for persons aged 65 and older, totally disabled persons, expectant mothers from the beginning of the sixth month, and tubercular patients during curative treatment. Also 20 percent above standard rates are those benefits applying to a couple who are responsible for two or three children under age 16; families with four or more children receive 40 percent more than the standard rate. Of interest, also, are provisions for special assistance under various circumstances, including preventive health care, family planning assistance, and assistance during pregnancy and confinement.

As Table 14.1 shows, West Germany's expenditures on social assistance rose significantly in relation to GDP from 1970 to 1975, but then fell back somewhat. German data for 1986 indicated that about half of social assistance expenditures were for general social aid, slightly more than a fifth for education and training, about a sixth for aid to youth, and most of the remainder for housing assistance (Bundesregierung, 1986d).

Social assistance rates in West Germany in the late 1970s tended to be somewhat lower than those in Britain in relation to average gross earnings of persons in manufacturing, but the differences for various types of individuals and families were not very great (Lawson, 1980, 216). More recent data for seven countries cited by C. Euzéby (1987) indicate that the guaranteed minimum income provided by public assistance for a couple with two children aged 10 and 16 was highest in West Germany, followed by the Netherlands, the United Kingdom, Belgium, France, Ireland, and Luxembourg. The gap between the countries was large, and the amount provided by France was less than half that in West Germany. Yet, as we noted in Chapter 9, reluctance to apply for assistance appears to be a more important factor in holding assistance expenditures down in West Germany than in Britain, along with the fact that the unemployment rate has been somewhat lower.

In Chapter 4, we commented on the "social market" theory, emphasized by Ludwig Erhard and other Christian Democrats, which favored social security measures that intervened minimally in the operation of the market and was influential in the adoption of benefits that were strictly earnings-related. Interestingly, according to Lawson (1980), there has been something of a shift away from this view among Christian Democrats in recent years amid discussions of the new social question (*Neue Soziale Frage*). Proponents of this more recent view argue that German social security policies have reflected the strength of organized labor and have neglected the needs of minorities in the labor force and of many people outside the labor force. This has led the Christian Democrats, like conservatives in a number of other countries, to advocate greater selectivity and discrimination in social policy – that is, the targeting of benefits more effectively to the poor. The recent adoption of supplementary family allowances for low-income families may well reflect the influence of this school of thought.

France and Italy

In both France and Italy, there is a complex array of public and private agencies providing assistance with very little coordination and relatively meager allocations of public funds.

As we saw in Chapter 11, however, France has a substantial program of assistance to the unemployed, and especially the older unemployed, under the solidarity program, of relatively recent origin. Provisions for other impoverished persons appear to be limited and uncertain. According to Sinfield (1980, 106), the *bureaux d'aide sociale* provide public assistance to the very poor, but ''their effectiveness is difficult to establish.'' The literature on poverty, which has been growing under the auspices of various research groups, includes allusions to the need for those without income from other sources to seek charity from the mayor of the commune. The *Petits Frères des Pauvres* and other charitable groups organize mass signing of form letters for the aged poor, with the result that local public assistance funds are quickly exhausted. Moreover, the problem of reluctance to apply is apparently acute, and ''take-up'' rates are very low.

There is also a problem of ignorance of entitlement, and this may be particularly serious among the families of foreign workers, many of whom have entered the country illegally, and among whom there is a problem of acute poverty. There is also a high incidence of poverty among the very old, who may not be eligible for a pension, or may be eligible only for a very meager pension. On the other hand, it is important to recognize that there would undoubtedly be a much more serious problem of poverty among families with children were it not for the relative generosity of the family allowance system.

In Italy the situation is, if anything, more complex than in France. According to Moss and Rogers (1980, 162–3), Italian Catholics continue to believe that the ''alleviation of poverty through individual care and action'' is a Christian duty, and therefore ''it must not be the task of the state to assume all responsibility for welfare. . . .'' Nor have Italian Marxists displayed concern for the general problem of poverty. Rather, they have tended to adhere to the concept of ''class'' over ''individual need'' and to display the ''traditional distaste of the working-class movement for the problems of the disorganised, often politically hostile, sub-proletariat.'' And yet, as we saw in Chapter 9, poverty continues to be widespread in Italy, despite economic growth.

Moreover, as in France, Italy's social assistance system involves a complex assortment of public and private institutions, using differing criteria for granting assistance or relief. Benefit levels are very low, and applicants sometimes manage to obtain assistance from several agencies, public and private, without achieving a subsistence level as a result. In addition, administrative costs eat up very large proportions of the available funds, greatly reducing amounts available for the needy.

United States

Public assistance in the United States, unlike the situation in a number of other countries, is largely categorical (available only for defined groups of people under special programs), and leaving some people effectively uncovered by any program. Moreover, it is comprised of a mixture of federal, federal–state, state–local, or entirely local programs.

The Social Security Act of 1935 provided for federal grants-in-aid to the states to meet half the cost of state benefits to the needy aged and blind, up to $15 per month per person. This amount was raised from time to time, and, in 1950, eligibility was extended to the permanently and totally disabled. Although the law provided for certain general standards (e.g., that the program should apply throughout the state), eligibility conditions and standards of payment varied greatly from state to state. President Nixon's family assistance proposal of 1969, which would have provided for federal payments for families with children, as well as the aged and disabled, was rejected by Congress, but was clearly influential in leading to the adoption in 1972 of the supplemental security income (SSI) program, which provided for standard federal benefits (federally financed and administered) for the less controversial groups – the aged, blind, and disabled. These benefits could be supplemented by the states if they so chose, and many of those, especially the states with more liberal assistance, did elect to supplement the federal benefits.

The Social Security Act also provided for aid to dependent children under the age of 16 who were deprived of parental support because of the death, incapacity, or absence from the home of a parent. The law was amended to extend coverage to a needy parent or other relative with whom the child was living in 1950, and in 1961 to permit the states to assist families in which a parent was in the home and unemployed if the state so elected. The program came to be called Aid to the Families of Dependent Children (AFDC) and the unemployed parent segment was called AFDC-UP, as we have seen.

AFDC was a successor to mothers' aid laws that had previously existed in some of the states and that had provided aid chiefly for widows with children. Gradually, however, after 1935, widows and their children became eligible for social security survivors' insurance benefits, and the AFDC program came to assist chiefly families in which the parents were divorced or separated, or in which there had never been a husband. It is the largest of the cash assis-

Table 14.2. *Cash and noncash benefits for persons with limited income,
United States, 1983*

Type of assistance	Total expenditures (millions)	Average monthly recipients (thousands)	Average monthly amount per recipient[a]
Total	$102,302		
AFDC	15,385	10,639	$107.17
SSI	10,101	3,873	214.69
Food stamps	13,267	22,200	42.77
General assistance	2,110	1,275	127.18[b]
Earned income tax credit	1,803	19,000	
Housing benefits	12,723		
Jobs and training	4,169	1,173	
Low-income energy assistance	1,898	8,700	
Medicaid	34,956	22,324	
Miscellaneous	5,890[c]		

[a] These data relate to the fiscal year, whereas other data are for the calendar year.
[b] 1980.
[c] Includes maternal and child health services; Indian health services, community health centers; school lunch programs; food program for women, infants, and children; and nutrition program for the elderly.
Sources: *Statistical Abstract of the United States, 1985* (p. 357); *SSB: Annual Statistical Supplement, 1984–85* (Sec. 5). Data do not include education aid, aid to veterans, or social services.

tance programs, by far the most controversial, and the program to which we shall devote most of our discussion.

Table 14.2 shows that expenditures on social aid programs in 1983 amounted to $102.3 billion, or 3.1 percent of GDP. It also reveals the wide variety of programs involved. Clearly, it has been easier politically to provide assistance in a variety of ways than to liberalize the major cash assistance programs. The food stamp program is a clear example. Started very modestly in 1961, the program has gradually expanded to major dimensions, although it has been cut back somewhat in recent years. Unlike the main AFDC program, it provides benefits for intact families as well as for single-parent families. Medicaid (hospital and medical assistance for the poor) is the other most important example.

Critics of AFDC fall into two quite separate groups: liberals, who emphasize the inadequacy of benefits; and conservatives, who tend to view the "welfare" population as a group of people who shun work and are content to stay "on welfare" for indefinite periods.

Among those who stress the inadequacy of benefits is Senator Daniel P.

Moynihan, who pointed out in his recent book that maximum benefits for a four-person family declined 33 percent in real terms in the median state from 1970 to 1985 (Moynihan, 1986, 15). He has introduced legislation that would require the states to provide training, job programs, and child care for welfare recipients, make families with unemployed fathers eligible for welfare payments for limited periods, and would call for more adequate enforcement of child support provisions. However, his bill is weaker in some respects than legislation that has passed in the House, and calls for a considerably more modest increase in expenditures.

A noteworthy development in the past few years has been increasing recognition – for too long absent in my opinion[2] – of the need for more adequate provision of child care services if welfare mothers are to be required to work. Several states, including California, Massachusetts, and Wisconsin, as we saw in Chapter 13, have recently adopted programs to improve opportunities for training and jobs, as well as more adequate provision for child care centers.[3]

Meanwhile, the differences in average payments per recipient among the states have continued to be glaring and, even in the highest-paying states, to be well below the official poverty threshold. Although related to differences in per capita income, they are much wider than those differences.

The literature in criticism of "welfare" is vast and only a few central points can be considered here. Let us start with a basic misconception, that welfare supports numerous able-bodied men, especially black men; in fact, the only significant source of assistance for able-bodied men is AFDC-UP, and, until unemployment rates shot up in the early 1980s, very few men were supported by this highly restrictive program. As Levy (1980, 27) has shown, only 3 percent of the families receiving AFDC in 1978 were headed by able-bodied men and were on the AFDC-UP rolls.

There are three other main lines of criticism of AFDC: (1) that it supports an underclass of people who are content to live on government largesse; (2) that it encourages family splitting because of the unavailability of aid in most cases to two-parent families; and (3) that many recipients are in a "poverty trap" because they might lose eligibility not only for AFDC but also for food stamps, Medicaid, and in some cases housing assistance, if they get a job (the "notch" problem).

As Levitan (1985, 27) has pointed out, however, "most families do not languish forever on welfare." In 1979, nearly three of every ten AFDC families had received welfare benefits for less than one year, and a majority had remained on the rolls for less than four years. The charge that AFDC has encouraged family splitting may have somewhat more credibility, but a care-

---

[2] See my supplementary statement in U.S. President's Commission . . . (1969, 79–83).

[3] For an extensive analysis of these issues in Massachusetts, see Carballo and Bane, eds. (1984).

ful review of a number of studies by MacDonald and Sawhill (1978) indicated mixed findings on this point. The third problem has been emphasized particularly by Aaron (1980, 53–4), who points out, however, that some states have provisions that do not automatically remove eligibility for Medicaid if a family goes off AFDC.

An important problem that cannot be solved by welfare reform alone is that of teenage pregnancies. It has been estimated that in 1975 about one-half of total AFDC payments went to women who were either teenage mothers or who had borne their first children while still teenagers. A very large proportion of these women were not high school graduates, and the evidence indicated that the majority of births to teenage mothers were unplanned and unwanted (see especially Moore, 1978).

There is a need not only for greater emphasis on sex education in the schools, as we pointed out in Chapter 13, but also for programs (which some schools have) aimed at assisting high school students who become pregnant to complete their high school education. There is abundant evidence of the disastrous impact of early marriages and early pregnancy on poverty among young people (e.g., Schorr, 1966). Moreover, a recent Census Bureau survey showed that it was the never-married mothers who were particularly unlikely to benefit from child-support awards. Fewer than one-fifth of these women had child support awards, compared with four-fifths of the women who were divorced or remarried (*San Francisco Chronicle,* August 21, 1987).

Attracting widespread attention since it appeared in 1984 has been Charles Murray's *Losing Ground,* which argues that the social programs of the past two decades have had the unintended and perverse effect of slowing and even reversing earlier programs in reducing crime, poverty, and discrimination. His attack is not just on public assistance but on income maintenance programs in general (as they affect the working age population and children, not the aged), on affirmative action policies, and much else.

Murray's conclusion is that all income maintenance programs except those for the aged should be discontinued, although he makes an exception for unemployment insurance. How he reached this sweeping conclusion is perhaps better understood if one considers his treatment of the disabled. Noting that there had been advances in rehabilitation programs that should have reduced the number of disabled, he cites figures showing an enormous increase in the number of disability beneficiaries and concludes that "something odd was happening to the way Americans used the disability insurance program and the way the government administered it" (ignoring altogether the results of research on the reasons for the increase that were cited in Chapter 6).

There have been many excellent criticisms of the way in which he interprets the data. Particularly worthy of close attention are those of Wilson (1987, 17), who points out that Murray "neglects the key facts that contradict his message," namely that the unemployment rate in 1980 was twice that of 1968. He goes on to identify the interrelated economic and social factors that have been responsible for the deteriorating conditions in urban ghettos since the early 1970s – that is, the growing problems of the urban "underclass." They include (1) the extraordinary rise in the black teenage population (almost 75 percent) in the 1960s and in the number of black young adults aged 20 to 24 (about two-thirds) in the same period, exacerbating the problem of unemployment among black youth in the 1970s; (2) the tendency for the crime rate to be high in the youthful population; (3) teenage pregnancies; (4) the declining ratio of the number of employed young black men to the number of young black women, reducing the pool of "marriageable" (economically stable) men; (5) the outmigration of black professionals and also of stable working-class blacks from ghetto areas, where they had formerly been a socially stabilizing influence; and (6) the fact that federal antidiscrimination and affirmative action programs have benefited chiefly those blacks "best qualified for valued positions, such as college admissions, higher paying jobs, and promotions" (Wilson, 1987, 147).

Wilson goes on to advocate major emphasis on a macroeconomic policy designed to promote both economic growth and a tight labor market – a policy that will benefit all segments of the population and not just disadvantaged urban blacks. In addition, major emphasis in manpower programs should be on relating these programs more closely to opportunities in the private sector, although there will be a need for transitional public programs, such as public service employment programs, for those who have difficulty finding immediate employment in the private sector. He also advocates a program of welfare reform that would overcome weaknesses such as the lack of provision for poor two-parent families and would call for a national AFDC benefit standard indexed for inflation. In addition, he calls attention to the demonstration project in Wisconsin, which provides a guaranteed minimum benefit per child to single-parent families, regardless of the income of the custodial parent, and collects from the absent parent through withholding a portion of wages (see also Bergmann, 1986).

Canada

The Canada Assistance Plan, enacted in 1966, incorporated several previously existing federal–provincial categorical assistance programs into a far more comprehensive program with a very broad definition of who is in need. Included are one-parent families, mentally and physically disabled persons, the aged, children who are in care or who are in need of protection because of abuse or neglect, the unemployed, families or individuals in crisis, low-income workers, and battered women (Canada, Health and Welfare, 1985a).

Under the program, the federal government has entered into agreements with the provinces and territories to meet 50 percent of the costs incurred by provinces and municipalities in providing social assistance and welfare services. The plan also provides for the federal government to share 50 percent of the cost of work activity projects. Although standards of payments vary among the provinces, the differences are not nearly as pronounced as those among the states in the AFDC program.

Total federal–provincial expenditures under the plan have increased steadily and in 1984–5 amounted to more than $8 billion. However, total social aid expenditures, as reported by OECD (see Table 14.1) amounted to $22.3 billion, or about 5.1 percent of GDP. They included such items as the guaranteed income supplement for the aged and the income-tested allowance for spouses aged 60 to 64, which are financed entirely by the federal government.

Under the Canada Assistance Plan, over 1.9 million Canadians received income support in 1985, not including those provided for in institutions. Persons defined as employable rose from 33.7 percent of the cases in 1980 to 46.5 percent in 1984. Of the one million adults on welfare, more than half were single individuals, and most of these were young. Most of the young recipients had never been eligible for unemployment insurance, but their average duration of unemployment was shorter than that of older adults. Other major groups receiving assistance were older women without husbands and single mothers with children. The single mothers made up 25 percent of the welfare caseload, and a large number of them were very young. According to Powell (1986), the number of teenage out-of-wedlock births doubled over the period from 1975 to 1985, despite the fact that the proportion of teenagers in the overall population has been declining.[4] There were also a large number of single mothers in their 20s or 30s who had experienced recent separation from their husbands, but women in this group tended to receive social assistance only for short periods. The remaining 20 percent of the cases included couples or two-parent families, and typically the males in these families had experienced long-term employment difficulties or been adversely affected by regional employment dislocation.

Cutting across all of these groups were the permanently disabled, who made up about 22 percent of the social assistance population.

Overall, according to Powell, turnover in the welfare population in Canada is high, as in the United States. Many provinces have indicated that at least half of new welfare cases move back into the world of work within a year of welfare enrollment. Although a large proportion of the population is likely to make use of one or more of the safety nets, there is not a well-defined and permanent welfare class. Nevertheless, concern over the impact of unemploy-

---

[4] This discussion is based partly on an interview with Powell in Ottawa in October 1986.

ment on the welfare rolls led the government in 1985 to adopt the Canadian Jobs Strategy program, discussed in Chapter 12.

Additional comments

Before leaving the subject of public assistance, it is important to recognize that comparisons of relative expenditures on public assistance, or of the number of persons receiving public assistance, must be treated with great caution because needs that are met by public assistance in some countries may be met by other programs elsewhere.

This consideration is particularly important in relation to health services. Where there is a national health service, as in Britain and a few other Western countries, or a national health insurance system that provides in one way or another for persons who are not currently employed, there is little need for a special hospital and medical assistance program, as in the United States.

This is a particularly important consideration in relation to Eastern Europe. In general, the Eastern European countries do not have large expenditures on cash public assistance, but they do provide hospital and medical care largely free of charge. They also have relatively generous programs of free public education, including the university level, and of stipends for students. Moreover, the family income supplement for low-income families with children in the Soviet Union is a significant move toward provision for the poor in a country that has generally emphasized earnings-related social insurance programs (for an interesting account of the gradual recognition of the problem of poverty and steps to alleviate it in the Soviet Union, see McAuley, 1977).

Since the mid-1960s, and to a certain extent influenced by developments in the United States, there has been increasing interest in, and some movement toward, various versions of a guaranteed minimum income, to which we now turn.

Guaranteed minimum income policies

In 1962, in his *Capitalism and Freedom,* economist Milton Friedman proposed the abolition of all existing social security and welfare measures and their replacement by a negative income tax. He was especially opposed to compulsory social insurance programs. His proposal for a negative income tax aroused considerable interest, especially among economists in the United States, and also in Britain, but most economists who favored the negative income tax did not advocate discontinuing all existing income maintenance programs.

Under a negative income tax scheme, a family with no earnings or other sources of income would receive a government grant through the income tax system – that is, a negative tax – that would provide a guaranteed minimum income. To the extent that a low-income family had any other income, the grant would be reduced by some percentage of that income.

The three essential characteristics that may vary among negative income tax proposals are (1) the amount of the income guarantee, (2) the rate at which existing family income is reduced (or taxed) when it exceeds zero, and (3) the break-even level of income at which eligibility for a grant disappears.[5] Proponents generally favor taxing existing income at a rate considerably under 100 percent, in order to preserve incentives to work. With a tax rate of less than 100 percent, the family always benefits from more earnings. Let us assume that the guaranteed income is $10,000 for a family of four (roughly the official poverty threshold for that size family in 1984) and that the tax rate on other income is 50 percent. Then the family income will vary as follows:

Earnings	Grant	Total family income
0	$10,000	$10,000
$ 2,000	9,000	11,000
5,000	7,500	12,500
8,000	6,000	14,000
10,000	5,000	15,000
15,000	2,500	17,500
20,000	0	20,000

As the table indicates, the break-even point is twice the guaranteed income amount, and this will always be true if the tax rate is 50 percent. If all families with income up to $20,000 were to receive a grant, though of declining size, something like 40 percent of all families would have qualified for grants in 1984. Such a program would be exceedingly costly, and yet economists tend to look upon a tax much higher than 50 percent as creating a disincentive to work. In their 1967 article, Tobin, Pechman, and Mieszkowski proposed a 40 percent tax, which would result in grants even farther up in the income scale.

This problem was faced by the U.S. President's Commission on Income Maintenance Programs, appointed by President Johnson in 1968. After much debate and extensive study, the commission recommended a universal income supplement program (essentially a negative income tax) with a 50 percent tax rate and a guaranteed minimum income of $2,400 for a family of four, or considerably below the poverty threshold of $3,553 at the time. The commission explained:

This level was not chosen because we feel that it is an adequate income, but because it is a practical program that can be implemented in the near future. . . . To set pay-

---

[5] This discussion of the negative income tax is based in large part on my statement in Greenwald, ed. (1982, 697–9).

ment levels at the poverty line immediately would cost an estimated $27 billion, and provide income transfers to a total of 24 million households. We believe that a program of that potential magnitude must be adopted in steps.

(U.S. President's Commission . . . , 1969, 7)

By the time the commission issued its report, a new president had been elected and had sent a proposal for a family assistance program to Congress, as we noted earlier.

An alternative approach to a guaranteed minimum income was proposed by Lady Rhys-Williams of Great Britain (1943), as we noted in Chapter 13. Under her proposal, every family would receive a "social dividend," or tax credit, that would replace all other social security benefits and would be financed by a proportional income tax on all other income. This approach has been regarded favorably by some economists (e.g., Peacock, 1952, in Britain, and Rolph, 1967, in the United States) and in recent years seems to have gained ground over the negative income tax.

Meanwhile, however, the negative income tax has been the subject of the most expensive social science experiments ever conducted, financed by the U.S. Office of Economic Opportunity and carried out by nonpublic research groups. The earlier experiments (in New Jersey and elsewhere) were focused chiefly on the impact of support payments on work incentives and indicated a slight tendency for work effort to be reduced as a result of income maintenance, chiefly on the part of wives. (The results were based on comparisons between experimental groups and control groups.) Later experiments in Seattle and Denver showed more significant negative effects on work incentives, along with a greater tendency for couples in the experimental group than for those in the control group to split up (Robins et al., eds., 1980).

However, in a meticulous reworking of the data, Cain (1986) found only small and inconsistent effects on marital stability, although he did find a statistically significant destabilizing effect among blacks. On the whole, he maintained, as have others, that the findings on the impact on marital stability seem inconclusive.

Meanwhile, we have traced the development of tax credit programs in a number of countries in Chapter 13. And yet, none of these programs embraces the entire population or provides for a guaranteed minimum income that would support at least a subsistence level of living, as the Rhys-Williams proposal did. Proponents of such a program tend to regard it as less likely to have an adverse effect on work incentives or to encourage family splitting than a negative income tax.

What we seem to be observing is the development of programs that combine elements of a negative income tax and a tax credit. This was true of the guaranteed income recommendation of the Australian Government Committee on Inquiry into Poverty (1975), which has not been adopted. The Canadian tax credit program incorporates an element of the negative income tax by reducing the tax credit gradually for amounts of income over the ceiling, thereby seeking to avoid a notch problem. The program is aimed at targeting additional income to low-income and middle-income families with children, avoiding the much higher cost of a tax credit program that would embrace the entire population and that would provide tax credits for adults as well as for children.

The U.S. earned income credit applies only to low-income families with children and at least one adult worker, but it, too, incorporates a feature of the negative income tax by reducing the credits gradually as income rises above $6,925. Conceivably, this program might be broadened to resemble the Canadian program, perhaps in a series of steps. Developments in the 1988 presidential campaign have focused attention on child care and tax credit issues.

The main point to be stressed is that countries are groping for ways of providing a minimum income that avoid the stigma of public assistance but that also avoid the problem involved in guaranteeing a specified minimum income and cutting off any assistance above that income level. It seems probable that versions of tax credit programs that also incorporate negative income tax features are likely to spread. Clearly, the debates over these proposals have served to call attention to the advantage of avoiding a sharp cutoff of public assistance at a specified income level and of permitting the retention of a percentage of earnings by public assistance recipients.

In a realistic analysis of the negative income tax and universal allowances (or tax credits), C. Euzéby (1987) concluded that both approaches are monetaristic and take too little account of the different circumstances of families. She advocated a modified version of a minimum income guarantee which would be closely tied to labor market programs and linked with existing social security measures.

CHAPTER 15

International linkages

Thus far we have been considering social security provisions on a country by country basis, with little reference to how those moving between countries might acquire social security rights or how the provisions of a given country might be affected by bilateral or multilateral agreements. On occasion, we have referred to ILO or ISSA reports and to the directive of the European Economic Community relating to equality of treatment of men and women in social security matters, but there is a broad field of international cooperation and agreements that has yet to be explored.

Over the course of the present century, there has developed a network of bilateral agreements, under which workers moving from one country to another may become eligible for benefits in the country to which they have moved, or in some cases may receive credit for contributions made to social security schemes in the country from which they have moved. Second, international organizations have developed regulations providing for the social security rights of migrant workers and for minimum social security standards that become effective in the countries ratifying them. The oldest and largest of these organizations is the ILO, dating from 1919 and including (as of 1983) 144 countries, or the vast majority of members of the United Nations. Also active in developing social security standards is the Council of Europe, dating from 1949 and including 22 European countries.

More recently the European Communities have become active in this field. They include the European Coal and Steel Community, dating from 1952, and the European Economic Community (EEC) or Common Market, established under the Treaty of Rome of 1957, which became effective in 1958. The European Communities also include the European Community for Atomic Energy (Euratom). Beginning with six countries – France, West Germany, Italy, Belgium, the Netherlands, and Luxembourg – the European Communities since have added the United Kingdom, Ireland, Denmark, Greece, and most recently Spain and Portugal.

Also important in protecting the rights of workers moving from country to country is the multilateral convention of the Scandinavian countries and a convention among the countries bordering the Rhine for the protection of the rights of the Rhine boatmen.

Bilateral agreements

The first bilateral agreement providing for the protection of the social security rights of migrant workers was the Franco-Italian Treaty of 1904 (Watson, 1980, 8). France had been experiencing the importation of Italian goods produced more cheaply than similar French goods because of the lower levels of compensation in Italy. The situation created hostility toward Italians working in France on the part of French workers who resented the competition of Italian imports. The treaty provided for equal treatment of nationals of the two countries in industrial accident compensation and for the free movement of workers' savings from one country to another. It also aimed at improving the working conditions of young workers and women, as well as strengthening the system of factory inspection. In addition, there was mention of cooperation in relation to pension schemes and unemployment benefits, but France did not yet have a pension scheme, and neither country had an unemployment compensation system.

The treaty was pathbreaking and was followed by the signing of similar agreements between other pairs of countries, especially where emigration and immigration were involved. The agreements signed following World War I tended to relate at first to industrial accidents or to working conditions generally, but later there was a movement to provide specifically for various social security programs, including the coordination of pension rights accumulated in more than one country.

According to Watson (1980, 11), more than 400 bilateral agreements concluded after June 1946 were still in effect. However, there has been an increasing tendency during the postwar period for social security relations between states to be regulated by international organizations. This has resulted from the formation and expansion of economic unions both on a regional and on an international basis.

The International Labor Office (ILO)

The International Labor Conference, which brings together annually the representatives of the countries belonging to the ILO (chosen on a tripartite basis), has adopted many important conventions relating to the rights of migrants under social security systems and to minimum standards in social security policies, but they are not effective in a country until that country has acted to ratify the convention, and some of the more significant agreements have been ratified only by a few countries.

At its first session in Washington in 1919, the conference adopted a general agreement designed to secure for foreign workers the benefits of national laws and regulations in the country in which they were employed. There followed in 1925 a convention relating to workers' compensation, under which a migrant worker was entitled to benefits without any length of residence requirement. More complex was a convention adopted in 1935, calling for the transfer of pension rights from one country to another. This involved (1) "aggregation," or the adding together of insurance contributions paid in different countries; and (2) "proraterization," or the equitable distribution of the cost of pensions among the countries involved, according to the number of contributions paid by the worker while employed in each country. The 1935 convention, however, was ratified by only eight countries and two of these later withdrew (Watson, 1980, 17). Nevertheless, it has played a significant role as a model for a number of other international and bilateral agreements. In fact, the technical assistance of the ILO has been sought in the drafting of instruments adopted by the Council of Europe, the European Communities, and other regional and international organizations. Moreover, the 1935 convention was followed by a broader measure in 1939 (amended in 1949), which aimed at providing equality of treatment for migrants in all major branches of social security, and which had been ratified by 30 countries by 1980.

The significance of the ILO should not be measured solely on the basis of the number of countries that have ratified its conventions. It plays an important role in research and publication relating to social security issues, including its valuable reports on *The Cost of Social Security*. Along with its affiliated organization, the ISSA, it brings together groups of experts on various aspects of social security, and it also renders valuable services, particularly to less developed countries, in assisting them to formulate social security policies.

The Council of Europe

Social policy plays an important role in the activities of the Council of Europe, which dates from the signing of an agreement in London in May 1949, initially involving 15 countries and gradually increasing to 22 Western European countries. Article 1 of its statute provides that the aim of the council is to "achieve a greater unity between its members for the purpose of facilitating . . . their social progress" (Watson, 1980, 20). There followed, in March 1950, the creation of a Committee of Governmental Experts on Social Security, which was made responsible for studying the possibilities of extending bilateral and multilateral agreements already existing between or among member states. Interim agreements were adopted and became effective in July 1954, under which (1) nationals of any one country would receive within the territory of any other contracting country equal treatment with the nationals of the latter state under its social security laws, and (2) the benefits of bilateral and multilateral conventions on social security matters would be extended to nationals of all member states. The first of these agreements applied to benefits under sickness schemes, employment injury schemes, unemployment benefit schemes, and family allowances, whereas the second related to OASD benefits.

Also negotiated in the early years of the council was the European Convention on Social and Medical Assistance, involving a commitment to provide the nationals of other contracting parties who needed assistance and who lacked sufficient resources with social and medical assistance equal to and under the same conditions as their nationals. Because it involved no residence requirement, but merely lawful presence in the country in which the need arose, it applied to tourists as well as to immigrants.

After extensive study and negotiation, the European Code of Social Security was signed in April 1964 and came into effect in March 1968. Its aim was to extend the scope of national social security legislation gradually until it covered the entire working population, including the self-employed, and eventually the entire population. The code lists the type of benefits affected and the minimum number of types that must be included by a member state, as well as the minimum percentage of the population that must be covered against the risk in question. It also includes a protocol that provides for higher standards and that applies to countries already possessing higher standards than those called for by the code. Watson (1980) reported that it had been ratified by only nine member states. Even less effective was the European Convention on Social Security, which was adopted in 1972 to replace the interim agreements on rights of migrants, but which has been ratified by only a few countries.

Thus, the Council of Europe, although maintaining high aspirations in its social policies, has had an experience similar to that of the ILO in that some of its instruments have not been implemented by many of its member countries.

The European Economic Community (EEC)

The European Economic Community, like the ILO and the Council of Europe, has aimed at providing for equal treatment of migrants and at encouraging minimum standards in social security matters, but it has gone beyond this in the development of the European Social Fund, through which grants are made by the EEC to member states to encourage training and job creation programs. It is this aspect of its program that is of special interest, since it has tended to be expanded over the years and may well become even more significant in the future.

The Treaty of Rome, establishing the European Economic Community, embodied a number of provisions aimed at improvement of the conditions of life and employment, including (Office des Publications Officielles . . . , 1983, 8 – my translation from the French):

1. The progressive realization of the free circulation of workers, including the guarantee of their rights under social security regimes
2. Promotion of the exchange of young workers in the framework of a common program
3. Promotion of close collaboration among the member states in the social domain, in order to encourage improvement in conditions of life and work, leading toward equalization
4. Application of the principle of equality of remuneration between male and female workers
5. Institution of a European social fund having for its mission the promotion within the community of employment facilities and the geographical and occupational mobility of workers
6. Establishment of general principles for the development of a common policy in occupational training.

Earlier the Coal and Steel Community had adopted similar goals, including the financing of programs of job creation and retraining. The European Community for Atomic Energy (Euratom) aimed at encouraging the formation and rapid growth of nuclear industries in order to raise the level of life in the member states and the development of exchanges with other countries. It need scarcely be added that these aims have become highly controversial in a number of countries in recent years, especially following the Chernobyl disaster.

Following the example of the Coal and Steel Community, the Council of Ministers of the EEC reached a decision in October 1968 providing for the right of all workers of the community to respond to offers of employment whatever their nationality, including the right to spend time in another state for this purpose, to move there and be joined by their families, and to benefit from the same rights as nationals in relation to conditions of work and employment. An innovation adopted by the EEC Commission at the end of 1972 was the creation of a European system for the dissemination of offers and applications for employment. The system, known as SEDOC, had for its purpose the granting of priority to workers from other member states in access to jobs that could not be filled by national manpower. A uniform language is used in the reciprocal announcements of job offers and employment applications, and the terms of employment are publicized simultaneously in the placement offices of the member states.

Unfortunately, this move came at a time when rising unemployment in Western Europe seriously impaired job opportunities for migrant workers and led in many cases to discontinuation of their work permits.

During the 1960s, under the highly favorable employment conditions then prevailing, the EEC Commission sponsored a series of studies of conditions of work and social protection, as well as many seminars and work groups involving national experts. It adopted a number of recommendations addressed to the member states, relating to the protection of young workers, healthy conditions of work within enterprises, social assistance in favor of migrant workers and their families (including their housing), and adoption of a European list of occupational diseases. However, these recommendations have rarely been translated into legislative changes within member countries, although there has been progress with respect to industrial accidents within the Coal and Steel Community and under Euratom with respect to work safety.

During the 1970s, as the problems of slower growth and rising unemployment confronted the member states, steps were taken to strengthen the mission and functioning of the European Social Fund, as well as to place greater emphasis on a program of social action. In a reform based on a decision of the Council of Ministers in February 1971 and effective in May 1972, decisions as to allocations from the Social Fund were no longer to be based on criteria established by individual member states but were to be based on community criteria. Moreover, the fund's activities were to be broadened through allocations to private organizations and even to private enterprises, and its budget was to be substantially increased.

The fund was given the responsibility to intervene when the employment situation was affected, or threatened, by community policy, or when there appeared to be a need to achieve a better balance between the supply and demand for manpower within the community. More specifically, the council has made decisions to support measures of vocational retraining or reemployment for the benefit of the following groups:

> Persons shifting from agriculture to nonagricultural activities
> Displaced workers in the textile and clothing industries
> Migrant workers
> Handicapped persons
> Unemployed or jobseeking youth under age 25
> Women

In addition, the fund could intervene to meet certain difficult employment situations, including (1) regions facing slowing development or declining economic activity, (2) difficulties encountered by certain groups of enterprises, (3) adaptation to technical progress, and (4) handicapped persons, older workers, and women over 35 years of age. All in all, nearly 90 percent of the fund was allocated to training and occupational upgrading.

As time went on, and the problem of youth unemployment became more serious, increasing emphasis was given to programs for youth. In December 1978, a new type of aid in favor of youth was approved, providing for job creation programs for young persons under age 25, with emphasis on combining job creation and training, as well as emphasis on the types of jobs that responded to community needs.

By 1982, the share of allocations from the fund reserved for youth for the first time reached the share allocated for backward regions. At the same time, policies were adopted calling for closer coordination between the fund and community priorities in occupational training, to ensure consistency with the economic, industrial, and sectoral policies being pursued and more effective coordination between expenditures of the fund and other financial instruments of the community. At the same time, as a commission decision in April 1985 made clear, "absolute priority regions" continued to include Greece, the French overseas departments, Ireland, the Mezzogiorno, and Northern Ireland. These areas were eligible for assistance at a rate 10 percent higher than that applied to the other regions of the community, even though priority was also given to other regions with economic problems, including substantial long-term unemployment.

How much has actually been expended by the fund in recent years? In 1984, the amount of assistance approved totaled 1,855 million ECU, at a time when the ECU was worth slightly less than the U.S. dollar. Of this total amount, 1,606 million was actually committed, the remainder being carried over to the next year. The Social Fund budget represented 6.9 percent of the total community budget. The fund was not in a position to approve all of the applications for assistance, which amounted to a total of 3,358 million ECU (Commission of the European Communities, 1985).

Interestingly, two-thirds of the sums involved in total applications and 76 percent of the total commitments related to programs for young people under 25 years of age. Moreover, of the total amounts allocated, 40 percent went to the "absolute priority" regions. It should be kept in mind that there is overlapping between programs for youth and priority regions because some of the programs in priority regions are for youth.

Of the 1,606 million actually committed in 1984, a surprisingly large amount – 610 million, or 38 percent of the total – went to the United Kingdom. Of the amount allocated to the United Kingdom, 503 million related to programs for youth. We have discussed in Chapter 12 the large-scale nature of the job and training programs for youth in Britain, and it also has more than its share of depressed regions. Following the United Kingdom in shares of committed funds were Italy, with 23 percent; France, with 14 percent; and Ireland, with 8 percent. It turns out that a major reason for the large share of commitments received by the United Kingdom, France, and Italy was that they were very active in submitting applications. For example, among the number of applications to support programs of vocational training and youth employment in 1984, the United Kingdom accounted for 42 percent; France, for 17 percent;

and Italy, for 12.5 percent (Commission of the European Communities, 1985, 31).

The activities of the European Communities in the social field have by no means been confined to the European Social Fund. We have noted in Chapter 4 the directive calling for equality of treatment of women in social security programs. The council has also adopted a number of recommendations relating to such problems as programs for the handicapped, the occupational and social integration of migrant workers and their families, aid to the most disadvantaged, the need for greater participation of the social partners in decision-making at the community level, and reduced hours of work.

In spite of much activity at the community level, there is serious dissatisfaction with the lack of implementation of recommendations at the level of the member states, as well as dissatisfaction at the lack of progress in overcoming the social and economic problems of the European Communities. In Chapter 1, I quoted Jacques Delors (president of the Commission of the European Communities) on the reasons for the European crisis. In the volume of papers to which he was contributing (Delors, 1984) there were many recommendations made for more effective and more imaginative social policies, including broadening the functions of the European Social Fund to include such activities as programs for the more constructive use of leisure time in the face of reduced hours of work and long-term unemployment.

CHAPTER 16

Conclusions

Since the mid-1970s, social security policies in industrial countries have been forced to adjust to changing economic and social circumstances that have frequently placed a strain on their resources. Not only has there been the problem of rising unemployment, but also severe inflation in the late 1970s and early 1980s inhibited many governments from pursuing expansionary fiscal policies. Of special concern, for its social as well as its economic implications, has been the severity of the youth unemployment problem. Another serious problem has been the growth of family instability, resulting from rising illegitimacy rates, increasing divorce and separation rates, and cohabitation.

How national policies reacted to these problems has been the subject of much of the discussion in this volume. The problems are not likely to "go away," and there will be a continuing need for adjustments to meet them. And yet, there is growing evidence that the countries that have pursued vigorous policies to combat unemployment on both the demand and the supply sides of the labor market have succeeded in holding down the level of joblessness.

Although we have not found a very consistent inverse relationship between social security expenditures and military expenditures as a percentage of GNP, it is pertinent to observe that the three Western European countries identified by Soskice (1987) as pursuing policies that held the unemployment rate to low levels – Austria, Norway, and Sweden – all had relatively low military expenditures as a percentage of GNP in 1982 (*Statistical Abstract . . . , 1985*, 866). Austria's military expenditures were especially low (only 1.2 percent of GNP). These three countries also spent a comparatively large percentage of GNP on social security.

On the other hand, the United States had relatively low social security expenditures and relatively high military expenditures as a percentage of GNP (6.4 percent in 1982 and somewhat more in later years). Far higher were the military expenditures of the Soviet Union as a percentage of GNP, but Israel ranked at the top in terms of military expenditures.

Additional progress toward arms control agreements between the United States and the Soviet Union could pave the way for a reduction in military expenditures in both countries, and it seems clear that this is one of the aims of Gorbachev, so that increased resources can be devoted to economic development. In the United States, a reduction in military expenditures could contribute substantially to a reduction in the budget deficit and to improvement in some of our social security programs, provided that politically there is a will to move in this direction.

One of the serious social problems that has developed in the 1980s is a very significant increase in the number of homeless people. That such a problem should develop in the United States is not surprising in view of the weakness of our public assistance provisions, but it *is* surprising in Western Europe, given the more comprehensive social assistance programs and the greater use of housing subsidies in many Western European countries. Recently the U.S. Department of Housing and Urban Development estimated the number of homeless persons in this country at about 350,000, but other estimates have run considerably higher (*The Economist,* February 7, 1987). In Western Europe, it was said in 1983 that tens of thousands were homeless, and even in West Germany, with its comprehensive income maintenance provisions, the number of homeless was estimated at about 260,000 (Tennison, 1983).

In both the United States and Western Europe, the homeless included thousands of young people who had never held jobs, people who had worked too little to qualify for unemployment insurance, self-employed workers who had gone bankrupt, released prisoners and mental patients, unemployed workers who could not meet their mortgage payments, and single mothers with children. Housing was either not available or simply too expensive for these people, in an era when rents had been rising rapidly. Even in more favorable periods, large numbers of the poor cannot afford available housing, and government programs have provided either rent subsidies or public housing.

In both Britain and the United States, appropriations for housing subsidies have been cut back sharply in recent years, and in the United States, much of the effort to provide emergency housing has been carried out by private agencies, although local governments have contributed in some cases. Only very recently (early 1987) has the federal government begun to act by appropriating funds to assist the homeless.

The problem of homelessness is more difficult to understand in Britain, where supplementary benefits have including a housing allowance that is added to the basic assistance payment so that it can be varied in accordance with local differences in rents. The problem seems to have been that, given shortages of low-cost housing, some recipients of supplementary benefits have had to resort to various types of emergency makeshift housing (Tennison, 1983).

This problem is mentioned here, even though housing policies have not been included in this study, because it is a problem that calls out for attention from central governments and not just local groups, with solutions that must involve both income maintenance policies and housing programs, as well as policies toward the mentally ill.

In the remainder of this concluding chapter, I shall avoid repetition of concluding remarks in a number of chapters and will concentrate on five problems that are certain to demand attention in the coming years: (1) attacks on earnings-related social insurance programs, (2) targeting benefits to the poor, (3) the plight of disadvantaged youth, (4) the need for more consistent labor market policies, (5) health and safety issues, and (6) tax reform and social security.

Attacks on earnings-related pensions

Earnings-related pension schemes have been subject to attack by some social security critics in the United States, by opponents of the mandatory supplementary earnings-related pension program in Britain, and to some extent by critics in other countries. Given the probability (though not certainty) of a sharp increase in the ratio of the retired population to the working population in the first quarter of the next century, these attacks are likely to be intensified and will probably play a role in bringing about changes in the financing and benefit structure of existing earnings-related pension programs.

One line of attack, not necessarily stemming from right-wing circles, criticizes such programs for their failure to target benefits more effectively to the poor. An interesting example of this is found in the useful study by Beckerman et al. (1979), in which it was argued that the Belgian social security system was relatively "inefficient" in reducing poverty because a large proportion of its benefits went to the nonpoor.

A similar charge is frequently made in the United States. An example is the book by Boskin (1986, 69), in which he argues that "huge transfers to well-off elderly people . . . are hidden from view." His proposed solution – a two-tiered system combining a program of benefits tightly related to contributory taxes paid over one's lifetime and a means-tested transfer program financed from general revenues for elderly individuals and families whose resources are deemed insufficient – would clearly not eliminate benefits for the wealthy, although it would tie them much more directly to their contributions. It leaves open large questions, however, as to how such a scheme would be phased in.

As I pointed out in Chapter 3, social insurance programs are not designed to eliminate poverty at a given point in time, but rather to protect the stability of income over the life cycle. Through social insurance programs, large proportions of the population are prevented from falling into poverty. At the same time, countries have come to recognize that some type of provision must be made for those who have not succeeded in accumulating rights to social insurance benefits.

Some of those who oppose social security benefits for affluent people would deny benefits to those with incomes above a certain level, but this would almost certainly lead to a situation in which high earners would want to opt out of the system and rely on employer pensions and personal savings. The result would be a two-class system, as well as intense controversy over the income ceiling above which benefits would be denied. Moreover, earners who opted out of the system might find themselves and their families inadequately protected in the event of disability or death. Even a move to deny cost-of-living increases to those with higher benefits would have a destabilizing effect on the system and, in the United States, where the benefit formula is heavily tilted toward the low earner, would gradually tilt benefits even more toward the low earner.

As a practical matter, in country after country there is strong political support for earnings-related schemes, especially on the part of workers who do not want to see a sharp drop in their incomes at the time of retirement. Any major moves away from existing earnings-related systems seem, for this reason, unlikely. As numerous writers have pointed out, programs that benefit the middle class along with the poor tend to have strong political support (see especially Goodin and Le Grand, 1987).

Even so, there is little question that many countries are seeking ways of reforming their pension systems in anticipation of far heavier costs in the future (Holzmann, 1986). In West Germany, and to some extent elsewhere, there is discussion of a plan that would index the per capita net benefits of the retired person to the per capita net earnings of the worker.[1]

Other changes that I consider worthy of consideration include the following:

1. Taxation of old-age benefits under the same rules as taxation of other income, eliminating special tax exemptions for the elderly or complete exemption of benefits from taxation. In the United States, this would mean taxing the benefits of elderly couples, for example, with taxable income of about $7,500 or more, rather than just those with taxable income of $32,000 or more. Because American workers, unlike those in most other countries, pay taxes on their social security contributions, only half of their benefits should be taxed, as at present.

2. Consideration of eliminating the income ceiling on contributions, as

[1] For a discussion of various economies in OASDI that have been adopted or are under consideration in West Germany, see Fisher (1984).

has been done in Belgium, Italy, Sweden, and Switzerland. This would make pension programs more redistributive of income and would be controversial for that reason, but it would substantially increase the revenue of the system.

3. Careful reconsideration of policies relating to spouses and widows, in view of the increased labor force participation of women, as has been done by a special commission in Sweden. Ball (1978), for example, has recommended reducing the spouse's benefit from one-half to one-third of the primary insurance amount in the United States, and Britain in 1986 placed new restrictions on benefits for widows.

4. Setting contributory taxes at rates that would build up a surplus between now and say, 2000, as has been done in the United States under the 1983 amendments, *and* refraining from using that surplus to finance improvements in benefits. (This would be more difficult to accomplish in countries where contributory rates are far higher than they are in this country.)

5. Raising the normal retirement age, along the lines of the policy that has been adopted in the United States, but *only* if labor market opportunities for older workers improve and only if early retirement provisions are retained for those with impaired earnings capacity. (See the discussion of a proposal by Staples, p. 109.)

6. Consideration of a partial pension scheme for workers in the five years prior to reaching the normal retirement age, like that in Sweden. Sweden's experience indicates that the scheme has proved attractive to workers who might otherwise have sought disability benefits or reduced early retirement benefits. Clearly, however, it requires the cooperation of employers and unions.

These suggestions, especially the first, are made partly in recognition of the improved income status of the aged in most industrial countries. They no longer need the benefit of special tax provisions, especially in view of the fact that those with low incomes would not be subject to the tax to any significant degree under the policies of most countries.

Targeting benefits to the poor

Although a strong movement away from earnings-related benefit programs appears unlikely, we have noted indications of a movement toward targeting certain types of benefits to low-income families. There has been a widespread movement in this direction, as we have seen, in family allowance schemes, and there has been a more modest movement toward raising benefits in universal pension programs on an income-tested basis rather than raising the universal pension for all who meet the age requirements. The imposition of modest charges for services, with exemptions for those with low incomes, in national health insurance and national health service systems is another example of a movement away from universal benefits.

This movement is likely to continue, and, as noted in Chapter 14, is especially likely to take the form of tax credits for families with children, but it is important not to lose sight of the advantages of universal benefits as countries move toward more targeting to those with low incomes. We have noted that universal family allowances are neutral with respect to marital status of the parents, whereas there is at least a possibility of a family-splitting effect when benefits are directed to the poor or are limited to single-parent families. We have also noted the evenhandedness of universal old-age and disability benefits in relation to marital status; they are available, for example, for divorced, separated, or never-married women along with all others who meet the age or disability requirements.

An important consideration, increasingly noted in a number of countries, is the advantage of moving toward more income-redistributive systems by taxing benefits such as family allowances – taxes that will be paid largely by middle- and upper-income families under the income tax policies of most countries. Similarly, the growing attention to the combined effect of social security contributory taxes and income taxes is to be commended.

The problem of disadvantaged youth

One of the most serious problems facing many industrial countries is that of disadvantaged youth. It is particularly acute in inner city – "ghetto" – areas in the United States, but on a somewhat smaller scale it is clearly apparent and a source of concern in Britain, France, and West Germany, and to some extent elsewhere. I have long been convinced that it is a serious mistake to regard the youth unemployment problem, which is discussed at some length in Chapter 12, as a problem that can be solved by labor market policies alone. The attack on the problem must begin in the schools and requires a high degree of cooperation between the education authorities and the labor market authorities.

Black teenage unemployment rates in the United States have been above 40 percent since the early 1980s, and the improvement in the overall unemployment rate has had only a slight effect in reducing these rates. Indeed, a conspicuous development of the past several decades is the growing contrast in the black population between the deteriorating social and economic conditions in the ghetto and the increase in the number of middle-class blacks who have graduated from college and moved into managerial and professional positions.

As Trow has pointed out, the black youth unemployment rates may be somewhat exaggerated because of underground employment (Gordon, with Trow, 1979), but there is little question that a serious social problem is involved, including what appears to be an increasing problem of drug trafficking and drug use. Unemployment rates are also high for young Hispanics, though somewhat lower than among blacks, and, among both blacks and Hispanics, the problem is particularly severe in inner city areas.

The evidence is clear that the youth unemployment problem is particularly acute for those who have dropped out of school or have been chronic absentees.

The problem is not confined to ghetto areas, nor is it confined to the United States. Throughout Western Europe, it has been found that the least educated young people, and especially those who have dropped out of school, are the most likely to be unemployed (Gordon, with Trow, 1979, xiv). The prolongation of compulsory education uncovered the fact that by no means all young people benefited from continuing their education beyond age 14 or 15. Prolonged education turned out to be ill suited to many young people (especially those from low socioeconomic backgrounds). Particularly revealing is the analysis by Henri Janne (1979) of the data on "laggers" in the Belgian schools, indicating that, even in a country without racial differences, the problem of children who fall behind in school is serious and highly influenced by the socioeconomic status of the parents (and may in this case be influenced by language differences).

As a result of recognition of this problem, there has been a movement away from any more prolonging of compulsory education in Western Europe and a tendency to focus on the appropriate "mix" of vocational and general education. In North Rhine Westphalia, students have been given an opportunity to try out several types of vocational programs before choosing one, and in Sweden students have been given an opportunity for actual work experience in the last year of compulsory education or even earlier before deciding whether to continue in school and what educational "stream" to choose.

The problem of youth unemployment is not likely to disappear, even though the numbers of teenagers is declining in some countries and before long will decline in others. In a period of rapid technological change, the youngsters who have dropped out of school or who have been chronic truants will become even more disadvantaged in the labor market. There needs to be a concerted effort to provide combinations of education and work experience for those who have become bored with school. Classroom vocational education alone is not likely to improve the holding power of the schools, but those who are given opportunities for work experience are likely in many cases to recognize the need for more education – at least there is some evidence to suggest that this happens in some cases.

Combinations of education and work experience, however, should not be regarded as the only solution. There are many examples in the United States, and to some extent elsewhere, of such developments as "magnet" schools and other types of experimental schools. We need to recall, also, the favorable view of Wilensky (1985) and others, mentioned in Chapter 12, of the close link between secondary schools and apprenticeships in West Germany, Austria, and Switzerland. A future goal of the European Social Fund, with its growing emphasis on youth programs, might be the extending of this close link in other countries.

The future of labor market policies

As we have seen, some countries such as Sweden and West Germany have had continuous and consistent emphasis on labor market policies, whereas others, like Britain and the United States, have had "stop and go" policies that have shifted with changes in the political party in control of the government. Stop-and-go policies should not be allowed to continue. There is a persistent need for training and retraining programs, not only for the unemployed and persons entering the labor force, but also for the employed. Stop-and-go policies result in deficiencies of training personnel and facilities.

Under conditions of technological change, workers need to be given opportunities for temporary release from their jobs for purposes of retraining. We have noted that Canada is seeking to provide such opportunities, and a number of European countries have followed the lead of France in providing for sabbaticals for workers, though these have not been utilized very much. Swedish experts have been stressing the need for greater attention to retraining of those who are employed.[2]

A vigorous move in this direction could help to reverse the trend toward earlier retirement and help to meet the possible emergence of a shortage of qualified older workers as the size of the teenage population declines. As is being recognized by some British experts, it could also help to reduce the extent of dependency on means-tested public assistance.

Even so, under conditions of high and persistent unemployment, the difficulty of placing workers who have completed training may be a serious problem. We noted in Chapter 15 that the European Social Fund is encouraging programs that not only combine job creation and training for youth but also meet community needs. More generally, the case for public service employment in periods of prolonged unemployment is very strong, even though it is

---

[2] As my interviews have indicated, Rehn and Meidner have both been stressing this need, and Karl-Olof Faxén, former chief economist of the Swedish Employers Federation, has been doing research on retraining for high-technology industries.

recognized that projects must be carefully planned to meet real needs and not merely displace existing employees.

In our discussion of labor market policies, we noted that some countries have given much greater emphasis to rehabilitation of the disabled than others, and the countries that have had the greatest success in rehabilitation have been those in which the labor market authorities, or an agency closely associated with the labor market authorities, make certain that a worker's need for rehabilitation is assessed at a very early stage after the onset of disability, and that he or she is referred to an appropriate program. In many countries, there is a need to reorganize the administration of both occupational and nonoccupational disability programs to ensure early assessment of the individual's need for rehabilitation and adequate funds and facilities to meet his or her need.

Health and safety issues

In spite of the expansion of health insurance and national health service programs and the enormous increase in expenditures on health care, there have not been commensurate improvements in health, as Abel-Smith (1983b) has concluded on the basis of his comparative studies of health policies. Differences in mortality rates among social classes have not, with some exceptions, been reduced, and a large part, though not all, of the difficulty seems to be the lack of understanding of the need for health care among lower socioeconomic groups and the less healthy environment in which they live, as well as differences in life-styles (Fuchs, 1974). That is not the entire picture, however. There is also evidence of shortages of health professionals and hospital facilities in low-income and ghetto areas, in at least some countries.

Here again, the importance of educational policies enters the picture. We have noted the need for sex education in the schools in connection with the problem of teenage pregnancies, but more generally there is a need, varying, perhaps, from country to country, for greater emphasis on teaching youngsters about healthy patterns of living. I can remember vividly being given reading assignments on the dangers of drug use in the eighth grade, and yet there appears to have been too little emphasis on this type of education in more recent years. Belatedly, as noted in Chapter 13, the growth of the AIDS crisis is leading to a greater recognition in this country of the need for education on how to avoid exposure to this threat.

What it comes down to, as the ILO experts emphasized (ILO, 1984b), is the need for far greater attention to prevention. There is little question, moreover, that some health policies are more effective in this respect than others. Free dental care for children in the schools – found in New Zealand and to some extent elsewhere – along with education of children on the need for regular dental care is a good example of a preventive approach. Government policies and those of nonprofit organizations can also play an important role: Witness the gradual progress toward limiting smoking on planes and in offices and toward curbing advertising of cigarettes.

Equally important, as was recognized in Chapter 7, is the need for effective safety programs in workplaces. As I write these concluding lines, a controversy is continuing in California over the governor's move to delete funds for "Cal OSHA," the state's occupational health and safety program, and to rely exclusively on the federal OSHA program, considered by experts to be considerably less vigorous and effective than the state program.

Finally, I believe that the time will come when the United States will cease to be the only industrial country that lacks a comprehensive national health insurance or health service program. Although very recent developments, such as provision for catastrophic illness, may broaden the protection for the aged, they will not solve the fundamental problem posed by government provision for high-risk groups, while most of the rest of the population is covered by private insurance, and some groups, such as employees of small firms, are not protected at all. There is a need to bring all within a single program that averages the risk groups and provides more effective protection against inflation. Employers are becoming increasingly concerned about their high health benefit costs, and younger physicians, as we observed in Chapter 10, are increasingly joining the staffs of HMOs. Eventually, we are likely to move toward a system that combines nationwide insurance, as Enthoven (1980) has urged, with policies that encourage the expansion of HMOs. The issue is relevant not only to the adequacy and efficiency of access to health care, but also to the future of OASDI, which is threatened with diversion of its surplus funds to meet a possible deficit in Medicare.

Tax reform and social security

Throughout this volume, I have said nothing about the wave of tax reform legislation in industrial countries, largely because it is so recent that it is just beginning to be recognized. The importance of this movement has been shown clearly in a volume edited by Pechman (1988).

To the extent that the legislation in the 11 countries covered by the volume has been influenced by the United States tax reform legislation of 1986, it has emphasized a reduction in top marginal income tax rates and in the number of income tax brackets. The American legislation reduced the top marginal tax rate from 50 percent to 28 percent (effective in 1988), but with a 5 percent addition for those with relatively high incomes. For most taxpayers, except those subject to the 5 percent addition, there would be only two tax brackets, compared with 15 in 1986.

Proponents of the change argued that high marginal tax rates led those with high incomes to seek ways of avoiding the high rates in various ways – some legal and some illegal. It was also argued that personal saving and investment took place largely among those with upper-middle and high incomes (as we noted in Chapter 9) and that somewhat lower marginal tax rates would induce more saving and investment. We have also called attention in Chapter 9 to the tendency for savings rates to be low in some of the countries with very high top marginal tax rates. Thus the tax reform movement may have the effect of encouraging more saving and investment, and hence more rapid economic growth. It is too early to appraise its effects, and the American experience, which began with substantial tax reductions under 1981 legislation, has been complicated because of sharply rising military expenditures, which, along with the lowered tax rates, resulted in mounting budget deficits, despite reductions in spending on some domestic programs.

Among the 11 countries included in the volume edited by Pechman, most are in the process of reducing individual income tax rates, particularly in the top brackets, and compressing the number of brackets. The reduction will not be nearly as large as the 22 percentage point reduction in the U.S. top rate, and top rates will continue to be considerably higher than the American top rate, ranging from 45 percent in Canada to 75 percent in Sweden and 76 percent in Japan in 1989 (Pechman, ed., 1988, 4). (The American top rate will be 33 percent when adjusted to include state and local taxes, and the top rate for the other countries includes local taxes in most cases, along with provincial or state rates in West Germany, Canada, and Australia).

My purpose in calling attention to this development is to suggest that as countries undertake income tax reform, it is important for them to review the entire tax structure, including social security contributory taxes. Some countries have begun to do this, as we noted in Chapter 4. To the extent that income tax reform reduces the tax burden of those with higher incomes, it may strengthen the case for more progressive financing of social security. This could be accomplished by increasing the relative contribution from general government revenues, or by removing the ceiling on income subject to the contributory taxes, or by reducing contributory tax rates for low earners, or some combination of the three. There is a case, in view of high youth unemployment, for eliminating contributory taxes in the case of youth, as has been tried in France.

Another important development that is likely to have a positive impact on saving, as we noted in Chapter 5, is the increased labor force participation of women in the age group from 45 years to the early 60s. When couples in this age group are both earning, their capacity to save is enhanced, their prospective social security benefits are increased, and both husband and wife in many cases may be likely to qualify for employer pensions. This trend may call for reconsideration of provisions for spouses' and widows' benefits, as we noted earlier.

At the 1980 annual meeting of the American Economic Association, Moses Abramovitz devoted his presidential address to the problem of a possible conflict between welfare policies and economic growth, emphasizing that the goal of a mixed economy "is to obtain a measure of distributive justice, security, and social guidance of economic life without losing too much of the allocative efficiency and dynamism of private enterprise and market organization" (Abramovitz, 1981, 13). The outlook for achievement of this goal may be more promising than it was in 1980, not only because of the trends we have been discussing here, but also for other reasons, particularly the fact that inflation is much less threatening than it was in 1980. For those concerned with the future of social security, the challenge is to meet emerging problems with a view toward adaptation to changing circumstances and toward avoidance of abrupt or radical changes.

Appendix 1. *Social security expenditures as a percentage of gross domestic product, by type of program, selected industrial countries, 1959–60 and 1979–80*

Country and year	Health benefits	Pensions	Unem-ployment benefits	Family allowances	Public assistance	Total[a]
Sweden						
1959–60	3.8%	3.6%	0.1%	1.1%	1.3%	10.0%
1979–80	11.4	9.7	0.4	1.6	5.2	28.6
Denmark						
1959–60	3.1	4.0	0.5	0.4	1.4	9.6
1979–80	6.7	7.8	3.2	0.8	6.3	25.0
Netherlands						
1959–60	2.5	3.8	0.2	1.5	0.5	8.8
1979–80	7.5	11.3	1.1	2.1	1.7	24.2
France						
1959–60	2.2	2.6		2.9	0.7	9.0
1979–80	7.1	7.7	1.2	2.7	4.0	22.7
Belgium						
1959–60	2.9	3.1	1.0	2.1	0.4	10.1
1979–80	6.3	6.6	3.5	2.6	0.7	20.6
Germany (Fed. Rep.)						
1959–60	3.1	5.9	0.2	0.3	1.0	11.0
1979–80	5.8	9.5	1.4	1.1	0.9	19.4
Czechoslovakia						
1959–60	5.3	7.0		2.6	0.3	15.2
1979–80	5.8	9.9		2.8	0.5	18.9
Norway						
1959–60	3.4	2.4	0.2	0.6	0.6	7.5
1979–80	8.1	7.5	0.4	1.0	1.7	18.8
Ireland						
1959–60	2.9	2.3	0.7	1.1	0.5	7.7
1979–80	9.2	5.3	2.0	1.0	0.5	18.4
Hungary						
1959–60	3.9	2.9		0.9		7.7
1979–80	5.6	9.5		3.0		18.1
Germany (Dem. Rep.)						
1959–60	5.0	7.8		1.4		14.4
1979–80	6.9	9.3		0.8		17.0

348

Appendix 1. (*cont.*)

Country and year	Health benefits	Pensions	Unemployment benefits	Family allowances	Public assistance	Total[a]
Austria						
1959–60	2.6	4.6	0.5	1.4	0.5	10.0
1979–80	3.7	8.8	0.6	2.5	0.7	16.7
United Kingdom						
1959–60	3.7	3.1	0.2	0.5	1.1	8.8
1979–80	4.9	5.6	0.4	1.5	2.6	15.3
Finland						
1959–60	2.0	2.3	0.1	1.4	1.2	7.1
1979–80	5.0	6.2	0.5	0.7	2.3	15.0
Poland						
1959–60	3.9	2.8		2.0		8.7
1979–80	6.8	7.0		0.7	0.3	14.9
Italy						
1959–60	2.1	3.3	0.3	2.1	0.3	8.4
1979–80	5.4	6.2	0.5	0.7	0.7	13.8
USSR						
1959–60	4.7	4.8		0.3		9.8
1979–80	6.2	7.3		0.3		13.8
New Zealand						
1959–60	3.9	4.1		2.6		10.9
1979–80	4.9	6.7	0.3	0.9		13.0
Canada						
1959–60	2.1	2.1	1.2	1.4	1.0	8.1
1979–80	3.6	3.2	1.5	1.1	2.6	12.3
Switzerland						
1959–60	2.0	2.4		0.0[b]	1.1	6.1
1979–80	2.6	7.5	0.1	0.0[b]	1.1	12.0
United States						
1959–60	0.8	2.3	0.5		1.0	4.8
1979–80	2.1	3.9	0.6		3.0	10.0
Australia						
1959–60	2.0	2.2		1.0	0.2	5.8
1979–80	2.2	3.8	0.7	1.0	0.5	9.8[c]
Israel						
1959–60	3.5	0.8			0.4	5.4
1979–80	3.7	3.2	—	2.1	0.3	9.6

Appendix 1. (*cont.*)

Country and year	Health benefits	Pensions	Unem- ployment benefits	Family allowances	Public assistance	Total[a]
Greece						
1959–60	1.8	4.8		0.5	0.2	7.3
1979–80	2.0	5.5	—[d]	0.6	0.8	8.9
Japan						
1959–60	1.7	0.1	0.3		0.6	2.9
1979–80	3.5	2.3	0.4	0.1	1.2	7.7

[a]Totals include industrial injuries benefits, which are not shown separately. Data do not include administrative expenses.

[b]Less than 0.05%.

[c]There is a discrepancy between amounts of expenditures in two tables. I have chosen the higher figure.

[d]Included under family allowances.

Source: ILO, *The Cost of Social Security* (selected issues).

Appendix 2. *Types of provisions for early retirement, selected countries, 1985*

Early retirement with reduced pension
Belgium: 60 (m), 55 (w), 5% a year
Canada: 60, 0.5 percent a month (Quebec only before 1987)
Finland: 60, 6% a year
Greece: 60 (m), 55 (w), 6% a year
Japan: 60, actuarial reduction (national pension program)
Spain: reduced pension if under age 65
Sweden: 60, 6% a year
United States: 62, 6.7% a year

Early retirement contingent on long service
Austria: 60 (m), 55 (w), 35 years of contributions, 24 months in last 3 years
Belgium: 64 (m), 45 years of employment
Germany (Fed. Rep.): 63, 35 years of employment
Greece: 62 (m), 57 (w), 10,000 days of contributions (1,000 in last 10 years) or 58 (w), 10,500 days
Italy: any age, 35 years of contributions
Poland: 60 (m) 55 (w), 25 years of employment
Yugoslavia: any age, 40 years of insurance (m), 35 years (w); 55 (m) 50 (w), 35 years of insurance (m), 30 years (w)

Early retirement contingent on prolonged unemployment
Austria: 60 (m), 55 (w), after year of unemployment
Canada: 54, under redundancy provisions for certain industries
Finland: 55 in 1983, increasing to 60 in 1985, unemployed at least 200 days in last 60 weeks
Germany (Fed. Rep.): 60, unemployed 1 year in last 18 months
Italy: 55 (m), 50 (w), if unemployed as a result of economic crisis or industrial reorganization
Sweden: 60, if unable to cope with job or unemployed with no prospect of job

Prepension payments (usually through unemployment insurance or collective agreements)
Austria: 60 (m), 55 (w), after year of sickness
Belgium: 60 (m), 55 (w), if stipulated in collective agreement and worker discharged
Denmark: voluntary retirement, member of unemployment fund for 5 out of last 10 years, or 10 of last 15 if becoming member after April 6, 1980
France: 56 (55 in certain cases) up to age 65
Germany (Fed. Rep.): 58
Netherlands: 60–2
Spain: 60
Sweden: 55

Early retirement contingent on disability
Austria: 55 (m), 50 (w), if unemployed for economic or structural reasons
Belgium: 60 (m), 55 (w), if disabled more than one year
Denmark: 18 to 67, if earning capacity reduced by at least 50 percent; 50 to 66, if state of health or social situation justifies it
Finland: 55, if cannot reasonably be expected to continue working in his or her profession
France: 60, less than 37.5 years of insurance, if uncapacitated for work in usual occupation and loss of 50 percent of capacity for any work

351

Appendix 2. (*cont.*)

Germany: (Fed. Rep.) 60, with 35 years of contributions
Norway: 64, partial disability
Sweden: 63, partial disability

Early retirement of workers in arduous or unhealthy occupations
Austria: 57 (m), 52 (w), if 15 years of such employment in last 30
Belgium: 64 (m) if 5 out of last 15, or any 12, years of employment in an unhealthy occupation
Czechoslovakia: 55 to 58 (m), if in unhealthy or arduous work
Germany (Dem. Rep.): 50 to 65, miners, according to length of employment
Greece: 60 (m), 55 (w), with 3,240 of 4,050 days of employment in arduous or unhealthy work
Hungary: age reduced for those in unhealthy work
Japan: 55, miners
Poland: 60 (m), 55 (w) for underground or unhealthy work[a]
Spain: lower age for difficult or dangerous work
USSR: age and years of employment requirements reduced for work in the far north, difficult, or
    dangerous work
Yugoslavia: lower age requirements for arduous or unhealthy work

Early retirement contingent on employment of an unemployed worker
Belgium: 60 (m), if replaced by unemployed worker under age 30
Finland: farmers' scheme, 55
Germany (Fed. Rep.): 58
Spain: 64, if employer replaces retiree with youth seeking first employment
United Kingdom: 62 to 64 (m), 60 to 61 (disabled men), 59 (w), voluntary job release scheme
    under which job must go to an unemployed worker

Partial pension or allowance scheme for partial early retirement[b]
France: 55, having worked at least 10 years in insured employment
Spain: 62, wages and working hours reduced by 50 percent
Sweden: 60, reduced work, employed at least 5 of 12 months before entitlement, and 10 years'
    earnings-related coverage after age 45
United Kingdom: same age and sex criteria as job release scheme, but worker shifts to part-time
    work and receives allowance

Early retirement provisions for women, or women who have raised many children
Czechoslovakia: 53 to 57, according to number of children raised
Germany (Fed. Rep.): 60, with 10 years of insurance in last 20
Greece: 55, with dependent children and 5,500 days of contributions
USSR: age and years of employment requirements reduced for mothers of 5 or more children

No special provisions for early retirement
Australia, Ireland,[c] Israel, New Zealand, Romania, Switzerland

---

Note: (m), men; (w) women.
[a] Also includes teaching, aviation, and maritime work, and, since 1978, workers in social enterprises if there is an important reason for early retirement.
[b] Schemes in Denmark and Finland were not effective until 1987.
[c] With a normal retirement age of 66, a worker is permitted to retire at age 65 if he or she
withdraws from work entirely and receives his or her flat-rate pension.
Sources: Tracy (1978, 1979); ISSA (1985); USSSA (biennial, 1986); other sources.

352

References

Aaron, Henry J. 1967. "Social Security: International Comparisons." In *Studies in the Economics of Income Maintenance*, edited by Otto Eckstein. Washington, D.C.: Brookings Institution.

——— 1980. *On Social Welfare*. Cambridge, Mass: Abt Books.

——— 1982. *Economic Effects of Social Security*. Washington, D.C.: Brookings Institution.

——— 1984. "Social Welfare in Australia." In *The Australian Economy: A View from the North*, edited by Richard E. Caves and Lawrence B. Krause. Washington, D.C.: Brookings Institution.

——— 1986. "When Is a Burden Not a Burden? The Elderly in America." *Brookings Review, 4* (Summer): 17–24.

Abel-Smith, Brian. 1981. *Social Security Provision for the Longer-Term Disabled in Eight Countries of the European Community*. Brussels: EEC, V/566/81.

——— 1983a. "Assessing the Balance Sheet." In *The Future of the Welfare State*, edited by Howard Glennester. London: Heinemann.

——— 1983b. "Economic Efficiency in Health Care Delivery." *ISSR, 36* (2): 165–79.

——— 1984. *Cost Containment in Health Care: A Study of Twelve European Countries*. London: Bedford Square Press.

Abramovitz, Moses. 1981. "Welfare Opportunities and Productivity Concerns." *American Economic Review, 71* (March): 1–17.

Alber, Jens. 1982. *Vom Armenhaus zum Wohlfahrstaat: Analysen zur Entwicklung der Sozialversicherung in Westeuropa*. Frankfurt: Campus Verlag.

Aldrich, J. 1982. "Earnings Replacement Rate of Old-Age Benefits in 12 Countries, 1969–80." *SSB, 45* (November): 3–11.

Allan, Kathryn. 1976. "First Findings of the 1972 Survey of the Disabled: General Characteristics." *SSB, 39* (October): 18–37.

American Council on Life Insurance. 1984. *Pension Facts, 1984/1985*. Washington, D.C.

Andersen, H. 1910. "Subvention à la vieillesse en Danemark." In *Assistance et prévoyance sociale en Danemark*, edited by A. Kreigen. Copenhagen: J. H. Schultz.

Anderson, Maxine. 1973. "Broad Accident Compensation Law Enacted in New Zealand." *Monthly Labor Review, 96* (August): 77–8.

Anderson, Odin W. 1972. *Health Care: Can There be Equity? The United States, Sweden, and England*. New York: John Wiley.

Ando, Albert, and Modigliani, F. 1963. "The 'Life Cycle' Hypothesis of Saving:

Aggregate Implications and Tests." *American Economic Review, 53* (March): 55–84.

Annuaire Statistique de la France. Paris.

Armstrong, Barbara N. 1932. *Insuring the Essentials: Minimum Wage Plus Social Insurance – A Living Wage Program.* New York: Macmillan.

1939. *The Health Insurance Doctor.* Princeton, N.J.: Princeton University Press.

Australian Government Commission on Inquiry into Poverty. 1975. *First Main Report.* Canberra.

Ball, Robert M. 1978. *Social Security Today and Tomorrow.* New York: Columbia University Press.

Barth, Peter S., with Hunt, H. Allan. 1980. *Workers' Compensation and Work-Related Illnesses and Diseases.* Cambridge, Mass.: The MIT Press.

Beattie, R. A. 1974. "France." In *Pensions, Inflation, and Growth: A Comparative Study of the Elderly in the Welfare State,* edited by Thomas Wilson. London: Heinemann.

Beckerman, Wilfred, with van Ginneken, Wouter, Szal, Richard, and Garquel, Michel. 1979. *Poverty and the Impact of Income Maintenance Programmes in Four Developed Countries.* Geneva: ILO.

Beller, Daniel J. 1981. "Coverage Patterns of Full-Time Employees Under Private Retirement Plans." *SSB, 44* (July): 3–11, 47.

Bentzel, R., and Berg, L. 1983. "The Role of Demographic Factors as a Determinant of Savings in Sweden." In *The Determinants of National Saving and Wealth,* edited by Franco Modigliani and Richard Hemming. London: Macmillan.

Berghman, Jos. 1980. "Poverty and Inequality in Belgium." In *Poverty and Inequality in Common Market Countries,* edited by Vic George and Roger Lawson. London: Routledge & Kegan Paul.

Bergmann, Barbara R. 1986. *The Economic Emergence of Women.* New York: Basic Books.

Bernstein, Irving. 1960. *The Lean Years: A History of the American Worker, 1920–1933.* Boston: Houghton Mifflin.

Beveridge Report, The. 1942. See *Social Insurance and Allied Services . . .*

Blaustein, Saul J., and Craig, Isabel. 1977. *An International Review of Unemployment Insurance Schemes.* Kalamazoo, Mich.: W. E. Upjohn Institute for Employment Research.

Booth, Charles. 1894. *The Aged Poor in England and Wales.* London: Macmillan.

Borowczyk, Ewa. 1986. "State Social Policy in Favour of the Family in East European Countries." *ISSR, 39* (2): 164–82.

Boskin, Michael J. 1986. *Too Many Promises: The Uncertain Future of Social Security.* Homewood, Ill.: Dow Jones-Irwin.

Boullot, Michel, et al. 1976. "L'âge de la retraite." *Revue française des affaires sociales, 30* (July–September): 457–534.

Bouquet, Rolande. 1979. "Insurance Against Incapacity for Work in European Law." *ISSR, 32* (4): 445–64.

Boyd, J. H. 1913. *Workmen's Compensation and Industrial Insurance.* New York: Bobbs-Merrill.

References

355

Bradshaw, Jonathan, and Piachaud, David. 1980. *Child Support in the European Community*. London: Bedford Square Press.

Bratfisch, Oswald. 1981. *New Organization for Vocational Rehabilitation in Sweden*. Stockholm: National Labor Market Board.

Brewster, Agnes W. 1959. "Canada's Federal–Provincial Program of Hospitalization Insurance." *SSB, 22* (July): 12–16.

Brittain, J. A. 1972. *The Payroll Tax for Social Security*. Washington, D.C.: Brookings Institution.

Brown, Joan C. 1983. *Family Income Supplement*. London: Policy Studies Institute.

Bryson, Lois, and Mowbray, Martin. 1986. "Who Cares? Social Security, Family Policy and Women." *ISSR, 39* (2): 183–200.

Bullock, Paul. 1985. *Youth Training and Employment: From New Deal to New Federalism*. Los Angeles: Institute of Industrial Relations, University of California, Los Angeles.

Bundesregierung. 1986a. *Familienpolitik als Zukunftsaufgabe*. Bonn: Presse- und Informationsamt, September 15.

1986b. *Gezielte Arbeitsmarkhilfen für Jugendliche und Frauen*. Bonn: Presse- und Informationsamt, August.

1986c. *Politik für Arbeitnehmer*. Bonn: Presse- und Informationsamt, August.

1986d. *Sozialbericht*. Bonn: Presse- und Informationsamt, August.

Bureau of National Affairs. 1974. *Highlights of the New Pension Reform Law*. Washington, D.C.

Burns, Eveline M. 1968. "Childhood Poverty and Children's Allowances." In *Children's Allowances and the Economic Welfare of Children*, edited by Eveline M. Burns. New York: Citizens' Committee for Children of New York.

Burtless, Gary. 1986. *Jobless Pay and High European Unemployment*. Paper presented at a conference on Impediments to European Economic Growth. Brookings Institution, Washington, D.C., October 9–10.

Bushell, Robert. 1986. "Evaluation of the Young Workers Scheme." *Employment Gazette* (May): 145–52.

Cagan, Phillip. 1965. *The Effect of Pension Plans on Private Saving: Evidence from a Sample Survey*. New York: Columbia University Press for the National Bureau of Economic Research, Occasional Paper 95.

Cain, Glen. 1986. "The Issues of Marital Stability and Family Composition and the Income Maintenance Experiments." In *Lessons from the Income Maintenance Experiments*, edited by Alicia H. Munnell. Boston: Federal Reserve Bank of Boston, and Washington, D.C.: Brookings Institution.

Canada, Government of. 1970. *White Paper on Income Security*. Ottawa.

1986. *Cooke Task Force on Child Care Releases Report*. Ottawa: March 7 (press release).

Canada, Health and Welfare. 1985a. *Canada Assistance Plan: Annual Report, 1984–85*. Ottawa.

1985b. *Canadian Jobs Strategy*. Ottawa.

1985c. *Social Security Statistics of Canada and the Provinces: 1958–59 to 1982–83*. Ottawa.

1986. *Basic Facts on Social Security Programs.* Ottawa.

Carballo, Manuel, and Bane, Mary Jo (eds.). 1984. *The State and the Poor in the 1980s.* Boston: Auburn House.

Carnegie Commission on Higher Education. 1970. *The Open-Door Colleges: Policies for Community Colleges.* New York: McGraw-Hill.

Carnegie Council on Policy Studies in Higher Education. 1976. *Progress and Problems in Medical and Dental Education: Federal Support Versus Federal Control.* San Francisco: Jossey-Bass.

1979. *Giving Youth a Better Chance: Options for Education, Work and Service.* San Francisco: Jossey-Bass.

Carroll, John J. 1960. *Alternative Methods of Financing Old-Age, Survivors, and Disability Insurance.* Ann Arbor, Mich.: Institute of Public Administration, University of Michigan.

Cartwright, William S. 1984. "Saving, Social Security, and Private Pensions." *ISSR, 37* (2): 123–38.

Casey, Bernard, and Bruche, Gert. 1985. "Active Labor Market Policy: An International Overview." *Industrial Relations, 24* (Winter): 37–61.

Centre d'Étude des Revenues et des Coûts. 1982. *L'indemnisation du chomage en France et à l'étranger.* Paris.

Chambers, Rosalind. 1948. "Workmen's Compensation." In *Social Security,* edited by W. A. Robson. London: Allen and Unwin.

Charles, Jean-François. 1984. "Social Security in Switzerland: Main Features of the Schemes and Current Problems." *ISSR, 37* (2): 178–93.

Cheit, Earl F., and Gordon, Margaret S. (eds.). 1963. *Occupational Disability and Public Policy.* New York: John Wiley.

Clark, Robert M. 1960. *Economic Security for the Aged in the United States and Canada: A Report Prepared for the Government of Canada.* Ottawa: The Queen's Printer, 2 vols.

Clarke, R. D. 1982. "Worker Participation in Health and Safety in Canada." *ILR, 121* (March–April): 199–206.

Collier, Joe. 1973. "Inspection and Enforcement at the Workplace." *Monthly Labor Review, 96* (August): 35–42.

Collins, Katharine P., and Erfle, Anne. 1985. "Social Security Disability Benefits Reform Act of 1984." *SSB, 48* (April): 5–32.

Collot, Claudette, and Le Bris, Hannelore Jani. 1981. "La femme agée isolée dans trois pays européens." *Revue française des affaires sociales, 35* (July–September): 101–14.

Comanor, William S. 1980. *National Health Insurance in Ontario: The Effects of a Policy of Cost Control.* Washington, D.C.: American Enterprise Institute.

Commission of the European Communities. 1985. *Thirteenth Report on the Activities of the European Social Fund: Financial Year 1984.* Brussels.

Condliffe, John B. 1959. *The Welfare State in New Zealand.* London: Allen and Unwin.

Copeland, Lois S. 1981. "International Trends in Disability Program Growth." *SSB, 44* (October): 25–36.

D'Anastasio, Mark. 1987. "Red Medicine: Soviet Health System, Despite Early Claims, Is Riddled by Failures." *Wall Street Journal*, August 18.

Danziger, Sheldon, Haveman, Robert, and Plotnick, Robert. 1981. "How Income Transfers Affect Work, Savings and the Income Distribution." *Journal of Economic Literature, 19* (September): 975–1028.

Danziger, Sheldon, et al. 1982. *Implications of the Relative Economic Status of the Elderly for Transfer Policy.* Paper presented for the Brookings Institution Conference on Retirement and Aging, October 21–2.

David, Miriam, and Land, Hilary. 1983. "Sex and Social Policy." In *The Future of the Welfare State,* edited by Howard Glennester. London: Heinemann.

Davis, Karen. 1975. *National Health Insurance: Benefits, Costs, and Consequences.* Washington, D.C.: Brookings Institution.

Davis, Karen, and Rowland, Diane. 1986. *Medicare Policy: New Directions for Long-Term Care.* Baltimore and London: Johns Hopkins University Press.

Dawson, W. Harbutt. 1912. *Social Insurance in Germany, 1885–1911.* London: T. Fisher Unwin.

Delors, Jacques. 1984. "Avant propos." In *Pour une nouvelle politique sociale en Europe,* edited by Jacques Vandamme. Paris: Economica.

Denison, Edward F. 1967. *Why Growth Rates Differ: Postwar Experience in Nine Western Countries.* Washington, D.C.: Brookings Institution.

de Schweinitz, Karl. 1943. *England's Road to Social Security: From the Statute of Laborers in 1549 to the Beveridge Report of 1942.* Philadelphia: University of Pennsylvania Press.

Dixon, John. 1983. "Australia's Income-Security System: Its Origins, Nature and Prospects." *ISSR, 36* (1): 19–44.

Doeringer, Peter B., and Piore, Michael J. 1971. *Internal Labor Markets and Manpower Analysis.* Lexington, Mass.: Lexington Books.

Dumont, J. P. 1987. "The Evolution of Social Security During the Recession." *ILR, 126* (January–February): 1–20.

Dupriez, F. 1977. "Les travailleurs du secteur privé en pension anticipée ou en prépension." *Revue du travail, 118* (May): 289–327.

Durand, Paul. 1953. *La politique contemporaine de sécurité sociale.* Paris: Librarie Dalloz.

Dworkin, Peter. 1985. "Job Stress Claims on the Increase." *San Francisco Chronicle,* March 1.

Eisner, Robert. 1981. "Discussion." In *Saving for Retirement,* edited by Philip Cagan. Washington, D.C.: American Council on Life Insurance.

Emanuel, Han. 1980. "Factors in the Growth of the Number of Disability Beneficiaries in the Netherlands." *ISSR, 33* (1): 41–60.

Enthoven, Alain C. 1980. *Health Plan: The Only Practical Solution to the Soaring Cost of Medical Care.* Reading, Mass.: Addison-Wesley.

Epstein, Lenore A., and Murray, Janet H. 1967. *The Aged Population in the United States: The 1963 Social Security Survey of the Aged.* Washington, D.C.: USSSA.

Eriksen, T. E. 1981. "Some Reflections on the Role of the National Supplementary Pension Scheme in the Swedish Pension System." *ISSR, 34* (4): 410–26.

Esposito, Louis, Mallan, Lucy B., and Podoff, David. 1980. "Distribution of Increased Benefits Under Alternative Earnings Tests." *SSB, 43* (September): 3–9.

Euzéby, Alain, and Euzéby, Chantal. 1984. "Social Security Financing Methods, Labour Costs, and Employment in Industrialised Market Economy Countries." In *Financing Social Security: The Options. An International Analysis*. Geneva: ILO.

Euzéby, Chantal. 1987. "A Minimum Guaranteed Income: Experiments and Proposals." *ILR, 126* (May–June): 253–76.

Feldstein, Martin. 1974. "Social Security, Induced Retirement, and Aggregate Capital Accumulation." *Journal of Political Economy, 82* (September–October): 905–26.

    1976. "The Unemployment Caused by Unemployment Insurance." *Proceedings of the Twenty-Eighth Annual Meeting of the Industrial Relations Research Association*, 225–33. Madison, Wis.: IRRA.

Ferge, Zsuzsa. 1978. "Hungary." In *Family Policy: Government and Families in Fourteen Countries*, edited by Sheila B. Kamerman and Alfred J. Kahn. New York: Columbia University Press.

Fields, Gary S., and Mitchell, Olivia S. 1984. *Retirement, Pensions, and Social Security*. Cambridge, Mass.: MIT Press.

Filler, Louis (ed.). 1964. *The President Speaks: From William McKinley to Lyndon B. Johnson*. New York: Putnam.

Fisher, Paul. 1973. "Major Social Security Issues: Japan, 1972." *SSB, 36* (March): 26–38.

    1984. "Financing the Federal Republic of Germany's Old Age, Survivors and Disability Program." *Aging and Work, 7* (1): 47–63.

    1986. *Social Security Protection of Youth*. Geneva: ILO.

Forsyth, Gordon. 1973. "United Kingdom." In *Health Service Prospects: an International Survey*, edited by I. Douglas-Wilson and Gordon McLachlan. London: The Lancet, and Boston: Little Brown.

Fragonard, Bertrand. 1983. "Family Benefit Schemes and Contemporary Family Needs in France." In *Social Security and Family Policy*. Geneva: ISSA.

Frank, W. F. 1953. "Employers' Liability in Great Britain." *Law and Contemporary Problems, 18* (3): 324–49.

Fried, Albert, and Elman, Richard. 1968. *Charles Booth's London*. New York: Pantheon Books.

Friedman, Milton. 1957. *A Theory of the Consumption Function*. Princeton, N.J.: Princeton University Press.

    1962. *Capitalism and Freedom*. Chicago: University of Chicago Press.

Friis, Henning. 1969. "Issues in Social Security in Denmark." In *Social Security in International Perspective: Essays in Honor of Eveline M. Burns*, edited by Shirley Jenkins. New York: Columbia University Press.

Fuchs, Anke. 1982. "Reform of Social Security Coverage for Women and Survivors in the Federal Republic of Germany." *ILR, 121* (September–October): 553–64.

Fuchs, Victor R. 1974. *Who Shall Live? Health, Economics, and Social Choice*. New York: Basic Books.

1986. *The Health Economy*. Cambridge, Mass.: Harvard University Press.

Futro, Aleksander. 1964. *Invalid's Cooperatives in Poland*. Warsaw: Publishing House of the Central Agricultural Union of Cooperatives.

Gajda, Anthony J. 1988. "The Hidden Costs of Health Coverage for the Elderly: New Employee Benefit Might Not Be." *Wall Street Journal*, April 28.

Galbraith, John K. 1958. *The Affluent Society*. Boston: Houghton Mifflin.

Galenson, Marjorie. 1973. *Women and Work: An International Comparison*. Ithaca, N.Y: New York State School of Industrial and Labor Relations, Cornell University.

George, Vic. 1980. "Poverty and Inequality in the UK." In *Poverty and Inequality in Common Market Countries*, edited by Vic George and Roger Lawson. London: Routledge & Kegan Paul.

George, Vic, and Lawson, Roger (eds.). 1980. *Poverty and Inequality in Common Market Countries*. London: Routledge & Kegan Paul.

Gevers, J. K. M. 1983. "Worker Participation in Health and Safety in the EEC: The Role of Representative Institutions." *ILR, 122* (July–August): 411–28.

Gilbert, Bentley B. 1966. *The Evolution of National Insurance in Great Britain: The Origins of the Welfare State*. London: Michael Joseph.

Gill, Derek G. 1980. *The British National Health Service: A Sociologist's Perspective*. Washington, D.C.: National Institutes of Health.

Ginsburg, Helen. 1983. *Full Employment and Public Policy: The United States and Sweden*. Lexington, Mass.: Lexington Books.

1985. "Flexible and Partial Retirement for Norwegian and Swedish Workers." *Monthly Labor Review, 108* (October): 33–43.

Glaser, William A. 1970. *Paying the Doctor: Systems of Remuneration and Their Effects*. Baltimore: Johns Hopkins University Press.

Goodin, Robert E., Le Grand, Julian, with Dryzek, John, et al. 1987. *Not Only the Poor: The Middle Class and the Welfare State*. London: Allen and Unwin.

Gordon, David M. 1972. *Theories of Poverty and Underemployment*. Lexington, Mass.: Lexington Books.

Gordon, David M., Edwards, Richard, and Reich, Michael. 1982. *Segmented Work: Divided Workers: The Historical Transformation of Labor in the United States*. Cambridge: Cambridge University Press.

Gordon, Margaret S. 1963a. "Income Security Programs and the Propensity to Retire." In *Processes of Aging: Social and Psychological Perspectives*, edited by Richard H. Williams, Clark Tibbitts, and Wilma Donahue. New York: Atherton Press, Vol. 2.

1963b. "Industrial Injuries Insurance in Europe and the British Commonwealth Before World War II," and "Industrial Injuries Insurance in Europe and the British Commonwealth After World War II." In *Occupational Disability and Public Policy*, edited by Earl F. Cheit and Margaret S. Gordon. New York: John Wiley.

1963c. *The Economics of Welfare Policies*. New York: Columbia University Press.

1965a (ed.). *Poverty in America*. San Francisco: Chandler Publishing.

1965b. *Retraining and Labor Market Adjustment in Western Europe*. Washington, D.C.: Manpower Automation Research Monograph, No. 4. U.S. Department of Labor.

1967. "The Case for Earnings-Related Social Security Benefits Restated." In *Old Age Income Assurance*, Part 2, U.S. Congress, Joint Economic Committee.

Gordon, Margaret S., with Trow, Martin. 1979. *Youth Education and Unemployment Problems: An International Perspective.* Berkeley, Calif.: Carnegie Council on Policy Studies in Higher Education.

Gordon, Robert J. 1986. *Productivity, Wages, and Prices Inside and Outside of Manufacturing in the U.S. and Europe.* Paper presented to the International Seminar on Macroeconomics, Namur, Belgium, June 23–4.

Gould, R. 1981. "The Background and Work History of Persons Applying for Disability Pensions in Finland." *ISSR, 34* (3): 320–35.

Gourley, John B. 1986. "Current Issues in Old-Age Protection in New Zealand." *ISSR, 39* (2): 201–15.

Grad, Susan. 1984. "Incomes of the Aged and Nonaged, 1950–82." *SSB, 47* (June): 3–17.

Grana, John M. 1983. "Disability Allowances for Long-Term Care in Western Europe and the United States." *ISSR, 36* (2): 207–21.

Greenhouse, Steven. 1985. "Crisis Over Pensions." *San Francisco Chronicle*, November 19.

Greenough, William C., and King, Francis P. 1976. *Pension Plans and Public Policy.* New York: Columbia University Press.

Greenwald, Douglas (ed.). 1982. *Encyclopedia of Economics.* New York: McGraw-Hill.

Haanes-Olsen, Leif. 1972. "Children's Allowances: Their Size and Structure in Five Countries." *SSB, 35* (May): 17–28.

1978. "Earnings-Replacement Rates of Old-Age Benefits, 1965–75." *SSB, 41* (January): 3–14.

1979. "Taxation and Pensions." *ISSR, 32* (1): 32–49.

Haber, Lawrence D. 1967. *Relationship of Disability and Retirement.* Paper presented at Conference on Interactions of Health and Retirement, New Orleans, December 11–12.

Hahn, F. H. 1987. "On Involuntary Unemployment." *Economic Journal, 97* (Conference 1987): 1–16.

Harrington, Michael. 1962. *The Other America: Poverty in the United States.* New York: Macmillan.

Harrod, R. F. 1948. *Towards a Dynamic Economics.* London: Macmillan.

Hart, Maurice C. 1961. "Old-Age, Survivors, and Disability Insurance: Early-Retirement Provisions." *SSB, 24* (October): 4–13.

Haveman, Robert H., Halberstadt, Victor, and Burkhauser, Richard V. 1984. *Public Policy Toward Disabled Workers: Cross-National Analyses of Economic Impacts.* Ithaca, N.Y.: Cornell University Press.

Haveman, Robert H., and Saks, Daniel H. 1985. "Trans-Atlantic Lessons for Employment and Training Policy." *Industrial Relations, 24* (Winter): 20–36.

Hax, Herbert. 1982. "The Burden of Social Policy on the Firm." *Zeitschrift für die Gesamte Staatswissenschaft, 138* (September): 469–77.

Hazen, Charles D. 1923. *Europe Since 1815.* New York: Henry Holt.

Heclo, Hugh. 1974. *Modern Social Politics in Britain and Sweden: From Relief to Income Maintenance.* New Haven, Conn.: Yale University Press.

Heidenheimer, Arnold J., with Layson, John. 1982. "Social Policy Development in Europe and America: A Longer View on Selectivity and Income Testing." In *Income-Tested Transfer Programs: The Case For and Against,* edited by Irwin Garfinkel. New York: Academic Press.

Hemming, Richard. 1984. *Poverty and Incentives: The Economics of Social Security.* Oxford: Oxford University Press.

Hemming, Richard, and Harvey, Russell. 1983. "Occupational Pension Scheme Membership and Retirement Saving." *Economic Journal, 93* (March): 128–44.

Heubeck, Georg. 1984. "Occupational Pension Schemes in the Context of the Evolution of the National Economy." In *Occupational Pension Schemes.* Geneva: ISSA.

Höjer, Karl J. 1952. *Den Svenska Socialpolitiken.* Stockholm: Norstedt.

Holzmann, Robert. 1986. "Pension Reform: Sharing the Burden." *OECD Observer,* January, 3–10.

Honig, Marjorie, and Shamai, Nira. 1978. "Israel." In *Family Policy: Government and Families in Fourteen Countries,* edited by Sheila B. Kamerman and Alfred J. Kahn. New York: Columbia University Press.

Horlick, Max. 1973. "Supplementary Security Income for the Aged: Foreign Experience." *SSB, 36* (December): 3–12.

1980. *Private Pension Plans in West Germany and France.* Washington, D.C.: USSSA, Research Report No. 55.

Horlick, Max, and Skolnik, Alfred M. 1979. *Mandating Private Pension Plans: A Study of European Experience.* Washington, D.C.: USSSA.

Hughes, James J., and Perlman, Richard. 1984. *The Economics of Unemployment: A Comparative Analysis of Britain and the United States.* Cambridge: Cambridge University Press.

Hume, Ellen. 1986. "New Regimen: The AMA Is Laboring to Regain Dominance Over Nation's Doctors." *Wall Street Journal,* June 10.

Husén, Torsten. 1977. *Changing Attitudes to Education and Work Among Youth in the Achievement-Oriented Society.* Paper presented for the High Level Conference on Youth Unemployment, preparatory group, October 20–21. Paris: OECD.

Iams, Howard M. 1985. "Characteristics of the Longest Job for New Retired Workers: Findings from the New Beneficiary Survey." *SSB, 48* (March): 5–21.

ILO. Annual. *Year Book of Labor Statistics.* Geneva.

1948. *Legislative Series* – U.K. 1.

1956. *Legislative Series* – Swe. 1.

1973. *Legislative Series* – Swe. 3.

1974. *Legislative Series* – Ger. F. R. 2.

1975. *Legislative Series* – Cz. 3.

1983. *Legislative Series* – Ger. F. R. 1.

1981. *The Cost of Social Security, 1975–1977.*

1984a. *Financing Social Security: The Options.*

1984b. *Into the Twenty-First Century: The Development of Social Security.*

1984c. *World Labor Report.*

1985a. *Analyse comparée des systèmes de santé,* unpublished paper.

1985b. *The Cost of Social Security, 1978–1980.*

1986[4]. *Bulletin of Labor Statistics.*

ISSA. 1982. *Social Security and the Elderly.* Geneva.

1984a. *Long-Term Care and Social Security.* Studies and Research, No. 21. Geneva.

1984b. *Occupational Pension Schemes.* Geneva.

1985. *Lowering the Age of Cessation of Activity and the Financial Equilibrium of Social Security Schemes Providing Replacement Income.* Provisional Report. Geneva.

James, Frank E. 1987. "Study Lays Groundwork for Tying Health Costs to Workers' Behavior." *Wall Street Journal,* April 14.

Janne, Henri. 1979. *Education and Youth Employment in Belgium.* Berkeley, Calif.: Carnegie Council on Policy Studies in Higher Education.

Johnson, Paul. 1985. *Modern Times: The World from the Twenties to the Eighties.* New York: Harper Colophon Books.

Jones, Elise F., et al. 1985. "Teenage Pregnancy in Developed Countries: Determinants and Policy Implications." *Family Planning Perspectives, 17* (March–April): 53.

Jones, Mary G. (ed.). 1983. *Social Security: The Long View.* College Park, Md.: Center for Business and Public Policy, University of Maryland.

Juster, Thomas F. 1981. "Current and Prospective Financial Status of the Elderly Population." In *Saving for Retirement,* edited by Phillip Cagan. Washington, D.C.: American Council on Life Insurance.

Kamerman, Sheila B. 1983. *Meeting Family Needs: The Corporate Response.* Work in America Institute Studies in Productivity, Vol. 33. New York: Pergamon Press.

Kamerman, Sheila B., and Kahn, Alfred J. (eds.). 1978. *Family Policy: Government and Families in Fourteen Countries.* New York: Columbia University Press.

1981. *Child Care, Family Benefits, and Working Parents: A Study in Comparative Policy.* New York: Columbia University Press.

1982. "Income Transfers, Work and the Economic Well-Being of Families with Children." *ISSR, 35* (3): 345–82.

Kato, Hidetoshi. 1978. *Education and Youth Employment in Japan.* Berkeley, Calif.: Carnegie Council on Policy Studies in Higher Education.

Katona, George. 1964. *The Mass Consumption Society.* New York: McGraw-Hill.

Kewley, T. H. 1973. *Social Security in Australia, 1900–72.* Sydney: Sydney University Press; 2nd edition.

Keynes, John M. 1936. *The General Theory of Employment, Interest, and Money.* New York: Harcourt Brace Jovanovich.

Killingsworth, Charles C. 1966. "Discussion." In *Prosperity and Unemployment,* edited by R. A. and M. S. Gordon. New York: John Wiley.

Kleiler, Frank M. 1978. *Can We Afford Early Retirement?* Baltimore: Johns Hopkins University Press.

Koch-Nielsen, Inger. 1980. *Opvaekstvilkar og Erhvervsbaggrund: Invalidepensionistundersogelserne, 7.* Copenhagen: Danish National Institute of Social Research [English summary included].

Köhler, Peter A., and Zacher, Hans F. 1982. *The Evolution of Social Insurance,*

1881–1981: Studies of Germany, France, Great Britain, Austria, and Switzerland. London: Frances Pinter, and New York: St. Martin's Press.

Korpi, Walter. 1985. "Economic Growth and the Welfare State." *Labor and Society, 10* (May): 195–209.

Krute, Aaron, and Burdette, Mary Ellen. 1978. "1972 Survey of Disabled and Non-disabled Adults: Chronic Disease, Injury, and Work Disability." *SSB, 41* (April): 3–17.

Kubernátová, Marta. 1986. "The Occupational Integration of Disabled Citizens in Czechoslovakia." *ISSR, 39* (3): 287–301.

Kudrle, Robert T., and Marmor, Theodore. 1981. "The Development of Welfare States in North America." In *The Development of Welfare States in Europe and America,* edited by Peter Flora and Arnold J. Heidenheimer. New Brunswick, N.J.: Transaction Books.

Kurilin, Mikhail N. 1986. "Young Working People in the USSR: Socioeconomic aspects." *Labor and Society, 11* (May): 221–36.

Lando, Mordechai E., Coate, Malcolm B., and Kraus, Ruth. 1979. "Disability Applications and the Economy." *SSB, 42* (October): 3–10.

Lansbury, Russel. 1980. "Older Workers: The Australian Experience." *Labor and Society, 5* (January): 69–84.

Laroque, Pierre. 1948. "From Social Insurance to Social Security: Evolution in France." *ILR, 57* (6): 565–90.

1962. *Politique de la vieillesse.* Paris: Documentation Française.

Laurent, André. 1982. "European Community Law and Equal Treatment for Men and Women in Social Security." *ILR, 121* (July–August): 373–86.

Lauterbach, H. 1960. "Compulsory Industrial Accident Insurance in the Federal Republic of Germany." *Bulletin of the ISSA, 13* (October–November): 498–521.

Lawson, Roger. 1980. "Poverty and Inequality in West Germany." In *Poverty and Inequality in Common Market Countries,* edited by Vic George and Roger Lawson. London: Routledge & Kegan Paul.

Layard, Richard. 1986. *How to Beat Unemployment.* Oxford: Oxford University Press.

Leimer, Dean R., and Lesnoy, Selig D. 1980. *Social Security and Private Saving: A Reexamination of the Time-Series Evidence Using Alternative Social Security Wealth Variables.* USSSA. Working Paper No. 19.

Lesnoy, Selig D., and Leimer, Dean R. 1985. "Social Security and Private Saving: Theory and Historical Evidence." *SSB, 48* (January): 14–30.

Lester, Richard A. 1962. *The Economics of Unemployment Compensation.* Princeton, N.J.: Industrial Relations Section, Princeton University.

1966. *Manpower Planning in a Free Society.* Princeton, N.J.: Princeton University Press.

Leve, M. 1981. "The Situation in the Federal Republic of Germany." In *Unemployment Protection Schemes and Employment Policies.* Geneva: ISSA.

Levitan, Sar A. 1969. *The Great Society's Poor Law: A New Approach to Poverty.* Baltimore: Johns Hopkins University Press.

1985. *Programs in Aid of the Poor.* Baltimore: Johns Hopkins University Press.

Levy, Frank. 1980. *The Logic of Welfare Reform.* Washington, D.C.: The Urban Institute.

364   **References**

Liberska, Barbara. 1979. *Education and Youth Employment in Poland.* Berkeley, Calif.: Carnegie Council on Policy Studies in Higher Education.

Liefmann-Keil, Elizabeth. 1961. *Ökonomische Theorie der Sozial Politik.* Berlin: Springer-Verlag.

Liljeström, Rita. 1978. "Sweden." In *Family Policy: Government and Families in Fourteen Countries,* edited by Sheila B. Kamerman and Alfred J. Kahn. New York: Columbia University Press.

Lindbeck, Assar. 1985. "What is Wrong with the West European Economies?" *The World Economy, 8* (June): 153–69.

Ljung, Bengt. 1986. "Swedes Not So Sexy Now." *San Francisco Chronicle,* August 28.

Lucas, Robert, and Rapping, Leonard. 1969. "Real Wages, Employment, and Inflation." In *Microeconomic Foundations of Employment and Inflation,* edited by Edward S. Phelps. New York: Norton.

Lundberg, Erik. 1985. "The Rise and Fall of the Swedish Model." *Journal of Economic Literature, 23* (March): 1–36.

Lynes, Tony. 1967. *French Pensions.* Occasional Papers on Social Administration, No. 21. London: G. Bell.

⸺ 1968. "Family Allowances in Great Britain." In *Children's Allowances and the Economic Welfare of Children,* edited by Eveline M. Burns. New York: Citizens Committee for Children of New York.

MacDonald, Maurice, and Sawhill, Isabel V. 1978. "Welfare Policy and the Family." *Public Policy, 26* (Winter): 89–119.

Mackintosh, Margaret. 1939. "Workmen's Compensation in Canada." *ILR, 40* (July): 1–31.

Maclure, Stuart. 1979. *Education and Youth Employment in Great Britain.* Berkeley, Calif.: Carnegie Council on Policy Studies in Higher Education.

Maddison, Angus. 1964. *Economic Growth in the West.* New York: Twentieth Century Fund.

⸺ 1983. "Economic Stagnation Since 1973, Its Nature and Causes: A Six Country Survey." *De Economist, 31* (4): 585–608.

Madison, Bernice. 1968. *Social Welfare in the Soviet Union.* Stanford, Calif.: Stanford University Press.

Maguire, Maria. 1987. "Making Provisions for Ageing Populations." *OECD Observer,* October–November.

Makkaveyskiy, P. 1981. "The Employment of Disabled Persons in the USSR and Their Rehabilitation." *ISSR, 34* (3): 301–7.

Malloy, Michael T. 1988. "Health, Canadian Style." *Wall Street Journal,* April 22.

Marmor, T. R., and Rein, Martin. 1969. "Post-War European Experience with Cash Transfers: Pensions, Child Allowances, and Public Assistance." In Presidents' Commission on Income Maintenance Programs. *Technical Studies.* Washington, D.C.

Marsh, L. C. 1943. *Report on Social Security for Canada.* Report prepared for the Advisory Committee on Reconstruction. Ottawa: Edmond Cloutier.

Marshall, T. H. 1967. *Social Policy in the Twentieth Century.* London: Hutchinson University Library, 2nd edition.

Mattyasovszky, G. 1985. *Family Benefits Provided for One-Parent Families*. Report of the 16th meeting of the Permanent Committee on Family Allowances. Geneva: ISSA.

McAuley, Alastair. 1977. *Soviet Anti-Poverty Policy*. Madison, Wis.: Institute for Research on Poverty, University of Wisconsin, Discussion Papers.

McCallum, John. 1986. "Unemployment in the OECD Countries in the 1980s." *Economic Journal, 96* (December): 942–60.

McCrostie, J. J., and Peacock, Alan. 1984. "Disability Policy in the United Kingdom." In *Public Policy Toward Disabled Workers: Cross-National Analyses of Economic Impacts*, authored by Robert H. Haveman, Victor Halberstadt, and Richard V. Burkhauser. Ithaca, N.Y.: Cornell University Press.

Menzies, Anne M. 1974a. "The Federal Republic of Germany." In *Pensions, Inflation, and Growth*, edited by Thomas Wilson. London: Heinemann.

1974b. "The Netherlands." In *Pensions, Inflation, and Growth*, edited by Thomas Wilson. London: Heinemann.

Messere, Kenneth, and Owens, Jeffrey. 1979. "The Treatment of Children Under Income Tax and Social Welfare Systems." *ISSR, 32* (1): 50–9.

Meyerson, Per-Martin. 1985. *Eurosclerosis: The Case of Sweden*. Stockholm: Federation of Swedish Industries.

Mills, C. 1983. "Le système social à l'épreuve de la crise." *Revue française des affaires sociales, 37* (July–September): 103–32.

Miry, Raoul. 1945. "The First Reconstruction Measures in Liberated Belgium." *ILR, 51* (April): 419–32.

Mitton, Roger, Willmott, Peter, and Willmott, Phyllis. 1983. *Unemployment, Poverty and Social Policy in Europe: A Comparative Study in Britain, France, and Germany*. London: Bedford Square Press.

Modigliani, F., and Sterling, A. 1983. "Determinants of Private Saving with Special Reference to the Role of Social Security: Cross-Country Tests." In *The Determinants of National Saving and Wealth*, edited by Franco Modigliani and Richard Hemming. London: Macmillan.

Moon, Marilyn. 1986. "Impact of the Reagan Years on the Distribution of Income of the Elderly." *The Gerontologist, 26* (February): 32–7.

Moore, K. A. 1978. "Teenage Childbirth and Welfare Dependency." *Family Planning Perspectives, 10* (4): 233–5.

Moss, David, and Rogers, Ernesta. 1980. "Poverty and Inequality in Italy." In *Poverty and Inequality in Common Market Countries*, edited by Vic George and Roger Lawson. London: Routledge & Kegan Paul.

Moy, Joyanna T. 1985. "Recent Trends in Unemployment and the Labor Force, 10 Countries." *Monthly Labor Review, 108* (August): 9–22.

Moynihan, Daniel Patrick. 1986. *Family and Nation*. New York: Harcourt Brace Jovanovich.

Munnell, Alicia H. 1982. *The Economics of Private Pensions*. Washington, D.C.: Brookings Institution.

Murray, Charles. 1984. *Losing Ground: American Social Policy, 1950–1980*. New York: Basic Books.

Myrdal, Alva. 1941. *Nation and Family: The Swedish Experiment in Democratic Family and Population Policy*. New York: Harper; and revised edition, 1968, Cambridge, Mass.: MIT Press.

Nagorski, Z. 1981. "Counterrevolution." *New York Times*, 30 December.

Nagy, Olga, and Szabady, Egon. 1983. "Current Trends in Family Policy and the Role of Social Security in Hungary." In *Social Security and Family Policy*. Geneva: ISSA.

National Commission on Social Security Reform, Report of. 1983. Washington, D.C.

National Conference on Social Welfare. 1985. *The Report of the Committee on Economic Security of 1935: 50th Anniversary Edition*. Washington, D.C.

National Foundation for Unemployment Compensation and Workers' Compensation. 1985. *Highlights of State Unemployment Compensation Laws*. Washington, D.C.

Office des Publications Officielles des Communautés Européennes. 1983. *La politique sociale de la Communauté Européenne*. Luxembourg; 3rd edition.

Olsson, Bertil. 1967. "Labor-Market Policy in Modern Society." In *Toward a Manpower Policy*, edited by R. A. Gordon. New York: John Wiley.

Ontario Workers' Compensation Board. 1985. *Vocational Rehabilitation Services: Annual Report*. Toronto.

OECD. 1972. *Labor Force Statistics, 1959–70*. Paris.

1976. *Public Expenditure on Income Maintenance Programs*. Paris.

1985a. *Social Expenditure, 1960–1990*. Paris.

1986. *The Tax and Benefit Position of Production Workers, 1981–1985*. Paris.

1987a. *Financing and Delivering Health Care*. Paris.

1987b. *Labor Force Statistics, 1965–1985*. Paris.

1987c. *National Accounts Statistics, 1973–1985*. Paris.

1987d. *OECD Economic Outlook, 42* (December).

Orshansky, Mollie. 1966. "Recounting the Poor – a Five-Year Review." *SSB, 29* (April): 20–37.

Paltiel, F. L. 1982. "Women and Pensions in Canada." *ISSR, 35* (3): 333–44.

Peacock, Alan T. 1952. *The Economics of National Insurance*. London: William Hodge.

Pechman, Joseph A. (ed.). 1988. *World Tax Reform: A Progress Report*. Washington, D.C.: Brookings Institution.

Pechman, Joseph A., Aaron, Henry J., and Taussig, Michael K. 1968. *Social Security: Perspectives for Reform*. Washington, D.C.: Brookings Institution.

Perlman, David. 1988. "Candidates Blasted on Health 'Chaos.' " *San Francisco Chronicle*, March 19.

Perrin, Guy. 1984a. "A Hundred Years of Social Insurance." *Labor and Society. 9* (October–December): 399–410.

1984b. "Rationalisation of Social Security Financing." In *Financing Social Security: The Options. An International Analysis*. Geneva: ILO.

Pfaff, Martin, and Huber, Walter. 1984. "Disability Policy in the Federal Republic of Germany." In *Public Policy Toward Disabled Workers: Cross-National Analyses of Economic Impacts*, authored by Robert H. Haveman, Victor Halberstadt, and Richard V. Burkhauser. Ithaca, N.Y.: Cornell University Press.

Pisca, L. 1965. "Some Remarks on the Development of Social Security in Czechoslovakia." *ILR, 92* (July–August): 223–33.

Popay, Jennie, Rimmer, Lesley, and Rossiter, Chris. 1983. *One Parent Families:*

Parents, Children, and Public Policy. London: Study Commission on the Family.

Porter, Sylvia. 1985. "Why Pension Plans Are in Trouble." *San Francisco Chronicle,* August 23.

Powell, Brian J. 1986. *Welfare and Employment: Recent Changes in Canadian Policy.* A discussion paper for the International Workshop on Welfare and Employment, Vienna, September 27 to October 1. Policy, Planning, and Information Branch, Health and Welfare, Canada.

Price, Daniel N. 1980. "Workers' Compensation: 1978 Program Update." *SSB, 43* (October): 3–10.

Questiaux, Nicole, and Fournier, Jacques. 1978. "France." In *Family Policy: Government and Families in Fourteen Countries,* edited by Sheila B. Kamerman and Alfred J. Kahn. New York: Columbia University Press.

Rathbone, Eleanor F. 1947. *The Case for Family Allowances.* London: Penguin Books.

Rehn, Gösta. 1985. "Swedish Active Labor Market Policy: Retrospect and Prospect." *Industrial Relations, 24* (Winter): 62–89.

Rehn, Gösta, and Petersen, K. Helveg. 1980. *Education and Youth Employment in Sweden and Denmark.* Berkeley, Calif.: Carnegie Council on Policy Studies in Higher Education.

Reno, Virginia P. 1971. "Why Men Stop Working At or Before Age 65: Findings from the Survey of New Beneficiaries." *SSB, 34* (June): 3–17.

Reno, Virginia P., and Grad, Susan. 1985. "Economic Security, 1935–85." *SSB, 48* (December): 5–20.

Reubens, Beatrice G. 1970. *The Hard-to-Employ: European Programs.* New York: Columbia University Press.

1974. "Vocational Education for *All* in High School?" In *Work and the Quality of Life: Resource Papers for Work in America.* Cambridge, Mass.: MIT Press.

1983. (ed.) *Youth at Work: An International Survey.* Totowa, N.J.: Rowman and Allanheld.

Rhys-Williams, Lady Juliet. 1943. *Something to Look Forward To.* London: Mac-Donald.

Ricci, Lelia. 1981. "The Situation in Italy." In *Unemployment Protection Schemes and Employment Policies.* Geneva: ISSA.

Rikkert, H. K. 1981. "The Situation in the Netherlands." In *Unemployment Protection Schemes and Employment Policies.* Geneva: ISSA.

Rimlinger, Gaston V. 1971. *Welfare Policy and Industrialization in Europe, America, and Russia.* New York: John Wiley.

Rimmer, Lesley, and Wicks, Malcolm. 1983. "The Challenge of Change: Demographic Trends, the Family and Social Policy." In *The Future of the Welfare State,* edited by Howard Glennester. London: Heinemann.

Rivlin, Alice M. 1987. "Overview." In *The Swedish Economy,* edited by Barry P. Bosworth and Alice M. Rivlin. Washington, D.C.: Brookings Institution.

Roberts, John. 1986. "Apprenticeships in West Germany." *Employment Gazette* (March): 109–16.

Robins, Philip K. et al. (eds.). 1980. *A Guaranteed Annual Income: Evidence from a Social Experiment.* New York: Harcourt Brace Jovanovich, Academic Press.

Rolph, Earl R. 1967. "The Case for a Negative Income Tax Device." *Industrial Relations, 6* (February): 155–65.

Roter, Raphael, and Shamai, Nira. 1976. "The Reform in Tax-Transfer Payments in Israel." *ISSR, 29* (4): 360–77.

Rouast, André, and Durand, Paul. 1960. *Sécurité Sociale.* Paris: Dalloz; 2nd edition.

Rowntree, B. Seebohm. 1922. *Poverty: A Study of Town Life.* London: Longmans Green; new edition.

Rundle, Rhonda L. 1987. "Medical Debate." *Wall Street Journal,* October 6.

Sako, Mori, and Dore, Ronald. 1986. "How the Youth Training Scheme Helps Employers." *Employment Gazette* (June): 183–4.

Saunders, Peter, and Klau, Friedrich. 1985. *The Role of the Public Sector: Causes and Consequences of the Growth of Government.* Paris: OECD.

Schobel, Bruce D., and McKay, Steven F. 1982. "Characteristics of Newly Awarded Recipients of the Social Security Regular Minimum Benefit." *SSB, 45* (June): 11–19.

Schober, Karen. 1983. "Youth Employment in West Germany." In *Youth at Work: An International Survey,* edited by Beatrice G. Reubens. Totowa, N.J.: Rowman and Allanheld.

Schorr, Alvin. 1966. *Poor Kids.* New York: Basic Books.

Shanas, Ethel et al. 1968. *Old People in Three Industrial Societies.* New York: Atherton Press.

Sherman, Sally R. 1985. "Assets of New Retired-Worker Beneficiaries: Findings from the New Beneficiary Survey." *SSB, 48* (July): 27–43.

Shinohara, M. 1983. "The Determinants of Post-War Savings Behaviour in Japan." In *The Determinants of National Saving and Wealth,* edited by Franco Modigliani and Richard Hemming. London: Macmillan.

Sinfield, Adrian. 1980. "Poverty and Inequality in France." In *Poverty and Inequality in Common Market Countries,* edited by Vic George and Roger Lawson. London: Routledge & Kegan Paul.

Skidmore, Felicity (ed.). 1981. *Social Security Financing.* Cambridge, Mass.: MIT Press.

Smith, Randall. 1984. "Business Reduces Pension Funding To Cut Costs, Fend Off Takeovers." *Wall Street Journal,* October 11.

　　　1985. "Experts Advise Taking Some Risk in Your Profit-Sharing Account." *Wall Street Journal,* January 17.

Social Insurance and Allied Services: Report by Sir William Beveridge. 1942. New York: Macmillan; American edition.

Solcher, Hans. 1978. "Sharing of Pension Rights in the Event of Divorce Under German Law." *ISSR, 31* (3): 308–17.

Solow, Robert M. 1980. "On Theories of Unemployment." *American Economic Review, 70* (March): 1–11.

　　　1985. *Unemployment: Getting the Questions Right.* Paper presented at White House Conference Centre, Chelwood Gate, Sussex, May 27–31.

Somers, Herman M., and Somers, Anne R. 1954. *Workmen's Compensation: Prevention, Insurance, and Rehabilitation of Occupational Disability.* New York: John Wiley.

Soskice, David. 1987. "Flexibility and Unemployment: The View from Western Europe." In *Industrial Relations Research Association Series: Proceedings of the 39th Annual Meeting*, 93–100.

Staples, Thomas G. 1978. "Trends in the Definition of Risk in Old-Age and Invalidity Schemes." *ISSR, 31* (2): 173–86.

Statistical Abstract of the United States. Annual. Washington, D.C.

Statistisches Jahrbuch der Bundesrepublik Deutschland. Wiesbaden.

Stecker, Margaret L. 1955. "Why Do Beneficiaries Retire? Who Among Them Return to Work?" *SSB, 18* (May): 3–12, 35–6.

Steele, Earl C. 1963. "Benefit Administration." In *Occupational Disability and Public Policy*, edited by Earl F. Cheit and Margaret S. Gordon. New York: John Wiley.

Stein, Bruno. 1980. *Social Security and Pensions in Transition: Understanding the American Retirement System*. New York: Free Press.

Steiner, Peter O., and Dorfman, Robert. 1957. *The Economic Status of the Aged*. Berkeley: University of California Press.

Sulzbach, W. 1947. "German Experience With Social Insurance." In *Studies in Individual and Collective Security*. New York: National Industrial Conference Board.

Sutch, W. B. 1941. *Poverty and Progress in New Zealand*. Wellington: Modern Books.

Svahn, J. A., and Ross, M. 1983. "Social Security Amendments of 1983: Legislative History and Summary of Provisions." *SSB, 46* (July): 3–48.

Sweden, Delegation for Labor Market Policy and Research, Ministry of Labor. 1984. *Labor Market Policy Under Reconsideration*. Stockholm.

Sweden, National Labor Market Board. 1985. *Labor Market Training*. Stockholm.

Tamburi, G. 1985. *The Two-Tier Pension Protection: Trends and Comparisons*. Geneva: ILO, unpublished paper.

Tanzi, Vito. 1982. *The Underground Economy in the United States and Abroad*. Lexington, Mass.: D. C. Heath.

Tennison, Debbie C. 1983. "Homeless People Grow Numerous in Europe, Despite Welfare States." *Wall Street Journal*, April 25.

The College Board. 1987. *Trends in Student Aid: 1980–1987*. Washington, D.C.

Thompson, W. E., and Streib, G. F. 1958. "Situational Determinants: Health and Economic Deprivation in Retirement." *Journal of Social Issues, 4* (2): 18–34.

Tierney, Brian. 1959. *Medieval Poor Law*. Berkeley: University of California Press.

Titmuss, Richard M. 1958. *Essays on 'The Welfare State.'* London: Unwin University Books.

1963. *Essays on 'The Welfare State.'* London: George Allen and Unwin; 2nd edition.

Tobin, James, Pechman, Joseph A., and Mieszkowski, Peter M. 1967. "Is a Negative Income Tax Practical?" *Yale Law Journal, 77* (November): 1–27.

Townsend, Peter. 1979. *Poverty in the United Kingdom: A Survey of Household Resources and Standards of Living*. Harmondsworth, Middlesex, U.K.: Penguin Books.

Tracy, Martin. 1978. "Flexible Retirement Features Abroad." *SSB, 41* (May): 18–36.

1979. "Trends in Retirement." *ISSR, 32* (2): 131–59.

Uhr, Carl G. 1966. *Sweden's Social Security System: An Appraisal of Its Economic Impact in the Postwar Period.* Washington, D.C.: USSSA, Research Report No. 14.

Ulman, Lloyd (ed.). 1973. *Manpower Programs in the Policy Mix.* Baltimore: Johns Hopkins University Press.

Umetani, Shun'ichiro, and Reubens, Beatrice G. 1983. "Youth Employment in Japan." In *Youth at Work: An International Survey,* edited by Beatrice G. Reubens. Totowa, N.J.: Rowan and Allanheld.

United Kingdom, Department of Employment. 1983a. *Job Release Scheme.* London.

1983b. *Part-Time Job Release Scheme.* London.

United Kingdom, Department of Health and Social Security. 1982a. *Social Security Statistics, 1982.* London.

1982b. *Which Benefit: 60 Ways to Get Cash Help.* London.

United Kingdom, Government of. 1972. *Proposals for a Tax-Credit System.* London, Cmnd. 5116.

1974. *Report of the Committee on One-Parent Families.* London.

United Kingdom, Manpower Services Commission. 1981. *Employment Rehabilitation: A Review of the Manpower Services Commission's Employment Rehabilitation Services.*

United Kingdom, Ministry of Pensions and National Insurance. 1954. *Reasons for Retiring or Continuing at Work.* London.

United Kingdom, Office of the Minister of Reconstruction. 1944. *Employment Policy.* London, Cmnd. 6527.

United Kingdom, Royal Commission on the Distribution of Income and Wealth. 1977. Report No. 5. *Third Report on the Standing Reference.* London.

1978. Report No. 6. *Lower Incomes.* London.

United Nations. 1978a. *Demographic Yearbook, 1977.* New York.

1978b. *Statistical Yearbook, 1977.* New York.

1984. *Demographic Yearbook, 1983.* New York.

U.S. Bureau of Labor Statistics. 1978. *International Comparisons of Unemployment.* Bulletin 1979. Washington, D.C.

1984. *Employee Benefits in Medium and Large Firms, 1983.* Bulletin 2213. Washington, D.C.

1986. *Consumer Expenditure Series.* Bulletin 2173. Washington, D.C.

U.S. Bureau of the Census. 1986. "Marital Status and Living Arrangements." *Current Population Reports.* Series P-20, No. 410. Washington, D.C.

U.S. Commissioner of Labor. 1911. *Twenty-Fourth Annual Report, 1909: Workmen's Insurance and Compensation Systems in Europe.* Washington, D.C., Vol. I.

U.S. Employment Standards Administration. 1984. *State Workers' Compensation Laws.* Washington, D.C.

U.S. National Commission on Social Security. 1981. *Final Report.* Washington, D.C.

U.S. National Commission on Unemployment Compensation. 1980. *Unemployment Compensation: Final Report.* Washington, D.C.

U.S. Office of Management and Budget. 1985. *Budget of the United States Government, Fiscal Year 1986.* Washington, D.C.

U.S. President's Commission on Income Maintenance Programs. 1969. *Poverty Amid Plenty.* Washington, D.C.

U.S. President's Commission on Pension Policy. 1980. *An International Comparison of Pension Systems.* Working Papers. Washington, D.C.

U.S. President's Committee to Appraise Employment and Unemployment Statistics. 1962. *Measuring Employment and Unemployment.*

USSSA. Biennial. *Social Security Programs Throughout the World.* Washington, D.C.

    1976. *Reaching Retirement Age: Findings from a Survey of Newly Retired Workers.* Washington, D.C.

    1982. *Initial Effects of Elimination of the Dependency Requirement on Entitlement to Husbands' and Widowers' Benefits.* Washington, D.C.

Upp, Melinda. 1983. "Relative Importance of Various Income Sources of the Aged." *SSB, 46* (January): 3–10.

Van Der Reijden, P. 1983. "Social Security and Family Policy: Integration and Co-ordination Questions in the Netherlands." In *Social Security and Family Policy.* Geneva: ISSA.

Venediktove, D. 1973. "Union of Soviet Socialist Republics." In *Health Service Prospects: An International Survey,* edited by I. Douglas-Wilson and Gordon McLachlan. London: *The Lancet,* and Boston: Little Brown.

Villars, Charles. 1979. "Ninth Amendment to the Swiss Old-Age and Survivors' Insurance." *ISSR, 32* (1): 72–9.

Voirin, Michel. 1980. "What is the Future of the Employment Accident Branch in the Light of the Extension of Compensation by Social Security for Personal Injury?" *ISSR, 33* (1): 3–40.

von Dohnanyi, Klaus. 1978. *Education and Youth Employment in the Federal Republic of Germany.* Berkeley, Calif.: Carnegie Council on Policy Studies in Higher Education.

von Moltke, Konrad, and Schneevoigt, Norbert. 1977. *Leaves for Employees: European Experience for American Consideration.* San Francisco: Jossey-Bass.

Vroman, Wayne. 1976. "Work Injuries and Wage Losses for Partially Disabled California Workers." *Proceedings of the Twenty-Ninth Annual Winter Meeting of the Industrial Relations Research Association,* 228–35.

    1986. *The Funding Crisis in Unemployment Insurance.* Kalamazoo, Mich.: W. E. Upjohn Institute for Employment Research.

Wadensjö, Eskil. 1984a. "Disability Policy in Sweden." In *Public Policy Toward Disabled Workers: Cross-National Analyses of Economic Impacts,* authored by Robert H. Haveman, Victor Halberstadt, and Richard W. Burkhauser. Ithaca, N.Y.: Cornell University Press.

    1984b. *Labor Market Policy Toward the Disabled in Sweden.* Stockholm: Swedish Institute for Social Research, University of Stockholm, discussion paper.

Walters, Vivienne. 1980. *Class Inequality and Health Care: The Origins and Impact of the National Health Service.* London: Croom Helm.

Watson, Philippa. 1980. *Social Security Law of the European Communities.* London: Mansell.

Webb, Sidney, and Webb, Beatrice. 1910. *The English Poor Law.* London: Longmans, Green.

Wilensky, Harold L. 1975. *The Welfare State and Equality: Structural and Ideological Roots of Public Expenditures.* Berkeley: University of California Press.

——— 1981. "Leftism, Catholicism, and Democratic Corporatism: The Role of Political Parties in Welfare State Development." In *The Development of Welfare States in Europe and America,* edited by P. Flora and A. J. Heidenheimer. New Brunswick, N.J.: Transaction Books.

——— 1985. "Nothing Fails Like Success: The Evaluation Research Industry and Labor Market Policy." *Industrial Relations 24* (Winter): 1–19.

Wilensky, Harold, and Turner, Lowell. 1987. *Democratic Corporatism and Policy Linkages.* Berkeley Calif.: Institute of International Studies, University of California, Berkeley.

Williams, Gertrude. 1963. *Apprenticeship in Europe: The Lesson for Britain.* London: Chapman and Hall.

Wilson, Dorothy J. 1974. "Sweden." In *Pensions, Inflation, and Growth: A Comparative Study of the Elderly in the Welfare State,* edited by Thomas Wilson. London: Heinemann.

Wilson, Thomas J. (ed.). 1974. *Pensions, Inflation, and Growth: A Comparative Study of the Elderly in the Welfare State.* London: Heinemann.

Wilson, William J. 1987. *The Truly Disadvantaged: The Inner City, the Underclass, and Public Policy.* Chicago: University of Chicago Press.

Zeitzer, Ilene R. 1983. "Social Security Trends and Developments in Industrial Countries." *SSB 46* (March): 52–62.

Index